D1602378

Race Is . . . Race Isn't

Race Is . . . Race Isn't

Critical Race Theory and Qualitative Studies in Education

EDITED BY

Laurence Parker

Donna Deyhle

Sofia Villenas

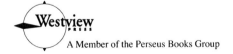

Westview
PRESS

A Member of the Perseus Books Group

Copyright © 1999 by Westview Press, A Member of the Perseus Books Group

Published in 1999 in the United States of America by Westview Press, 5500 Central Avenue, Boulder, Colorado 80301-2877, and in the United Kingdom by Westview Press, 12 Hid's Copse Road, Cumnor Hill, Oxford OX2 9JJ

Library of Congress Cataloging-in-Publication Data
Race is . . . race isn't : critical race theory and qualitative studies in
  education / edited by Laurence Parker, Donna Deyhle, Sofia Villenas.
    p. cm.
  Includes bibliographical references and index.
  ISBN 0-8133-9069-9
  1. Minorities—Education—United States. 2. Racism—United
States. 3. United States—Race relations. 4. Discrimination in
education—United States. I. Parker, Laurence. II. Deyhle, Donna.
III. Villenas, Sofia A.
LC3731.R27 1999
306.43—dc21   99-11946
                                                                              CIP

The paper used in this publication meets the requirements of the American National Standard for Permanence of Paper for Printed Library Materials Z39.48-1984.

Contents

Acknowledgments

Many friends and colleagues deserve thanks for their help and assistance on this project. First of all, we would like to thank the staff at Westview Press, including Lisa Wigutoff and Rebecca Ritke, our production and copy editors, respectively; and especially Catherine Murphy, for taking an interest in our prospectus and working with us toward publication. Second, we thank the editors of the *International Journal of Qualitative Studies in Education (QSE)*, especially James Joseph Scheurich and Douglas Foley, for giving us the opportunity initially to pursue this project through a special issue of the journal devoted to critical race theory and educational research. We also would like to thank the many authors who contributed to that special issue—most notably, Daniel Solórzano, Greg Tanaka, and Cindy Cruz at UCLA, and Kristin Nebeker at the University of Utah—particularly for their efforts to expand the boundaries of critical race theory into areas such as the social construction of whiteness, Chicano/Chicana perceptions of racism and sexism in postgraduate education, and gay/lesbian polyphonic textual narratives. For reasons of space, we were not able to reprint all of these contributions in the present volume. We believed it was absolutely necessary, however, to include chapters on key policy issues such as higher education desegregation and tracking. We also wanted to open and close the volume with an introduction and a conclusion that would provide readers with an overview of how educational research and policy can be connected to critical race theory in the law. The introductory chapter to the book was written by an emerging voice in the area of Latino/Latina critical legal theory. The concluding chapter, based on an article that appeared in the *Review of Research in Education* (1997), also suggests salient points of research, policy, and practice for future critical scholarship on race.

Many people gave us technical assistance in preparing the manuscript, most notably Claudia Torres of *QSE*. Very special appreciation goes to Joyce Atkinson, whose editorial suggestions were invaluable in helping us to focus, tighten, and strengthen the manuscript. We also must acknowledge a number of other readers and advisers who provided helpful advice or critical insights during the writing and editing process.

Among them, Frank Margonis and Wanda Pillow deserve special mention. Others deserving of thanks for their reading of and comments on various drafts of the chapters are the Critical Cultural Studies Group at the University of Utah; and Kevin Brady, Tim Eatman, Janet Thomas, Chris Span, Livia Morales, Dave Stovall, Erica Collins, Nora Hyland, Dionne Danns, and Alejandro Padilla, students in the critical race theory and educational policy class at the University of Illinois at Urbana-Champaign (UIUC). Matt Garica, Arlene Torres, and the members of the Latino Studies Group at the University of Illinois at Urbana-Champaign should also be acknowledged for their important feedback and criticism on a number of draft chapters. Nick Burbules and William Trent, professors in the Department of Educational Policy Studies at UIUC, provided helpful suggestions in the project's initial stages. The discussions we had with Richard Delgado of the University of Colorado School of Law were also a great asset, suggesting linkages between the legal arena and that of educational research and policy. We thank him for his support of our project. Our special thanks also to the Department of Educational Studies at the University of Utah and the Department of Educational Policy Studies at the University of Illinois at Urbana-Champaign. James D. Anderson, the department head at UIUC, provided substantial support in the form of time and funding. Other resources for completing the preparation of this book came from the Targeted Opportunities Program research funds administered by the Office of the Chancellor at UIUC.

Finally, we feel particularly privileged to have collaborated with all of the authors who contributed to this volume, who represent a wide range of scholarly interests connected to critical race theory and educational policy. As we move into the twenty-first century, we believe that civil rights in education will once again figure prominently in public policy debate. We hope this volume will spur further collective efforts linking educational research, practice, and law, toward the achievement of social justice for people of color in education.

We also would like to thank Taylor and Francis, publisher of the *International Journal of Qualitative Studies in Education,* for permitting us to republish the following articles that first appeared in vol. 11, no. 1 (1998) of this journal. They are:

- Just What Is Critical Race Theory and What's It Doing in a Field Like Education?, by Gloria Ladson-Billings (pp. 7–24)
- "Chicana/o Power!": Epistemology and Methodology for Social Justice and Empowerment in Chicana/o Communities, by Marc Pizarro (pp. 43–56)

- Formations of *Mexicana*ness: *Trenzas de identidades múltiples* / Growing Up Mexicana: Braids of Multiple Identities, by Francisca E. González (pp. 81–102)
- Toward a Definition of a Latino Family Research Paradigm, by Nitza M. Hidalgo (pp. 103–120)
- Research Methods As a Situated Response: Toward a First Nations' Methodology, by Mary Hermes (pp. 137–154)

Laurence Parker
Donna Deyhle
Sofia Villenas

Introduction to Critical Race Theory in Educational Research and Praxis

DARIA ROITHMAYR

Critical race theory (CRT) is an exciting, revolutionary intellectual movement that puts race at the center of critical analysis. Although no set of doctrines or methodologies defines critical race theory, scholars who write within the parameters of this intellectual movement share two very broad commitments. First, as a critical intervention into traditional civil rights scholarship, critical race theory describes the relationship between ostensibly race-neutral ideals, like "the rule of law," "merit," and "equal protection," and the structure of white supremacy and racism. Second, as a race-conscious and quasi-modernist intervention into critical legal scholarship, critical race theory proposes ways to use "the vexed bond between law and racial power" (Crenshaw, Gotanda, Peller, and Thomas, 1995, p. xiii) to transform that social structure and to advance the political commitment of racial emancipation.

Critical race theory inherits much from critical legal scholarship and conventional legal principles generated during the civil rights movement, but it also represents a significant departure from these two movements. Like most of critical legal scholarship, critical race theory manifests a deep dissatisfaction with liberal legal ideology generally, and with contemporary civil rights thinking about race and racism in particular. When critical race theory emerged in the late 1980s, national conversations about race and racism were still very much tied to a conventional liberal model of law and society. Under this model, liberal political commitments focused on the universalism, objectivism, and race-neutrality of concepts like "equal opportunity," "merit," and "equal protection." Racism was understood to be a deviation from these race-neutral norms: To be racist was to irrationally assume on the basis of an irrelevant characteristic like skin color that people of color did not possess the universal characteristics of reason or merit. Law was supposed to eradicate these instances of race-consciousness in social decisionmaking, leaving behind an otherwise race-neutral way of distributing opportunities and resources.

Under this conventional civil rights ideology, community and national leaders condemned segregation in schools because it imposed on education and school life a racial face. Where segregationists tied to race the opportunity and ability to learn, integrationists believed that the ability to learn was universal and race-neutral and the "professional" classroom culture of good education did not take race into account. Indeed, civil rights thinking promoted integration as a way of educating whites to realize that "we are all brothers under the skin."

Similarly, in terms of workplace discrimination, the civil rights establishment insisted on ostensibly race-neutral, objective standards—that people of color be judged "on their merits" rather than on the color of their skin. As in education, merit represented the universal, impersonal side of distributing opportunities and resources in the workplace; merit standards were purported to measure one's potential ability without regard to race. In contrast, bias irrationally focused on the irrelevant characteristic of skin color or stereotype. Racism was a failure in reason, which resulted from ignorance, lack of education, or lack of exposure to people of color.

By the early 1980s, the color-blind vision of race relations had exhausted itself, as early critical race theorists have pointed out. Conservatives used the rhetoric of color blindness against affirmative action programs to argue that all race-conscious considerations in education were inconsistent with race-neutrality. The Supreme Court decided that racial disparity in the workplace was not enough to make out a case of discrimination, and that an employer or educational institution could rebut any presumption of discrimination by a minimal showing of workplace or educational necessity for the selection criteria that produced the disparity. Civil rights lawyers lost ground on issues for which they had recently made limited progress, particularly with respect to affirmative action evidentiary rules in antidiscrimination cases.

Beginning with Derrick Bell's work in the early 1980s, CRT scholars attempted to revive and expand the scope of the reformist commitment to racial emancipation. Critical race theory scholars demonstrated that concepts that the reformists had taken for granted as helpful—color blindness, formal legal equality, merit, integration—in fact reflected, created, and perpetuated institutional racial power. CRT scholars pointed out, for example, that the color-blind perspective represses and renders irrelevant the ways in which race shapes social relationships. In addition, they explained how formal legal equality in fact adopts the perspective of the perpetrator by requiring evidence of conscious racial animus in a discrete discriminatory act, and by ignoring those instances in which racism is built into the structure of social institutions.

In the area of education, for example, critical scholars have pointed out that courts are unwilling to find the need for a desegregation remedy in the absence of some specific and discrete action by an identifiable villain school district. CRT authors noted also how merit standards, which are purported to be race-neutral and objective, are actually race-specific because they were constructed in a context of racial exclusion, by elites who had acquired social power by explicitly excluding people of color.

Critical race theory is a product not only of civil rights thinking but of critical thinking as well. As with civil rights ideology, critical race theory takes many of its starting points from critical legal scholarship, but revises and transforms many of those concepts as well. During the late seventies, critical theory on issues of class had achieved a significant presence in the legal academy in the form of critical legal studies (CLS). The Critical Legal Studies Conference, put together by a collection of neo-Marxists, former New Left and law-and-society types, counterculturists, and newly emerging critical theorists, represented a predominantly white Left critical intellectual movement organized mostly around issues of class and market forces. CLS scholars demonstrated how ostensibly neutral and apolitical concepts like liberty of contract, consent, and duress were manifestations of a particular institutional political and class-based ideology. Extending and revising Realist insights from the twenties and thirties, CLS scholars methodically exposed the deeply political and contextual character of supposedly apolitical legal standards and free-market rules.

Critical race theorists took their leave from the umbrella movement of critical legal studies in 1989, a year that marked the first official CRT conference devoted exclusively to the issue of race. Many of the early thinkers in critical race theory had developed their ideas as part of the CLS movement. But although critical race theory had inherited much of its critical content from CLS, its ideology diverged in important ways. First, many critical race theorists believed that although critical legal scholars had done much to expose the relationship between law and social power, they had not developed any theory about the relationship between law and racial power. Relatedly, although scholars of color found useful the idea that legal consciousness helps to create social power by persuading victims to participate in their own oppression, some scholars found that this argument ignored the way in which racism and racial power coercively forced oppression on unwilling victims.

In addition, CRT took issue with the CLS critique of legal rights. CLS scholars criticized rights discourse as indeterminate—the legal definition of a right was indeterminate because it depended largely on social context and judicially interpreted meaning. In response, CRT scholars agreed with much of the indeterminacy critique but argued that CLS scholars had ignored the transformative power of rights for a group of disem-powered outsiders. For outsiders who had been denied recognition as full legal persons, the principle of possessing legal rights held great meaning in symbolic if not legally operative ways, even if those legal rights ultimately proved limiting.

Even as critical race theory can be traced to both the civil rights move-ment of the 1960s and the critical legal studies movement of the late 1970s, contemporary critical race theory has evolved to embrace much from the postmodern cultural revolution in the humanities. Contempo-rary currents in critical race theory have borrowed most recently from re-search in postcolonialism, geography and space, ethnicity studies of racial and ethnic identities, critical ethnography, and many other critical movements in the humanities. Just as Critical legal studies produced de-parture movements in critical race theory and components of radical feminism, critical race theory has produced smaller intellectual move-ments focusing on Asian American critical scholarship and LatCrit the-ory—Latina/o critical theory—each of which now sponsors its own con-ferences.

What can critical race theory, a movement that has its roots in legal scholarship, contribute to research in education? Plenty, as it turns out. Much of the national dialogue on race relations takes place in the context of education—in continuing desegregation and affirmative action battles, in debates about bilingual education programs, and in the controversy surrounding race and ethnicity studies departments at colleges and uni-versities. More centrally, the use of critical race theory offers a way to un-derstand how ostensibly race-neutral structures in education—knowl-edge, truth, merit, objectivity, and "good education"—are in fact ways of forming and policing the racial boundaries of white supremacy and racism. The chapters by Ladson-Billings; Villenas, Deyhle, and Parker; Pizarro; and other authors in this book provide an excellent example of this use of critical race theory.

To be sure, a number of chapters in this book point out limitations in the use of critical race theory to explore ethnicity, culture, nationality, and language issues related to specific populations (see González and Hi-dalgo on Mexicana and Latina/o schooling in the United States, and Her-mes on tribal nations' concerns in education). Nevertheless, these chap-ters demonstrate how schools teach students of color that what they learn in their homes is primitive, mythical, and backward but what they learn in their classrooms is objective, historically accurate, and universal. Students attend class in an atmosphere of "professionalism," which as the measure of their enlightenment, devalues what they bring to the classroom from their homes and neighborhoods as backward, deprived, and deficient.

Similarly, critical race theory can be used to "deconstruct" the meaning of "educational achievement." Disparities in the workplace are blamed on the differences in educational achievement between white candidates and applicants of color. However, as the educational research discussed in the chapter by Green demonstrates, tracking procedures (which separate the college-bound students from those who are not "college material") test for a culturally and racially contingent concept of ability and merit. In a similar vein, as the federal government seeks to wrest control from local communities of color over their neighborhood schools by invoking the notion of "national standards," education scholars are using critical race theory to demonstrate that these standards may in fact be a form of colonialism, a way of imparting white, Westernized conceptions of enlightened thinking.

In short, the classroom—where knowledge is constructed, organized, produced, and distributed—is a central site for the construction of social and racial power. Indeed, having understood racial power's connection to both law and education, critical legal studies and critical race theory scholars have devoted much energy toward challenge and resistance in law schools and the law school classroom.

Critical race theory also provides the theoretical justification for taking seriously oppositional accounts of race—for example, counterstories that challenge the conventional take on integration as a universalizing move to equalize education for all races. Oppositional counterstories provide one way to make good on critical race theory's commitment to use law to transform and move social institutions toward racial empowerment and emancipation. For many outside the legal field, critical race theory has become synonymous with the idea of counter-storytelling—challenging the stock story on merit or academic tracking or standardized testing by redescribing an experience or a social phenomenon from an outsider's perspective. Mari Matsuda, one of the founding mothers of critical race theory, exhorts social decision-makers to "look to the bottom" to evaluate the impact of policy on the disenfranchised and disempowered.

This volume takes Matsuda's call into the field of educational research by integrating the idea of counter-storytelling into the methodology of qualitative research (as demonstrated by its use in Choe's chapter, for example, and her discussions related to Korean American women and education). Using critical race theory and its intersections with gender and social class analysis as a framework on which to build research, the chapters by Banning and by Tate examine oppositional accounts and narratives in the classroom, the school, and the school district. These sections of the book illustrate how critical race theory's storytelling can be combined with meticulous qualitative research in the field of education to open exciting new areas of inquiry.

As education scholars begin to integrate the principles of critical race theory into their thinking, they in turn are contributing a great deal to critical race theory, enabling it to look far more systematically at the field of education than legal scholars ever could. This collaboration is a wonderfully exciting sign of the ever growing cross-fertilization in critical scholarship across the academic curriculum. Such multicultural relationships are essential to the achievement of racial liberation.

1

Just What Is Critical Race Theory, and What's It Doing in a *Nice* Field Like Education?

GLORIA LADSON-BILLINGS

Almost five years ago a colleague and I began a collaboration in which we grappled with the legal scholarship known as "critical race theory" (Delgado, cited in Monaghan, 1993). So tentative were we about this line of inquiry that we proceeded with extreme caution. We were both un-tenured and relatively new to our institution. We were unsure of how this new line of inquiry would be received both within our university and throughout the educational research/scholarly community. Our initial step was to hold a colloquium in our department. We were pleasantly surprised to meet with a room filled with colleagues and graduate students who seemed eager to hear our ideas and help us in these new theoretical and conceptual formulations.

That initial meeting led to many revisions and iterations. We presented versions of the paper and the ideas surrounding it at conferences and professional meetings. Outside the supportive confines of our own institution, we were met with not only the expected intellectual challenges but also outright hostility. Why were we focusing only on race? What about gender? Why not class? Are you abandoning multicultural perspectives? By the fall of 1995 our much discussed paper was published (Ladson-Billings and Tate, 1995). We have held our collective intellectual breaths for almost a year because, despite the proliferation of critical race scholarship in legal studies, we have seen scant evidence that this work has made any impact on the educational research/scholarly community. Thus, seeing critical race theory (CRT) as a theme in an educational journal represents our first opportunity to "exhale."

Race Still Matters

It had been a good day. My talk as a part of the "Distinguished Lecture" Series at a major research university had gone well. The audience was receptive, the questions were challenging, yet respectful. My colleagues were exceptional hosts. I spent the day sharing ideas and exchanging views on various phases of their work and my own. There had even been the not so subtle hint of a job offer. The warm, almost tropical climate of this university stood in stark contrast to the overly long, brutal winters of my own institution. But it also had been a tiring day—all that smiling, listening with rapt interest to everyone's research, recalling minute details of my own, trying to be witty and simultaneously serious had taken its toll. I could not wait to get back to the hotel to relax for a few hours before dinner.

One of the nice perks that comes with these lecture "gigs" is a decent hotel. This one was no exception. My accommodations were on the hotel's VIP floor—equipped with special elevator access key and private lounge on the top floor overlooking the city. As I stepped off of the elevator I decided to go into the VIP lounge, read the newspaper, and have a drink. I arrived early, just before the happy hour, and no one else was in the lounge. I took a seat on one of the couches and began catching up on the day's news. Shortly after I sat down comfortably with my newspaper, a White man peeked his head into the lounge, looked at me sitting there in my best (and conservative) "dress for success" outfit—high heels and all—and with a pronounced Southern accent asked, "What time are y'all gonna be servin'?"

I tell this story both because storytelling is a part of critical race theory and because this particular story underscores an important point within the critical race theoretical paradigm—race still matters (West, 1992). Despite the scientific refutation of race as a legitimate biological concept and attempts to marginalize race in much of the public (political) discourse, race continues to be a powerful *social* construct and signifier:

> Race has become metaphorical—a way of referring to and disguising forces, events, classes, and expressions of social decay and economic division far more threatening to the body politic than biological "race" ever was. Expensively kept, economically unsound, a spurious and useless political asset in election campaigns, racism is as healthy today as it was during the Enlightenment. It seems that it has a utility far beyond economy, beyond the sequestering of classes from one another, and has assumed a metaphorical life so completely embedded in daily discourse that it is perhaps more necessary and more on display than ever before. (Morrison, 1992, p. 63)

I am intrigued by the many faces and permutations race has assumed in contemporary society. Our understanding of race has moved beyond the biogenetic categories and notions of phenotype. Our "advanced ideas" about race include the racialization of multiple cultural forms. Sociologist Sharon Lee (1993) suggests that "questions of race have been included in all U.S. population censuses since the first one in 1790" (p. 86). Although racial categories in the U.S. census have fluctuated over time, two categories have remained stable—Black and White. And although the creation of the category does not reveal what constitutes membership within it, it does create for us a sense of polar opposites that posits a cultural ranking designed to tell us who is White or, perhaps more pointedly, who is *not* White!

But determining who is and is not White is not merely a project of individual construction and/or biological designation. For example, in early census data citizens of Mexican descent were considered White. Over time, political, economic, social, and cultural shifts have forced Mexican Americans out of the White category. Conversely, Haney Lopez (1995) pointed out that some groups came to the United States and brought suit in the courts to be declared White. Omi and Winant (1994) argued that the polar notions of race as either an ideological construct or an objective condition both have shortcomings. Thinking of race strictly as an ideological concept denies the reality of a racialized society and its impact on people in their everyday lives. On the other hand, thinking of race solely as an objective condition denies the problematic aspects of race—how to decide who fits into which racial classifications.

Our notions of race (and its use) are so complex that even when it fails to "make sense" we continue to employ and deploy it. I want to argue that our conceptions of race, even in a postmodern and/or postcolonial world are more embedded and fixed than in a previous age. However, this embeddedness or "fixedness" has required new language and constructions of race so that denotations are submerged and hidden in ways that are offensive without identification. Thus, we develop notions of "conceptual whiteness" and "conceptual blackness" (King, 1995) that both do and do not map neatly on to biogenetic or cultural allegiances. "School achievement," "middle classness," "maleness," "beauty," "intelligence," "science" become normative categories of whiteness, whereas "gangs," "welfare recipients," "basketball players," "the underclass" become the marginalized and delegitimated categories of blackness.

The creation of these conceptual categories is not designed to reify a binary but rather to suggest how in a racialized society where whiteness is positioned as normative *everyone* is ranked and categorized in relation to these points of opposition. These categories fundamentally sculpt the extant terrain of possibilities even when other possibilities exist. And, although there is a fixedness to the notion of these categories, the ways in which they actually operate are fluid and shifting. For example, as an African American female academic, I can be and am sometimes positioned as conceptually White in relation to, perhaps, a Latino, Spanish-speaking gardener. In that instance, my class and social position override my racial identification and for that moment I become "White."

The significance of race need not be debated at length in this chapter. But as Toni Morrison argues, race is always already present in every social configuring of our lives. Roediger (1991, p. 3) asserts, "Even in an all-white town, race was never absent." However, more significant/problematic than the omnipresence of race is the notion that "whites reach the conclusion that their whiteness is meaningful" (Roediger, p. 6). It is because of the meaning and value imputed to whiteness that CRT becomes an important intellectual and social tool for deconstruction, reconstruction, and construction—deconstruction of oppressive structures and discourses, reconstruction of human agency, and construction of equitable and socially just relations of power. In this chapter I am attempting to speak to innovative theoretical ways for framing discussions about social justice and democracy and the role of education in reproducing or interrupting current practices.

I will provide a brief synopsis of critical race theory[1] and discuss some of its prominent themes. Then I will discuss its importance to our understanding of the citizen in a democracy, and its relationship to education; and finally, I will offer some cautionary implications for further research and study. As is true of all texts, this one is incomplete (O'Neill, 1992). It is incomplete on the part of both the writer and the reader. However, given its incompleteness, I implore readers to grapple with how it might advance the debate on race and education.

What Is Critical Race Theory?

Most people in the United States first learned of critical race theory (CRT) when Lani Guinier, a University of Pennsylvania law professor, became a political casualty of the Clinton administration. Her legal writings were the focus of much scrutiny in the media. Unschooled and unsophisticated about the nature of legal academic writing, the media vilified Guinier and accused her of advocating "un-American" ideas. The primary focus of the scorn shown Guinier was her argument for proportional representation.

Guinier (1991) asserted that in electoral situations where particular racial groups were a clear (and persistent) minority, the only possibility for an equitable chance at social benefits and fair political representation might be for minority votes to count for more than their actual numbers.

Guinier first proposed such a strategy as a solution for a post-apartheid South Africa. Because Whites are in the obvious minority, the only way for them to participate in the governing of a new South Africa would be to insure them some seats in the newly formed government.

Guinier made a similar argument in favor of African Americans in the United States. She saw this as a legal response to the ongoing lack of representation. Unfortunately, her political opponents attacked her scholarship as an affront to the American tradition of "one person, one vote." The furor over Guinier's work obscured the fact that as an academic, Guinier was expected to write "cutting-edge" scholarship that pushed theoretical boundaries (Guinier, 1994). Her work was not to be literally applied to legal practice. However, in the broad scope of critical race legal studies, Guinier may be seen as relatively moderate and nowhere near the radical that the press made her out to be. But, her "exposure" placed critical race theory and its proponents in the midst of the public discourse.

According to Delgado (1995, p. xiii), "Critical race theory sprang up in the mid-1970s with the early work of Derrick Bell (an African American) and Alan Freeman (a White), both of whom were deeply distressed over the slow pace of racial reform in the United States." They argued that the traditional approaches of filing amicus briefs, protests, marching, and appealing to the moral sensibilities of decent citizens produced smaller and fewer gains than in previous times. Before long they were being joined by other legal scholars who shared their frustration with traditional civil rights strategies.

CRT is both an outgrowth of and a separate entity from an earlier legal movement called critical legal studies (CLS). Critical legal studies is a leftist legal movement that challenged the traditional legal scholarship that focused on doctrinal and policy analysis (Gordon, 1990) in favor of a form of law that spoke to the specificity of individuals and groups in social and cultural contexts. CLS scholars also challenged the notion that "the civil rights struggle represents a long, steady march toward social transformation" (Crenshaw, 1988, p. 1334).

According to Crenshaw (p. 1350), "Critical [legal] scholars have attempted to analyze legal ideology and discourse as a social artifact which operates to recreate and legitimate American society." Scholars in the CLS movement decipher legal doctrine to expose both its internal and external inconsistencies and to reveal the ways that "legal ideology has helped create, support, and legitimate America's present class structure" (Crenshaw, p. 1350). The contribution of CLS to legal discourse is in its analysis of legitimating structures in the society. Much of the CLS ideology emanates from the work of Gramsci (1971) and depends on the Gramscian notion of "hegemony" to describe the continued legitimacy of oppressive structures in American society. However, CLS fails to provide pragmatic strategies for material social transformation. Cornel West (1993, p. 196) asserts:

> Critical legal theorists fundamentally question the dominant liberal paradigms prevalent and pervasive in American culture and society. This thorough questioning is not primarily a constructive attempt to put forward a conception of a new legal and social order. Rather, it is a pronounced disclosure of inconsistencies, incoherences, silences, and blindness of legal formalists, legal positivists, and legal realists in the liberal tradition. Critical legal studies is more a concerted attack and assault on the legitimacy and authority of pedagogical strategies in law school than a comprehensive announcement of what a credible and realizable new society and legal system would look like.

CLS scholars critiqued mainstream legal ideology for its portrayal of U.S. society as a meritocracy but failed to include racism in its critique. Thus, CRT became a logical outgrowth of the discontent of legal scholars of color.

CRT begins with the notion that racism is "normal, not aberrant, in American society" (Delgado, 1995, p. xiv) and because it is so enmeshed in the fabric of our social order, it appears both normal and natural to people in this culture. Indeed, Bell's major premise in *Faces at the bottom of the well* (1992) is that racism is a permanent fixture of American life. Thus, the strategy becomes one of unmasking and exposing racism in its various permutations.

Second, CRT departs from mainstream legal scholarship by sometimes employing storytelling to "analyze the myths, presuppositions, and received wisdoms that make up the common culture about race and that invariably render blacks and other minorities one-down" (Delgado, 1995, p. xiv). According to Barnes (1990, pp. 1864–1865), "Critical race theorists . . . integrate their *experiential knowledge* (emphasis added), drawn from a shared history as 'other' with their ongoing struggles to transform a world deteriorating under the albatross of racial hegemony." Thus, the experience of oppressions such as racism or sexism is important for developing a CRT analytical standpoint. To the extent that Whites (or in the case of sexism, men) experience forms of racial oppression, they may develop such a standpoint. For example, the historical figure John Brown suffered aspects of racism by aligning himself closely with the cause of African American liberation.[2] Contemporary examples of such identification may occur when White parents adopt transracially. No longer a White family, by virtue of their child(ren) they become racialized others. A final example was played out in the infamous O. J. Simpson trials. The criminal trial jury was repeatedly identified as the "Black" jury despite the presence of one White and one Latino juror. However, the majority White civil case jury was not given a racial designation. When Whites are exempted from racial designations and become "families," "jurors," "students," "teachers," etc., their ability to apply a CRT analytical rubric is limited. One of the most dramatic examples of the shift from non-raced to CRT perspective occurred when Gregory Williams (1995) moved from Virginia where he was a White boy to Muncie, Indiana where his family was known to be Black. The changes in his economic and social status were remarkable, and the story he tells underscores the salience of race in life's possibilities. The primary reason this story is deemed important among CRT scholars is that it adds necessary contextual contours to the seeming "objectivity" of positivist perspectives.

Third, CRT insists on a critique of liberalism. Crenshaw (1988) argues that the liberal perspective of the "civil rights crusade as a long, slow, but always upward pull" (p. 1334) is flawed because it fails to understand the limits of current legal paradigms to serve as catalysts for social change and because of its emphasis on incrementalism. CRT argues that racism requires sweeping changes but liberalism has no mechanism for such changes. Rather, liberal legal practices support the painstakingly slow process of arguing legal precedence to gain citizen rights for people of color.

Fourth, and related to the liberal perspective, is the argument posed by CRT that Whites have been the primary beneficiaries of civil rights legislation. For example, although under attack throughout the nation, the policy of affirmative action has benefited Whites. The actual numbers reveal that the major recipients of affirmative action hiring policies have been White women (Guy-Sheftall, 1993). One might argue that many of these White women have incomes that support households in which other Whites live—men, women, and children. The ability of these women to find work ultimately benefits Whites in general.

Let us look at some of the social benefits African Americans have received due to affirmative action policies. Even after twenty years of affirmative action, African Americans constitute only 4.5 percent of the professoriate (Hacker, 1992). In 1991 there were 24,721 doctoral degrees awarded to U.S. citizens and noncitizens who intended to remain in the United States, and only 933 or 3.8 percent of these doctorates went to African American men and women. If every one of those newly minted doctorates went into the academy, it would have a negligible effect on the proportion of African Americans in the professoriate. The majority of the African Americans who earn Ph.D.'s earn them in the field of education, and of that group, most of the degrees are in educational administration, where the recipients continue as school practitioners.

Thus, CRT theorists cite this kind of empirical evidence to support their contention that civil rights laws continue to serve the interests of Whites. A more fruitful tack, some CRT scholars argue, is to find the place where the interests of Whites and people of color intersect. This notion of "interest convergence" (Bell, 1980) can be seen in what transpired in Arizona over the Martin Luther King, Jr. holiday commemoration.

Originally, the state of Arizona insisted that the King holiday was too costly and failed to recognize it for state workers and agencies. Subsequently, a variety of African American groups and their supporters began to boycott business, professional, and social functions in the state of Arizona. When members of the National Basketball Association and the National Football League suggested that neither the NBA All-Star Game nor the Super Bowl would be held in Arizona because of the state's failure to recognize the King holiday, the decision was reversed. Hardly anyone is naive enough to believe that the governor of Arizona had a change of heart about the significance of the King holiday. Rather, when his position on the holiday had the effect of hurting state tourist and sports entertainment revenues, the state's interests (to enhance revenue) converged with those of the African American community (to recognize Dr. King). Thus, converging interests, not support of civil rights, led to the reversal of the state's position.

A recent compilation of CRT key writings (Crenshaw et al., 1995) points out that there is no "canonical set of doctrines or methodologies to which [CRT scholars] all subscribe" (p. xiii). However, these scholars are unified by two common interests—to understand how a "regime of white supremacy and its subordination of people of color have been created and maintained in America" (p. xiii) and to change the bond that exists between law and racial power.

Legal scholars such as Patricia Williams (1991) and Derrick Bell (1987, 1992) were among the early Critical Race Theorists whose ideas reached the general public. Some might argue that their wide appeal was the result of their abilities to tell compelling stories into which they embedded legal issues.[3] This use of story is of particular interest to educators because of the growing popularity of narrative and narrative inquiry in the study of teaching (Connelly and Clandinin, 1990; Carter, 1993). But just because more people are recognizing and using story as a part of scholarly inquiry, it does not mean that all stories are received as legitimate in knowledge construction and advancement of a discipline.

Lawrence (1995) asserts that there is a tradition of storytelling in law and that litigation is highly formalized storytelling. The stories of ordinary people, in general, have not been told or recorded in the literature of law (or any other discipline). But their failure to make it into the canons of literature or research does not make them less important stories.

Stories provide the necessary context for understanding, feeling, and interpreting. The ahistorical and acontextual nature of much law and other "science" renders the voices of dispossessed and marginalized group members mute. Much of the scholarship of CRT focuses on the role of "voice" to bring additional power to legal discourse involving racial justice. Delgado (1990) argues that people of color speak with experiential knowledge that our society is deeply structured by racism. That structure gives their stories a common framework warranting the term "voice." Critical race theorists are attempting to interject minority cultural viewpoints, derived from a common history of oppression, with their efforts to reconstruct a society crumbling under the burden of racial hegemony (Barnes, 1990).

The use of voice or "naming your reality" is a way that CRT links form and substance in scholarship. CRT scholars use parables, chronicles, stories, counterstories, poetry, fiction, and revisionist histories to illustrate the false necessity and irony of much of current civil rights doctrine. Delgado (1989) suggests that there are at least three reasons for "naming one's own reality" in legal discourse:

1. Much of "reality" is socially constructed;
2. Stories provide members of out-groups a vehicle for psychic self-preservation; and
3. The exchange of stories from teller to listener can help overcome ethnocentrism and the dysconscious (King, 1992) conviction of viewing the world in one way.

The first reason for naming one's own reality involves how political and moral analysis is conducted in legal scholarship. Many mainstream legal scholars embrace universalism over particularity. According to Williams (1991), "theoretical legal understanding" is characterized in Anglo American jurisprudence by the acceptance of transcendent, acontextual, universal legal truths or procedures. For instance, some legal scholars might contend that the tort of fraud has always existed and that it is a component belonging to the universal system of right and wrong. This worldview tends to discount anything that is non-transcendent (historical), or contextual (socially constructed), or non-universal (specific) with the unscholarly labels of "emotional," "literary," "personal," or false (Williams, 1991).

In contrast, critical race theorists argue that political and moral analysis is situational—"truths only exist for this person in this predicament at this time in history" (Delgado, 1991). For the critical race theorist, social reality is constructed by the formulation and the exchange of stories about individual situations (see, for example, Matsuda, 1989). These stories serve as interpretive structures by which we impose order on experience, and experience imposes order on us (Delgado, 1989).

A second reason for the "naming one's own reality" theme of CRT is the psychic preservation of marginalized groups. A factor contributing to the demoralization of marginalized groups is self-condemnation (Delgado, 1989). Members of minority groups internalize the stereotypic images that certain elements of society have constructed in order to maintain their power. Historically, storytelling has been a kind of medicine to heal the wounds of pain caused by racial oppression. The story of one's condition leads to the realization of how one came to be oppressed and subjugated, thus allowing one to stop inflicting mental violence on oneself.

Finally, naming one's own reality with stories can affect the oppressor. Most oppression, as was discussed earlier, does not seem like oppression to the perpetrator (Lawrence, 1987). Delgado (1989) argues that the dominant group justifies its power with stories, stock explanations that construct reality in ways to maintain their privilege. Thus, oppression is rationalized, causing little self-examination by the oppressor. Stories by people of color can catalyze the necessary cognitive conflict to jar dysconscious racism.

The "voice" component of CRT provides a way to communicate the experience and realities of the oppressed, a first step in understanding the complexities of racism and beginning a process of judicial redress. The voice of people of color is required for a deep understanding of the educational system. Delpit (1988) argues that one of the tragedies of the field of education is how the dialogue of people of color has been silenced. Delpit begins her analysis of the process-oriented versus the skills-oriented writing debate with a statement (or story) from an African American male graduate student at a predominantly White university who is also a special education teacher in an African American community (p. 280):

> There comes a moment in every class where we have to discuss "The Black Issue" and what's appropriate education for Black children. I tell you, I'm tired of arguing with those White people, because they won't listen. Well, I don't know if they really don't listen or if they just don't believe you. It seems like if you can't quote Vygotsky or something, then you don't have any validity to speak about your own kids. Anyway, I'm not bothering with it anymore, now I'm just in it for a grade.

The above comment and numerous other statements found in Delpit's analysis illustrate the frustration of teachers of color caused by being left out of the dialogue about how best to educate children of color. Further, Delpit raises several very important questions:

How can such complete communication blocks exist when both parties [Black and Whites] truly believe they have the same aims? How can the bitterness and resentment expressed by educators of color be drained so that all sores can heal? What can be done? (1988, p. 282)

Critical Race Theory and Citizenship

One of the places to begin understanding CRT is to examine how conceptions of citizenship and race interact. Although the connections between race and citizenship are numerous and complex, in this chapter I will detail only one of the central connections that is important in understanding the relationship of critical race scholarship to educational issues. That central connection is the "property issue" (Ladson-Billings and Tate, 1995). CRT scholars assert that the United States is a nation conceived and built on property rights (Bell, 1987; Harris, 1993). In the early history of the nation only propertied White males enjoyed the franchise. The significance of property ownership as a prerequisite to citizenship was tied to the British notion that only people who *owned* the country, not merely those who *lived* in it, were eligible to make decisions about it.[4]

The salience of property often is missed in our understanding of the United States as a nation. Conflated with democracy, capitalism slides into the background of our understanding of the way in which U.S. political and economic ideologies are entangled and read as synonymous. But it is this foundation of property rights that makes civil rights legislation so painfully slow and sometimes ineffective. Civil rights are wedded to the construction of the rights of the individual. Bell (1987, p. 239) argues that "the concept of individual rights, unconnected to property rights, was totally foreign to these men of property," in his explanation of how men who expressed a commitment to liberty and justice could uphold the repression of African Americans, the indigenous peoples who inhabited the land, and women.

African Americans represented a particular conundrum because not only were they not accorded individual civil rights because they were not White and owned no property, but they were constructed *as* property! However, that construction was only in the sense that they could be owned by others. They possessed no rights of property ownership. Whites, on the other hand, according to Harris (1993, p. 1721), benefited from the construction of whiteness as the ultimate property. "Possession—the act necessary to lay basis for rights in property—was defined to include only the cultural practices of Whites. This definition laid the foundation for the idea that whiteness—that which Whites alone possess—is valuable and is property."

This thematic strand of whiteness as property in the United States is not confined to the nation's early history. Indeed, Andrew Hacker's (1992) exercise with his college students illustrates the material and social value the students place on their possession of whiteness. Hacker uses a parable to illustrate that although the students insist that "in this day and age, things are better for Blacks" (p. 31), none of them would want to change places with African Americans. When asked what amount of compensation they would seek if they were forced to "become Black," the students "seemed to feel that it would not be out of place to ask for $50 million, or $1 million for each coming Black year" (p. 32). Hacker continues:

> And this calculation conveys, as well as anything, the value that white people place on their own skins. Indeed, to be white is to possess a gift whose value can be appreciated only after it has been taken away. And why ask so large a sum? . . . The money would be used, as best it could, to buy protection from the discriminations and dangers white people know they would face once they were perceived to be black. (p. 32)

Thus, even without the use of a sophisticated legal rhetorical argument, Whites know they possess a property that people of color do not and that to possess it confers aspects of citizenship not available to others. Harris's (1993) argument is that the "property functions of whiteness"—rights of disposition, rights to use and enjoyment, reputation and status property, and the absolute right to exclude—make the American dream of "life, liberty, and the pursuit of happiness" a more likely and attainable reality for Whites as citizens. This reality also is more likely to engender feelings of loyalty and commitment to a nation that works in the interests of Whites. Conversely, Blacks, aware that they will never possess this ultimate property, are less sanguine about U.S. citizenship.

Patricia Williams (1995) explains these differential notions of citizenship as being grounded in differential experiences of rights because "one's sense of empowerment defines one's relation to law, in terms of trust-distrust, formality-informality, or right-no rights (or needs)" (pp. 87–88). An example of this differing relation (in this case to commerce) was shared in one of my classes.

We were discussing McIntosh's (1990) article on "White privilege." One White woman shared a personal experience of going into a neighborhood supermarket, having her items rung up by the cashier and discovering that she did not have her checkbook. The cashier told her she could take her groceries and bring the check back later. When she related this story to an African American male friend, he told her that was an example of the privilege she enjoyed because she was White. Her White property was collateral against the cart full of groceries. She insisted that this was the store's good neighbor policy and the same thing would have happened to him. Determined to show his friend that their life experiences were qualitatively different, the young man went shopping a few days later and pretended to have left his checkbook. The young woman was standing off to the side observing the interaction. The same cashier, who had been pointed out by the woman as the "neighborly one," told the young African American man that he could push the grocery items to the side while he went home to get his checkbook. The White woman was shocked as the African American male gave her a knowing look.

These daily indignities take their toll on people of color. When these indignities are skimmed over in the classrooms that purport to develop students into citizens, it is no wonder students "blow off" classroom discourse. How can students be expected to deconstruct rights "in a world of no rights" (Williams, 1995, p. 89) and construct statements of need "in a world abundantly apparent of need" (p. 89)?

African Americans represent a unique form of citizen in the United States—property transformed into citizen. This process has not been a smooth one. When Chief Justice Taney concluded in the *Dred Scott* decision that African Americans had no rights Whites were required to respect, he reinscribed the person-as-property status of African Americans. Later in *Plessy v. Ferguson* the high court once again denied full citizenship rights to African Americans as a way to assert White property rights—rights to use and enjoyment and the absolute right to exclude.

Even the laudable decision of *Brown v. Board of Education* comes under scrutiny in the CRT paradigm. Lest we misread *Brown v. Board of Education* as merely a pang of conscience and the triumph of right over wrong, it is important to set *Brown* in context. First, the *Brown* decision helped the United States in its struggle to minimize the spread of communism to so-called Third World nations. In many countries, the credibility of the United States had been damaged by the widely broadcast inequitable social conditions that existed in the United States in the 1950s. Both the government and the NAACP lawyers argued the *Brown* decision would help legitimize the political and economic philosophies of the United States with these developing nations (Bell, 1980).

Second, *Brown* provided reassurance to African Americans that the freedom and equality fought for during World War II might become a reality at home. Black veterans faced not only racial inequality but also physical harm in many parts of the South. And the treatment of African Americans after the war in concert with the voice of African American leaders such as Paul Robeson may have greatly influenced the *Brown* decision. Robeson argued: "It is unthinkable . . . that American Negroes would go to war on behalf of those who have oppressed us for generations ... against a country [the Soviet Union] which in one generation has raised our people to the full human dignity of mankind" (Foner, 1978, pp. 17–18).

According to Bell (1980), it is not unreasonable to assume that those in positions of power would recognize the importance of neutralizing Robeson and others who held similar views. Robeson's comments were an affront to the "national interests." Thus, racial decisions by the courts were pivotal in softening the criticism about the contradiction of a free and just nation that maintained a segment of its citizenry in second-class status based on race. Finally, there were White capitalists who understood that the South could only be transformed from an agrarian society to an industrialized sunbelt when it ended the divisive battle over state-supported segregation. Here, segregation was read as a barrier obstructing the economic self-interest of U.S. profit makers.

At this writing, the electorate of California have passed Proposition 209, calling for an end to "preferential treatment" in state employment and state university admission policies based on race or gender. The trope of preferential treatment has helped create a perception that ending affirmative action will lead to a more fair and equitable society; but in reality, the proposition will be used to instantiate the hierarchical relations of power that once again privilege whiteness as the most valued property. Citizenship for people of color remains elusive.

Critical Race Theoretical Approaches to Education

Thus far in this chapter I have attempted to explain the meaning and historical background of critical race theory in legal scholarship and the role of property rights in understanding citizenship. However, educators and researchers in the field of education will want to know what relevance CRT has to education. The connections between law and education are relatively simple to establish. Since education in the United States is not outlined explicitly in the nation's constitution, it is one of the social functions relegated to individual states. Consequently, states generate legislation and enact laws designed to proscribe the contours of education.

One of the earliest legislative attempts was Massachusetts' "old deluder Satan" act that required citizens of the state to provide education for its children to ensure they received moral and religious instruction. In the modern era the intersection of school and law provided fertile ground for testing and enacting civil rights legislation. Thus, the landmark *Brown* decision generated a spate of school desegregation activity in the late 1950s and early 1960s—the desegregation of Central High School in Little Rock, Arkansas, the New Orleans public schools, the University of Mississippi, the University of Alabama, and the University of

Georgia. By the 1970s, school desegregation/civil rights battles were being fought in northern cities. The fight for school desegregation in Boston schools was among the most vicious in civil rights annals.

One recurring theme that characterized the school/civil rights legal battles was "equal opportunity." This notion of equal opportunity was associated with the idea that students of color should have access to the same school opportunities—i.e., curriculum, instruction, funding, and facilities—as White students. This emphasis on "sameness" was important because it helped boost the arguments for "equal treatment under the law" that were important for moving African Americans from their second-class status.

But what was necessary to help African Americans to "catch up" with their White counterparts? Beyond equal treatment was the need to redress pass inequities. Thus, policies of affirmative action and the creation of African Americans and others as "protected classes" were adopted to ensure that African Americans were not systematically screened out of opportunities in employment, college admission, and housing. If we look at the way that public education is currently configured, it is possible to see the ways that CRT can be a powerful explanatory tool for the sustained inequity that people of color experience. I will use the areas of curriculum, instruction, assessment, school funding, and desegregation as exemplars of the relationship that can exist between CRT and education.

Curriculum

Critical race theory sees the official school curriculum as a culturally specific artifact designed to maintain a White supremacist master script. As Swartz (1992) contends:

> Master scripting silences multiple voices and perspectives, primarily legitimizing dominant, white, upper-class, male voicings as the "standard" knowledge students need to know. All other accounts and perspectives are omitted from the master script unless they can be disempowered through misrepresentation. Thus, content that does not reflect the dominant voice must be brought under control, *mastered*, and then reshaped before it can become a part of the master script. (p. 341)

This master scripting means stories of African Americans are muted and erased when they challenge dominant culture authority and power. Thus, Rosa Parks is reduced to a tired seamstress instead of a longtime participant in social justice endeavors as evidenced by her work at the Highlander Folk School to prepare for a confrontation with segregationist ideology. Or, Martin Luther King, Jr. becomes a sanitized folk hero

who enjoyed the full support of "good Americans" rather than a dis-
dained scholar and activist whose vision extended to social justice causes
throughout the world and who challenged the United States on issues of
economic injustice and aggression in Southeast Asia.

The race-neutral or color-blind perspective, evident in the way the curriculum presents people of color, presumes a homogenized "we" in a cel-
ebration of diversity. This perspective embraces a so-called multicultural
perspective by "misequating the middle passage with Ellis Island" (King,
1992, p. 327). Thus, students are taught erroneously that "we are all immigrants" and African American, Indigenous, and Chicano students are
left with the guilt of failing to rise above their immigrant status like
"every other group."

But it is not just the distortions, omissions, and stereotypes of school
curriculum content that must be considered, it also is the rigor of the
curriculum and access to what is deemed "enriched" curriculum via
courses and classes for the gifted and talented. In Jonathan Kozol's
(1991) words:

> The curriculum [the white school] follows "emphasizes critical thinking,
> reasoning and logic." The planetarium, for instance, is employed not simply
> for the study of the universe as it exists. "Children also are designing their
> own galaxies," the teacher says. . . .
>
> In my [Kozol's] notes: "Six girls, four boys. Nine White, one Chinese. I am
> glad they have this class. But what about the others? Aren't there ten Black
> children in the school who could *enjoy* this also?" (p. 96)

This restricted access to the curriculum is a good illustration of Harris's
(1993) explanation of the function of property in terms of use and enjoyment.

Instruction

CRT suggests that current instructional strategies presume that African
American students are deficient. As a consequence, classroom teachers
are engaged in a never-ending quest for "*the* right strategy or technique"
to deal with (read: control) "at-risk" (read: African American) students.
Cast in a language of failure, instructional approaches for African American students typically involve some aspect of remediation.

The race-neutral perspective purports to see deficiency as an individual phenomenon. Thus, instruction is conceived as a generic set of teaching skills that should work for all students. When these strategies or
skills fail to achieve desired results, the students, not the techniques, are
found to be lacking.

Fortunately, new research efforts are rejecting deficit models and investigating and affirming the integrity of effective teachers of African American students.[5] This scholarship underscores the teachers' understanding of the saliency of race in education and the society and the need to make racism explicit so that students can recognize and struggle against this particular form of oppression.

Examples of pedagogical countermoves are found in the work of both Chicago elementary teacher Marva Collins and Los Angeles high school mathematics teacher Jaime Escalante. Although neither Collins nor Escalante is acclaimed as a "progressive" teacher, both are recognized for their persistence in believing in the educability of all students. Both remind students that mainstream society expects them to be failures, and prod them to succeed as a form of counterinsurgency. Their insistence on helping students achieve in the "traditional" curriculum represents a twist on Audre Lorde's notion that one cannot dismantle the master's house with the master's tools. Instead, they believe one can only dismantle the master's house with the master's tools.

Assessment

For the critical race theorist, intelligence testing has been a movement to legitimize African American students' deficiency under the guise of scientific rationalism (Gould, 1981; Aleinikoff, 1991). According to Marable (1983) one purpose of the African American in the racial/capitalist state is to serve as a symbolic index for poor Whites. If working-class Whites are "achieving" at a higher level than Blacks, then they feel relatively superior. This allows Whites with real power to exploit both poor Whites and Blacks. Throughout U.S. history, the subordination of Blacks has been built on "scientific" theories (e.g., intelligence testing), each of which depends on racial stereotypes about Blacks that makes their condition appear appropriate. Crenshaw (1988) contends that the point of controversy is no longer that these stereotypes were developed to rationalize the oppression of Blacks but rather "the extent to which these stereotypes serve a hegemonic function by perpetuating a mythology about both Blacks and Whites even today, reinforcing an illusion of a White community that cuts across ethnic, gender, and class lines" (p. 1371).

In the classroom, a dysfunctional curriculum coupled with a lack of instructional innovation (or persistence) adds up to poor performance on traditional assessment measures. These assessment measures—crude by most analyses—may tell us that students do not know what is on the test but fail to tell us what students actually know and are able to do. A telling example of this mismatch between what schools measure and what students know and can do is that of a 10-year-old African American girl who was repeatedly told by the teacher that she was a poor math student. However, the teacher was unaware that the girl was living under incredible stresses where she was assuming responsibilities her drug-addicted mother could not. To ward off child welfare agents, the child handled all household responsibilities including budgeting and paying all the household bills. Her ability to keep the household going made it appear that everything was fine in the household. According to the teacher she could not do fourth grade math, but the evidence of her life suggests she was doing just fine at "adult" math!

School Funding

Perhaps no area of schooling underscores inequity and racism better than school funding. CRT argues that inequality in school funding is a function of institutional and structural racism. The inability of African Americans to qualify for educational advancements, jobs, and mortgages creates a cycle of low educational achievement, underemployment and unemployment, and substandard housing. Without suffering a single act of personal racism, most African Americans suffer the consequence of systemic and structural racism.[6]

Jonathan Kozol's *Savage inequalities* (1991) created an emotional and ethical stir within and beyond the education community. White colleagues talked of how moved both they and their students were as they read Kozol's descriptions of inequity in school settings. Some talked of being "moved to tears" and "unable to read more than a few pages at a time." Others talked of how difficult it was for their students to read the book. Interestingly, many African American colleagues indicated that, although Kozol had been precise and passionate in his documentation, he had not revealed anything new about the differences that exist between African American and White schools. But Kozol's research did give voice to people of color. His analysis of funding inequities provides insight into the impact of racism and White self-interest on school funding policies.

CRT argues that the import of property provides another way to consider the funding disparity. Schooling, as a function of individual states, is differentially administered by the various state legislatures. But one of the most common aspects of these 50 different schooling agencies is the way they are funded. Almost every state funds schools based on property taxes. Those areas with property of greater wealth typically have better-funded schools. In the appendix of Kozol's book are comparisons showing the disparities within three different areas. In the Chicago area for the 1988–89 school year the funding disparity was almost $4,000 per pupil: Chicago schools were spending $5,265 per pupil, whereas the suburban Niles Township High School District was spending $9,371. In the New Jersey area the differences between Camden schools and Princeton schools was about $4,200 in per pupil spending. In the New York City area the difference was almost $6,000 in per pupil spending.

Talking about the disparity between per pupil spending often invites the critique that money doesn't matter. Studies as far back as Coleman et al. (1966) and Jencks et al. (1972) have argued that family and individual effects are far more powerful than schools in determining poor school performance. Whether or not school spending is a determining factor in school achievement, no one from the family and individual effects camp can mount an ethical case for allowing poor children to languish in unheated, overcrowded schools with bathrooms that spew raw sewage, whereas middle-income White students attend spacious, technology-rich, inviting school buildings. If money doesn't matter, then why spend it on the rich?

CRT takes to task school reformers who fail to recognize that property is a powerful determiner of academic advantage. Without a commitment to redesign funding formulas, one of the basic inequities of schooling will remain in place and virtually guarantee the reproduction of the status quo.

Desegregation

Although desegregation is not occurring in every school district, its impact on the national level is important enough to be included with the more common school experiences of curriculum, instruction, assessment, and funding. Despite the recorded history of the fight for school desegregation, CRT scholars argue that, rather than serving as a solution to social inequity, school desegregation has been promoted only in ways that advantage Whites (Bell, 1980).

Lomotey and Staley's (1990) examination of Buffalo's "model desegregation" program revealed that African American students continued to be poorly served by the school system. African American student achievement failed to improve, and suspension, expulsion, and drop-out rates continued to rise. What, then, made Buffalo a model desegregation program? In short, the benefits that Whites derived from the program and their seeming support of desegregation. As a result of the school desegregation program Whites were able to take advantage of special magnet school programs and free extended child care. Thus, a model desegregation program is one that insures that Whites are happy (and do not leave the system altogether).

The report of school desegregation in Buffalo is not unlike the allegorical story presented by CRT dean Derrick Bell (1987). The story entitled

"The sacrificed Black children" illustrates how the failure to accept African American children into their community schools causes a White school district to ultimately end up begging the students to come because their presence was tied intimately to the economic prosperity of the community. It is this realization that civil rights legislation in the United States always has benefited Whites (even if it has not always benefited African Americans) that forms the crux of the CRT argument against traditional liberal civil rights legislation. The CRT argument provides an important segue into the final section of this chapter—the need for caution in proceeding with the integration of CRT into educational research.

Words of Caution

It is the pattern in educational research for a new idea or innovation to take hold and proliferate. Sometimes an idea takes a while to take root, but once it does, most likely its creators lose control of the idea. Consider what happened with the notion of cooperative learning. When Cohen and Roper (1972) proposed cooperative classroom structures to equalize the status of White and African American students, their work held great promise for helping teachers to develop curricular and instructional strategies for improving the academic performance of all children in desegregated classrooms. However, somehow their findings got distilled into day-long workshops and five-step lesson plans. School systems throughout the United States were adopting cooperative learning without any thought to improving the performance of children of color.

A similar transmutation of theory is occurring in the area of multicultural education. Although scholars such as James Banks, Carl Grant, and Geneva Gay[7] began on a scholarly path designed to change schools as institutions so that students might be prepared to reconstruct the society, in its current practice iteration, multicultural education is but a shadow of its conceptual self. Rather than engage students in provocative thinking about the contradictions of U.S. ideals and lived realities, teachers often find themselves encouraging students to sing "ethnic" songs, eat ethnic foods, and do ethnic dances. Consistently, manifestations of multicultural education in the classroom are superficial and trivial "celebrations of diversity."

What, then, might happen to CRT in the hands of educational researchers and school personnel? Well, to be honest, like Lani Guinier, I doubt if it will go very far into the mainstream. Rather, CRT in education is likely to become the "darling" of the radical left, continue to generate scholarly papers and debate, and never penetrate the classrooms and daily experiences of students of color. But, students of color, their families, and their communities cannot afford the luxury of CRT scholars' ruminations any more than they could afford those of critical and post-modern theorists, where the ideas are laudable but the practice leaves much to be desired.

As excited as I may be about the potential of CRT for illuminating our thinking about school inequity, I believe educational researchers need much more time to study and understand the legal literature in which it is situated. It is very tempting to appropriate it as a more powerful explanatory narrative for the persistent problems of race, racism, and social injustice. If we are serious about solving these problems in schools and classrooms, we have to be serious about intense study and careful rethinking of race and education. Adopting and adapting CRT as a framework for educational equity means that we will have to expose racism in education *and* propose radical solutions for addressing it. We will have to take bold and sometimes unpopular positions. We may be pilloried, figuratively, or at least vilified for these stands. Ultimately, we may have to stand, symbolically, before the nation as Lani Guinier and hear our ideas distorted and misrepresented. We may have to defend a radical approach to democracy that seriously undermines the privilege of those who have so skillfully carved that privilege into the foundation of the nation. We will have to adopt a position of consistently swimming against the current. We run the risk of being permanent outsiders, but as Wynter (1992) suggests, we must operate from a position of *alterity* or *liminality* where we may "call into question the rules of functioning on whose basis the United States conceptualizes itself as a generically 'White' nation, and elaborate its present system of societal self-knowledge" (p. 19). But, I fear we (educational researchers) may never assume the liminal position because of its dangers, its discomfort, and because we insist on thinking of ourselves as permanent residents in a *nice* field like education.

Notes

1. For a richer description of critical race theory, see Tate, W. (1997), Critical race theory and education: History, theory, and implications. In M. Apple (Ed.), *Review of research in education* (vol. 23). Washington, DC: American Educational Research Association.

2. Scholars such as Peggy McIntosh (1990) and Ruth Frankenberg (1993) have begun to deconstruct whiteness through their position of otherness as women. Their work suggests possibilities for Whites to deploy a CRT analysis.

3. Williams is known for her Benetton story, which tells about how she was locked out of a trendy clothing store in New York because of her race. Some doubted the "generalizability" of Williams's story until television personality Oprah Winfrey reported a similar incident. Bell's "Space Traders" story is an allegorical tale that suggests that White America would gladly "give away" African Americans to space aliens if the aliens made a good enough trade.

4. Of course in America the concept of "ownership" of the land has to be contested by the indigenous people's rights to that land. However, that discussion is beyond the scope of this paper.

5. See for example, M. Foster and J. Newman (1989), "I don't know nothin' about it": Black teachers' code-switching strategies in interviews, Working papers in educational linguistics (WPEL) (Philadelphia: Graduate School of Education, University of Pennsylvania); A. Henry (1992), African Canadian women teachers' activism: Recreating communities of caring and resistance, *The Journal of Negro Education, 61*, 392–494; G. Ladson-Billings (1995), "But that's just good teaching!" The case for culturally relevant teaching, *Theory into Practice, 34*, 159–165.

6. The impact of racism generally is tied to the everyday lives of poor and underclass people of color. Recently, revelations of major U.S. corporations (Texaco, Avis) indicate that they systematically perpetuate racism in hiring, promotion, and customer service.

7. Banks, Grant, and Gay are but a few of the notables who were in the forefront of the intellectual genesis of multicultural education. Gwendolyn Baker, Carlos Cortez, and Margaret Gibson are others. Any attempt to name them all would fall short.

References

Aleinikoff, T. A. (1991). A case for race-consciousness. *Columbia Law Review, 91*, 1060–1125.

Barnes, R. (1990). Race consciousness: The thematic content of racial distinctiveness in critical race scholarship. *Harvard Law Review, 103*, 1864–1871.

Bell, D. (1980). *Brown* and the interest convergence dilemma. In Bell, D. (Ed.), *Shades of Brown: New perspectives on school desegregation* (pp. 90–106). New York: Teachers College Press.

_____. (1987). *And we are not saved: The elusive quest for racial justice.* New York: Basic Books.

_____. (1992). *Faces at the bottom of the well: The permanence of racism.* New York: Basic Books.

_____. (1993). The place of story in the study of teaching and teacher education. *Educational Researcher, 22* (1), 5–12.

Cohen, E. G., and Roper, S. S. (1972). Modification on interracial interaction disability: An application of status characteristics theory. *American Sociological Review, 37*, 643–657.

Coleman, J. S., Campbell, E. G., Hobson, C. J., McPartland, J., Mood, A. M., Weinfeld, F. D., and York, R. L. (1966). *Equality of educational opportunity.* Washington, DC: U.S. Government Printing Office.

Connelly, F. M., and Clandinin, D. J. (1990). Stories of experience and narrative inquiry. *Educational Researcher, 19* (5), 2–14.

Crenshaw, K. (1988). Race, reform, and retrenchment: Transformation and legitimation in antidiscrimination law. *Harvard Law Review, 101*, 1331–1387.

Crenshaw, K., Gotanda, N., Peller, G., and Thomas, K. (Eds.). (1995). *Critical race theory: The key writings that formed the movement.* New York: New Press.

Delgado, R. (1989). Symposium: Legal storytelling. *Michigan Law Review*, 87, 2073.

_____. (1990). When a story is just a story: Does voice really matter? *Virginia Law Review*, 76, 95–111.

_____. (1991). Brewer's plea: Critical thoughts on common cause. *Vanderbilt Law Review*, 44, 1–14.

Delgado, R. (Ed.). (1995). *Critical race theory: The cutting edge*. Philadelphia: Temple University Press.

Delpit, L. (1988). The silenced dialogue: Power and pedagogy in educating other people's children. *Harvard Educational Review*, 58, 280–298.

Foner, P. (Ed.). (1978). *Paul Robeson speaks*. New York: Citadel Press.

Foster, M., and Newman, J. (1989). "I don't know nothin' about it": Black teachers' code-switching strategies in interviews. *Working Papers in Educational Linguistics (WPEL)*. Philadelphia: University of Pennsylvania, Graduate School of Education.

Frankenberg, R. (1993). *White women, race matters: The social construction of whiteness*. Minneapolis: University of Minnesota Press.

Gordon, R. (1990). New developments in legal theory. In D. Kairys (Ed.), *The politics of law: A progressive critique* (pp. 413–425). New York: Pantheon Books.

Gould, S. J. (1981). *The mismeasure of man*. New York: W. W. Norton.

Gramsci, A. (1971). *Selections from the prison notebooks*. (Q. Hoare and G. N. Smith, Eds. and Trans.). New York: International Publishers.

Guinier, L. (1991). No two seats: The elusive quest for political equality. *Virginia Law Review*, 77, 1413–1514.

_____. (1994). *The tyranny of the majority: Fundamental fairness in representative democracy*. New York: Free Press.

Guy-Sheftall, B. (1993). *Black feminist perspective on the academy*. Paper presented at the annual meeting of the American Educational Research Association, Atlanta.

Hacker, A. (1992). *Two nations: Black and White, separate, hostile, unequal*. New York: Ballantine Books.

Haney Lopez, I. (1995). White by law. In Delgado, R. (Ed.), *Critical race theory: The cutting edge* (pp. 542–550). Philadelphia: Temple University Press.

Harris, C. (1993). Whiteness as property. *Harvard Law Review*, 106, 1707–1791.

Jencks, C., Smith, M., Acland, H., Bane, M. J., Cohen, D., Gintis, H., Heyns, B., and Michelson, S. (1972). *Inequality: A reassessment of the effect of family and schooling in America*. New York: Basic Books.

King, J. (1991). Dysconscious racism: Ideology, identity and the miseducation of teachers. *Journal of Negro Education*, 60, 133–146.

_____. (1992). Diaspora literacy and consciousness in the struggle against miseducation in the Black community. *Journal of Negro Education*, 61, 317–340.

_____. (1995). Culture-centered knowledge: Black studies, curriculum transformation, and social action. In J. Banks and C. M. Banks (Eds.), *Handbook of research on multicultural education* (pp. 265–290). New York: Macmillan.

Kozol, J. (1991). *Savage inequalities*. New York: Basic Books.

Ladson-Billings, G. (1995). "But that's just good teaching!" The case for culturally relevant teaching. *Theory into Practice*, 34, 159–165.

Ladson-Billings, G., and Tate, W. F. (1995). Toward a critical race theory of education. *Teachers College Record*, 97, 47–68.

Lawrence, C. (1987). The id, the ego, and equal protection: Reckoning with unconscious racism. *Stanford Law Review*, 39, 317–388.

———. (1995). The word and the river: Pedagogy as scholarship and struggle. In K. Crenshaw, N. Gotanda, G. Peller, and K. Thomas (Eds.), *Critical race theory: The key writings that formed the movement* (pp. 336–351). New York: New Press.

Lee, S. (1993). Racial classifications in the U.S. census: 1890–1990. *Ethnic and Racial Studies*, 16, 75–94.

Lomotey, K., and Staley, J. (1990, April). *The education of African Americans in Buffalo public schools.* Paper presented at the annual meeting of the American Research Association, Boston.

Marable, M. (1983). *How capitalism underdeveloped Black America.* Boston: South End Press.

Matsuda, M. (1989). Public response to racist speech: Considering the victim's story. *Michigan Law Review*, 87, 2320–2381.

McIntosh, P. (1990). White privilege: Unpacking the invisible knapsack. *Independent School*, Winter, 31–36.

Monaghan, P. (1993, June 23). "Critical race theory" questions the role of legal doctrine in racial inequity. *Chronicle of Higher Education*, pp. A7, A9.

Morrison, T. (1992). *Playing in the dark: Whiteness and the literary imagination.* Cambridge, MA: Harvard University Press.

Omi, M., and Winant, H. (1994). *Racial formation in the United States from the 1960s to the 1990s.* (2d ed.). New York: Routledge.

O'Neill, M. (1992). Teaching literature as cultural criticism. *English Quarterly*, 25 (1), 19–24.

Roediger, D. (1991). *The wages of whiteness: Race and the making of the American working class.* London: Verso Press.

Swartz, E. (1992). Emancipatory narratives: Rewriting the master script in the school curriculum. *Journal of Negro Education*, 61, 341–355.

West, C. (1992, August 2). Learning to talk of race. *New York Times Magazine*, pp. 24, 26.

———. (1993). *Keeping faith.* New York: Routledge.

Williams, G. H. (1995). *Life on the color line.* New York: Plume.

Williams, P. (1991). *The alchemy of race and rights: Diary of a law professor.* Cambridge, MA: Harvard University Press.

———. (1995). Alchemical Notes: Reconstructing ideals from deconstructed rights. In R. Delgado (Ed.), *Critical race theory: The cutting edge* (pp. 84–94). Philadelphia: Temple University Press.

Wynter, S. (1992). *"Do not call us Negros": How multicultural textbooks perpetuate racism.* San Francisco: Aspire.

2

Critical Race Theory and Praxis: Chicano(a)/Latino(a) and Navajo Struggles for Dignity, Educational Equity, and Social Justice

SOFIA VILLENAS, DONNA DEYHLE,
AND LAURENCE PARKER

During the 1980s and 1990s, race-based scholarship generally was viewed as a form of identity politics not worthy of serious discussion in academic and public policy discourse (see, for example, Chen, 1996). However, this notion was challenged by a number of works that have offered solid interdisciplinary theoretical frameworks on race in the U.S. context (Omi and Winant, 1994; Winant, 1994; Goldberg, 1997). Critical race theory (CRT) has contributed to the theorizing about race as it has garnered increasing attention from various academic circles and disciplines as an emerging perspective in jurisprudence scholarship addressing race (Crenshaw, Gotanda, Peller, and Thomas, 1995; Delgado, 1995; Solórzano, 1998; Tate, 1997). The main tenets of CRT are described in other parts of this book, so the purpose of our chapter is to point to ways in which education research and policy can be linked to CRT for the purpose of racial social justice in educational practice. We contend that relating CRT to education can indeed foster the connections of theory to practice and activism on issues related to race (as well as ethnicity, gender, social class, language, and the like). Through our analysis, we hope to facilitate an understanding of CRT as a valuable tool with which to view and analyze issues related to land, human rights, and nationalism and how these connect with Chicano/a and Latino/a civil rights and education. We will also attempt to show how the legal tools and framework of CRT can provide valuable racial discrimination "data" in ongoing legal struggles for equal educational opportunity and equity for the Navajo tribal nation in the western United States. The ultimate goal of this chapter is to give readers not only a sense of what CRT is but of what/how struggles for education equity and social justice can form the basis of critical race praxis. We hope to demonstrate what the field of education has to offer to the discourse on race and the law.

Our chapter proceeds as follows: The first part provides readers with an overview of CRT and its importance to educational research, policy, and practice. The second section shows how the CRT lens is useful in analyzing Chicana and Chicano students' struggles for equity and social justice in the classroom and at the state and national levels as legislation (such as Propositions 187, 209, and 227 in California) assaults their identity, national origin, and culture. The third part links critical race theory with gender and class analysis through examining how Latina mothers in North Carolina create spaces for reclaiming dignity amidst the framing of their families as deficient. In the last part, we explore the legal and political fight for equity of Navajo students and community members in southern Utah and northern Arizona, and we examine civil rights and desegregation court cases to highlight how education and civil rights struggles can be linked to CRT. Critical race theory in education may not provide a new set of methodological tools (e.g., interviews, document analysis, survey questions, or statistical data analysis) for the qualitative or quantitative researcher. However, the theory does provide educational researchers with an interdisciplinary, race-based interpretive framework aimed toward social justice. This perspective has generally been absent from mainstream educational research, legal theory, and policy (Tate, 1997).

The Importance of CRT in Education

Most current research and policy orientations in education have been empirically driven in the hopes of establishing education as a science that is grounded in divisions and hierarchy based on race (Scheurich and Young, 1997). To be sure, the democratic ideal of equity and social justice is evident both in the efforts of the federal government to create equal opportunity initiatives and in the increasing focus of states on setting levels of adequacy in education for student success. However, U.S. society is also governed by a powerful ideology of competition that is stratified by race-ethnicity, social class, and gender divisions (Cicchino, 1996). Part of the role of K–12 and postsecondary education is to prepare students to compete in this system of winners and losers that is strongly correlated with the standards of racial-ethnic, social class, and gender hierarchy (Olivas, 1997; McQuillan, 1998).[1]

Furthermore, the current tendency is to assert that everyone has a fair opportunity to succeed in school, or that the effectiveness of educational policies and practices has to be based on variables (e.g., curriculum and instruction, enforcing school rules) that school administrators and teachers can control in order to ensure success for students regardless of race (Bennett, 1993). CRT is an important tool for dismantling prevailing notions of educational fairness and neutrality in educational policy, practice, and research. CRT partially builds on the previous race-/culture-based critiques of schooling and minority power relations with White authorities (Shujaa, 1994) by analyzing links between adherence to various ideological or empirical positions that appear fair and race neutral but often turn out to have a discriminatory impact on racial minorities. A central tenant of CRT methodology is to provide countertruths of racism and discrimination faced by African Americans, Latinos/as, and others, through racial storytelling and narratives.[2] The narratives of racism and racial discrimination play an important role in challenging the prevailing notion of racial neutrality in administrative policy decisions and legal actions in the schools. In fact, these narratives comprise part of the historical and current legal evidentiary findings in many racial discrimination cases. To be sure, given the current conservative nature of the federal courts and recent legal setbacks in the area of civil rights, minority groups should be skeptical of their chances to promote change through legislation and the courts (Halpern, 1995). However, we feel that CRT, in concert with social justice efforts in education, has the potential to be a strong force, continually pressing for the rights of poor people and racial minority groups at the micro and macro levels.

At the micro level, a CRT analysis of local schooling practice can reveal the racism undergirding typical schooling practices related to tracking or ability grouping, disciplinary procedures, testing, and curriculum and instruction. In the effort to treat all kids fairly and adhere to zero-tolerance policies regarding student behavior and work in the classroom, many administrators routinely uphold rules of order at all cost. Larson (1997) presents an example of this phenomenon in a case study of White school administrators at a midwestern high school. The administrators rigidly follow bureaucratic strategies of control by enacting disciplinary procedures against African American students despite growing evidence of racial tension due to outright prejudice by White teachers and tracking placements that stunted African American student progress and eventually caused the community to rise up and demand change. In their adherence to bureaucratic rules of school governance, the administrators were blind to racial issues and tensions. Introducing a CRT approach to educational research requires examining narratives of racism along with other forms of "data" to analyze racial dynamics and patterns of discrimination.[3] CRT strategies also require that teachers, administrators, and community members inquire seriously into the nature of the problems related to race and into the racial impact of school policies. In addition, school staff and community members are challenged to develop the racial knowledge, compassion, and capacities needed to engage in difficult dialogue and to make changes in school practices that seriously attempt to address racial discrimination there.

CRT analysis in education also calls for challenging broad societal inequities that are related to urban poverty and its impact on communities of color. The stranglehold that racism and poverty have in many urban communities makes it very difficult for entire neighborhood areas to improve their overall socioeconomic status in terms of employment, housing, and schools; and this phenomenon results in a "web of urban racism" (Darden, Duleep, and Galster, 1992, p. 490). This "web of urban racism" has a deleterious impact on schools because they have fewer resources (e.g., money for the arts, computers, academic materials, school physical plant improvements), and the minority communities lack the political power to force change at the state and local levels. Viewing education through the CRT lens would challenge the "market metaphors" that present school choice as solving urban education problems by creating equal opportunity for the best and brightest students in poverty-stricken areas.[4] Instead, a CRT perspective would be linked to participation in ongoing community efforts to improve urban education. This perspective also is manifest in efforts to effect changes in the electoral status quo that would allow racial minorities to have a chance not only to participate but to take their turn at governance and policy formation in political institutions (Guinier, 1991, 1994).[5]

In sum, critical race theory has emerged from the legal arena to uncover the deep patterns of exclusion and to challenge what is taken for granted with respect to race and privilege. As illustrated, CRT borrows from and expands to include a number of other critical epistemologies and seeks intersections and conjunctions with other areas of difference to push a social justice agenda into the legal and public discourse on race, gender, and other social divides (Crenshaw, Gotanda, Peller, and Thomas, 1995a; Wing, 1997). Through revealing legal narratives of racial discrimination and how the power of the law is used against persons of color, critical race theorists seek to break the dominance of stories about the success of merit, equality, the market, and objectivity that are so deeply entrenched and are accepted without question by society at large. The key role played by narrative in efforts to achieve social justice, and the implications of intersections and conjunctions related to difference are two aspects of critical race theory that have important ramifications for educational research and action.

The examples in the subsequent sections illustrate the role narrative can play in educational research, particularly when studies using ethnographic inquiry and method are viewed through a critical race theory lens. Good ethnographic studies capture the ways in which people make meaning of their lives, and pay close attention to the relations of power against and within which people operate. Ethnography also captures the stories of people of color—stories that are about both the daily indignities that communities of color suffer as well as the ways in which families maintain their dignity and cultural integrity. Critical race theorists argue that these stories of discrimination and cultural survival and resilience are essential for uncovering institutionalized and endemic racism. CRT legitimates storytelling as a method for examining how racism works against people of color in the everyday, and ethnography provides the rich data to show how ideologies of racism work to marginalize and disenfranchise children and families of color. Yet, most importantly, these data are also crucial to a rethinking of social action: The stories illustrate how communities' preservation of their cultural integrity has enabled them to survive hundreds of years of enslavement and genocide.

A Reinterpretation of Latino Education

The lens of CRT is critical to interpreting the schooling experiences of Chicano/a and Mexican students in ways that situate family education, culture, and language as strengths while pointing the finger at schools and the ways in which schools function to disenfranchise these students and their families. Recent ethnographic studies of Latino schooling and family education are filled with the voices and testimonies of Chicano/a and Mexican students and parents articulating the racism they encounter in schools, including lowered teacher expectations; dumbed-down curriculum; vocational tracking; and the absence of Chicano/Mexican history, culture, and language (see Villenas and Deyhle, in press).[6] As Ladson-Billings argues in the present volume, CRT is a useful approach toward understanding how children of color are situated within a system built upon race-based IQ testing, a Eurocentric curriculum, and unequal, race-based distribution of money and resources to schools. CRT is also useful in making clear how Latino students become recipients of the fury of an anti-immigrant, anti-Latino, xenophobic rhetoric that is gripping the nation and turning back the clock on the gains made for civil and human rights. The 1996 documentary film by Laura Simón, *Fear and learning at Hoover Elementary*, shows how teachers' fears about the "browning" of the United States translate into culturally assaultive lectures in the classroom. And yet, as Suárez-Orozco and Suárez-Orozco (1995) assert, Latino children must develop positive identities under this psychological assault to their humanness. CRT helps to name the racism underlying the barriers Latino children and families face in schools; at the same time, CRT links the pervasive and insidious practice of racism to the ongoing struggles for social justice through the resilience and resistance of families and communities at all levels. This section focuses on ethnographic studies that detail the structural racism that Latino children and their parents face in the schools, and ultimately connects CRT to potential practices of social justice in the schools.

Villenas and Deyhle (in press) reinterpret seven ethnographic studies of Latino family education and schooling through the lens of CRT, concluding that racism in the schools is an extension of racism in larger society. For Latinos/as and Chicanos/as, racism is evident in how they are monolithically constructed as racial Others. By representing Latinos/as and Chicanos/as as lazy, undeserving, and criminal, the public rhetoric justifies the real and symbolic violence committed against Latino families by immigration and police officers and through legislation. One example of such violence is the proliferation of English-only laws across the country. California, in particular, has passed oppressive legislation: Proposition 187 denies medical and educational services to the undocumented, Proposition 209 dismantles affirmative action, and Proposition 227 does away with bilingual education in the state. All of these attacks on the culture, history, and language of Latino and Chicano/Mexicano families are embedded within the history of the colonization and racialization of Chicanos/Mexicanos as indigenous people of the Americas.

CRT not only names the racialized ideologies and discourses that subjugate Latino families but also plays a critical role in uncovering how these racist discourses permeate and structure institutions such as the schools. Ladson-Billings in this volume argues that "if we look at the way that public education is currently configured, it is possible to see the ways that CRT can be a powerful explanatory tool for the sustained inequity that people of color experience." Configuration of the curriculum is one area of visible inequity. At the curriculum level, the absence of Chicano/Mexicano culture and language makes Latino children and their families invisible. The history and worldviews of Chicanas/os and Mexicanas/os are completely left out, subsumed under what Ladson-Billings refers to as the "immigrant" master script. Chicanos/as are taught the narrative of "we are all immigrants," thus denying Chicano communities' native and indigenous status in Aztlan, the region now known as the Southwest. This narrative also denies that Spanish is a language protected under the 1848 Treaty of Guadalupe Hidalgo, which ended the North American invasion of Mexico and legalized U.S. annexation of the Southwest. According to Ladson-Billings, the narrative that "we are all immigrants" blames Latino immigrants themselves for their marginalization by saying they do not work as hard as previous European immigrants. In this way, Ladson-Billings (in this volume) argues that CRT "sees the official school curriculum as a culturally specific artifact designed to maintain a White supremacist master script."

Yet despite such cultural assault in the curriculum, ethnographic studies portray Latino families and children as strong and healthy, with high aspirations. Delgado-Gaitan and Trueba (1991), for example, have for many years documented the teaching and learning that goes on in Mexicano/Chicano families, showing these as vibrant, creative, and completely appropriate activities that are cultural strengths. Other studies (Delgado-Gaitan, 1994; Romo and Falbo, 1996; and Valdés, 1996) also talk about how parents socialize their children through *consejos*, narrative advice or homilies meant to guide children on the "correct" path in life by teaching them cultural and moral values. Contrary to the public rhetoric that Latino parents do not care about their children's education, the parents in these studies use *consejos* to push their children to succeed in school, often using stories of themselves or of older siblings as examples of what happens when one does not study.

Moreover, many working-class Mexican families have worldviews of success and proper socialization that differ dramatically from those of White, middle-class, mainstream families (Valdés, 1996). Valdés (1996) argues that "for most ordinary Mexican families, individual success and accomplishment are generally held in lesser esteem than are people's abilities to maintain ties across generations and to make an honest living" (p. 170). The story Valdés presents is not a tale of uncaring parents but instead a narrative of how cultural differences work so that schools take as a prototype the worldviews of White, middle-class, mainstream families and devalue the worldviews of working-class Mexican families. One parent, for example, was belittled when trying to work in behalf of her son:

> I called there [school] but one of his counselors responded to me, how can I say it, very ugly, really. . . . Because, she said I was at fault, that I should have hit him when he was small, that I should have smacked him or swatted him on his bottom when he was little, . . . she was wrong to have answered me that way. I was asking for help and I want him to return to school and complete his school, . . . and this is what she answered me, "Well, you are to blame for not teaching them"(Romo and Falbo, 1996, p. 188).

In this manner, cultural differences that become borders in a racist society serve institutionally to keep parents out of schools, and the stated need for parent involvement in education becomes empty rhetoric.

Vasquez, Pease-Alvarez, and Shannon (1994) also argue that Mexicano families are embedded in creative and dynamic linguistic milieus. In act-ing as translators and cultural brokers, bilingual children handle not only two language registers but also demonstrate knowledge of the different languages of particular institutions, such as clinics and various agencies. The authors assert Mexicano families' "linguistic and cultural flexibility and adaptability in the use of language" (p. 6). Yet, as Vasquez and colleagues ask, "What happens when the school bell rings and language-minority children like those we have described enter the world of the classroom?" (1994, p. 143). Villenas and Deyhle argue that as monoculturalism and monolingualism uphold White privilege, these linguistically and culturally sophisticated families are relegated to an inferior status. They argue that "CRT as an explanatory tool helps us position schools' and larger society's negative perceptions of cultural differences in family socialization and education within a framework of power relations and the castification of Latinos in the United States" (Villenas and Deyhle, in press).

The data from these ethnographic studies of Latino communities demonstrates that vocational tracking is rampant. Based on the results of IQ tests and standardized tests, Latino/a students were channeled into lower-level courses for those who were not considered "college material" (Romo and Falbo, 1996). Ladson-Billings argues that the movement for intelligence testing has been motivated by a desire to legitimize the labeling of "raced" children as deficient. Using a CRT lens, Villenas and Deyhle argue that "deficit explanations on the part of teachers and school administrations are patterns connected to White strategies of maintaining privilege. As Mexican students are placed in lower tracks, White students are placed in upper tracks with the justification that this will prepare each for the sorts of jobs they are capable of" (in press). One youth who left school commented, "If you're Mexican, they put you lower. If you're White, they put you higher, right?" (Romo and Falbo, 1996, p. 192). Teachers looked at the cultural differences of their students and hoped that they would "snap out of it" and become "normal," meaning like White middle-class students. Teachers expressed the view that Mexican kids were "held back" by their families: "I think they hold him back [pause] well, unwillingly . . . I think they want what's best for him but they're unwilling [pause] or not able to help. I'm sure everything is in Spanish" (Carger, 1996, pp. 86–87). Villenas and Deyhle conclude that requiring assimilation becomes "a strategic way of dismissing Mexican culture and entrenching the 'normalcy' of white middle-class norms."

For Villenas and Deyhle, reinterpreting Latino ethnographic studies through a CRT lens serves as a valuable tool for exposing the racism that pervades the unequal power relations in society and that permeates schools and classrooms. They argue that "in essence, a CRT frame entails an analysis of the totality of racism and the interplay of the macro (anti-immigrant xenophobia, anti-bilingualism, anti-affirmative action, the job ceiling) and the micro (school policies and organization) in the lives of Latino children and families" (Villenas and Deyhle, in press). By putting race at the center of their analysis, Villenas and Deyhle redirect the ethnographic research they examine and open the possibility for action directed at social justice. As the next section illustrates, however, seeking social justice amid overt and benevolent racism is difficult. For the Latina mothers in Villenas's (n.d.) ethnographic research, social justice remained elusive in terms of real structural changes, yet their resistance to control and denigration enabled them to maintain dignity and cultural integrity.

CRT and Women of Color Feminisms:
Latina Mothers and Small-Town Racism in North Carolina

Well, I think that the way I educated my children is like when someone goes to a mountain where there are a lot of little trees, and the one that's soft, you can straighten, right? But when it's soft; when it's big, you can't straighten it because the tree is already too hard. And I think that the family is the same way. . . . (Doña Carmen, in Villenas, n.d.)

Doña Carmen is a single mother of 17 children. Most of her children are grown except for her two youngest daughters, who were under the age of sixteen at the time of our interview, quoted above. She immigrated from El Salvador to Hope City (pseudonym), a rural community in central North Carolina. Doña Carmen took pride in describing herself as an "educated" person who raised her children well despite her own illiteracy and civil war in her country. She explained:

When they [my children] could work, it was to give them two, two educations, one for work from the morning until noon, and from noon on [to school]. I taught them from when they were very little to say *usted* [the formal "you"]. . . . And now, thanks to God, I don't have any that can't read or write. Yes, I gave them all *crianza* (upbringing education). Even the very last children.

To Villenas, who spent two and a half years in Hope City conducting ethnographic research in the Latino community, Doña Carmen epitomized the sense of security that many Latina immigrant mothers had in their knowledge about raising children properly. Doña Carmen was in fact highly respected by the younger mothers in the community, who often left their children in her care. In parenting classes for Latina mothers conducted by the health and social service agencies of Hope City, there were many Doña Carmens—mature women and grandmothers who had generations of knowledge about how to raise children who are healthy and *bien educados* (that is, educated in the norms of morality, good manners, and loyalty to kin and community). However, as a participant-observer in these classes, Villenas witnessed conversations about Latina mothers framed in deficit terms. A conversation between two agency professionals concerned about finding a childcare provider while the women attended classes in parenting and in English as a second language illustrates this deficit view. While sitting around a table and planning for the programs, one health-care provider from South America (who was an upper-middle-class professional from outside the Latino community) used racially coded language in commenting, "We have to make sure we hire the appropriate person to do the child care." A woman social worker who was sitting across from him answered, "We really need to find someone to set a good example for these mothers, to be a role model in caring for the children," to which the health-care provider responded, "I know, because sometimes I see these mothers just put their kids in front of the TV." These providers ignored the wealth of knowledge Latina mothers carried. At the same time, newspaper headlines proclaimed, "Program enables Hispanic women to become better mothers," signaling to the public that the newly arrived Latina immigrants were not good mothers. In the public rhetoric of the town, Latina mothers were racialized under discourses of "problem" and "deficit."

Moreover, as Kimberlé Crenshaw (1995) and other feminist critical race theorists assert, racial, gender, and class oppression cannot be separated or teased out when analyzing the lives of women of color. CRT not only aids in naming the insidious form of benevolent racism operating in Hope City but also in naming the racialization and gendering of transnational labor and the racialization of patriarchy for women who are far from the centers of power. Finally, CRT provides a framework for understanding the importance of Latina mothers' stories of a moral education as cultural self-preservation in a town that considers their family education inadequate, lacking, and simply inferior. Through a CRT lens, we can see how the mothers' counterstories of a moral and "better" education are a powerful resistance to hegemonic discourses of their inferiority. In the daily practices of survival and resilience, these mothers' reclamations of dignity are critical to maintaining cultural integrity, community, and memory.

Racism in Hope City ranges from the activities of White supremacist groups in the county to rampant institutionalized discrimination in the areas of housing, law enforcement, and employment. These forms of racism as they played out in the everyday lives of Latino immigrant residents made up the experiential stories of discrimination that circulated in the community. As an English instructor in Hope City, Villenas heard many stories of police harassment. She also learned the mapping of the town in terms of who could live where and which places did not rent to Latino families. However, the most popular brand of racism in Hope City and the most publicly accepted was the benevolent kind. Hope City health, social service, and education professionals were ready to "help" Latina mothers and garner the resources and money needed to provide health and education services. Yet the "helping" attitude of these agencies also came with the paternalistic "we know what's best" tag, which devalued Latina mothers' ways of knowing. The zeal by which Latina mothers were solicited for the various programs sponsored by the health department signaled to the public that Latina mothers have poor child-rearing practices. Critical race theory in this ethnographic study is important in uncovering the different manifestations or brands of racism operating with the emergence of a third race in a community whose politics was previously framed in biracial terms. In uncovering the insidious benevolent and paternalistic brand of racism, we can see how the targeting of Latina mothers for parenting classes is what Dennis Carlson (1997) calls a colonial form of education for racial others in the United States. This colonial education includes the policing or "the surveillance, disciplining, and control of racialized bodies" (p. 137).

In addressing the policing of racialized, gendered bodies under neocolonialism, critical race theory becomes important in understanding immigrant women as transnational workers and the larger picture of the racialization of global and transnational labor. Crenshaw and colleagues argue that we need to pay serious attention to "the racial and ethnic character of the massive distributive transformations that globalization has set in motion" (Crenshaw, Gotanda, Peller, and Thomas, 1995b, p. xxx). Immigrant women are the most vulnerable in these global transformations where the racialization of patriarchy and capitalism serve to subjugate these women in every way—during immigration, in their job situations, and in their interactions with social services. It is critical to consider how racialized ideologies, such as those that justify the intense patrolling of the U.S. border in the South, deeply impact Latina immigrant women who occupy the lowest rung in the labor market and are considered disposable.

In the context of Hope City, Southern racism is shaped by labor exploitation. The recruitment of Latino immigrants to the local poultry plants, where the majority of Latino men and women are employed, is thus historically shaped by new neocolonial patterns of racism and patriarchy embedded in global capitalist expansion. The owners think they will get a hardworking labor force cheaply by recruiting Latinos, and they reason that women are even cheaper than men. Undocumented women confront immense barriers to employment, decent wages, and job security. Latinas in Hope City are channeled into the lowest-level jobs at a plastics manufacturing company, a textile company, a hosiery company, meat processing plants, and the two large poultry factories. In all of these jobs, immigrant women get paid less than the Latino men, who in turn are paid less than their Anglo counterparts. It is little wonder that the women I interviewed did not invest their sense of self in these jobs, although many expressed pride in doing a job well. As will be discussed, the women claimed their sense of self in the home and in their network of family and kin. In essence, the mothers' stories of dignity were a realization of their position in global capitalism as undocumented transnational women workers.

The forceful reclaiming of dignity was most evident in the life histories of twelve Latina mothers in Hope City. In these narratives the women constructed themselves as "educated" people—that is, they emphasized that they were intelligent human beings who knew how to raise children well. Doña Carmen, for example, expressed her feelings about getting a driver's license despite her illiteracy:

> And I don't know how to read and I went and got my driver's license. And people are surprised, how did I get my license. . . . My nephew is very intelligent . . . and he tells me, you're going to tell me what letters to choose on the [practice exam] . . . and so NOW I helped him more in getting his driver's license.

Doña Carmen's philosophy was that "you learn everything by having common sense," and she described herself as possessing the intelligence (i.e., common sense) that enabled her to raise seventeen children under conditions of poverty and civil war and to make her way in a foreign country. The mothers also talked about the family and community education they provided as good and even superior to that of the United States. They all spoke of the collective raising of children; of the high moral standards their children were held to, including an ethic of hard work, respect for elders, and responsibility to family and community; and of the good things about their customs and traditions. Their biggest fear was that their children would adopt the customs and manners of the United States. Lydia Torres commented, "The change [of immigration] is more difficult when the children grow up and *se acostumbran*, they get used to life here." Lastly, the women situated themselves in *el hogar* (the home) in their roles as mothers. Irma Lopez, for example, expressed the important lesson concerning her role in *el hogar*: "And like I tell you, my *suegra* (mother-in-law) and my father . . . they taught me . . . to *enfrentar el hogar* (face the challenge of the home)." From *el hogar*, women imparted what they considered to be the most important education. Therefore, women who are centers of their *hogar* have a powerful role in the home and community. They are in charge of imparting a moral education, something no other institution is charged to provide. The education of the home space becomes critical for the maintenance of cultural integrity in the midst of cultural assault (Baca Zinn and Dill, 1994).

Critical race theory and its intersections with the feminisms of women of color helps to reconceptualize these Latina mothers' appropriation of the home space and their pride and dignity in domestic labor. Because racism has reconfigured these women's home lives such that there is no such thing as a public/private distinction, an understanding of women's claim to the home requires a race-based perspective. For example, Hurtado (1996) argues that the public/private distinction is not relevant for women of color because historically the state has always intervened in the private lives of the working class, particularly in the private lives of women of color. Instead of being inspired by the slogan "the personal is political," Hurtado posits that the activism of women of color stems from the realization that the public sphere is personally political. That is, public policy has historically invaded the lives of families of color. Hurtado gives the examples of welfare programs and policies, unauthorized sterilization, disproportionate numbers of people of color in jail—all of which have affected women of color directly. For women of color, there has never been such a thing as the private sphere "except that which they manage to create and protect in an otherwise hostile environment" (Hurtado, p. 18). Indeed, an understanding of Hope City's Latina mothers, who forcefully distinguish the private in reclaiming *el hogar,* is to see how it is an appropriation of their own space. The space from which they impart a moral education is critical to the cultural and psychological preservation of Latino families in the South. These mothers' stories are no less significant than political altercations in producing collective action for social change.

In naming the insidious form of benevolent racism, and in exploring the ways in which Latina mothers are racialized and engendered as "brown" transnational workers in the process of global capitalist expansion, a CRT lens is critical to naming the intersectionality of oppressions and the diverse gendered and classed racisms these women confront. In turn, and most importantly, the naming of the oppression of indigenous peoples of the Americas under neocolonialism helps people who struggle for social justice name the ways in which communities resist commodification and exploitation and continually and dynamically recreate culture.

In the following section, a Navajo community's struggle against Anglo racism illustrates a similar resistance to exploitation. By naming racism as central to an understanding of Navajo school failure, Deyhle's (1995) ethnographic research became a tool used by the community in a legal battle against a school district over economic and educational equity.

Critical Race Theory and Educational Equity: Navajos Fight a School District

It was 1993 when the newly appointed director of bilingual education, an Anglo who spoke no Navajo, attended a parent meeting at an all-Navajo elementary school. More than thirty Navajo parents and their children were also in attendance. The director stood and spoke to the group. "We want to do what your kids need. So we are going to develop a bilingual program. So your kids can learn better in their classes. We think it will help." Navajo parents expressed disbelief. One said, "But you were supposed to be doing that when I was in school. And you still aren't. How do we know you will use Navajo to teach our kids?" Another angrily snapped, "You were supposed to be doing that bilingual education because of the court case. But it still isn't going on." Visibly uncomfortable, the director shook his head in agreement. "Yes. I know it wasn't done. But we are going to do it now. Trust us. We are now sincere." These Navajo parents had reason to question the sincerity of the district's efforts at educating their children. In an out-of-court settlement the district had agreed to such a program seventeen years earlier and it still did not exist.

In 1974 legal action was brought in the U.S. district court for southern Utah alleging that this school district discriminated against American Indian children (*Meyers v. Bd. of Educ. of the San Juan Sch. Distr.*, 1995). At the time of the case there were no high schools in the southern portion of the county, where most American Indians lived, and the few elementary schools were inadequate. Although several other issues were involved in the complaint (including the district's failure to provide a legally sufficient bilingual program for Navajos), the most important issue in the case revolved around the long distances Navajo children had to travel to attend high school. The two longest bus routes are instructive. In one, Navajo students were bussed up to 166 miles round-trip each day. In the other, Navajo students were bussed as far as 112 miles round-trip each day. The 220 Navajo high school students who were bussed by the district rode on the bus an average of 86 miles each day of the school year. The average Navajo student traveled four times as far to school as did the average non-Indian student. Each year, on average, Navajo students traveled more than 15,000 miles, spending the equivalent of 120 school days physically sitting on a bus in order to attend school. For the students at the end of the longest bus routes, the figures rise to 30,000 miles each year and 240 school days on a bus. The complaint in this lawsuit was based on the premise that the failure to construct high schools in the Navajo portion of the district denied Navajo children an equal educational opportunity and constituted illegal racial discrimination.

Attached to this out-of-court settlement requiring the district to build two high schools on the Navajo reservation was a bilingual-bicultural and cultural awareness program. By 1978 the district agreed to have a bilingual-bicultural program, utilizing both Navajo and English, operating in grades K–6 in elementary schools that Navajo students attended. A cultural awareness plan was to be developed and used for all students, Anglo and Navajo, in the district.

When Deyhle started ethnographic research in this community in 1984 she was told by the superintendent: "Go talk to the Director of the Curriculum Materials Center. He can tell you about our bilingual program." Arriving at his office she was invited in and was asked, "Are you friend or foe?" He laughed at her stunned silence and continued, "I always ask, because it's not popular here. I am only one of two in the district that is supportive of the bilingual program. None of the principals are in support of bilingual education. One elementary school has one, but it is just total immersion in English. Navajo will be used as a last resort, but it is not stressed or taught." He reached behind his desk and pulled a packet off the bookcase, dusted it off, and handed it to her. "Here is a copy of the plan we developed after the court case." Over the next several years, showing them the manual, she asked teachers in the district about the bilingual plan they were required to use. Responses ranged from surprise to disbelief; few of the teachers remembered seeing the district's bilingual plan, but all resisted the idea of bilingual education. Teachers and administrators ignored research that indicates that, at the very least, incorporating minority students' culture and language into the school curriculum does not impede academic success. They instead held firmly to racial folk myths about Navajo youth, arguing that Navajo culture and language were the reasons for academic failure, and refusing to implement the court-ordered bilingual program or any other effective program for Navajo students. In this case, racially driven educational policy served to maintain unequal educational and economic opportunities for Navajo students. Over the next decade and a half of her fieldwork, she saw no uniform bilingual-bicultural program in existence in the district, even though the district reported to the courts of its existence.

During Deyhle's time in the field, she moved race from the borders to the center of her analysis using critical race theory as her theoretical lens. In the process she replaced a "cultural difference" standpoint—a more neutral position—with one of "racial warfare." Within this "war," she observed cultural differences being twisted and used by Anglos to maintain racial inequities within educational, political, economic, and social institutions. Culture had become the explanation for school failure, masking the fact that racism was the true cause of this failure.

In 1992 Navajo parents, frustrated with the high dropout rate and low achievement rate of their children, filed to reopen the 1974 Sinajini court case and requested that the court hold the school district in contempt for its refusal to obey the terms of the agreement. Deyhle joined the parents in the case as an expert witness. The Navajo Nation also joined the parents' battle. At the same time the directors of the Utah Division of Indian Affairs (UDIA) and of the Office for Civil Rights were informed of the lack of a bilingual-bicultural program in the district. The district superintendent wrote the UDIA a letter saying

> The decree does mandate a bilingual-bicultural educational program in the schools. This program exists and has been operating since 1975. Like all programs, the degree of success can be measured by the quality of the people who are available to make it go. In the past fifteen years, the program has had ups and downs, as people come and go, but it has always been present.

The Office of Civil Rights (OCR) in the Department of Education did not agree with the superintendent. Its investigations concluded that the district was in violation of Title VI of the Civil Rights Act of 1964, and it is implementing regulations with regard to the issue of providing limited-English-proficient students with meaningful access to the district's educational program. After three years of unacceptable language plans from the district, the OCR issued a citation of noncompliance and turned the investigation over to the Education Litigation Division of the Justice Department. During the summer of 1994, Attorney General Janet Reno authorized the Justice Department, on behalf of the United States of America, to intervene as a party-plaintiff in the Sinajini case. Based on a preliminary investigation, the Justice Department believes the school district has discriminated against Indian students, violating federal law and the Fourteenth Amendment by failing to adopt and implement an alternative language program for limited-English-proficient students. The district was accused of denying American Indian students the same educational opportunities and services provided to Anglo students, such as equal access to certain academic programs, as well as of denying qualified American Indian persons employment opportunities equal to those provided to Anglos.

Deyhle's ethnographic research has been important in verifying the "facts" in this case. For fifteen years she has gathered the stories of Navajo adults and children documenting racial discrimination in the community and schools. Navajos live with periodic roadblocks and car searches on the only road leading to the reservation. Caught in one roadblock, Deyhle was told by the sheriff, "We do this to catch the Navajos, you know, no driver's license and insurance and stuff." Even the right to vote was not a guarantee for Indians in this county. After a voter discrimination lawsuit in 1989, the U.S. Justice Department now maintains poll watchers to make certain that Navajos and Utes are allowed to vote. In 1996, seventeen officials from the U.S. Justice Department monitored voting places to ensure that proper information was provided to Navajos. Since 1935 only five Navajos have served on county juries, even though Navajos make up almost 50 percent of the county's population. Even in recent history Navajo homes were not safe. In the 1950s more than 100 Navajo families were "rounded up" by Anglo ranchers and cowboys and forced to relocate across a river. They lost their homes, their livestock, and the land their ancestors had inhabited for centuries. This picture of racial warfare spilled over into the schools that Navajo children attended.

The stories that Deyhle collected from administrators and teachers also documented educational policies and practices that were discriminatory. Ten years of school course offerings illustrated a race-based curriculum—college preparatory classes for the Anglo schools and vocational education for the Navajo schools. Untrained and uncertified teachers filled the Navajo schools. The lowest reading scores in the state pointed to a lack of appropriate language instruction in the Navajo schools. The dropout rate for Navajo students was five times higher than that for Anglo students. And, Deyhle's data clearly showed the nonexistence of the court-required bilingual-bicultural curriculum.

In April 1997 all parties in this case came to a court-approved agreement. In a unique agreement that combined three different lawsuits against the school district, three committees—bilingual education, curriculum, and special education—were formed to develop new school district instructional plans. Each committee consists of three school-appointed and three Navajo Nation–appointed educational experts. Deyhle was appointed by the Navajo Nation to serve on the curriculum committee. If consensus on the plans cannot be reached during the 1998–99 school year, the case will be brought back to the court.

This case illustrates the importance of a critical race theory perspective for understanding and exposing the unequal power relations in the community and its schools, and thus for achieving social justice. From the advocacy position of CRT, critique and transformation are goals of research. These goals, however, are not neatly and easily reached. Different groups benefited from Deyhle's research results. Over a ten-year period the school district used her finding of a 50-percent Navajo dropout rate to successfully obtain federal grants, including a $3 million dropout prevention grant. Although the grant required Navajo-speaking instructors, none were found, and the district hired an all-Anglo staff for the three years of the grant. In this case, the powerful colonized and co-opted the grant. Navajo parents also used the high dropout rate in their case to prove discrimination in the schools and to demand equity for their youth. Now those who are institutionally disenfranchised are using Deyhle's data to support their struggles. The Navajo Nation is challenging the dominant racial ideology of the inferiority of Navajo culture and language through the Sinajini case, using the court to "further the goal of eradicating the effects of racial oppression" (Crenshaw, 1988, p. 134).

Critical Race Theory and Educational Practice

The field of education has much to offer critical race theory and legal scholarship, precisely because schooling and "colonial" education are the greatest normalizers of White supremacy. We have argued in this chapter that applying critical race theory to educational research moves the researcher's gaze from a deficit view of people of color to a critical view of discriminatory social practices that limit people's educational and life opportunities. The ethnographies we reviewed open the windows for the reader to see inside the lives of people of color, or as Delgado asserts, "to see the world through others' eyes" (1989, p. 2439). These individuals' narratives play a critical role in challenging the deficit of mainstream thought about people of color. Throughout the ethnographies, their voices echoed the frustration and struggle with institutionalized racism that they experienced as they sought dignity and educational equity. Latina mothers resisted and rejected the claims that they were "poor mothers." Latino/a youth rejected the view that they belonged at the bottom of educational tracking. Latino communities worked collectively to maintain their cultural traditions and histories by resisting assimilation and rejecting the "immigrant" master script. Navajo people resisted the dismissal of their language and culture. These cases illustrate how ethnographic research can serve to expose and to name the racism that frames the lives of people of color within the dominant society. Only by naming the problem correctly is it possible to undertake social action that will lead to educational equity and social justice.

Notes

1. For example, in 1993, 16.9 percent of White children in the United States lived below the poverty level along with 46.6 percent of African American children and 41 percent of Latino children. Furthermore, poor children in general are far more susceptible to factors associated with poor school performance and academic failure at an early age (Cicchino, 1996, pp. 23–27).

2. Storytelling and narratives have been sources of recent commentary and debate in the fields of education and law. For example, in education, Stanfield (1993,

1994), Foster (1994), and Casey (1995) pointed to the past weakness of storytelling as an exploitative tool used by White European American researchers, as well as its strengths in providing key detailed insights into the lives of African American students and teachers. However, in the legal arena, there has been some criticism of the "storytelling," or narrative, method used in CRT because of falsehoods told through some of the narratives and because of how certain CRT proponents have tried to silence debate around race by not allowing other minority viewpoints to be heard (Farber and Sherry, 1997).

3. See for example the qualitative and quantitative data on student track placement and ability-grouping, collected by minority plaintiffs, that documented the racial disparities and harmful racial impact of racial segregation caused by the tracking system in Rockford, Illinois, in *People Who Care v. Rockford Bd. of Educ.* (1994).

4. We are not saying that we are against efforts by individual minority families to choose public or private education in terms of what is best for their children. We are, however, skeptical of the claims by conservatives that vouchers and school choice will cure the crisis in urban education, because these types of school choice plans will once again sort low-income minority students and families into winners and losers in terms of who gets to take advantage of public-private choice plans (Margonis and Parker, 1995).

5. Currently this is the emerging debate surrounding the issue of at-large school board elections versus district-elected representatives on the Urbana, Illinois school board. The at-large system impedes the representation of Whites and African Americans of low socioeconomic status who reside in one census-track area, and these individuals have had a limited impact on community-wide local school elections (Wirt, 1997).

6. Villenas and Deyhle (in press) looked at the following ethnographic studies of Latino education: Carger's (1996) *Of borders and dreams*; Delgado-Gaitan's (1996) *Protean literacy*; Romo and Falbo's (1996) *Latino high school graduation*; Suárez-Orozco and Suárez-Orozco's (1995) *Transformations*; Trueba, Rodriquez, Cintron, and Zou's (1993), *Healing multicultural America*; Valdés's (1996) *Con respeto*; and Vasquez, Pease-Alvarez, and Shannon's (1994) *Pushing boundaries*.

References

Baca Zinn, M., and Dill, B. (1994). *Difference and domination.* In M. Baca Zinn and B. Dill (Eds.), *Women of color in U.S. society* (pp. 3–12). Philadelphia: Temple University Press.

Balkin, J. M. (1992). What is postmodern constitutionalism? *Michigan Law Review,* 90, 1966–1990.

Bennett, W. (1993). *Report card on American education.* Washington, DC: American Legislative Exchange Council.

Carger, C. L. (1996). *Of borders and dreams: A Mexican-American experience of urban education.* New York: Teachers College Press.

Carlson, D. (1997). Stories of colonial and postcolonial education. In M. Fine, L. Weis, L. Powell, and L. Mun Wong (Eds.), *Off white* (pp. 137–146). New York: Routledge.

Casey, K. (1995). The new narrative research in education. In M. W. Apple (Ed.), *Review of research in education*, vol. 21, pp. 211–253. Washington, DC: American Educational Research Association.

Chen, J. (1996). Diversity and damnation. *UCLA Law Review*, 43, 1839–1912.

Cicchino, P. M. (1996). The problem child: An empirical survey and rhetorical analysis of child poverty in the United States. *Journal of Law and Policy*, 5, 5–105.

Crenshaw, K. W. (1988). Race, reform and retrenchment: Transformation and anti-discrimination law. *Harvard Law Review*, 101, 1331–1387.

_____. (1995). Mapping the margins: Intersectionality, identity politics and violence against women of color. In K. Crenshaw, N. Gotanda, G. Peller, and K. Thomas (Eds.), *Critical Race Theory: Key writings that formed the movement* (pp. 357–383). New York: New Press.

Crenshaw, K., Gotanda, N., Peller, G., and Thomas, K. (Eds.). (1995a). *Critical race theory: Key writings that formed the movement.* New York: New Press.

Crenshaw, K., Gotanda, N., Peller, G., and Thomas, K. (1995b). Introduction. In K. Crenshaw, N. Gotanda, G. Peller, and K. Thomas (Eds.), *Critical race theory: Key writings that formed the movement* (pp. xiii–xxxii). New York: New Press.

Darden, J. T., Duleep, H. O., and Galster, G. C. (1992). Civil rights in metropolitan America. *Journal of Urban Affairs*, 14, 469–496.

Delgado, R. (1989). Storytelling for oppositionists and others: A plea for narrative. *Michigan Law Review*, 87, 2411–2441.

Delgado, R. (Ed.). (1995). *Critical Race Theory: The cutting edge.* Philadelphia: Temple University Press.

Delgado-Gaitan, C. (1994). *Consejos:* The power of cultural narrative. *Anthropology and Education Quarterly*, 25, 298–316.

_____. (1996). *Protean literacy: Extending the discourse on empowerment.* London: Falmer Press.

Delgado-Gaitan, C., and Trueba, H. (1991). *Crossing cultural borders: Education for immigrant families in America.* London: Falmer Press.

Deyhle, D. (1995). Navajo youth and Anglo racism: Cultural integrity and resistance. *Harvard Educational Review*, 65, 403–444.

Farber, D. A., and Sherry, S. (1997). *Beyond all reason: The radical assault on truth in American law.* New York: Oxford University Press.

Foster, M. (1994). The power to know one thing is never the power to know all things: Methodological notes on two studies of Black American teachers. In A. Gitlin (Ed.), *Power and method: Political activism and educational research* (pp. 129–146). New York: Routledge.

Goldberg, D. T. (1997). *Racial subjects: Writing on race in America.* New York: Routledge.

Guinier, L. (1991). The triumph of tokenism: The Voting Rights Act and the theory of black electoral success. *Michigan Law Review*, 89, 1077–1154.

_____. (1994). *The tyranny of the majority: Fundamental fairness in representative democracy.* New York: Free Press.

Halpern, S. C. (1995). *On the limits of the law: The ironic legacy of Title VI of the 1964 Civil Rights Act.* Baltimore: Johns Hopkins University Press.

Hurtado, A. (1996). *The color of privilege: Three blasphemies on race and feminism.* Ann Arbor: University of Michigan Press.

Ladson-Billings, G. (1998). Critical race theory: What's it doing in a *nice* field like education. *International Journal of Qualitative Studies in Education*, 11, 7–25.

Larson, C. L. (1998). Is the land of Oz an alien nation? A sociopolitical study of school community conflict. *Educational Administration Quarterly*, 33, 312–350.

Margonis, F., and Parker, L. (1995). Choice, privatization, and unspoken strategies of containment. *Educational Policy*, 9, 375–403.

McQuillan, P. J. (1998). *Educational opportunity in an urban American high school: A cultural analysis*. Albany: State University of New York Press.

Meyers v. Bd. of Education of San Juan Sch. Dist. (1995). 905 F. Supp. (D. Utah).

Olivas, M. A. (1997). Research on Latino college students: A theoretical framework and inquiry. In A. Darder, R. Torres, and H. Gutierrez (Eds.), *Latinos and education: A critical reader* (pp. 468–486). New York: Routledge.

Omi, M., and Winant, H. (1994). *Racial formation in the United States: From the 1960s to the 1990s.* (2d ed.). New York: Routledge.

People Who Care v. Rockford Bd. of Educ., 851 F. Supp. 905 (N.D. Ill. 1994).

Romo, H., and Falbo, T. (1996). *Latino high school graduation.* Austin: University of Texas Press.

Scheurich, J. J., and Young, M. D. (1997). Coloring epistemologies: Are our research epistemologies racially biased? *Educational Researcher, 26,* 4–17.

Shujaa, M. J. (Ed.). (1994). *Too much schooling, too little education: A paradox of black life in white societies.* Trenton, NJ: Africa World Press.

Solórzano, D. G. (1998). Critical race theory, race and microaggressions, and the experience of Chicana and Chicano scholars. *International Journal of Qualitative Studies in Education*, 11, 121–136.

Stanfield, J. H., II (1993). Methodological reflections: An introduction. In J. H. Stanfield and R. M. Dennis (Eds.), *Race and ethnicity in research methods* (pp. 175–188). Newbury Park, CA: Sage.

———. (1994). Response: Empowering the culturally diversified sociological voice. In A. Gitlin (Ed.), *Power and method: Political activism and educational research* (pp. 166–175). New York: Routledge.

Suárez-Orozco, C., and Suárez-Orozco, M. (1995). *Transformations: Migration, family life, and achievement motivation among Latino adolescents.* Stanford, CA: Stanford University Press.

Tate, W. F., IV (1997). Critical race theory and education: History, theory, and implications. In M. W. Apple (Ed.), *Review of research in education,* vol. 22, pp. 195–250. Washington, DC: American Educational Research Association.

Trueba, H., Rodriguez, C., Zou, Y., and Cintron, J. (1993). *Healing multicultural America: Mexican immigrants rise to power in rural California.* Washington, DC: Falmer Press.

Valdés, G. (1996). *Con respeto: Bridging the distances between culturally diverse families and schools.* New York: Teachers College Press.

Vasquez, O., Pease-Alvarez, L., and Shannon, S. (1994). *Pushing boundaries: Language and culture in a Mexicano community.* Cambridge: Cambridge University Press.

Villenas, S. n.d. *Small town racism and* mujeres *in struggle: Creating counter-stories of dignity and moral education in North Carolina.* Unpublished manuscript.

Villenas, S., and Deyhle, D. (in press). Critical race theory and ethnographies challenging the stereotypes: Latino families, schooling, resilience and resistance. *Curriculum Inquiry.*

Winant, H. (1994). *Racial conditions: Politics, theory, comparisons.* Minneapolis: University of Minnesota Press.

Wing, A. (1997). *Critical race feminism: A reader.* New York: New York University Press.

Wirt, F. M. (1997). *The political dynamics of American education.* Berkeley, CA: McCutchan.

3

"¡Adelante!": Toward Social Justice and Empowerment in Chicana/o Communities and Chicana/o Studies

MARC PIZARRO

Chicanas/os have fought vicious oppression within the borders of the United States since the nineteenth century. More recently, researchers have attempted to address the concerns of the Chicana/o community, perhaps most tangibly through the creation of a new field: Chicana/o studies. Unfortunately, despite the important work of Chicana/o studies scholars, problems of oppression have remained. Although the violence of racism has largely shifted from physical to psychological assaults, it is just as damaging. The persistence of this dramatic reality spurred my investigation of the connection between academic and intellectual traditions and methodology, on the one hand, and the continued oppression of Chicanas/os in the schools, on the other.[1]

The positivist tradition leaves contemporary researchers carrying baggage of which we are not always cognizant. For example, even the most innovative qualitative researchers tend to be overly concerned about standards—such as validity and reliability, embedded in the larger construct of objectivity—as they have been problematically and ethnocentrically defined within a positivist tradition (see Gitlin, Siegel, and Boru, 1989; Ladwig and Gore, 1994; Usher, 1996). As Gitlin (1990) argues, despite the shift begun in recent theoretical discussions of innovative research, "these changes in educational research methods have done little to alter the alienating relationship between the researcher and the researched" (p. 443). Gitlin adds, "Educational research is still a process that for the most part silences those studied, ignores their personal knowledge, and strengthens the assumption that researchers are the producers of knowledge" (p. 444). That is the impetus for this chapter: From the perspective of the current project, the most problematic shortcoming of even interactive research is that despite the potential impact of the methodological innovations, these models (with very good reason) have rarely produced research that is participatory *and* transformative, particularly with regard to Chicanas/os and their concerns related to social justice and educational empowerment. Chicanas/os have seen little substantial change in their condition in the United States despite years of scientifically acceptable research and numerous corresponding policies and policy changes that affect them. In the words of Anzaldúa: "In trying to become 'objective,' Western culture made 'objects' of things and people when it distanced itself from them, thereby losing 'touch' with them. This dichotomy is the root of all violence" (1987, p. 37).

With the support of critics like Anzaldúa, I assert that traditional epistemology and its corresponding impact on method (limiting efforts at innovation) continue to negatively affect Chicana/o communities. The university currently plays a critical role in allowing the continued oppression of the Chicana/o community as it does nothing to confront its traditions of "objectivity," which support both unconscious and blatant manifestations of racism. Furthermore, academic tradition directly opposes the efforts of Chicanas/os to empower themselves and has become an unconscious, scientific rationale for the violence directed at Chicanas/os. As a very overt example, current efforts of anti-Mexican and anti-Chicana/o groups in California are being explained and supported by prominent faculty at Stanford University and the University of Chicago (Lechuga, 1997). The overwhelming obstacles Chicanas/os face in the United States, just in trying to obtain an education, suggest that there is an urgent need to confront our epistemological and methodological obstacles.

The objectives of this chapter are to describe the ways in which epistemological tradition influences contemporary research, and through the example of my own work with Chicanas/os, to suggest why and how we can begin to move beyond these limitations. The ultimate goals of this project are to demonstrate that social justice[2] must become the measure by which we evaluate the strength of research in Chicana/o communities, and to show, through the development of a new method, how a reconstructed Chicana/o studies might create the context in which this can happen. In pursuing these goals, I am challenging the epistemological framework[3] that underlies contemporary research in academia and suggesting the potential for Chicana/o epistemology and methodology to transform the academy and, hopefully, to empower Chicana/o communities.

Personal Battles with Epistemological Tradition

Although these methodological and epistemological conflicts need be considered in the context of previous research, they can be more practically understood through a concrete example: my own evolving methodological turmoil. This section describes the limitations and contradictions I faced in attempting to engage in more dialogical/interactive research with and for Chicanas/os.

I am a Chicano who comes from a working-class background. Despite my school "success," I grew up very aware of the multiple forces at work in Chicana/o school failure. As an undergraduate studying Chicanas/os and the schools, I became acutely concerned when I realized the widespread "problems" Chicanas/os faced in the schools. Later, as a teacher in an almost entirely Chicana/o school in Los Angeles, I saw the daily practices and subtle manifestations of the hegemonic ideology that devastated the children and families with whom I worked. I wanted to do something about this but had little confidence in institutional possibilities for empowering Chicanas/os. I also had little faith in traditional research methods and their ability to help Chicanas/os in our efforts toward empowerment. I believed that we needed to find ways that we, as Chicanas/os, could empower ourselves and I hoped that research innovations might assist in this process.

As a beginning researcher, I started to consider how we might initiate this process. I was disturbed, although not surprised, by the fact that Chicanas/os and their voices had been almost completely excluded from educational research. Even the research that addressed the critical problems facing Chicanas/os in the schools did not include the students' perspectives to any substantial degree. My interest in addressing the troubling history of Chicana/o school performance led to this discovery. I found that the high school completion rates of Chicanas/os had improved little since the Chicana/o communities protested the 50-percent (and higher) dropout rates prevalent in "Chicana/o schools" throughout the southwestern United States in the late 1960s. As I reviewed the research and saw both the continuing problems and the lack of active Chicana/o inclusion in research, I began to see potential connections. Our disinterest and inability to see the world of school through the eyes of Chicana/o students might be related to their persistent failure. I knew that interactive research had the potential to provide both more detailed understandings of the school experiences of Chicanas/os and, in turn, ideas as to how we might make change for these students. From experience, I also knew these students were bright and had critical insights to share.

Conducting my first significant research project, I wanted to present Chicana/o students with the opportunity to talk about their school experiences and to expose the obstacles they encountered as well as the resources that assisted them. Through surveys and interviews, I asked students open-ended questions, shaped by my own research, questions that allowed me to look at the school through their eyes. Students talked about classes, teachers, and administrators, as well as the difficulties they faced in and out of school. During this same time, several studies that employed similar tactics, relying more heavily on what Chicana/o students themselves experienced and said about their schooling, were published (Delgado-Gaitan and Trueba, 1991; Foley, 1990; Padilla, 1992; Patthey-Chavez, 1993). This research was powerful and revealing because it clearly exposed not just the harsh reality faced by many Chicanas/os in the schools but also the cutting perceptiveness of these students and the multiple levels at which they critiqued their schooling.

Still, I found myself frustrated with the research being conducted with Chicana/o students (including my own). First of all, I felt that as researchers we still held onto the notion that we had the ability and right to contextualize, critique, and explain the experiences and descriptions provided by Chicana/o students. In my own work, after students discussed their school experiences, I then categorized their racial consciousness and suggested its connection to school outcomes. I felt I had "allowed" students to *tell* their stories, but I did not acknowledge that I had made it impossible for them to engage in *analyzing* their stories. I later saw the implicit hypocrisy of this process: I spoke of the significance of including the students in the research process more actively but still confined and constrained the ways in which they could participate. I, like other researchers working with Chicana/o students, decided what was significant, how it was significant, and how it should be discussed; in essence, I told their stories for them. In my work, the students' lives were reduced to catch-phrases and penetrating stories. They, therefore, remained excluded from the majority of the research process. I only recently realized that the strength of methodological tradition unconsciously shaped my methods. I deceived myself into believing I had arrived at some innovation, when in fact I had only replicated traditional methodology using new subjects (see Ladwig and Gore, 1994, for a discussion of this trend in "innovative," qualitative educational research).

At the same time, I was also frustrated by the fact that most of our research only exposed the world of Chicana/o students and did little to address racist school structures and practices and their effects on Chicana/o school performance. More importantly, research almost never actually engaged in the process of fighting the racism that we as Chicanas/os know permeates our schools. Research rarely attempted to assist in empowering Chicana/o students to deal with this "reality." As time passed, these two concerns (lack of student voice/analysis and lack of change) became increasingly intertwined and, together, guided my efforts at methodological innovation.

More recently, as I embarked on a new project with Chicana/o students, I wanted to address these concerns more adequately. I wanted my research project not simply to rely on Chicana/o students' voices but to engage them in the analysis as part of an empowering process. A few innovative researchers who shared these interests (e.g., Delgado-Gaitan and Trueba, 1991; Galindo and Escamilla, 1995; Padilla, 1992; Ronda and Valencia, 1994) provided a base for me to build on in my work with Chicana/o students.

Delgado-Gaitan and Trueba (1991), in particular, helped me see new possibilities through their "Ethnography of Empowerment." The method itself was important, but with regard to the struggles I was facing, the fundamental contribution of this research was not in method but in defining the intent of research. They explain newly emerging goals for ethnographic research: the improvement of the context in which the disempowered find themselves. They suggest that research must look at the possibilities and processes of empowerment and disempowerment seen in the educational system.

In addition to Delgado-Gaitan and Trueba, researchers like Romo and Falbo (1996) and Suárez-Orozco (1989) have been helpful in that they too are concerned about notions of social justice (as seen in the policy recommendations of Romo and Falbo and in the important community work Suárez-Orozco performed during his time as an ethnographer in the schools). Thus, although researchers in the Chicana/o community began to push methodological approaches and in so doing provided deeper insights into individuals' lives, their greatest contribution with regard to the struggles I have been describing is that they initiated an attack against separating research from efforts at social change.

Delgado-Gaitan (1993) provides one of the most important methodological discussions relevant to the issues I struggled with in developing my own methods. She introduces us to her dilemmas as a researcher as she engages in the "Ethnography of Empowerment." Her primary concern as an ethnographer was understanding the family-school interconnections in a Spanish-speaking community and their relationship to literacy. A shift in Delgado-Gaitan's position in the community created methodological dilemmas for her that are pertinent to my own dilemmas as I have been discussing them. As parents decided to form an organization that would address their needs and concerns regarding the education of their children, she was asked and felt compelled to participate. Upon doing so, not only did she see the degree to which her own

identity shaped her interpretations of the social contexts she was trying
to understand but she also discovered an approach among the parents
that, in my estimation, is an important lesson for us as researchers:

> (1) their interactions at the meetings showed respect for each other's voice
> and viewpoint while minimizing the authority of the leader, and (2) their
> collective effort to solicit input from as many families as possible repre-
> sented a commitment to a democratic voice among Latino parents. (Del-
> gado-Gaitan, 1993, p. 406)

Delgado-Gaitan concludes that "to counter our own ignorance and biases as researchers, we must integrate into our research rigorous and systematic joint analysis with our participants" (p. 409). Researchers who
challenge the oppressive tendencies of education and research (e.g., Chi-
canas/os) or the limiting epistemology underlying the positivist traditions of the academy itself (e.g., post-positivists) must also be willing to
challenge our own approaches and assumptions if we are to move
knowledge in new directions.

Chicana/o educational researchers, therefore, helped me move my
thinking forward as I realized that not only do we need the type of research *on* empowerment that they undertook, but we also need to recognize the potential of research *as* empowerment. What we had not done,
and what I slowly came to believe was needed, was to allow the participants themselves to analyze and explain their world as part of their empowerment. Our interviewees are rarely involved in coanalysis. They are
not typically "allowed" to push for a deeper level of interpretation or to
uncover the ways in which not just those in the future but they themselves can engage in transformative processes. Instead of empowerment
occurring in spite of the research, or through application of the research
findings and recommendations, or (most often) not at all, empowerment
should be aided by the research process itself. Since there are few opportunities for most Chicanas/os to engage in empowering and transformative processes, we should not simply wait or hope that our research will
eventually lead to these.

Building on the emerging methodological evolution in Chicana/o educational research, I began to better develop my own methods. The tac-
tic I next employed was to ask Chicana/o students not simply to describe their experiences in the school but also to answer general,
open-ended questions that closely resembled the research questions of
the project.[4] Again, I found that the students had critical insights to
share.[5] Still, I was frustrated. This frustration was grounded in the con-
strictions of institutional life. Although I was attempting to challenge
traditions of how we engage our subjects in the research and how much

we let them know about our objectives, both the students and I were limited by the institutions in which we found ourselves.

I was limited by the fact that my responsibilities to the university (and my own survival therein) made it difficult for me to continually dialogue with students over time. These responsibilities made it hard to establish deep and long-lasting connections with the students that would allow us to better deconstruct their world and to work toward a reconstruction that would be helpful and realistic. I was forced to engage in most analyses alone, without the help of the students. Dialogue was not impossible, only difficult. It was simply easier to succumb to institutional pressures. In addition, the institutions in which the students found themselves had taught them that they do not create knowledge. These institutions told them that, as Chicana/o students, they are not authorities. These are just two examples of the way in which the university and the school subtly maintain the status quo and, in so doing, participate in the continued oppression of the Chicana/o.

Although I was frustrated on multiple levels and saw the need for change, my institutional location *and* the understanding of the nature of research that was embedded in my academic consciousness made it difficult for me to place this frustration within my own methodological and (more importantly) epistemological limitations. I, like many other researchers, did not see how my own methods and my struggles with method in the institution were shaped by methodological tradition and its underlying epistemology. Thus, my methods remained limited, even when shaping my most recent research project. I had been unconsciously affected by research traditions that suggest the impossibility of complex participant analysis. It was only through this critique that I realized how I incorrectly decided that there were certain questions students could not answer.

Recent scholarship in critical race theory (CRT) has helped me more concretely understand the forces underlying the frustrations and limitations I have encountered in my research. In addition, this work has allowed me to move toward methods and epistemological frameworks that more fully address the concerns I have uncovered in my research and in the literature.

The Lessons of Critical Race Theory

Critical race theory was essential to my methodological self-critique on two levels. On the more simplistic and obvious level, CRT provides examples of the strength of new narratives and perspectives and their contributions to developing transformative knowledge. Critical race theorists argue that only by looking at the narratives of those who have been victimized by the legal system can we understand the "socially in-grained" and "systemic" forces at work in their oppression. Central to the CRT project are the notions that (1) racism is an endemic facet of life in our society; (2) "neutrality," "objectivity," "color blindness," and "mer-itocracy" are all questionable and nebulous constructs, whereas social re-ality is created only through the stories we tell as individuals and as a so-ciety; (3) context must be understood in searching for the deeper meanings that underlie contemporary social problems; and (4) race and the "experiential knowledge of people of color" is critical to understand-ing the law and society (see Delgado, 1995; Matsuda, Lawrence, Delgado, and Williams, 1993).

In both simple and complex ways, critical race theorists challenge the notion of the supposed biased subjectivity of narratives from the disfran-chised. Since reality as we understand it is primarily a socially con-structed entity, critical race theorists argue that we must acknowledge the multiplicity of realities that exist in order to better understand specific manifestations of the interactions of these realities (Ladson-Billings and Tate, 1995). Only by listening intently to people of color, for example, can we begin to see that dominant "realities" too are constructions and that they often exist at the expense of the reality of others. As Tate (1997) ex-plains, "The voice of the individual can provide insight into the political, structural, and representational dimensions of the legal system, espe-cially as they relate to the group case" (p. 235). This analysis informed my methodological evolution as it validated the need to listen to Chi-canas/os.

These ideas, however, expand on the work of critical ethnographers only slightly by focusing more specifically on the centrality of race. Thus, simply reading the CRT work did little to assist me in developing my methods because critical race theorists have not attempted to define how we can engage in methodological efforts at empowerment.

As I thought about my methodological struggles, however, CRT subtly helped me get to the heart of my turmoil and assisted me at another level. Much of CRT has been propelled by the critical standpoint that de-mands that these legal scholars ask who they are writing for and why. They have concluded that they are writing for *los de abajo* (my interpreta-tion): those who, by virtue of the oppressive structures that relegate them to the bottom of the socioeconomic ladder, reveal the unjust nature of our legal system. CRT researchers have emphasized the importance, for ex-ample, of Proposition 187's[6] "real" rationale, goals, and effects on Chi-canas/os through a Chicana/o-oriented analysis. These researchers have attacked the explicit and implicit racism of Proposition 187 and have de-manded social justice for Chicanas/os (Garcia, 1995). Furthermore, CRT suggests the significance of research that emphasizes social justice not simply as an objective but as a process. In short, much of the work of critical race theorists informs us that we cannot arrive at any degree of social justice if the means we employ in pursuing this goal are not also imbued with the principles of this justice. CRT, therefore, challenges the epistemology underlying the academy as it suggests that justice is a more essential measure of the strength of research than is objectivity.

CRT does not provide us with a method, but it questions traditional epistemology's top-down tendencies and, in so doing, gives us the rationale for a method of *los de abajo* that is grounded in social justice.

Challenging Tradition: Chicana/o Epistemology and a New Chicana/o Studies

Applying the revelations of critical race theory to my research on the educational concerns of the Chicana/o community helped me address frustrations I experienced with Chicana/o educational research and my own work. I explained earlier that my two primary frustrations with method in educational research with Chicanas/os were (1) that the students were never fully engaged in the research as co-researchers who "analyze data" and shape the findings, and (2) that the process itself was not helping Chicana/o students improve their situation in any significant way or contributing to their empowerment in general. Eventually—as I more fully understood my critiques of method and the possibilities suggested by innovative work such as that of CRT—I saw that my frustration was grounded in the lack of social justice Chicanas/os experience in their schools and communities and the role that institutions and research play in this process.

Critical educational ethnographers, CRT, and Chicana/o educational researchers all were essential to my evolving methodological thinking, but it was Chicanas/os outside of the academy who helped me confront the limitations of traditional methodology. For, as I thought about the problems involved in methodological change, I continually returned to the history of the Chicana/o in the United States and the interactions I had with Chicanas/os in my research, teaching, and personal life. Through this process, I realized that it was an unacknowledged nontraditional epistemology that was underlying my recurring methodological unrest. My efforts to seek a new method were unknowingly shaped by working-class Chicana/o epistemology itself.[7]

It is not my intent to describe all the nuances of a Chicana/o epistemology or the evolution of this epistemology (although this must be done). Rather, I hope simply to reveal the uniqueness of this epistemology by considering some of its central facets as they relate to this project.

The excerpt from Delgado-Gaitan's (1993) work discussed earlier can help in developing this analysis. The parents Delgado-Gaitan worked with were very concerned about the welfare of their children and engaged in efforts to improve their situation. They were also determined to coordinate these efforts as democratically as possible. This approach is one I have witnessed in a number of working-class Chicana/o communities. These Chicanas/os are intimately connected as an extended family, they are dedicated to achieving justice and equality (more for their children than for themselves), and they pursue this justice in ways that reflect their respect and love for each other. Knowledge that is sought and passed down within Chicana/o communities is grounded in these shared understandings.[8]

Thus, in the process of moving toward a new method and framework for research, I came to understand that my own efforts were informed by a Chicana/o epistemology and that my struggles resulted from the blatant contradictions between this way of thinking and the traditional epistemology I had been fighting. Citing Galeano extensively, Burciaga (1995) addresses this conflict when he discusses the common separation of the intellectual and the political as

> a mutilation of the human being, an objective of the ruling class who have us convinced that there are people who are "head" and people who are "hands." ... And I believe that we can be everything at once. I am political and many more things. I cannot cease being political because I am in solidarity with my own and because I hurt as if their needs were mine. (p. 132)

Through my self-critique, I finally realized that research and its underlying method and epistemology must be grounded on the epistemology of those with whom we work.

As I have attempted to understand the linkages between my methodological interests and a Chicana/o epistemology, I have looked back at Chicana/o history for clarification. One of the oldest forms for expressing Chicana/o values and histories is the *corrido* (the Mexican ballad). The *corrido* was and continues to be a means of passing on history for a people who rely heavily on the oral tradition. Typically, the stories sung in *corridos* tell of how individual Chicanas/os have fought against oppression in the United States (Peña, 1996). These stories give us insights into Chicana/o epistemology as they are grounded in principles of respect and love (through the oral tradition itself) and show the significance of pursuing justice.[9]

This is further reflected in the fact that many of the greatest achievements Chicanas/os as a group have made in the United States have been through group protest. In 1939 Chicanas fought the stereotype of their docility as they struck and picketed one of the largest canning companies in the Los Angeles area. Their victory was sealed as they brought their children to the home of the company's owner. Carrying signs that said, "I'm underfed because my Mama is underpaid," these children picketed in the wealthy neighborhood of the owners. Eventually, their mothers won the strike and met their goal of securing a brighter future for their families (Ruiz, 1990). This notion that families must fight together against oppression and injustice is central to the epistemology of working-class Chicanas/os.

The Chicana/o epistemology also has strong links to schooling itself. As many as 10,000 Chicanas/os walked out of schools in East Los Angeles in the spring of 1968 (Muñoz, 1989). They were protesting the inadequate education Chicana/o youth received in their schools. The students criticized an irrelevant curriculum, inadequate resources, and racist teachers and counselors. Chicanas/os in the 1960s sought an education (knowledge) that reflected their experiences and was relevant to their efforts to succeed and improve the conditions of their communities. In so doing, they created new knowledge and understandings about who they were.

In the 1990s this same epistemic approach is prevalent. In 1993, a group of Chicana/o students at UCLA, frustrated with the university's double-talk, began a hunger strike. They too sought the opportunity to have the curriculum reflect the Chicana/o history of struggle and to apply that history to their interests in improving the appalling conditions faced by many Chicanas/os in the Los Angeles area. Through the re-creation of their history, they wanted to develop new knowledge that reflected the strength of their indigenous roots. With nothing to gain for themselves as individuals, this small community of Chicanas/os endangered their long-term health by going fourteen days without food, until the university made significant steps toward creating a strong Chicana/o studies emphasis (Acuña, 1996). In the barrios of Los Angeles, I have seen this same sacrifice as *Guadalupanas*[10] give money they desperately need to help feed the children of a neighbor who has lost her job.

In looking at this history of Chicana/o resistance, I realized that there is a Chicana/o epistemology that exists in dramatic opposition to the dominant epistemology innovative researchers have been attempting to fight. I saw in my own experience that love, family, and social justice are not only embodied in our goals but are at the foundation of our epistemology itself. In addition, a central component of this epistemology is the oral tradition through which Chicana/o epistemology is passed on in the context of respect and love. As I began to see major facets of Chicana/o epistemology that I had only unconsciously understood earlier, I also looked back at my previous research experiences. I realized that this epistemology created a connection between myself and Chicana/o students—a community-oriented interest in making change in working-class Chicana/o communities—that at times virtually superseded ideology and power.

Burciaga (1993) provides another example of the uniqueness of Chicana/o epistemology. After deciding to paint a mural at Stanford University dedicated to Chicana/o heroes, he turned the task of identifying these heroes over to students and activists. Included in the lists of heroes/heroines were "mothers, fathers, grandparents, Vietnam veterans, *braceros, campesinos,* and *pachucos.*" These nominations revealed a Chicana/o epistemology that defined who we are, regardless of ideology, within the notions of family, love/honor/respect, and Chicana/o efforts to create new knowledge and seek empowerment. The mural's dedication submitted as the heroes of one student "all the people who died, scrubbed floors, wept and fought so that I could be here at Stanford" (Burciaga, 1993, p. 95).

Revisiting my experiences, my research, and the research of others in the Chicana/o community, I realized that there is a unique Chicana/o epistemology that is grounded in the pursuit of new knowledge toward group empowerment; that this was creating the disjuncture between the traditions under which I had been trained and my own methodological and research interests; and that, despite the fact that social justice was important to many of us doing Chicana/o research, Chicana/o epistemology had not shaped our methodology. I understood that Chicana/o researchers have rarely had the luxury to engage in this critique because they have been fighting for survival and legitimation. Whereas early interactive researchers continually had to justify their work and were therefore unable to focus solely on developing method itself (Scheurich and Young, 1997), Chicana/o researchers have been even more suspect, and the idea of a Chicana/o epistemology might only be seen by the mainstream as poor training and substandard scholarship by "unqualified, affirmative-action faculty."

Still, the persistence of the problems faced by Chicanas/os in and outside of academia suggests that we consider how a Chicana/o epistemology can help us redefine our place in the academy and reclaim our roles in Chicana/o empowerment. In fact, as I have argued elsewhere (Pizarro, 1998b), an essential step in this process will be to reconstruct Chicana/o studies upon the foundation of this epistemology. Although Chicana/o studies was intended to serve as a bridge between the university and the community—pursuing community empowerment by identifying, nurturing, and validating Chicana/o perspectives—it has typically been mired in the stagnant waters of traditional academic disciplines. The field tends to rely heavily on traditional disciplines and the frameworks and methodologies they employ in attempting to answer questions. I believe that this is because Chicana/o studies was not founded on the basic reality that Chicana/o epistemology is unique and demands alternative approaches to intellectual pursuits. Nevertheless, Chicana/o studies offers perhaps the best possibility for attacking and moving beyond the racism implicit in traditional epistemology.

To realize the original goals of Chicana/o studies, we must first deconstruct Chicana/o epistemology. I have begun this process in my work on methodology (as revealed in this chapter) and have started to decipher the connection between the cultural and political forces that have influenced Chicana/o epistemology (Pizarro, 1998b), but significantly more work needs to be done in this area. As that task is accomplished, it will allow us to use Chicana/o epistemology as the foundation for creating a paradigm for Chicana/o studies—propelled by and addressing the real-world struggles of Chicanas/os who are daily victims of the hyper-racialized context in which we now live. With the development of this paradigm, Chicana/o studies and Chicana/o communities will, for the first time, be able to develop theories, pedagogies, and methodologies that acknowledge and are grounded in a Chicana/o way of life and make realistic solutions attainable. Clearly, these goals extend beyond the emphasis of this chapter. Still, it is important that we keep these goals in mind as we address methodology. Returning to methodology, Chicana/o epistemology demands that we not choose between academic integrity and seeking justice, because in the Chicana/o community they are one and the same.

Chicana/o Social Justice Research

Although there is much work to be done and I have yet to fully develop a method that is based on Chicana/o epistemology through a long-term research project, I want to turn to a proposed method for Chicana/o social justice research. The method is divided into five phases.[11] As I describe each phase, I will explore the possible difficulties and shortcomings of the method as well.

Identifying "Subjects"

As we choose general areas of investigation related to Chicanas/os, researchers must begin by asking who are the parties involved in/affected by the context we will be exploring. In particular, we should ask who is experiencing "difficulties" or "problems," who is being exploited/victimized/oppressed, who is seeking change out of sheer necessity, and whose knowledge is being ignored and drowned out by hegemonic ideology and epistemology? Those who are most negatively involved/affected have the most light to shed on the investigation. As CRT suggests, they can expose the factors involved in their marginalization. Laura Simón's recent documentary film (Trench and Simón, 1997) provides strong support for this idea, as Latina/o students respond to the vicious assault being waged against Latinas/os through the ballot and Proposition 187. These students show us a world very different from that described by school staff.

Those "in power" within these contexts may have lessons to share, but they are also not fully invested in seeing the complexities of this context because it demands questioning their own power and authority. Simón's documentary demonstrates this process as teachers ignore the violent struggles for survival Latinas/os in Los Angeles must face and as they misinterpret the impact of these families on the local economy because of their own xenophobically constructed self-interests. It is often exceptionally difficult and of no interest to those with the most to lose to consider the way in which their own privilege is based on the denigration of others. Sleeter (1996) provides an excellent example as she explains white discourse on race at an interpersonal level and the way in which it allows for the maintenance of inequalities. In another work, Sleeter (1992) describes how political discourse in the United States also shapes social problems and the way we think about them so as to further empower the advantaged at the expense of the disadvantaged. Most people engaged in the discussion do not ever acknowledge that this may be the most significant result of our public political discourse. In looking at white teachers, Sleeter later shows that they create unconscious racialized understandings that privilege themselves and white students over students of color. In short, teachers, administrators, and schools have done very little to improve the educational opportunities of Chicanas/os over the years. There is a long history of school staff being formally and informally trained to blame Chicanas/os for their failure and to ignore the staff's complicity in the process.

With these examples in mind, in Chicana/o school research we have to work with specific segments of the Chicana/o student population. Our primary concern must be to engage in research that investigates and helps to shift social injustice as part of a larger effort to empower Chicana/o students. As researchers, our contributions to these attempts at social change may be greatest when we consider how we can "co-create" new knowledge and challenge racist epistemologies with those of the Chicanas/os with whom we are working.

Project Definition and Descriptive Phase

Next, we must develop a means by which we can begin to talk with Chicanas/os about their lives in and out of school. That is, the researcher and students have to construct a comfortable context in which students can engage in preliminary discussions about their world. The starting point must be to acknowledge, attempt to understand, and build on the unique epistemology of those with whom we are working. The researcher shows that s/he understands and shares the epistemological traditions in which Chicana/o students have been raised. We simultaneously explain our interests in learning from their experiences and in developing strategies (together) for changing and improving any conditions they deem problematic. In establishing trust, it is critical that Chicanas/os see the researcher as someone who is interested in what they have experienced.

An essential step in this phase is for participants to define themselves as authorities. They must know that we are turning to them for guidance. By starting with broad and general issues facing the participants, they begin to acquire a certain level of comfort with their own voice, and in this way we can establish a context in which they can assert their authority. [12] Most importantly, the researcher and participants must define the project as one that seeks to improve conditions for Chicanas/os and their communities. The research, therefore, is not seen as extraction from but as enrichment of the individuals and their communities. This facilitates breaking through the implicit power differential in the researcher-participant relationship. It can also, ideally, help the researcher avoid possible ideological conflicts with participants at this early stage of the project.

For me, the most powerful example of the potential of this phase came outside of what is considered formal research, during a preliminary presentation I made on these ideas. Having been accepted to present a paper on student voice at an academic conference, I considered alternative ways of making the presentation. Since I was teaching a Chicana/o studies course on education at the time and we were dealing with some of these issues, I asked if any of the students were interested in helping me with the presentation and if they thought the high school students they were working with would be interested. Many students were. Prior to the presentation, I met with the students and explained that I would not tell them what to say. I went on to say that I did not even want to know what they were going to say. I simply told them that their ideas and experiences were important, that the audience wanted to hear what they had to say about school, and that they would each have a few minutes to talk.

The students' presentations were enlightening (as reported by the session participants afterward). The high school students relished the opportunity to be heard, and to be heard by an audience that was concerned about the social inequalities that they have witnessed and experienced. They gained strength from the fact that they were able to demand that their epistemological framework be acknowledged. These students provided vivid images of their school lives as they described how schools "undermine the culture of the students" to create contexts in which they "always feel uncomfortable in school." School staff do not realize, as the students informed us, that "every Latino is smart." The college students validated the idea that schools set obstacles for Chicana/o students, but countered with the intelligence of the high school students they were mentoring, as they explained, "We even learned from them." Perhaps most important of all, after the presentations were over, there was an extensive question-and-answer period during which academics interacted directly with the students. Throughout the session, students revealed their ability to move beyond critical description and to effectively engage in analysis as they would if they were "researchers."

Thinking about this presentation and alternative means of research, we must be open to any number of forms of nontraditional research and to redefining our interests. The concerns of Chicanas/os, grounded in their own epistemology, can exist on many levels and in many arenas of their lives. Chicanas/os today face racist school staff; familial difficulties; legislation that classifies all Chicanas/os (based on appearance) as social leeches; limited economic opportunities; struggles with language acquisition; increased gang activity in Chicana/o communities; and a continued history of exploitation through a legal system that has stripped Chicanas/os of land, rights, and even humanity. Research with Chicana/o students may have to confront any number of these and other critical issues.

With regard to the goal of seeking social justice, participants may already be engaged in efforts at empowerment in which the researcher may then become participant.[13] Chicana/o students may also identify a specific need that transforms the researcher's role into that of advocate. They may want to pursue justice and empowerment by documenting their experiences on film, providing a needed community service, creating *teatros*, developing tutoring programs, painting murals, or through other expressions we have yet to consider as research. Alternatively, Chicanas/os may deem it critical to look within their families and communities and then to reinterpret their own lives through the experiences and knowledge of elders. In short, we must be open to any number of options. It is also possible that participants will not be interested in empowerment. In this case, it will be critical to question this position from the perspective of individuals who are seeking empowerment and vice versa.[14]

Through any of these processes, both researcher and participants can begin to more clearly define the questions that they will attempt to answer. Participants are asked broad, open-ended questions that are related to their specific experiences so that they can talk easily about a variety of issues that are significant to them. Even though a number of concerns may arise that extend beyond the initial interests of the researcher, participant discussions will be pivotal to the further development of the project. Thus, all participants are involved in the conceptualization and formation of the study.

Analytical Phase

The project must then consider the participants' perspectives and look to identify central themes and areas of concern. This should be done *with* the participants through researcher-participant conversations. Participants need to revisit their initial explanations and to agree and disagree with each other as to the heart of the issues at hand as they relate to their lives. The focus will be to identify the relationships that are critical to their own experiences.

In a recent follow-up interview I had with a Chicano college student, he volunteered an insight that was central to our efforts to understand the world of Chicana/o students and to begin to transform it. This student explained that as we looked at the forces shaping Chicana/o students' identities (which we agreed were important to consider), we needed to consider the specifics of the value system passed on to them by their families. He explained that although identity was important, it was their value system that would determine the actions students would take in response to the identity they had developed. These values would therefore shape the nature of our efforts at transformation and empowerment. His analysis was critical to the project—allowing us to consider the forces we might have to incorporate or fight against in activist efforts— and the principles described here (particularly our shared epistemology) were necessary for us to create a context in which he felt comfortable providing it.

A crucial component of this step in the research process is the challenging of participants' views and, subsequently, the development of stronger, more detailed explanations. One way of engaging in this process is to challenge participant views with those of other participants, with the understanding that this is essential to arriving at our agreed upon goals and that it is grounded in our respect for each other. In this way, the participants again are seen as authorities and they do not need to concern themselves with offending or overly challenging the researcher. So, the researcher will ask the participants to discuss, challenge, and/or reconstruct the relationships that the students as a group suggest are critical and to do so through the lens of their individual experiences. [15]

Most important, through the analysis, researcher and participants will focus attention on how empowerment can be achieved for their commu-

nity. As mentioned, there are many options here. Researcher and students may directly confront issues (such as racism or sexism, for example) in the arenas of institutional policy or individual behavior, or in unacknowledged climates of subordination. This confrontation may take
the form of challenging school personnel, initiating community-based
programs, coordinating social protest, assisting individuals in need, and
other processes of empowerment. Chicana/o students—like those who
participated in the conference presentation, like the student who provided me with additional considerations on the link between identity
and action, and like Laura Simón's fourth-graders who were fighting
against a system that detested them—have critical contributions to make
to understandings of their world and efforts to change it.

Meta-Analytical Phase

The "research" will continue as the researcher and the participants begin
to conduct meta-analyses of the area of investigation by reevaluating the
entire research process. The challenge here is to not simply incorporate a
feedback loop in research but to view the construction of themes and
analyses as an interactive process.

Returning to Chicana/o epistemology, we must see that the knowledge that is created and passed on through the Chicana/o oral tradition
is evolutionary. It is often through the telling of the story that its meaning
is first understood. Therefore, by returning to, retelling, and reinterpreting this story, its deeper meaning is often revealed. Similarly, research
with Chicanas/os must consider the evolutionary nature of the meaning
constructed by students. The story that I have told in this chapter is one
example of this phenomenon: It has taken continual reanalysis at multiple levels for me to arrive at the meaning of my experience as a Chi-
cana/o researcher.

This phase of the research, therefore, begins by asking participants if
they still believe the research questions they started with to be relevant
and subsequently critiques each stage of the research. It moves toward a
place where, as meaning is constructed in these conversations, the researcher and the participants push their discussion in the direction of
concrete implications and interventions that they can then propose
through the research.[16]

The "Product" and Empowerment Efforts

The most difficult and problematic area of this method is the "product."
In order for articles, books, research reports, and the like to mesh with
the principles undergirding this approach, they must be written in a dia-

logical fashion.[17] This requires that, in the writing, the researcher carefully recreate the processes and problematics involved in the coconstruction of knowledge during the research. As with the other steps in the research process, researchers need to share their writing with the participants, to have them respond to these representations, and to have them "rewrite" them, all through substantive *discussions*. Caring is the critical tool for addressing the concerns of power inherent in these discussions. I have seen young Chicanas/os take on many of these challenges in earnest once they realize that I am not doing the research for myself as a removed researcher. When they see that I am not on an expedition but that I share their concerns and experiences, they openly commit to the process of pursuing social justice (as they did in the conference presentation mentioned earlier).[18] They assume authority and ignore, challenge, or move beyond my perspective, ideology, and "authority" simply because they are engaged in an oral tradition that is embedded in their own epistemology. I am, therefore, arguing that when the Chicana/o researcher enters into her/his work as a caring individual who shares the concerns of the community in which s/he is working—as reflected in the reliance on their epistemology—issues of ideology and power can be addressed in revelatory ways.[19] This is facilitated when we come from and live in the communities that we "research," so that participants know we are researching together "for survival" as a Chicana/o community.

With regard to the "product" of research, we must also recognize that it may actually not be writing at all. Participants may be far less interested in documenting their experiences than in transforming their environment. Researchers may have to negotiate with participants to find avenues for sharing the "research" that are in line with a Chicana/o epistemology. One possibility might be creating and/or publishing in Chicana/o journals so that our experiences can be shared with other Chicana/o communities. In addition, we might also initiate dialogical interactions with other Chicana/o communities. Simultaneously, we will have to fight with our institutions to have this work "accepted." Finally, when appropriate, we may have to negotiate with our funding sources to ensure that participants are paid (especially for intervention efforts).

In this final and ongoing phase of research, researcher and participants together are pushing toward knowledge, understanding, and interventions that are directed at improving the conditions of Chicanas/os and their communities. Researcher and students are collaborating to expose the nuances of both Chicana/o epistemology and the Chicana/o experience because this has not been done and because it is necessary to our united effort to change our world. As this research process is grassroots-oriented, so too must be the subsequent efforts at change.

The students at the conference presentation provide one type of example. Just having the opportunity to be authorities was empowering for them. This process helped them see their own possibility and further clarified the need for their advancement as a part of the move toward the social changes that they deemed essential to their communities. In addition, I have since talked with some of these students, and they have gone on to develop Chicana/o studies programs for high schools as a means of empowering Chicana/o students who are struggling with the same issues they identified in their personal analyses at the conference.[20]

Ideally, researcher and participants will work together in establishing intervention efforts designed to address the issues that came out of the research. Overall, through methods that evolve from the epistemology of Chicanas/os themselves, we are attempting to move beyond traditional research and academic roles, and the idea that traditional research can make productive change for Chicanas/os. We are seeking to create new knowledge from within a Chicana/o epistemology that, although it attacks tradition, is helpful to Chicanas/os in their activist efforts. We are simultaneously trying to move beyond the reactionary activism that has become so common in the conservative sociopolitical climate of the 1990s. Chicanas/os and researchers who look to Chicana/o epistemology must see that empowerment will not be achieved solely through protests against racism or racist legislation (e.g., Proposition 187 and English-only efforts). It will be achieved when we redefine activism, research, knowledge, and empowerment to push us toward community-based changes that move us forward and focus on what we can do for ourselves rather than simply responding to racism. This can take the form of creating community-based centers that provide workshops and discussion groups designed to confront racism in schools, in the job market, and in obtaining services, coupled with proactive strategies for group empowerment.

This model is unquestionably general and undefined as it has just been presented. The general description without substantive examples is quite limited. Myriad options are available to the researcher at each step. The goal of this project, however, is not to provide a list of all these options. In fact, because participants are defining the project and may actually engage in it by allowing the researcher to participate in activism, most of the research process described here may only occur informally rather than as a scripted, step-by-step procedure. The entire process may occur through informal conversations that take place during community-based activism, for example. Because of these multiple possibilities, I have attempted to simply lay out a general model, to discuss potential critiques of the approach, and to consider its shortcomings. Furthermore, I have

not presented any innovative methods, only replaced traditional epistemology and in the process revealed the way in which Chicana/o epistemology can reshape how methods are employed and for what purposes.

Conclusion

The positivist foundations of the academy have created a significant obstacle to innovative methodological shifts in the research community.
This obstacle is grounded in epistemological immobility. Without question, traditional research has provided insights into the human condition
in a vast number of ways. Simultaneously, however, the positivist tradition has revealed the limits of "scientific" approaches to understanding
and, in particular, transforming humanity (as efforts to acquire knowledge that can lead to productive social change have proven largely un-
successful for Chicanas/os).

I have argued that we must move beyond the current theoretical discussions about the need for innovative and interactive methods. I suggest
that we look at epistemology and the way that it actually shapes most of
our efforts at innovation. Researchers who challenge the oppressive tendencies of education and research must also be willing to challenge our
own approaches and assumptions if we are to move thought and action in
new directions. I am attempting to initiate a process of self-critique
through which those of us who challenge academic traditions of objectivity, for example, also investigate how those traditions shape the very nature of our contestations. Not until we challenge the social injustices implicit in epistemological and methodological traditions will our work
uncover the transformative possibilities we seek in researching inequality.

The primary obstacle for researchers studying the world of Chicana/o
youth, for example, is the fact that even as we begin to increasingly incorporate the participation of these youth, most of us have not expressed
concern that our methods be as true to notions of social justice as we are
asking schools and institutions to be. We have not given much thought to
the way in which epistemology not only ignores but works against social
justice through our own methods. We have not considered how Chi-
cana/o epistemology might redirect our methods and move us in new
directions.

As we use the knowledge of Chicanas/os to challenge traditional epistemology, we confront a disturbing social reproduction head-on. It is evidenced in hardships faced by Chicanas/os that mirror those of previous
generations and (to mention only certain aspects) include:

- racist legislation at local, state, and national levels that hides a
  subtext currently implicating all brown-skinned residents as

criminals within a nicely wrapped package of preserving "America";

- directed assault on the psychological and physical well-being of Chicanas/os by alcohol companies and distributors that specifically target Chicana/o communities; and
- a comprehensive denial of educational opportunity in the schools through testing, special education, ESL and bilingual education, tracking, and the biased organization of daily school life as I have seen in my own experiences as a student and teacher.

At an individual level, Chicanas/os in the post–Proposition 187 era are confronted with a toxic racism—because of their skin color alone, *U.S.-born* Chicana/o students have been assigned the task of reporting on their parents' immigration status for homework; they have been taken to the Immigration and Naturalization Service for deportation, for not having a green card; and they have been told by school security that "we don't have to let fucking Mexicans in here anymore."

Chicana/o epistemology—grounded in shared notions of love, family, and the need for justice—suggests a new way of understanding how our society is organized. The Chicana/o experience betrays the popular color-blind discourse of modern "America" as well as the notion that it is acceptable to distance ourselves from racialized atrocities under the guise of "objectivity." Furthermore, the rich history of spiritual, cultural, and physical survival in this hostile climate, points to a number of lessons and characteristics that Chicanas/os can share and, through efforts for social justice, translate into greater group empowerment. An analysis of the Chicana/o experience can, therefore, assist us in forging a new epistemological approach to academic life and can help us construct a Chicana/o studies paradigm upon which to found a methodology, theories, and pedagogies that are true to and helpful in the struggle of Chicanas/os.

The method I propose has evolved from this goal as researchers and participants are engaged in social justice research, as Chicanas/os fighting together for survival. Although the issues of power inherent in research can never be fully resolved, I have incorporated tools to address them: Implicit in the method are attempts to attack issues of power and method through critical dialogue. More important, in using a Chicana/o epistemology as part of this process, I have been able to construct a model that helps us attack the racism of traditional epistemology (and of the university that supports it) in seeking empowerment for Chicanas/os.

In pursuing this objective, we must acknowledge that the empowerment of the disenfranchised is antithetical to the goals of the university.

For this reason, efforts at empowerment must emerge from the community itself, as they always have. Chicana/o Social Justice Research, however, shares the same objectives of community-based activism. It seeks to participate in the creation of new knowledge and "truth" that attacks tradition and, therefore, helps activist efforts by confronting the intellectual rationales and arguments that support, for example, an anti-Chicana/o hysteria (see Lechuga, 1997). Finally, Chicana/o Social Justice Research further assists community efforts at empowerment by providing opportunities for community-based Chicanas/os to participate in the intellectual exploration of Chicana/o epistemology that can support the development of those efforts. Chicana/o researchers must, therefore, realize that our role in the empowerment of Chicana/o communities is limited but important. We must also see that engaging in Chicana/o Social Justice Research makes us suspect in our institutions, but that we have little choice other than to challenge the system and policies that call our work into question. There are no comprehensive answers as to how Chicanas/os can survive in the institution and engage in Chicana/o Social Justice Research, but we must seek them. Critical race theory has provided us with the understanding that the racist structures of our society have influenced institutions and individuals to engage in a race war against Chicanas/os and other people of color. Although CRT has laid bare the overwhelming obstacles that confront researchers who want to break through the barriers to the empowerment of the disenfranchised, it has also demanded that we take on this difficult task. We can use the approach discussed here as a way of fulfilling the objectives of CRT and Critical Theory by understanding the limitations of our institutional location and pursuing realistic efforts at exposing new epistemologies and "truths"—considering social justice as both process and product.

It is not my intent to suggest that Chicana/o Social Justice Research is the only method of educational research worth pursuing: Much research on the state of education for Chicanas/os has been very insightful. Nor is it my belief that we can ever fully address the complex problematics of social research (e.g., the role of power). Even more important, I am not suggesting that research is itself empowering or that it can necessarily be made integral in efforts at social change. Chicana/o researchers (and others pursuing social justice) must, however, confront our complicity in the continued school failure of Chicanas/os. We must seek "the truth" as Chicanas/os experience it and attempt to disrupt epistemological tradition and racism. As part of this process, we have to create new spaces in which it is safe to engage in these efforts; building a new Chicana/o studies that is grounded in its own paradigm (based on a Chicana/o epistemology) from which we can then develop our own theories, pedagogies, and methods. It is my hope that this analysis and method will help researchers and disenfranchised communities confront the social injustices in method, epistemology, institutions, and society as part of our multifaceted efforts to empower ourselves.

Notes

1. In this text, *Chicana/o* refers to females and males of Mexican descent who are living, and have been socialized, in the United States. Demographic research over the past twenty-five years, and historically, shows that Chicanas/os and Latinas/os have the highest dropout rates of any major ethnic/racial group in the United States (California Postsecondary Education Commission, 1994; Carter and Segura, 1979; Duran, 1983; Gey, Oliver, Highton, Tu, and Wolfinger, 1992; Los Angeles Unified School District, 1985; Schick and Schick, 1991; U.S. Commission on Civil Rights, 1971; Valencia, 1991). The national dropout rate for Chicanas/os (often underreported) approaches 50 percent, whereas in some urban areas (such as Los Angeles) it is as high as 70 percent (Bennett, 1988; Chapa and Valencia, 1993; Los Angeles Unified School District, 1985; National Commission on Secondary Education for Hispanics, 1984; Schick and Schick, 1991). Alarmingly, 61 percent of Chicana/o adults (those older than 24) have not completed high school (Gey et al., 1992, p. 33). Even more shocking, in 1990 Latinas/os made up 62 percent of the dropout population in California (among 16- to 19-year-olds), despite the fact that they constituted only 35 percent of all 16- to 19-year-olds in the state (California Postsecondary Education Commission, 1994, p. 65). Most important of all, the educational outcomes (especially graduation rates) of Chicana/o students have improved little, if at all, over the past fifty years (Carter and Segura, 1979; Chapa and Valencia, 1993; National Center for Education Statistics, 1989), and the significant disparity between Chicana/o and white students' educational outcomes has not narrowed (Valencia, 1991).

2. By *social justice,* I mean social relations that are based on equality. This contrasts sharply with life in modern American society, which demands empowerment of selected groups at the expense of others through the abuse of power (e.g., via race-based hierarchies). With regard to methods, *social justice* refers to methods that seek knowledge and develop empowering strategies to move us toward greater equality through processes in which researcher and participant are equals at all stages of the data collection, analysis, and intervention. This requires that researchers and participants deconstruct the epistemology of the participants and use it as the basis for the entire project, and that we redefine our roles in institutions and daily life so that empowerment is central to our work and lives. It further demands that we challenge the assault currently being leveled on the Chicana/o community at sociopolitical and intellectual levels (see Lechuga, 1997). Social justice (in general and as method) will be further explained through the description of the Chicana/o experience and Chicana/o epistemology that follows.

3. The traditional epistemological framework I am describing here will become clear over the course of this discussion. Briefly, I am referring to the commonly accepted academic notions that "objectivity" is desirable (if not attainable); that knowledge exists independent of the subjectivities of individuals (implicitly referring to people of color and the disenfranchised in particular); and that mem-

bers of the academy are those best equipped to acquire and explain that knowledge.

4. I worked with Chicana/o students in a high school, community college, and university in the Los Angeles area. They ranged in age from mid-teens to late twenties. Most of the students were working-class, second-generation Chicanas/os (or first-generation Chicanas/os who had moved to the United States before coming of school age).

5. I have chosen not to include examples here because I cannot address the concerns of this chapter while also explaining the process in which I and the students engaged. Furthermore, as mentioned, I have only recently begun to identify and confront the methodological issues I have been discussing, and so my forthcoming research will be a better example of the method. I do, however, include one minor example in a later section.

6. Proposition 187 was an initiative on the 1994 California ballot. It was designed to deny social services and aid to undocumented immigrants. Among other things, the initiative called for denying undocumented students access to public education and for schools to confirm the "legal" status of all students' parents. It was passed by a majority of California voters and has since been partially upheld by the U.S. district courts (albeit with most of the legislation being deemed unconstitutional).

7. We can argue either that there are distinctions between working-class and middle-/upper-class Chicana/o epistemology or that some middle-/upper-middle-class Chicanas/os have surrendered to and adopted mainstream epistemology in the United States. Regardless, there are important connections between class and epistemology that must eventually be considered; but given the focus of this paper, I refer to working-class Chicana/o epistemology exclusively.

8. As mentioned, there are many nuances to Chicana/o epistemology that must be addressed in future works. There are also a number of critical Chicana/o characteristics that inform this epistemology (e.g., spirituality, duality, language, work ethic, and so on) and that must be integrated into a more comprehensive model. Perhaps most important to this model will be an analysis of gender and sexism within Chicana/o culture and of their links to Chicana/o epistemology. The female is central to the survival and strength of Chicanas/os in the United States; but at the same time, Chicanas face a significant degree of sexism within their own communities. This must be confronted as we move toward a more holistic model of Chicana/o epistemology and also attempt to translate it into methodology and empowerment.

9. The significance of interracial conflict and social justice is similarly reflected in most forms of Chicana/o expression: theater, art, literature, music, film, graffiti, dress, and others.

10. These are organizations of women in the Catholic church. They find strength in the *Virgen de Guadalupe*, who cares for and helps Mexicanas/os in need. Among other things, these women honor *La Virgen* through their efforts to help others in their community.

11. No aspect of this method is truly unique, although the rationale underlying it redefines the concept of method in a way that may allow for greater innovation. Freire (1970, 1994) inspired the approach I am pursuing. Also, some of the prob-

lematics implicit in the initial phases of the method are addressed in the explanation of the final phases. Furthermore, an earlier version of this paper (Pizarro, 1998a) goes into greater depth in addressing issues such as false consciousness and power.

12. With regard to the proposed method, of great concern is the fact that the world of research exists outside the world of most individuals, particularly that of students. An earlier version of this work (Pizarro, 1998a) explains how to address this dilemma and suggests that it is through continual dialogue that both researchers and participants get beyond superficial descriptions to the deeper meaning underlying our experiences.

13. Because research typically exists in unconscious opposition to Chicana/o empowerment, social justice research may often entail activism itself; and when method is innovative and not constricted by epistemological tradition, it can assist in these efforts.

14. It is essential that we respect and attempt to understand the position of those who are not interested in empowerment. Although upper-middle-class Chicanas/os, for example, may tend to be less interested in empowerment, it is important to acknowledge that most Chicanas/os are not upper-middle-class and that in many disenfranchised Chicana/o communities empowerment is a common goal. For a great deal of Chicana/o research, then, it is the differences in the definitions of empowerment with which the researcher and participants will have to struggle.

15. Researchers often raise the concern that these types of innovative methods may be limited by the "false consciousness" of the participants. This method, however, does more to cut through "false consciousness" than most, as it never takes a reply or position at face value and the researcher constantly questions students on multiple levels (see Pizarro, 1998a, for an extended discussion).

16. Of course, there are issues of power, whether real or perceived, that exist in research. Paulo Freire (1994) has provided strong examples of how to address issues of researcher-participant power *with* participants—examples that I applied to the method in an earlier version of this work (Pizarro, 1998a). Through this method, researchers and participants attempt to deconstruct these power-laden aspects of our relationship.

17. Fine (1994) points to an important dilemma: the process of attempting to accurately reflect and include our research subjects' voices can limit or eliminate our own voices. Fine resolves that there is a need for researchers to take authorial ownership of their work. In an earlier version of my work (Pizarro, 1998a), I contend that if our intent as researchers is to uncover and obliterate social injustice and improve the human condition in whatever way is possible (via our areas of emphases), then by allowing our voice (that is our writing) to be a true conduit for those with whom we engage in critical dialogues, our voice becomes representative of its intent and remains intact.

18. Naples (1996) provides another example in her research. Interestingly, she entered into the project she describes in her work not as a researcher but as a concerned individual who shared the trauma and obstacles of her "participants." In other words, Naples began her "work" as a caring person rather than an interested researcher.

19. Ellsworth (1989) addresses this possibility as she considers Christian's (1987) idea that she writes "for survival." When we do our research "for survival," it can transform our methodological framework and inform our efforts to address power inequities in our work. Still, the impact of power on our lives and work is unavoidable, as discussed and addressed in an earlier version of this chapter (Pizarro, 1998a).

20. This example is not meant to be a model of the method itself. My own inability to continue working with these students made this impossible. Rather, the example is intended to suggest the possibilities of pursuing methods that are socially more just and more interactive.

References

Acuña, R. F. (1996). *Anything but Mexican: Chicanos in contemporary Los Angeles.* New York: Verso.

Anzaldúa, G. (1987). *Borderlands/La frontera: The new mestiza.* San Francisco: Spinsters/Aunt Lute.

Bennett, W. [Secretary of Education]. (1988, April). *American education, making it work: A report to the president and the American people.* Washington, DC: U.S. Government Printing Office.

Burciaga, J. A. (1993). *Drink cultura: Chicanismo.* Santa Barbara: Joshua Odell Editions.

_____. (1995). *Spilling the beans: Loteria Chicana.* Santa Barbara: Joshua Odell Editions.

California Postsecondary Education Commission. (1994). *The state of the state's educational enterprise: An overview of California's diverse student population.* Sacramento, CA: California Postsecondary Education Commission.

Carter, T., and Segura, R. (1979). *Mexican Americans in school: A decade of change.* New York: College Entrance Examination Board.

Cervantes, L. D. (1981). Poem for a young white man who asked me how I, an intelligent, well-read person could believe in the war between the races. *Emplumada.* Pittsburgh, PA: University of Pittsburgh Press.

Chapa, J., and Valencia, R. (1993). Latino population growth, demographic characteristics, and educational stagnation: An examination of recent trends. *Hispanic Journal of Behavioral Sciences, 15,* 165–187.

Christian, B. (1987). The race for theory. *Cultural Critique, 6,* 51–63.

Delgado, R. (Ed.). (1995). *Critical race theory: The cutting edge.* Philadelphia: Temple University Press.

Delgado-Gaitan, C. (1993). Researching change and changing the researcher. *Harvard Educational Review, 63,* 389–411.

Delgado-Gaitan, C., and Trueba, H. (1991). *Crossing cultural borders: Education for immigrant families in America.* New York: Falmer Press.

Duran, R. (1983). *Hispanics' education and background: Predictors of college achievement.* New York: College Entrance Examination Board.

Ellsworth, E. (1989). Why doesn't this feel empowering? Working through the repressive myths of critical pedagogy. *Harvard Educational Review, 59,* 297–324.

Fine, M. (1994). Working the hyphens: Reinventing the self and other in qualitative research. In N. K. Denzin and Y. S. Lincoln, *Handbook of qualitative research* (pp. 70–82). Thousand Oaks, CA: SAGE Publications.

Foley, D. (1990). *Learning capitalist culture: Deep in the heart of Tejas.* Philadelphia: University of Pennsylvania Press.

Freire, P. (1970). *Pedagogy of the oppressed.* New York: Continuum.

――――. (1994). *Pedagogy of hope: Reliving pedagogy of the oppressed.* New York: Continuum.

Galindo, R., and Escamilla, K. (1995). A biographical perspective on Chicano educational success. *The Urban Review, 27,* 1–29.

Garcia, R. J. (1995). Critical race theory and Proposition 187: The racial politics of immigration law. *Chicano/Latino Law Review, 17,* 118–148.

Gey, F., Oliver, J., Highton, B., Tu, D., and Wolfinger, R. (1992). *California Latina/Latino demographic data book.* Berkeley: California Policy Seminar.

Gitlin, A. (1990). Educative research, voice and school change. *Harvard Educational Review, 60,* 443–466.

Gitlin, A., Siegel, M., and Boru, K. (1989). The politics of method: From leftist ethnography to educative research. *Qualitative Studies in Education, 2,* 237–253.

Ladson-Billings, G., and Tate, W. (1995). Toward a critical race theory of education. *Teachers College Record, 97,* 47–68.

Ladwig, J., and Gore, J. (1994). Extending power and specifying method within the discourse of activist research. In A. Gitlin (Ed.), *Power and method: Political activism and educational research* (pp. 227–238). New York: Routledge.

Lechuga, F. S. (1997, July 16). Anti-Mexican hate group stirring in California. *Salt Lake Tribune.* Available on line at http://utahonline.sltrib.com/97/jul/071697/27055.htm.

Los Angeles Unified School District. (1985). *A study of student dropout in the Los Angeles Unified School District.* Report presented to Dr. Harry Handler, superintendent, and Board of Education, Los Angeles.

Matsuda, M., Lawrence, C., Delgado, R., and Williams, K. (Eds.). (1993). *Words that wound: Critical race theory, assaultive speech, and the first amendment.* San Francisco: Westview Press.

Muñoz, C. (1989). *Youth, identity, power: The Chicano movement.* New York: Verso.

Naples, N. A. (with E. Clark). (1996). Feminist participatory research and empowerment: Going public as survivors of childhood sexual abuse. In H. Gottfried (Ed.), *Feminism and social change: Bridging theory and practice* (pp. 160–183). Chicago: University of Illinois Press.

National Center for Education Statistics. (1989). *Digest of education statistics* (25th ed.). Washington, DC: U.S. Government Printing Office.

National Commission on Secondary Education for Hispanics. (1984). *"Make something happen": Hispanics and urban high school reform.* Vol. 1. Washington, DC: Hispanic Policy Development Project.

Padilla, R. (1992). Using dialogical research methods to study Chicano college students. *The Urban Review, 24,* 175–183.

Patthey-Chavez, G. (1993). High school as an arena for cultural conflict and acculturation for Latino Angelinos. *Anthropology and Education Quarterly, 24,* 33–60.

Peña, M. (1996). Música fronteriza/border music. *Aztlan*, 21, 191–225.

Pizarro, M. (1998a). "Chicana/o Power!": Epistemology and methodology for social justice and empowerment in Chicana/o communities. *International Journal of Qualitative Studies in Education*, 11, 57–80.

_____. (1998b). Reconstructing the foundation of Latina/o Studies: Latina/o epistemology and intellectual rebirth. Paper presented at the first "Constructing Latina/Latino Studies: Location and Dislocation" Conference, Urbana-Champaign, Illinois.

Romo, H. D., and Falbo, T. (1996). *Latino high school graduation: Defying the odds.* Austin: University of Texas Press.

Ronda, M., and Valencia, R. (1994). "At-risk" Chicano students: The institutional and communicative life of a category. *Hispanic Journal of Behavioral Sciences*, 16, 363–395.

Ruiz, V. L. (1990). A promise fulfilled: Mexican cannery workers in southern California. In A. R. Del Castillo (Ed.), *Between borders: Essays on Mexicana/Chicana history* (pp. 281–298). Encino, CA: Floricanto Press.

Scheurich, J., and Young, M. (1997). Coloring epistemologies: Are our research epistemologies racially biased? *Educational Researcher*, 26 (4), 4–16.

Schick, F., and Schick, R. (1991). *Statistical handbook on U.S. Hispanics.* Phoenix: Oryx Press.

Sleeter, C. E. (1992). *Keepers of the American dream: A study of staff development and multicultural education.* Washington, DC: Falmer Press.

_____. (1996). White silence, white solidarity. In N. Ignatiev and J. Garvey (Eds.), *Race traitor* (pp. 257–265). New York: Routledge.

Suárez-Orozco, M. M. (1989). *Central American refugees and U.S. high schools: A psychosocial study of motivation and achievement.* Stanford, CA: Stanford University Press.

Tate, W. F. (1997). Critical race theory and education: History, theory, and implications. *Review of Research in Education*, 22, 195–247.

Trench, T., and Simón, L. A. (Producers). (1997). *Fear and learning at Hoover Elementary.* Los Angeles: Public Broadcasting Service.

U.S. Commission on Civil Rights. (1971). *Report II: Mexican American education study. The unfinished education: Outcomes for minorities in the five Southwestern states.* Washington, DC: U.S. Government Printing Office.

Usher, R. (1996). A critique of the neglected epistemological assumptions of educational research. In D. Scott and R. Usher (Eds.), *Understanding educational research* (pp. 9–32). New York: Routledge.

Valencia, R. (1991). The plight of Chicano students: An overview of schooling conditions and outcomes. In R. Valencia (Ed.), *Chicano school failure and success: Research and policy agendas for the 1990s* (pp. 3–26). London: Falmer Press.

4

Research Methods as a Situated Response: Toward a First Nations' Methodology

MARY HERMES

Looking back at my dissertation, now a full year after it is all said and done, I am still trying to sort out exactly where the "methods" are. It reminds me of the split I identified in my research as stifling: the content/methods split in educational practice. Why would I dissect what I teach from how I teach it? How could a worksheet on ricing replace going out in a canoe to collect wild rice?

When only content is implicated in curriculum, the question of culturally relevant curriculum becomes severely limited. It is as if the way you have done something (e.g., teach or research) should be extracted from what you did or, for that matter, why you did it. So that it can be replicated? or mass produced? These categories do not make sense to me. And so I write this article, this "piece," or slice of my research, with methods as a focus, but, moreover, to complicate through example how much the "way" of doing research was inextricable from the research and its context and cultural locations.[1]

My intention in going to the Lac Courte Oreilles (LCO) Ojibwe reservation, in northern Wisconsin, was not to do research. Being of mixed heritage (Lakota, Chinese, and White), I had many personal as well as professional reasons for wanting to "go back" to the reservation.

Going back means touching a place of the past and the future that belongs to all of us detribalized, adopted out, colonized, and made-not-to-feel-at-home people. "Going back" means remembering to touch the places that bring us together. "Going back" means I am not from there, the way someone raised there is, means I will never be a part of that community in that same way, but it also means no better and no worse.

I originally went to student teach, then to teach, then to stay, and in the process of all this, wrote a dissertation. This chapter is an attempt to continue the reflective element that was so much a part of the original work. It is a reflective retrospection on my methodology. The ways in which I did the research, the "methods," were not clearly delineated before I started the work. Instead, the goal of exploring a problem that was relevant to the community, in a way that was responsive to that particular context, guided my work. Now, a year after the entire dissertation process is done, and situated away from the community, I believe the "methods" still refuse a single category or any other formula that may make them a recipe for research. I am uncomfortable retrospectively naming one methodology or theoretical basis[2] to which I can pledge my allegiance. In this chapter I will refer to several influential academic research traditions (critical ethnography, activist methodology, and narrative inquiry) and suggest that no single, predetermined methodology would have accommodated the grounding of my research in Ojibwe culture and community.

As I came straight from graduate school, where I had been steeped in cultural studies and curriculum theory, my work on the reservation juxtaposed abstract theories with grounded teaching practice and made me shift my research agenda in ways that were responsive to the community. My presence on the reservation forced me to create a research methodology that was inspired by traditions (ranging from traditional Ojibwe culture to the culture of the University of Wisconsin—Madison's graduate school) but not clearly derived from any of them. I constructed the "methods" of this research project as a response to some of the problems associated with the question of developing a locally based curriculum as well as the historically negative reputation of research in Indian Country at large. Necessarily, my "response" was one deeply influenced by culture, or more appropriately, I would say, was itself a site of cultural production.

Throughout the text of the dissertation I use a multiplicity of voices (my own reflective notes; the words of other community members, Elders, and students; as well as the reflections of other writers) to represent the community involvement that I (being the sole author) was taking individual credit for. Due to space limitation, in this chapter I will imitate that format only by drawing on my own narrative voice (written in italics).

The model I used for writing was inspired by a model of editing a videotape (Bordowitz, 1988). By taking different but related "clips" of writing (for example, stories as told by myself or others, analytical writings and quotes, and examples of practices at the school), I created a montage in a way not dissimilar to editing a tape (sometimes smooth transitions, sometimes jarring juxtapositions). My hope was to capture some of the detail and complexity of the voices that exist around the competing ideas of "school." Further, Bordowitz's video production model is most compelling in that it brings together different perspectives, side by side, without resolving tensions or making sweeping generalizations. The research project itself was an attempt to bring together different perspectives, different voices, in hopes of forming an imaginary meeting ground among them. Through relating personal experiences, practices, and narratives (including lengthy quotes from community members' interviews), I hoped to be able to write in a style that expresses abstract, logical, and theoretical lines of thoughts even as it also validates as knowledge the expressive and emotional gestures that often outline the details of personal stories and community struggles over the meanings of "school."

How Was Theory Generated?
A Deeper Methods Question

When I started to limit "my" research problem to the most narrow definition, I realized the burning question (Haig-Brown, 1990; Haig-Brown and Archibald, 1996) was the question I took from the community: How to develop a curriculum that was relevant to Ojibwe culture within the confines of a tribal school? Twenty years ago when Native students walked out of the public school in Hayward, Wisconsin, discriminated against but not beaten, this was the same question they carried with them: Where is our school? Where is our knowledge? Can't we learn this inside of a school that is really ours? Since I did not own the question (the community did), the question of curriculum and community continually centered the project and, in this sense, made it an "activist" (Fine, 1994) research project. Whatever I could find out about the problem would also have to be channeled back into the community.

Back and forth between discussions, practice, observation, reading, and writing, theories emerged in ways similar to the "recursive" process that Doll suggests as a model for curriculum (1993). That is to say, the writing of the text did not simply reflect practice or theory, but the "method" was one of continually recycling thought/action/reflection/writing in ways that pointed to new theoretical directions. Since one goal of the dissertation project was to generate theory (as opposed to fixed answers), the reflective methods question becomes: How was theory generated? The short answer is that in this case, theory became empirically grounded through the practice of the research (Lather, 1991).

Every now and then my idealism gets stomped on. Internal colonization, distrust, dysfunctionalism, fighting against that legitimacy which is perceived as coming

only from the White man's system. . . . Harsh reality. Bitter feelings. Turning cyni-
cal, again. . . . Sometimes I find refuge in theory, in an understanding that is not
aimed at blaming an individual or anyone, but looks at history, generations, and the
expression of an entire way of being which expects and accepts struggle.

I think the project was a test of accountability for theory, or maybe a test of accountability for me. Could I make sense of theory in the context of life, not just the context of an argument? Could I put what I learned in graduate school to work? On my entry form for the *Holmes directory of minority scholars, 1991,* I wrote:

I refuse to separate the "theory" from the "practice," and so I find myself in the middle of trying to figure out what curriculum is relevant while tanning hides and collecting wild rice. . . . It is messy and confusing, but I am learning more here on the reservation than I would have asked for.

I believe the place of theory in methods/research is an important question because it exposes a commonsense assumption about methods: Methods are categorically distinct from theory. They are disinterested tools for extracting information, ways of doing (not ways of thinking about) that are implicitly a one-way interaction. In my research project, theory intersected with methods continuously. Methods were not held as a constant but rather were continually changing. Given the nature of my research problem, I felt that the methods acted as a situated response. It is the specific nature of that response to which I now turn my attention.

Problems with Research

Exploitative Research Methods

Gleaned from readings by Native scholars (see LaFromboise and Plake, 1983, for example) as well as through the oral traditions of the Indian "community" (meaning the grapevine, the oral tradition of Indian Country), there seems to be a growing, Native-oriented, or First Nations',[3] ethic for doing research in our own Native American communities (personal communication with Rosemary Christenson, a representative of the National Indian Education Association, November 1993). Deyhle and Swisher (1997) in a comprehensive review of research for, by, and about Native education wrote:

We started this chapter with voices that spoke of assimilation as the goal of Indian education. We end this chapter with the voices of Indian people who proposed a different goal, one that envisions equal coexistence and the maintenance of languages and cultures as effective means of achieving success in schools and communities. These Indian voices also call for an increase of both Indian researchers and perspectives. (p. 176)

My interpretation of this "ethic" is that the emphasis shifts from "research for research's sake" (read: knowledge in the abstract) to research that serves a specific purpose or need of the community within which it is situated. This ethic is at least in part contradictory to the historical circumstances of being continually colonized through "research." For example, the exploitative role of anthropology within Native communities has long been critiqued and at times undermined by Native peoples through oral traditions as well as written ones (see, for example, Deloria, 1973; LaFromboise and Plake, 1983). At this point many anthropologists, especially critical ethnographers, have become aware of this history and dynamic and have become more reflective of their positions and ethics accordingly (see Clifford and Marcus, 1986). However, Cultural Anthropology's subdiscipline, archeology, has not been so well behaved. And the battle to reorient archeological research methods according to the ethics of their "subjects" still rages, often ending up in the courts.[4]

As a Native American, this research ethic arises and is articulated *against* a colonial relationship; it also arises *for* Native self-determination in education (Deyhle and Swisher, 1997). Since the Indian Education Act of 1972, 31 tribal-controlled colleges (Ambler, personal communication, May 1997)[5] have been established as well as 66 tribal-controlled elementary or high schools (Indian Nations At Risk Task Force, 1990). A general mission of all of these schools is to serve various and particular Native American populations in ways that are culturally relevant. As a part of the colonial legacy of boarding schools, all of the tribal schools have adopted, at least in part, a Western European model of school "structure." Yet the idea of developing a "culture-based school" is a common goal, although the means toward this goal are consistently in flux.

The task of responding to this "dilemma," the task of Indian education, is enormous and the need is urgent for research on a variety of topics, including bias in educational testing; indigenous languages; the development of "inclusive" (of all races of people) texts; generational effects of boarding schools and alcoholism; learning styles and teaching methods; and inherent bias in school structures, to name a few. A well-articulated "ethic" that legitimates community-generated research questions and culturally appropriate research behaviors and holds researchers accountable to these standards would displace the current system of research projects that are accountable only to institutions of higher education or funding sources. Such an ethic would undercut imposed structures of power that continue to define Indian education through language and practices that carry the legacies of colonialism. In this way, much more community involvement and participation would become a necessary part of the process of research. This goal seems well within the grasp of Native communities as sovereign nations.

Coinciding with this emerging ethic and sense of purpose in Indian community-based research is the agenda of the academy—to fulfill the requirements to satisfy the degree of Ph.D. Along with this purpose comes yet another sense of protocol and expectations, a different set of research needs and a different ordering of priorities. And so I am left with the sense of a duality. I have organized my thoughts around the demands of meeting the needs of two distinct purposes, two distinct audiences, only rarely overlapping.

Situating Myself Within the Research: A Not-God Trick

The war is not between Indian and White, but between that which honors life and that which does not. It is fought within ourselves as well as within the world (Hampton, 1993, p. 296).

What is the purpose for doing this project anyway? To get a Ph.D., to get a job at a college, to take the time and put the thoughts with the experiences and the voices of community people and do some foundation work for cultural curriculum development that includes community building as part of the vision, part of the process, a part of the way the school changes and becomes a community cultural center. That's my vision.

Situating myself in the text of the dissertation (*not* as an abstract, all-knowing, unsituated voice) was an important and yet illusive goal for me. My intention was to avoid making sweeping generalizations about Indian education, or positioning myself as "expert" in any other way. This would be untrue to my experience and antithetical to the idea of community building through this research. For this reason, to be very clear and conscious of my positions (shifting, flexible, and dependent on context) within the school/community and within the text became another aspect of how I conducted research.

What it's like to suddenly become "Auntie" to 300 kids and know that in three years I'll have to write something about them, something which does not betray that trust and relationship. . . . What it's like to be a "mixed blood" in 1995 and in every community I live in feel that that is either "exotic" or somewhat looked down on (I heard a song about a HALF BREED on the radio just today), not quite "authentic," never quite completely respected. . . . And then what it's like to work at a tribal school where the real, the earth-shaking work is all about identity; finding a space and a place for yourself in the fast changing world without getting caught in the crossfire of tribal politics. What it's like to try ever so hard to fully, intelligently comprehend all this, while still maintaining the freedom and dignity to laugh, cry, sometimes not understand—and feel it all.

The Retelling of Methods

Gathering Stories . . . Community Visions

I conducted many formal and informal interviews over a period of three years. The first formal set was done with teachers in the beginning of my first year there as "cultural curriculum director." The job was just as broad and ambiguous as the title sounds—the main question interviewees often asked me was "What is your job, anyway?" Sometimes perceived as administration but, I believe, more often as associated with teaching,[6] I interviewed 30 teachers and staff members at the school. In these conversations I asked teachers some general questions about Ojibwe culture-based curriculum, but the format was very open and followed any direction they set. The second set was done at the beginning of my third year and involved 30 parents, students, Elders, teachers, and community members at large. In these interviews I asked to hear about people's dreams for the school, and sometimes heard about how their dreams had been stomped on.

In the face of an oftentimes pervasive feeling of hopelessness, I had to ask about hopes and dreams. In purposefully wanting to build dreams and visions for the community and school, I asked to hear them, to record them, and to tell them. What are the dreams of community members? Of the school community? How have they changed over time? Where do they come from? How do they connect or diverge? What are some examples of how they are being lived out? What are some roadblocks to their ever being tried out? Through gathering stories and visions, I hoped to strengthen the vision of the school as a part of the community. Further, it was my hope that the interviews be utilized as a reference for curriculum development at the school.[7]

I refer to "community" in a broad sense, as the school community includes both persons from the reservation community and outside of it. Although the school is situated on the reserve and serves approximately 100 percent Indian children (as self-identified), many of the teaching faculty are non-Indian and live outside of the reservation in nearby towns. So the school community includes a diverse group of people, people whose dreams and visions for the school should not be excluded.[8] This relationship between school and community is what I was aiming to strengthen through the act of gathering a diverse sampling of dreams and visions.

In some cases I found the interviewing process to be merely a way of blocking off some time and space for a conversation that was ongoing. Once I had found the time to sit with an interviewee it was not usually necessary to formally "ask" questions. The topic of culture-based curriculum was "in the air" but oftentimes not discussed due to the urgent nature of other issues. At times, the interview was an "excuse" to engage folks in some long conversations about the school.

At times, Elders thought individual interviews were redundant, saying that my past three years of working with them was an "asking" of what they thought of the school. This gave me permission to acknowledge some ideas that I was being overly cautious about presuming (for example, the idea among Elders that Indian identity and sobriety are priorities). So instead of sitting down with a tape recorder and asking questions, I often would merely "check in" with various sources to confirm my assumptions about their visions and hopes for school change. With teachers, on the other hand, or people I knew only in a professional setting, in-depth interviews provided a good tool for listening to their views more carefully.

At times during the research process, interviews and discussions were reflected back to the community in very direct ways. I circulated copies of my "proposal" among the most interested staff members and asked for comments. I gave transcribed interviews back to participants (second set) and had subsequent conversations where participants could clarify anything they perceived as ambiguous. I used interviews as curriculum and reading material in a class I taught for staff. I deposited several interview copies with administrators and the curriculum committee and a complete copy of the dissertation in the school library, inviting teachers and staff to use the information in their classes or in their continued curriculum efforts.

Observations

In my first semester at the school, I was a student teacher and graduate student at the same time. Although this did interesting things for my identity as a student teacher (see Britzman, 1991), it also gave me an entree to observe classes in a way that was familiar and comfortable to most teachers. From the observations and conversations that followed, I was invited into many hands-on instances of curricular development. Teaching examples included in the text of the research were generally initiated by teachers who invited me into their classrooms. By developing relationships with teachers in a variety of ways, I never clearly fit into any one particular category—just a researcher or teacher or community member, for example. Analogous to developing relationships with students in multiple contexts, this seemed to strengthen my position as a researcher with a bias and a purpose. I feel it clearly points to a methodology that involves more reciprocity than exists when a person solely comes to "research" a classroom.

Elders

In my desire "not to be the expert," I am extremely aware of the cultural traditions that position the Elders as teachers and authorities. In seeking to honor life and wisdom in researching (Haig-Brown and Archibald, 1996), it seemed obvious to me that the first source to consult was the Elders. Also conscious of the legacy of exploitation that has continued under the guise of research, I felt it morally and spiritually necessary to develop the qualities of submission[9] and reciprocity in my relationships with Elders. In my first year at the Ojibwe school, I was part of a community–tribal college–school collaborative group that started up the Elders' Council for the explicit purpose of bringing Elders together and inviting them into our schools. Through this work I often asked Elders about "curriculum" and got a variety of responses. My "method" or way of asking in these cases was guided more by cultural protocols than a particular methodology. I was grateful and listened to whatever I was told, and never consciously tried to guide discussion or interrupt with questions. Even the "formal" interviews I conducted after three years of working with Elders took on these forms of narrative or storytelling.

Teaching

Teaching was another role I played in the community, one that informed my theory and research on many levels. There was a teacher shortage and a desire to recruit more Indian teachers, and so after one semester of student teaching there, I was offered a job. In my various teaching positions over the next three years, I was given the opportunity to translate theory into practice and experiment with curriculum. Feedback from students was (of course) immediate and constant. Teaching was probably the one act that strengthened my relationships with community members the most; through students I was invited into many families. To veteran teachers, I was a "new teacher" and occupied a very different position than a "Ph.D. candidate."

Intersections with Critical Ethnography, Narrative, and Activist Research

In this section I will briefly describe how some recognized educational research methods served as models and inspiration for this method. I will also point out places where I feel that my work diverged. And finally, I want to emphasize places where these traditions intersected with ideas gleaned from First Nations researchers or traditions.

The post-positivistic methodological traditions I will discuss are critical ethnography, narrative inquiry, and activist research. These are broad, interdisciplinary methodologies, and I will not attempt to review all the educational research that links them, desirable as such a project would be. Rather, I want to focus my discussion on the ideas I found most useful in validating, legitimizing, and/or inspiring my methodology as a situated response.

Critical Ethnography

> *Critical ethnography is research which provides opportunity for the study participant to engage in dialectical interactions of action and reflection—praxis—in relation to both the research and their situations, thereby transforming those situations. (Haig-Brown and Archibald, 1996, p. 246)*

Apart from the obvious sort of "being there and participating" (participant observation), from critical ethnography I borrowed the important concept of "praxis" (Lather, 1991) and combined it with activist research. I believe that being in this particular community as a researcher (among other things) opened up venues of communication and reflection that had not previously existed for this community. Further, the conversations that took place were implicitly and explicitly about transforming the school. In a school setting where life's urgencies were a daily part of the unofficial curriculum, taking time for these conversations seemed like a necessary luxury. Working in the school together provided avenues for "action" that might emerge from group discussions or researcher/teacher reflections. One clear illustration of this is from the class I conducted for teachers. After reading and discussing some of the research from the school, teachers all developed their own culturally relevant curriculum projects, or at least "directions" for projects.

The goal of my research was to use method and theory to explore an educational problem in a way in which the concept of culture was fluid. Relationships grounded in Ojibwe culture produced knowledge, methods, and curriculum, which was a part of this research project, but my research was not intended to use an understanding of culture to interpret behaviors.

Ideas of power and respect were very helpful in legitimizing my thoughts on First Nations ethics. In the words of Haig-Brown and Archibald, "Critical ethnography in a First Nations context resists hierarchical power relations between study participants, including the principal researcher, and focuses on ethics sensitive to and respectful of the participants and their contexts" (1996, p. 246). I believe I challenged the idea of a rigid hierarchy of power by building relationships that had multiple dimensions or, perhaps, just in recognizing this multiplicity. For example, in Elders' meetings, at moments I was the "organizer" or facilitator and could control the agenda, but when it was time to eat I was just as easily a "waitress" or, at the meeting's end, a "driver." In many social contexts with the Elders I was simply a "young person" or a "helper." So, although I set the meeting dates or held the tape recorder in an interview, these positions of "power" could quickly vanish in a different setting. I believe this interpretation of "power relations" is a different one than a "power-blind" approach to research. That is to say, since I was the Ph.D. candidate, there were always certain economic and social privileges tied to my being a researcher that were not currently available to many of those who participated in the research. As already mentioned, I continually tried to involve community members in all levels of the project, to recognize my position as "not the expert," and to problematize the positions of power I did occupy. However, at some point I had to recognize that I did occupy them, even if I tried not to reinscribe them.

Narrative Inquiry and Oral Traditions

Ideas from narrative inquiry informed my work on many levels. Specifically, this approach gave me permission to insert my voice directly into the text (see Anzaldúa, 1987; hooks, 1990; Williams, 1991) and "name my own reality" (Delgado, in Tate, 1997.) This was important to my project in order to explore the insights only the situated positioning of a researcher can yield. That is to say, just as I was specific about the context of the school and community, my voice and bias also was a part of the context and was explicitly included for this reason. Second, I found validation to the idea that it was important to include a multiplicity of voices from the community directly in the text as well (in addition to including long quotes within the text, eighteen full interviews were included in the appendix).

The idea that "stories" are open to an infinite variety of interpretations, or especially to meanings that are not obvious ("ethnographic allegory," in the words of Clifford and Marcus, 1986), was very appealing to me. This seems to intersect with some Native American ideas about storytelling (Tafoya, 1989). In this particular Ojibwe tribal context, traditional stories were given much authority as teaching tools. In my research, however, I did not "ask" for stories (as someone using a narrative inquiry approach might). I asked questions and behaved in a way that often evoked stories as responses. I received these stories as gifts, feeling respected as a learner and as a person who could be entrusted to make sense of the stories myself. My first set of protocols for receiving stories were from Ojibwe traditions; perhaps in this sense my methods diverged from narrative inquiry. For example, I would not write down or record "wintertime," or traditional stories, and knew it would be disrespectful to ask for permission. Usually, I did not record any stories given to me by Elders unless instructed to do so. On certain occasions, if I felt I wanted to use what was said in the text, I would ask to later transcribe "what I heard," for this purpose. In many ways the seriousness, respect, and authority given to stories in my "methods" and in Ojibwe traditions is divergent from that of narrative inquiry. Stories as "myth" or "folklore" conjures up connotations with which I would take issue.

Activist Research

The emerging "ethic" around doing research as a Native person in Native communities was a starting point for developing a community-based research project. I define a "community-based" research project as one that revolves around the perceived needs of the community rather than one that is dictated by academic protocol or traditions. I understand the idea of community-based research as a way of devoting time, attention, thought, and sometimes actions to areas that are defined as problematic by the community itself.

   This ethic is similar to the "community grounding" efforts of participatory research, work which comes out of a Freirian school of thought (Kidd, 1982; Kidd and Kumar, 1982). This approach to research requires a constant back-and-forth movement between the research group and the community of origin. Topics for research are generated around community needs, as perceived by community members. Another approach that grounds research in community is called "activist research" (Fine, 1994; Tierney, 1994). The idea that I find useful from this methodology is that the researcher's objective is to work toward some stated change within the community: "Activist research unearths, interrupts and opens new frames for intellectual political theory and practice. . . . A move to activism occurs when research fractures the very ideologies that justify power inequalities" (Fine, 1994, p. 24). In my case, I am supporting the efforts of the tribal school to continue making changes to an Ojibwe culture-based curriculum.

   In grounding my research in what I perceive to be a community need, I make no claims to an unbiased or "objective" methodology. I hold a vision for the school that involves the (Native) community and the school community coming together and working toward the goal of building a school that is strong academically and culturally—whatever this means as determined by these "communities"—and through the process of creating a culturally specific curriculum. I surrender the "privileges" of trying to maintain and prove an "objective" position in this project to one that places me as an "activist" within the community, that is, a person working for change. The implication for this project is that it then contains a *performative* aspect—my objectives, biases, emotions, and creativity are all a part of this project. This written expression of the work was created with the school/community audience in mind, with the hope of supporting change—more specifically, supporting a paradigm shift in the curriculum from one currently based on a "modernist" paradigm to one that is based on Ojibwe relationships, culture, and values.

Reciprocity, Respect, and Native Research Methods

I have come to see creating a culture-based curriculum as a "process in motion," much as I see First Nations research methods as a situated response. My research was driven by the question of culturally based curriculum development, including all of the forms and shapes this question took throughout the writing of the dissertation. At the outset of this project I could not anticipate what steps I would need to take in order to explore these questions—some of the questions came about during the research, not before it. What I did articulate at the beginning of the research project was a sense of an emerging research ethic within Indian Country for Native peoples to conduct research in our own communities. I would like to revisit this ethic and articulate the methods that came about, in part, as a response to it. I do this in the spirit of wanting to contribute ideas about research ethics and methods to an ongoing discussion, not to define a new methodology.

Earlier, I wrote about going against, or contradicting, the history of being exploited by research processes. The contradiction to this history has been a starting point for my methodology: Relationships of reciprocity replace relationships of exploitation. Here I draw from Carl Urion's (1991) idea of a First Nations discourse of learning. Most importantly, the idea of reciprocity and mutual respect in the teacher/learning relationship is emulated in my research methodology. This meant that the people I "interviewed" or gathered stories from were involved in an ongoing, two-way exchange with me. These were people with whom I had some kind of relationship before the formal "interview." The interviews drew on a common interest (the school and the children there) and were intended to strengthen an existing relationship for the purpose of community building around the school, not to create a new or "artificial" relationship solely for the purpose of extracting information.

I am thinking of the time I went to "interview" Lucy. She was quite happy to have me visiting, but when I started to ask her "What should be taught at the school?"

she told me that in the past three years of working with the Elders I had been asking that question. The question was not new, and I had already been given the answers, in so many different ways. We spent our time sipping coffee and I listened to other stories that day. I was a little surprised, and somewhat delighted. It made me feel as if I had been doing, and asking, what I had wanted to all along, and that that was understood.

The relationships, of reciprocity and respect, ordered the methods. This made my research a "process" that cannot be replicated but that is situated within the particular relationships among other community members and myself. This brings up a second point in my methodology, one that responds to Robert Allen Warrior's call to be intellectually sovereign:

If our struggle is anything, it is the struggle for sovereignty, and if sovereignty is anything, it is a way of life. That way of life is not a matter of defining a political ideology or having a detached discussion about the unifying structures and essences of American Indian traditions. It is a decision—a decision we make in our minds, in our hearts, and in our bodies—to be sovereign and to find out what that means in the process. (Warrior, 1995, p. 123)

What I have done in my research is to constantly amend the process as responses from the community informed what I was doing.

In my interactions with the Elders I would ask a direct question about the meaning of culture-based curriculum or curriculum for the Lac Courte Oreilles Schools, for example, and oftentimes the response I got was not an "answer" but rather a story about the boarding schools. This is how the chapter on boarding schools came about. I interpreted their stories to my questions as a way of telling me that the boarding school stories were an important piece of the puzzle of curriculum and schooling at the tribal school today.

I was concerned with researching a question that originated with the community, while also being acutely attuned to their responses. I wanted to know how these responses might be incorporated and again reorient the research process. After hearing a half dozen stories about boarding school experiences, for example, I began to ask for these stories in my interviews and to ask myself how to organize the dissertation around them.

I tried to approach this research in ways that strengthened existing relationships of reciprocity, community relationships. My writing came from a process of being a part of discussions, listening to stories, and reflecting back on practices. This all happened within the context of being a part of the community I was writing about. I believe that going back and forth between stories, practices, and writings helped me to keep research grounded in the concerns of the community. Further, this research is only one moment in the process; teaching practices, school reform, and many more stories are to follow.

I approached the research methods as something that could change over the course of the research. To start, my only guide was that what I did and how I did it were "situated responses," specific to the culture, the problem, and the dynamics of the particular context. One other guiding principle emerged over time: Be in the community as a community member first and a researcher second. In this way the community itself influenced and shaped the methods. The relationships I enjoyed in the community were not designed just to extract information or to exploit an "insider" perspective. The work I did was based on mutual respect and reciprocity,[10] as a person who was deeply invested in studying a problem but not willing to prioritize this over the relationships created in the process. This meant that I had multiple responsibilities (not just to a university or a "committee") and relationships with people that had a variety of dimensions. Within this context, "methods" took on new meanings; methods were no longer simply tools for *taking* or *discovering*[11] something. As textbook and tradition took a backseat to ethics and responsibility, methods began to feel like a recursive process rather than one procedure, a part from a whole.

Maybe going back really means going back and forth, for me, for now. So publishing something on methods is not so much "selling out" as it is paving a way for other scholars/community members like myself. Feeling yet another version of a dualistic and fatalistic choice emerging—smart or pretty; Indian or raceless; scholar or community member—I rush to object! It must be time to evolve beyond impossible choices for women and people of color in the academy.

Notes

1. The writing in italics is used to demarcate an "insider" voice, one that calls on *epistemic privilege* to validate ideas, and considers emotions and "all the details of the ways in which [their] oppression is experienced" to be an essential way in which knowledge is constructed (Narayan, 1988, p. 36). Bound in concrete examples, these thoughts are often theoretically laden. Some of these are taken from the time of writing the dissertation, some are more recent.

2. At this point, I am thinking specifically of critical race theory. Since I first presented this work publicly (Hermes, 1997), scholars have commented on elements of critical race theory that they feel undergird it. Although critical race theory has been influential (as I indicate later in this chapter), to attribute the entire

theoretical basis to this emerging body of work would be artificial. I believe "Ojibwe traditions" were also influential at the theoretical level, for example. However, since these are much less accessible to the citation process (see the work of Delgado in Tate, 1997, for reference to structural determinism), it would be easy to negate their influence in comparison.

3. I was introduced to this term through the *Canadian Journal of Native Education*. It is a term more often used in Canada to refer to indigenous peoples, but I use it here since I credit many of those First Nations writings with ideas inspirational to this chapter.

4. The issue I refer to here is the return and reinterment of Native bones and sacred objects to their peoples and to the Earth. Some museums have begun the process of "giving back" the archeological "findings" that were stolen from Native gravesites. However, for the most part, the question of "ownership" is one that is currently raging between tribes and museums or, worse, has itself become buried in legal bureaucracy. See: http://www.repatriationfoundation.org/ or http://www.fws.gov/laws/digest/reslaws/natamer.html for more information.

5. Marjane Ambler, editor of *Tribal College Journal*. See http://www.fdl.cc.mn.us/tcj for more information.

6. One teacher gave me the nickname of "Father Confessor," since I was perceived as someone teachers could talk to without the same connotations of "power over" that many administrators bring to teacher-administrative relationships.

7. The idea of "schools as community" seems very akin to a "traditional" idea of Native education. (During pre-invasion times the idea of "education" was an integrated part of the daily functioning of the community; see Armstrong, 1987.) Currently, the idea of a school as a community, and the building of social and cultural relationships therein, is being heralded as a key to successful current "alternative schools" (Wehlage et al., 1989).

8. Dennis White, principal at the LCO Schools, in collaborating on this proposal, offered the suggestion to include the diversity of people who work at the school. This important idea—of a "School community" as both intersecting with and divergent from the community it serves—was developed throughout the research project.

9. After years of coming to "consciousness" of some of the dynamics of power and oppression, *submission* is not a term I use lightly. Learning to recognize that much of my life history was influenced by occupying "submissive" positions predetermined by a stratified society, choosing this position was a challenge. Nevertheless, I believe it positioned me to listen in a way in which I could simply absorb and not critique. I found direction for my research and meaning that went beyond a degree.

10. See Haig-Brown and Archibald (1996).

11. See Bill Bigelow (1995) on the biased meaning of discovery in the Columbus Day context.

References

Anzaldúa, G. (1987). *Borderlands: La frontera*. San Francisco: Spinster/Aunt Lute.
Armstrong, J. (1987). Traditional indigenous education: A natural process. *Canadian Journal of Native Education*, 14 (3), 14–19.

Bigelow, B. (1995). Discovering Columbus: Rereading the past. In D. Levine, R. Lowe, B. Peterson, and R. Tenorio (Eds.), *Re-thinking schools: An agenda of change.* New York: New Press.

Bordowitz, G. (1988). Picture a coalition. In D. Crimp (Ed.), *AIDS: Cultural analysis, cultural activism* (pp. 183–196). Cambridge: MIT Press.

Britzman, D. (1991). *Practice makes practice: A critical study of learning to teach.* Albany: State University of New York Press.

Clifford, J., and Marcus, G. (Eds.), (1986). *Writing culture: The poetics and politics of ethnography.* Berkeley: University of California Press.

Deloria, V. (1973). *God is red.* New York: Delta Books.

Deyhle, D., and Swisher, K. (1997). Research in American Indian and Alaska Native education: From assimilation to self-determination. In M. W. Apple (Ed.), *Review of research in education,* vol. 22, pp. 113–194. Washington, DC: American Educational Research Association.

Doll, W. E. (1993). *A post-modern perspective on curriculum.* New York: Teachers College Press.

Fine, M. (1994). Distance and other stances: Negotiations of power inside feminist research. In A. Gitlin (Ed.), *Power and method: Political activism and educational research* (pp. 15–35). New York: Routledge.

Haig-Brown, C. (1990). Border work. In W. H. New (Ed.), *Native writers and Canadian writing* (pp. 229–242). Vancouver, BC: University of British Columbia Press.

Haig-Brown, C., and Archibald, J. (1996). Transforming First Nations research with respect and power. *International Journal of Qualitative Studies in Education,* 9 (3), 245–267.

Hampton, E. (1993). Towards a redefinition of American Indian/Alaska Native education, *Canadian Journal of Education,* 20 (2), 261–309.

Hermes, M. (1997). *Making culture, making curriculum: Teaching through meaning and identity at a tribal school.* Unpublished Ph.D. dissertation. University of Wisconsin at Madison.

hooks, b. (1990). *Yearnings: Race, gender, and cultural politics.* Boston: South End Press.

Indian Nations At Risk Task Force. (1990). *Indian Nations at risk: An educational strategy for action.* Washington, DC: Department of Education. (ERIC Document Reproduction Service No. ED 339 378.)

Kidd, R. (1982). From outside-in to inside-out: The Benue workshop on theater for development. *Theaterwork,* 2, 44–54.

Kidd, R., and Kumar, K. (1982). Co-opting the ideas of Paulo Freire. *Ideas and Action,* 148 (5), 4–8.

LaFromboise, T., and Plake, B. (1983). Towards meeting the research needs of American Indians. *Harvard Educational Review,* 53, 45–51.

Lather, P. (1991). *Getting smart: Feminist research and pedagogy with/in the postmodern.* New York: Routledge.

Narayan, U. (1988). Working together across difference: Some considerations on emotions and political practice. *Hypatia: A Journal of Feminist Philosophy,* 3 (2), 31–47.

Tafoya, T. (1989). Coyote's eyes: Native cognition styles. *Journal of American Indian Education,* 22, 21–33.

Tate, W. F., IV. (1997). Critical race theory and education: History, theory, and implications. In M. W. Apple (Ed.), *Review of research in education*, vol. 22, pp. 195–250. Washington, DC: American Educational Research Association.

Tierney, W. (1994). On method and hope. In A. Gitlin (Ed.), *Power and method: Political activism and educational research* (pp. 97–115). New York: Routledge.

Urion, C. (1991). Changing academic discourse about Native education: Using two pairs of eyes. *Canadian Journal of Native Education,* 18 (2), 1–9.

Warrior, R. (1995). *Tribal secrets: Recovering American Indian intellectual traditions.* Minneapolis: University of Minnesota.

Wehlage, G., Rutter, R. A., Smith, G. A., Lesko, N., and Fernandez, R. R. (1989). *Reducing the risk: Schools as communities of support.* London: Falmer Press.

Williams, P. (1991). *The alchemy of race and rights: Diary of a law professor.* Cambridge: Harvard University Press.

5

Toward a Definition of a Latino Family Research Paradigm

NITZA M. HIDALGO

Through the process of education, qualitative researchers trained in traditional paradigms learn how Eurocentric forms of knowledge are supposed to be applied universally to all people (Stanfield, 1994). The educational researcher is positioned to frame the questions to be investigated in a supposedly "neutral" stance with little attention to the unique characteristics of the communities to be researched. But the research stance of neutrality serves to hide inherent privilege in the research process (Fine, 1994). Researcher neutrality masks an underlying conceptual framework that posits the behavior and experiences of people of color to be inferior to those of Whites (Tate, 1997). In recent years research that applies Eurocentric frameworks to Latinos[1] and other people of color without questioning intrinsic conceptual frameworks has been critiqued (Baca Zinn, 1996; Hurtado, 1995; Stanfield, 1994). In addition, there is controversy surrounding how "White" is defined as the cultural norm in colonial sites like Puerto Rico, at the expense and exclusion of people of Black and African origins (Torres, 1998).

The social construction of Whiteness relegates Latinos, as a multiracial people, to an inferior status on the social hierarchy. Within social institutions such as schools and social service organizations, Latinos are judged by their race and little attention is paid to their ethnic and national differences. Critical race theory is employed in this chapter to explore the

I would like to thank my colleagues, Aida Nevárez-La Torre and Klaudia Rivera, for their help in the initial formulation of this manuscript. I am also grateful to the editorial board of the *International Journal of Qualitative Studies in Education* (vol. 11, 1998) for their critical questions and suggestions.

counterstories of Latino families (Delgado, 1995), whose experiences have been constructed by traditional research and by the mind-sets operating in public schools as the monolithic "Hispanic" experience. This dominant, and supposedly neutral, monolithic view of Latinos has served as a racist means of oppression and colonialism against Latinos because it veils a deficit mentality. Dominant ideology justifies the continued marginalization of Latino families by classifying them as the racial other. But the increased presence of the Latino population in the United States, and the rise of critical researchers who create alternative approaches to how qualitative research is conceptualized, designed, implemented, and disseminated (Maack, 1995), moves us toward a research paradigm based on unique forms of Latino social organization and knowledge construction that is contextualized within historical and structural conditions, and employs ethnicity, race, class, and gender as central organizing constructs (Sherrard Sherraden and Barrera, 1995).

Latinos, who will soon be the largest "minority" population in the United States, are not one but rather many nationalities, cultures, and social statuses (Marín and Van Oss Marín, 1991). Their experiences in the United States have been both unique and complex. Latinos predate Anglo populations in the Western hemisphere, and they have not followed the assimilationist patterns of other immigrants. Numerous factors (e.g., continued immigration, resistance to marginalization) account for why Latinos continue to maintain self-identity, familism, and Spanish language (Hurtado, 1995). Oftentimes, the Latino experience in the United States has consisted of living between the hyphens. For example, third- and fourth-generation, U.S.-born Puerto Rican Americans may be considered "too American" in Puerto Rico and "not American enough" in the United States. This bicultural experience is shared among many Latinos.

Accordingly, there is sufficient evidence to suggest the need for a Latino family qualitative research paradigm that is grounded in an understanding of the structural, cultural, contextual, and gendered conditions of the Latino experience in the United States (Massey, Zambrana, and Alonzo Bell, 1995). This chapter analyzes some of the methodological requisites for qualitative research with Latino populations within educational and community settings and presents retrospective insights from my own research. In this chapter, a Latino family research paradigm is defined by an exploration of its philosophical premises, objectives, parameters, and the role of the researcher. The framework reveals an epistemology that is particularly sensitive to Puerto Rican cultural knowledge production. It challenges the imposition of dominant interpretations of Latino culture and knowledge, delineates the intragroup boundaries that Latinos share, and examines the continuities and discontinuities within the researcher/informant relationship from a Puerto Rican Latina perspective.

Arguments for a Latino Family Research Paradigm

In a recent conversation with a White friend about the O. J. Simpson verdict, my perspective was described as not being impartial when I included a consideration of racism within the legal system. Yet my colleagues' opinions were presented as being based on scientific evidence and thus considered objective and neutral. This dialogue exposes the philosophical basis of a Latino family research paradigm; its basic belief system rests on a critical theoretical approach that posits knowledge as political. Thus, each of our perspectives was shaped in relation to our race, ethnic, class, and gender experiences: We construct knowledge through our lived experiences. Research that stems from a White-privilege conceptual framework highlights one standard as if that standard is divorced from the racial, ethnic, class, and gendered conditions that give rise to it. Tate (1997), in an explanation of the historical development of critical race theory, states that objectivity and neutrality serve to camouflage the self-interest of dominant groups. For example, family studies' research that promoted the nuclear family as the standard viewed Latino families as dysfunctional and therefore responsible for their own lack of social progress (Baca Zinn, 1996). Behavioral changes in Latino families away from the supposed deficiency are interpreted as movement toward normal behavior (Hurtado, 1995). Dominant ideology hides the fact that race is a social construction and racism is pervasive in the United States (Tate, 1997). Misinformation about Latinos and other people of color is socially sanctioned and given validity through, among other areas, past scholarly research.

Although critical race theory developed within the field of legal studies, which borrowed elements from literature and narratives, its use within qualitative educational research promises to expand understanding of the Latino family experience in the United States. As employed in this chapter, "race" and "ethnicity" are understood as essential theoretical constructs in qualitative investigations of Latinos within the U.S. educational system. The Latino family qualitative research paradigm argues for the interrogation of the researcher's conceptual framework throughout the research process. Socioeconomic class and gender, in addition to race and ethnicity, are placed within the sociohistorical contexts of Latino families' lived experiences. Thus, the elements of critical race theory can be employed to reconstruct Latino family stories in order to counter dominant mythology (Tate, 1997).

A Latino family qualitative research approach examines how cultural constructs such as values, behaviors, language, and traditions are understood by Latinos. Families are interpreted as social productions and the adaptations they make are not solely cultural productions but are created in response to varying opportunity structures (Baca Zinn, 1996). A system of stratification is responsible for variations in family structures and their connections to resources; families adapt to and resist social and economic pressures (Baca Zinn, 1996). One effect of a racially stratified society is to limit opportunity structures based on the group's location within the racial hierarchy (Haney López, 1995). This paradigm shifts the research focus to the structural contexts that influence family patterns. It conceptualizes family members as active agents making adaptations to and resisting daily structural constraints. The adaptations families make to racial, economic, and other structural inequalities have been analyzed as sources of strength (Baca Zinn, 1996).

From the perspective of feminist standpoint philosophy, the researcher occupies multiple social locations as she translates and critiques data that also stem from multiple positions and may be full of contradictions (Fine, 1994). Thus, as researchers we should examine our own social locations and aim toward at least a partial understanding of the multiple views of our informants (Andersen, 1993). A Latino family research paradigm requires an acknowledgment and examination of the researcher's conceptual framework, since knowledge production—that is, data interpretation, evaluation, and analysis—is mediated by one's values, experiences, and learned theoretical constructs (Guba and Lincoln, 1994).

For example, I was part of a five-year, cross-cultural, qualitative research project investigating how parents support their children's school achievement.[2] The ethnic/racial groups studied were African American, Chinese American, Irish American, and Puerto Rican. Each of the researchers on the team was in charge of investigating the particular group of which she herself was a representative. I encountered a problem in the construction of the initial interview questions; as a team, we created a series of questions to be asked of all parents, all the while mistakenly assuming that the initial questions would be generalizable to all four groups. The problems fell into two different levels of meaning: Some of the questions were outside the realm of Puerto Rican cultural knowledge, and still others contained a subtle middle-class bias.

The paradigm applied in the creation of the interview questions was based on a universal, biracial understanding of race as a theoretical construct. But Puerto Ricans, as a multiracial group, have different conceptual categories through which to view race (Rodríguez, 1989). Race is sometimes seen as a continuum that is intermixed with socioeconomic class throughout Latin America and the Caribbean (Torres and Whitten, Jr., 1998). Thus, issues of race and its definition change within a Puerto Rican context, as evidenced in Ferré's (1995) historical fiction, where blue books were kept by Catholic Church representatives to trace the blood lines of prominent families.[3]

As a Puerto Rican researcher raised in the United States, I had internalized through schooling the U.S. biracial model.[4] I focused on race as a significant theoretical category, but most of the parents did not address issues of race with their children.[5] One mother said: "Yo no sabía mi color hasta que yo llegué aquí" (I did not know my color until I arrived here). Instead, the parents emphasized the importance of developing children's awareness of and pride in their ethnicity. They believed that a strong ethnic identification would fortify children against cultural assaults. These parents knew that within current social and educational settings their children might be relegated to an inferior status. Many of these parents had experienced some form of racism. Sometimes the discrimination took the form of linguistic chauvinism. This knowledge is exemplified by the following mother's desire to teach her son about his ethnicity:

> Yo lo que creo es que él aprenda, porque aquí hay la mala costumbre de enseñar de que tú eres puertorriqueño, tú no eres nadie. Tú eres americano, tú hablas inglés, tú eres todo. Pero si eres puertorriqueño, tú eres basura. Yo quiero que por lo menos, aunque él es muy pequeño, estoy tratando desde ahora de que sea orgulloso de las raíces que él tiene.
>
> [I believe that he is learning—because there is a bad habit here—that if you are Puerto Rican, you are nobody. If you are American, you speak English, then you are everything. But if you are Puerto Rican, you are garbage. I want him at least, although he is quite young, to feel proud of his roots.]

The parents' definitions of a Puerto Rican identity encompassed an awareness of the discrimination that Puerto Ricans face in the United States. The topic of Puerto Ricans' construction of race has not been studied. Rather, past research has focused on acculturation, especially Puerto Ricans' identification as Americans (Sabogal, Marín, and Otero-Sabogal, 1987; Rogler, Cooney, and Ortiz, 1980). Educational research with Latino family involvement in schools tends to focus on training parents about U.S. school culture—that is, how to negotiate and interact with schools (Gonzalez, 1986; Voiland-Sánchez, Sutton, and Ware, 1991; Rosales, 1991; McCollum and Russo, 1993). But, as my study suggests, the parents are operating within the racial hierarchy as it is translated onto ethnicity. Although they did not address race directly with their children, they fostered a strong sense of identity as a preventative measure against discrimination. The task of Puerto Rican parents is to deconstruct the deficit mythology while helping their children create a positive ethnicity.

A critical theoretical approach considers race, class, and gender as central theoretical constructs to be examined (Sherrard Sherraden and Barrera, 1995); however, caution must be used when researching the various Latino groups because they may be operating from a Latin American perspective of race, or informants may conflate race and ethnicity.[6] In the quote below, one mother, Natalia Rodríguez, identifies as Hispanic, not Puerto Rican. As she thinks through the question of identity in the following passages, she realizes that her choice of *Hispanic* is based on the negative construction of *Puerto Rican*. When used by outsiders, or "Americans" as she called them, *Puerto Rican* is riddled with stereotypes about the group.

> NMH: If I were to ask you what nationality you were, what would you say?
>
> NR: Hispanic. I know a lot of people consider like . . . Puerto Rican. I don't like that word. I know that's what I am, but it just doesn't sound right. Sort of like when Black people are called Negroes. I think Hispanic is the more proper word to be used for Hispanic people.
>
> NMH: What makes Hispanic better to you?
>
> NR: The way it sounds, and the way . . . it's said by certain people. You know the way people say it, they say it with *more respect* and it sounds better. People think Puerto Rican is like . . . "Oh, she's Puerto Rican." . . . I've learned to deal with that at my job. You know, a patient comes in, an American patient, and says, "Well, some Puerto Rican girl was helping me. You know, from Puerto Rico or something. She had the hair."
>
> `It's just maybe the way it's transformed. Maybe the way people use it. Where I've been around, I just don't like it. It's the way, who says it, and how they say it. I'm just pictured as the Puerto Rican girl who works there.
>
> NMH: So you've had to deal with that for a long time?
>
> NR: Yeah. Maybe that's the problem. I probably never would have thought about that before at all because I honestly believe different[ly]. That's what I am, and I am what I am.
>
> NMH: What would be a positive way of saying it?
>
> NR: Um, that's a good question. I guess I'm just used to hearing negative things about the way they use it. My parents, they use it a lot: *Puertorriqueña*, Puerto Rican.
>
> NMH: It sounds like *Puertorriqueña* sounds okay to you?
>
> NR: It sounds nice, I guess, when Hispanics, Puerto Ricans say it, 'cause they say *Puertorriqueña*. It's just the way American people say it. "Oh that, Puerto Rican girl, the Puerto Rican person." Just maybe the way they phrase it. It's sort of like, you're a nobody.

In this quote we find the intersection of ethnicity, race, and gender operating to construct negative social stereotypes about Puerto Ricans. Natalia identified as Hispanic because the term had positive connotations for her. After further discussion, she revealed that she thought of herself as *Puertorriqueña,* also a positive term her parents used at home as she was growing up. This young woman had created a public mask in English as Hispanic and a private persona in Spanish as *Puertorriqueña* in order to overcome the negative messages she received from dominant society about Puerto Ricans (Montoya, 1995; Nieto, 1998; Ramos-Zayas, 1998; Valle, 1998; Walsh, 1998; Perry, 1998). Critical race theory, when applied to Latinos, needs to incorporate the social construction of ethnicity, which includes the traditional aspects of identity, familism and other values, and Spanish language. Thus, the central theoretical constructs are redefined as ethnicity, race, class, and gender within the U.S. Latino experience.

Similarly, even though the strong influences of Catholicism and traditional cultural customs are social forces operating in the construction of traditional Latina/o gender roles, U.S. cultural values and the women's movement have influenced adaptations and accommodations of Latina/o gender role socialization. For example, in my study, Puerto Rican families transformed strict cultural orientations to accommodate the changes they faced. Young girls were taught both to be independent and to hold family obligations as primary values. Baca Zinn (1982) explored differences between Chicanas' actions and beliefs and found that employed wives questioned their husbands' authority, yet maintained a belief in patriarchy. For Latinas, these adaptations result in living in a bicultural, two-worlds orientation.

The theoretical construct of socioeconomic class and the related level of education of the researchers also posed problems in the creation and implementation of interview questions in my study. Although the interview instrument was translated into Spanish, early in the parent-interviewing process I found some parents, especially those without postsecondary education, had difficulty answering many of the questions in our instrument. I would have to explain what I meant or reword the questions. I discovered that some of the parents found the abstract nature of the questions difficult to answer. The instrument implicitly had a middle-class bias derived from my own and my colleagues' educational level. In order to make the interviews generalizable to all four groups, the questions were worded abstractly and contained terms unfamiliar to some of my informants. To correct this error, I compiled a second interview schedule; interview 2 tried to get at similar concepts but used more concrete questions and asked for more examples from the parents.[7] Thus, I found that in order to work effectively with some of the parents, the translation of instruments was a necessary but not a sufficient condition; it was also necessary to modify the interview instrument to remove its middle-class bias.

This experience was humbling to me. Research from a critical perspective should "contribute to the human development of the researcher" (Stanfield, 1994, p. 174). It took me the next two years of interviewing to contextualize and reconstruct Puerto Rican family meanings and knowledge production. The refocus of methodology led me to change the scope of my research from parental involvement practices to parenting within a community context. I included grandparents and other relatives as informants in the study. When appropriate, I would share information about my background so that at times the interaction was more like a dialogue than a formal question-and-answer format. My methods changed to include field trips with families, which generated much information about parents' actual socialization practices. My field notes documented my reflective process; my understanding was transformed by and led to a search for the awareness of the differences and contradictions between my own and my informants' worldviews (Fine, 1994).

A necessary paradigm shift should occur when researchers conceptualize Latino family organization and the social forces impacting families. The shift requires placing families, not individuals, at the center of analysis. The analysis should include extended family, community, friends, community members, and families' institutional participation. In my study, children's kindergarten pictures of their families all included a grandparent or aunt/uncle, and all parents included extended family members in their definitions of family. But within U.S. public schools a normative view of families still exists. Educators' expectations are still based on the "Leave It to Beaver" norm of two parents plus two children. For example, our research design required that kindergarten teachers refer us to the families of the potentially successful children in their classrooms (see endnote 3). At a subsequent visit to a popular kindergarten teacher's classroom, she informed me that she only referred me to the Puerto Rican children who came from two-parent families, implying that her definition of an academically successful Puerto Rican child was based on the "Ozzie and Harriet" family organization model. Research has to be conceptualized around families and communities, since the Latino individual identifies within a network of familial and social relationships (Hidalgo, Siu, Bright, Swap, and Epstein, 1995). Research that is conceptualized on the extended-family model begins to expand the norm so that Latino family organization is not seen as deficient but as a strength and resource to educators who must begin to see grandmothers, aunts, uncles, and other extended family members as valid representatives of the family and the child.

For example, during the first year of the aforementioned study, the four principal researchers created a conceptual framework that was designed in an effort to begin to determine some of the influences on children's school success. Guided by a consultant during a preliminary session, we were directed to graphically envision the possible influences upon the child's academic success. The three other researchers drew the child at the center of their graph with some of the influences being family, school, community, church, and so on. I originally drew the family at the center because of my own experience, but naively changed the graph to conform to the versions produced by my colleagues. After the first round of parent interviews, with evidence from the data, I reconceptualized the framework to a Latino family-oriented model.

A Latino family qualitative research paradigm recasts investigations of families from a dysfunctional model to one centered within ethnic, race, class, and gender systems of power. My own awareness of the pressures on families and the implementation of methodological changes developed slowly over the three years of data collection. Some constraints in the design of the study, such as how the informants were selected (see note 2), limited the development of a research design that was as fully informed as depicted here. Through an introspective process of questioning my own operating constructs and multiple positions, and referring back to my cultural socialization, I was able to understand some of the informants' intersubjective meanings.

The Objectives of Latino Family Research

Two objectives of research with Latino communities can be delineated: (1) to understand and represent authentic forms of Latino cultural knowledge, and (2) to promote transformative action for Latino community uplift. The first purpose of a Latino family research paradigm is to provide an understanding and interpretation of the validity of Latino knowledge. As members of historically subordinated groups, Latinos have unique understandings and insights about their experiences and about American society. The unique viewpoints of Latinos are not ethnically or racially determined but are constructed through lived experiences and as a result of the social locations they occupy (Andersen, 1993; Stacey, 1991). Vélez-Ibáñez and Greenberg (1992), working with Mexican American families, have formulated the concept of "funds of knowledge" to define cultural bodies of knowledge transmitted by families to their children. Valdés (1996) uses the phrase "family's collective wisdom" to refer to types of survival strategies that Mexican families acquire through their collective experiences in the United States.

Valdés's work (1996) has resulted in a reformulation of Puerto Rican mothering strategies within a community context (Hidalgo, in press). Parenting strategies of the working-class mothers stemmed both from their cultural traditions and their neighborhood context, in which the physical safety of their children was not assured. The mothers devised elaborate protection strategies in an effort to control negative social influences upon their children. From a Eurocentric perspective often found in schools, the mothers' strategies would be interpreted as overprotective; from the Puerto Rican mothers' point of view, the strategies were commonsense. Thus, one purpose of research is to gain an understanding of Latino norms, without reference or comparison to Eurocentric norms. The objective entails conceptualizing Latino norms, which moves qualitative research away from the mythology of one universal standard.

If we look for the inherent strengths of culturally diverse families and reject the deficit model of describing Latino communities and families (Auerbach, 1989; Delgado-Gaitan, 1993), we find a socioculturally meaningful organization of daily life from which we can reconceptualize Latino family knowledge production based on an authentic cultural framework. In this sense, the accumulated knowledge base that Latino families have derived from their historical, cultural, and social traditions puts families in the best position to guide the direction of research (Delgado-Gaitan, 1993).

The Latino family research paradigm acknowledges the validity of alternative knowledge production that is useful to the participants themselves (Tandon, 1988). This paradigm can best be illustrated by its potential to transform and reaffirm knowledge about Latinos: It gives serious consideration to research topics that are essential for the daily survival and uplift of Latino communities (Tandon, 1988). The research has to allow informants to guide the interviews into areas that they feel are significant to them. Some themes having particular significance to Latinos are ensuring the economic survival of the family; guarding the physical safety of children; and negotiating their way through U.S. institutions, such as immigration and schools. The interpretation of the voices of Latino communities brings awareness of the structures and existing inequalities that may constrain communal progress, and the adaptations that families create in response to the uneven benefits and rewards available to them in this society.

Thus, this qualitative research paradigm employs an understanding of Latino family practices to critique and change existing structures (Guba and Lincoln, 1994). The criteria for the research's validity depend on whether the work deconstructs misinformation and myths and whether the work promotes transformative action (Guba and Lincoln, 1994). In her review of research on Latino families, Hurtado (1995) states that many studies stem from an assimilationist model that compares Latinos to other immigrant groups of the past whose goals were to achieve White middle-class behavior patterns and who arrived during different economic times in the United States. According to Hurtado (1995), other research has employed the underclass model that equates persistent poverty within Latino communities to culture. Hurtado points to the work of Baca Zinn and others who critique the assimilationist and underclass approaches and posit the incorporation of structural and contextual analysis. The assimilationist and underclass explanations can be seen as justifications by dominant groups for the continued oppression of Latinos (Tate, 1997), whereas, from a critical race perspective, the unique viewpoints of Latinos can counter dominant explanations of the Latino experience. Future qualitative research on Latino families needs to incorporate the contextual and historical realities of Latinos in the United States. This paradigm argues for research on Latino schooling, for example, to change its focus from the individual determinants of school failure to the oppressive structures, within and outside schools, that limit opportunity and may exacerbate Latino student disadvantage. Given the demographic fact that by the year 2030 Latino students will make up 25 percent of the public school population in the United States (Archer, 1996),[8] researchers and educators should attend to identifying the strengths within Latino families and communities as resources for school improvement.

For example, stereotypes surface about Puerto Rican family organization being "enmeshed" when interpreted using a Eurocentric, nuclear family model. When such stereotypes are deconstructed, one finds that Puerto Ricans' dependency on extended family networks (when available) promotes the cultural value of unity of the family and may result from structural constraints such as poverty. Thus, families utilize familial networks to provide services that middle-class families can purchase, such as child care (Hidalgo, in press). Research that stems from the concerns of Latino informants may become a vehicle for the empowerment of Latinos in the United States by uncovering historical, political, and economic structures that tend to limit Latino opportunity.

In sum, the purposes of research within this framework require the discovery of Latinos' unique viewpoints and pay attention to the themes that have significance for the transformation of Latino lives. The voices of Latinos, when framed by their cultural knowledge, function to deconstruct stereotypes, which may be utilized toward the community's benefit.

The Contextualization of Latino Family Experiences

Parameters are contextual issues relevant in the lives of diverse Latino groups. A Latino family qualitative research paradigm cannot ignore the contextual issues relevant to this population because the context relates to how much or how little power is afforded to Latinos. All research must be placed in the context of Latinos' lives. The contextual factors help illustrate Latino informants' multiple social locations. The various contextual dimensions are sociohistorical, socioeconomic, linguistic, and cultural citizenship.

The sociohistorical context consists of the group's history and social relationship to the United States. For example, Puerto Ricans' experience of migrating to the United States as citizens differs from that of Mexicans. Regardless of these differences, immigration issues are central to the Latino experience in the United States (Zambrana, 1995). In work that meets many of the requisites of this paradigm, Pessar (1997) traces Dominicans' immigration to the United States by contextualizing their "chain migration" within the historical context of the Dominican Republic, their settlement patterns in New York City, and their activism to gain a voice in New York electoral politics (p. 133). An understanding of the historically situated structures (such as the historical period of immigration/migration for each Latino group, the group's colonial history or relationship to the United States, the different geographical points of entry to the United States, the annexation of the group's land by the United States, the group's ties to the mother country, and the generational changes that may occur) unveils the researcher's view of the Latino reality. Without this information, the understanding and interpretation of informants' meaning will remain decontextualized.

Latino groups' socioeconomic class position is another contextual factor to be critically examined with this paradigm (Massey, Zambrana, and Alonzo Bell, 1995), as the average Latino income is disproportionately low in comparison with that of the U.S. population as a whole. The socioeconomic context includes issues such as economic status, work history, work status, housing conditions, and the community's economic vitality. Poverty conditions limit access to health care, quality education, decent housing, and quality of life. The Puerto Rican families in my study were aware of the lack of resources available to them and struggled to ensure a better life for their children, as the following quotes show.

> Twenty-four-year-old single mother: With all the cutbacks and everything, pretty soon there's not going to be anything left. But then again, they want kids to continue their education. I know we're talking about the crime, drugs, all the race stuff, and everything else. But the majority of the people, Hispanics and Blacks, aren't making it. It's just frustrating, when everything is being cut back.
>
> NMH: Is it hard to be a parent these days?
>
> Twenty-eight-year-old father: Yeah, it is. It is. It is hard because sometimes you want to do things to get them [his daughters] a

> better education and stuff like that, and you just can't do it. And
> you feel the pressure. By not doing that, your kids ain't gonna
> make it, you know, in the outside world.

The pressures on poor families leave them unable to control some basic factors in their lives, such as the quality of education their children receive. Socioeconomic status is, like race and gender, a basic contextual category of social organization (Baca Zinn, 1996). For example, researchers have linked the increase in Puerto Rican single female heads of household in the Northeast to a decline in the manufacturing industry and the underemployment of Puerto Rican men (Amott and Matthaei, 1991). Thus, socioeconomic status intersects with the previous context when one considers the historical period during which the group immigrated or was annexed to the United States.

Cultural citizenship, a sense of commonality amid heterogeneity, depicts another important contextual factor. Latinos share cultural elements across all groups (Flores and Benmayor, 1997). Latinos, regardless of individual group membership, share several characteristics, such as retaining an ethnic identity, a tendency toward familism, and Spanish language maintenance. Hurtado (1995) finds that Latinos retain a strong ethnic identification; paraphrasing Rogler, Cooney, and Ortiz (1980), Hurtado states, "The endpoint of immigrant children's adaptation to the United States is not a total rejection of their ethnic origins and complete assimilation to the Anglo mainstream; rather the endpoint is stable biculturalism" (p. 48). Strong family unity and a preference for extended family networks are primary Latino cultural values. Sabogal, Marín, and Otero-Sabogal (1987) found Latinos seek to have close geographical proximity to family members and prefer a lot of family support. To what extent the particular Latino cultures differ and how these differences may be related to historical and regional factors are significant pieces of knowledge that stem from specific grounded experiences of each group.

The Spanish language is linked to cultural citizenship because Spanish is at the heart of Latino culture. The Spanish language cuts across all Latino group experiences in the United States, thereby making language a significant contextual factor (Massey, Zambrana, and Alonzo Bell, 1995). Hurtado (1995) notes that Latinos tend not to transit from Spanish to monolingual English but to bilingualism in both languages. Although patterns of Spanish language maintenance differ among the particular Latino groups and between generations, the continuity and maintenance of the Spanish language influences Latino adaptability in the United States.

The contextualization of Latino family experience serves to deconstruct a monolithic view of Latinos. Although Latinos share overlapping boundaries, their unique sociohistorical and socioeconomic experiences have resulted in vast differences between the particular subgroups. The differences between the current socioeconomic levels of Puerto Ricans and Cubans is an appropriate case in point; the causes can be traced, in part, to the educational levels of early immigrants and to the structural conditions found in the United States at the time of immigration.

Puerto Ricans have the highest percentage of all Latinos living in poverty (33 percent) (Chapa and Valencia, 1993). Mass migration to New York began in the 1940s.[9] Most Puerto Rican migrants were young, skilled, and literate in Spanish, with an average of eight years of schooling. They represented the range of Puerto Rican racial types. Although Puerto Rican migrants were likely to find work initially, the decline in the New York garment industry in the 1960s and 1970s limited later employment opportunities. Many low-skilled jobs were lost in the industrial and occupational sectors (Torres, 1988). The manufacturing sector lost 173,000 jobs in the 1960s. At that time over 60 percent of the Puerto Rican workforce was employed in manufacturing (Rodríguez, 1989). The deindustrialization of the economic strata, aided by the 1970 recession occurring in the United States, caused a decline in the formal semi-skilled employment opportunities. Thousands of Puerto Ricans found themselves without a livelihood.

Cuban Americans currently have the lowest percentage of people living in poverty (15 percent) of all the Latino groups (Chapa and Valencia, 1993). The first waves of Cuban immigrants to the United States were well educated, predominantly White, and represented the professional and entrepreneurial sectors of the Cuban economy (McGoldrick, Pearce, and Giordano, 1982). They were classified as refugees by the U.S. government, which granted them relocation assistance, such as low-interest loans to start businesses and purchase homes (McGoldrick, Pearce, and Giordano, 1982). Thus, the economic and educational capital that earlier Cubans brought with them and the conditions the group experienced in the United States have influenced, at least in part, their social status.

Stanfield (1994) notes that researchers should pay attention to the context in which their informants live, specifically to the "historical moments, political economies, ethnoregional and ecological locations, and community and institutional sites" (p. 170). Being able to contextualize Latino informants' meaning requires background research into their stories. For example, during the research design phase of my group research study mentioned earlier, I conducted extensive library research in order to understand Puerto Rico's colonial history, the mass migration to the United States, the conditions faced here, and the present educational status (Hidalgo, 1992). In my review of the literature, I emphasized work by Puerto Rican authors in the belief that their interpretations would not stem from the inferiority paradigm (Tate, 1997). This research was the beginning of my relearning process; having attended U.S. schools, I had little access to the history of Puerto Rico and the contributions of Puerto Ricans to the United States.

The contextual elements of a Latino family research paradigm relate to the overlapping boundaries among the various Latino groups. The historical relationship between the mother country and the United States; the Latinos' economic status as a disproportionately poor population; the shared cultural values that stress close family ties; and the maintenance of the Spanish language between generations all impact on the social locations of Latinos and their adaptability in the United States. The intergroup variations within the contextual levels refine our understanding of the U.S. Latino family experience.

The Researcher's Influence on the Research

The researcher's influence on the research is analyzed from the perspective of a Puerto Rican woman to discover the continuities and discontinuities within the researcher/informant relationship. The role of the researcher consists of two overlapping dimensions within a Latino family research paradigm: (a) as an insider-interpreter of Latino experience, because of membership within a Latino ethnic group; and (b) as an outsider, stemming from educational, national, and regional differences. A Latino family qualitative research paradigm, like all good ethnography, requires data collection that provides precise knowledge and deeper levels of understanding by encouraging informants to elaborate on concepts and terms important to their realities. As a Puerto Rican conducting research on Puerto Rican families, I bring the overlapping insider/outsider perspective to the research. As an insider, I share a similar cultural background with my informants resulting in common understandings and shared meanings about subtle cultural aspects. Through my cultural socialization, I learned the importance of *respeto* (respect) and reciprocity: These are fundamental Puerto Rican values that are part of all good interpersonal relationships. I implicitly employed insider constructs (Sherrard Sherraden and Barrera, 1995). For example, I used titles of respect, such as *don* and *doña*, within the context of the age hierarchy that exists within the Puerto Rican culture (Facio, 1993). As a Latina who raised two sons as a single mother and who was raised by three strong but quiet Puerto Rican women (mother, aunt, and sister), I was drawn to the stories of the mothers in the families I was researching. I perceived them as the unsung heroes, all of whom worked full time and held primary responsibilities as caregivers for their children, husbands, and other family members. Thus, my insider status was based on a shared Puerto Rican heritage and being raised within a low socioeconomic background similar to that of five of the nine families in the study. Yet, similar to what Foster (1994) found in her study of Black teachers, throughout the study my insider status was tested in numerous ways by the informants.

There existed a number of characteristics within my insider status that relegated me to an outsider's position (Foster, 1994). Some characteristics entailed the subtle differences that one finds within the Puerto Rican community in the United States. Being a newcomer to the Boston-based Puerto Rican community that I was researching, I was subject to initial suspicion since no one in the area knew me. Once a connection was made between me and people whom I knew and who were trusted within the community, the establishment of rapport could commence. More importantly, having been raised in New York (being considered a *Nuyorican*) and being English-language dominant led to a perceived difference in status as Puerto Rican, especially between those parents born and educated within Puerto Rico and me.[10] One of the consequences of being a Puerto Rican raised in the United States is "having an absence of Puerto Rico in my soul" (Son, 1996), which means that one internalizes some U.S. values in a subtractive process resulting in a loss of some cultural elements as these are expressed in Puerto Rico.[11] Montoya (1995) makes a similar point in reference to the legal profession: "The masks we choose can impede our legal representation and advocacy by driving a wedge between self, our *familias*, and our communities" (p. 532). In the eyes of some of my informants, my insider status was diminished by my U.S. socialization, such that my insider status was not a given; I had to show my informants that I knew what it meant to be Puerto Rican. A simple example of this is based on Puerto Rican generosity toward others. I and my research associate would never visit a family without some small token, usually a children's book or food, to repay the family for their generosity.[12]

My outsider status was a result of my education and training in traditional social science research, which may interfere with rapport and trust building between the researcher and informants (Foster, 1994; Villenas, 1996). Being highly educated in the United States created a difference in formal schooling level with some informants that affected the research design and the interview questions posed (see the example above). It was clear that my position as researcher granted me power over the relationship, but I tried to adjust the imbalance by making myself available to families for advice, favors, translation services, trips to community events, and so on. I found that some parents would defer to some of my statements out of respect for my status as a college professor. Realizing the imbalance, I felt a responsibility. When asked for advice or information, I gave it freely. Thus, my status contained certain reciprocal responsibilities vis-à-vis the families. I also found myself reassuring some families that there were no right answers that I sought, rather that I wanted to learn about what they thought was important in raising their children. In some cases I used my status as a Harvard University graduate to gain validity with the professional parents, especially those middle-class families who made distinctions between Puerto Ricans and *Nuyoricans*. My ethnic status was offset by my class/education status, which corresponds to a similar interplay of race and class that exists in Puerto Rico, where one can be considered "whiter" if one comes from a wealthy family, regardless of one's actual skin color (the intersection of race and class).

Finally, my outsider status interfered with the interpretation of interview data. The interviews were conducted in the language that the parent, child, or grandparent preferred to use. For this reason I and my research associate always visited the homes together: My associate[13] would conduct the Spanish interviews, and I the English ones. All the data were transcribed in the original language. Although I understand and speak Spanish, I have far greater fluency in English. Thus, the analysis of the Spanish data would take me about twice the time spent on the English data. I would constantly check with my research associate to assure myself that I had not missed the subtle connotations found in the transcriptions. In this study, triangulation included analysis by more than one researcher.

The researcher's outsider characteristics can be an obstacle to an authentic understanding of the informants' meaning. Also, the researcher's status can impede rapport-building and true interpretation of culturally bound practices, since what is learned through the process of education is how the Eurocentric forms of knowledge are supposed to be applied universally to all people (Delgado-Gaitan, 1993; Stanfield and Dennis, 1993). In her study of parental literacy practices, Delgado-Gaitan (1993) found that as a result of her own education, her initial interpretations of some parent behavior were shaped by Eurocentric cultural constructions. Without this insight, she could not have reached an authentic understanding of her informants' culturally bound practices. In a very real sense, I had to unlearn the teaching of the distanced researcher in order to appreciate, relearn, and gain strength from my cultural grounding.

Thus, the myth of researcher as a detached expert is deconstructed (Andersen, 1993). The distanced paradigm of the isolated researcher, not influencing what is researched, is changed to a consideration of how the values, agenda, and experiences brought by the researcher shape the production of knowledge (Fine, 1994). If the central focus of my research is the experiences of Latino families and communities, then my own experiences as a Latina are also relevant.

An End and a Beginning

An understanding and interpretation of forms of Latino family cultural knowledge that are grounded in the experiences and adaptations they make leads to an unveiling of what is considered normal by Latinos. The grounded theory stems from particular Latino experience and is not derived, in contrast to prevailing theoretical models developed from other populations. The aim is to discover authentic Latino forms of knowledge, not in relation to Eurocentric norms, but as grounded intersubjective meanings. From these understandings, the researcher reconstructs the stories of Latino families. These stories will be different for each of the Latino groups but may share overlapping themes. The knowledge created is used to deconstruct misinformation about Latino families. Latino stories are utilized to counter the inferiority paradigm in areas like teacher training and parental involvement policies, and to help educators and researchers arrive at a better understanding of Latino groups, the forces that shape their lives, and the resistance found in their actions.

The use of critical race theory in the development of this paradigm exposes the underlying racism in existing conceptualizations of Latino families. It challenges the deficit model of Latino family organization and points to the shared experiences of oppression that Latino families face. Within the area of teacher training, it can challenge operational definitions of what is considered normal; within teachers' expectations of children, it shifts the definition of achievement from an individualistic one to a family-centered one. Within educational policy, a Latino reformulation of family can expand the scope of parental involvement practices to one of family involvement regardless of the type of organization the family may have.

Future qualitative research with Latino families can be delineated along three trends: studies on Latino family socialization practices, studies on Latino school achievement, and studies on the juxtaposition of family and school contexts. Future qualitative research should continue to focus on the unique forms of Latino knowledge production to discover the adaptations families make to their ethnic, race, class, and gender positions within the U.S. social hierarchy. Studies on the intermixture of race and ethnicity within the major Latino groups can provide insights on how positive ethnic identity is created within an environment of cultural assaults. Latino family research that contextualizes the immigration experiences, both in the home country and in the United States, can provide insights on the present socioeconomic positions of Latinos.

Although Latino families' and students' characteristics account for some of the factors affecting school achievement levels, they are not the sole causes of the dismal levels of Latino school achievement, as the stories constructed from dominant ideology would have us believe. School research that contextualizes Latino school failure within the larger power structures impinging upon families and communities will lead educators away from flaccid, "blame-the-victim" findings to the structural causes of school failure. Studies on Latino identity formations in terms of the interplay of ethnic, race, class, and gender constructions, as these are defined by Latinos, may help schools address the needs of Latino students. Research on how Latino families and community-based organizations can be reconceptualized as helpers in finding answers to school improvement problems may begin to conceptualize public schools as part of the Latino communities they serve. Finally, how Latino family values can inform pedagogy can only be discovered when Latino parents are perceived as real partners in the education of their children, which occurs when educators accept the cultural contributions of the home as valid cultural capital. Yet it is imperative that research not solely focus on culture in an essentialist manner but that it study the juxtaposition of lived culture, race, class, and gender experiences of Latinos within their particular contexts.

The comprehensive nature of a Latino family qualitative research paradigm leads to complex understandings and interpretations because the demythification of long-held stereotypes demands that Latino groups be understood within their unique lived experiences. For me, after a three-year relationship with the families, after repeated mistakes and false starts, I have begun to rediscover Puerto Rican families' intersubjective meaning. With their help and the relearning of my history, among the many discoveries I have made is that their story is, in part, also my story.

Notes

1. The word *Latino* describes persons from the following groups: Puerto Rican, Mexican American (Chicana/o), Dominican, Cuban American, Central American, and South American.

2. The ethnographic study investigated how African American, Chinese American, Irish American, and Puerto Rican families supported their children's school success during the primary grades. The first year of the study was devoted to research design and a review of the literature. The selection of informants was accomplished by interviewing kindergarten teachers about the characteristics they sought in potentially successful students. In other words, each teacher defined success. We asked each teacher to refer us to students in her classroom who fit her definition of a potentially successful student. We then contacted individual families to negotiate entry. Qualitative, longitudinal data were collected on forty families (nine Puerto Rican families) in Boston, Massachusetts, between September 1991 and September 1994. The database consists of kindergarten and first- and second-grade teacher interviews; yearly classroom observations; review of school records; parent (both mother and father in year one), grandparent, uncle/aunt, and child interviews in grades K, 1st, and 2nd; field trip data; and field notes.

3. The Spanish tradition of the Catholic Church's maintenance of documentation on the purity of White racial stock within families served to keep wealth in the hands of White Puerto Ricans. For a more in-depth discussion of the salient

points of Puerto Rican racial representation and the creation of a White European identity that excluded Blacks, see Roy-Fequiere (in press) and Torres (1998).

4. This internalization contrasted my socialization as a Puerto Rican.

5. The African American parents in the study tended to prepare their children against racial stereotypes.

6. My research associate, Gladys Capella Noya, who came from Puerto Rico and attended postsecondary school here, and I agreed that asking informants to identify racially would be culturally inappropriate since the racial variations of Puerto Ricans do not have the same meaning within the U.S. context. So we asked about their nationality. All five first generation Puerto Rican–born informants identified as Puerto Rican, as did two out of four second-generation, U.S.-born informants. The last two of the four second-generation, U.S.-born informants identified as Hispanic and Black Hispanic, respectively. It may be that the second-generation parents' meaning included race mixed in with ethnicity.

7. In the first version of the parent interview, one question asked was "How is the child's temperament?" The revised version asked, "Does she/he have a temper?" Examples of the parents' responses were requested in the revised version.

8. A Latino majority in public school enrollments is a closer reality in states like California. By the year 2006 Latino students will be 48 percent of all public school students in California (Perez and De La Rosa Salazar, 1993).

9. The causes of immigration for Puerto Ricans and Cubans to the United States differed dramatically. In Puerto Rico among the causes was the rapid transformation of the Puerto Rican economy from an agricultural to an industrial base leaving many rural people without work (Maldonado-Dennis, 1975); and in Cuba the causes stemmed from the overthrow of the Batista regime by Fidel Castro's army, which resulted in the nationalization of many middle- and professional-class people's properties.

10. The U.S.-born informants did not differentiate my status since we shared common experiences growing up in large northeastern cities in the United States.

11. This is understandable, given that Puerto Rico has been under U.S. political and cultural dominance for close to one hundred years.

12. The research project paid families for their time and cooperation a small sum of $50 per year.

13. In the first year of the study Aida Ramos worked with me. In the following years Gladys Capella Noya was my research associate. Both women were graduate students at Harvard University Graduate School of Education at the time of the study. Both had grown up in Puerto Rico and were Spanish-language dominant.

References

Amott, T., and Matthaei, J. (1991). *Race, gender, and work: A multicultural economic history of women in the United States.* Boston: South End Press.

Andersen, M. (1993). Studying across difference: Race, class, and gender in qualitative research methods. In J. Stanfield, II, and R. Dennis (Eds.), *Race and ethnicity in research methods* (pp. 39–52). Newbury Park, CA: Sage.

Archer, J. (1996, March). Surge in Hispanic enrollments predicted. *Education Week,* p. 3.

Auerbach, E. (1989). Toward a social-contextual approach to family literacy. *Harvard Educational Review*, 59, 165–181.

Baca Zinn, M. (1982). Qualitative methods in family research: A look inside Chicano families. *California Sociologist*, 5, 58–79.

_____. (1995). Social science theorizing for Latino families in the age of diversity. In R. Zambrana (Ed.), *Understanding Latino families* (pp. 177–189). Thousand Oaks, CA: Sage.

_____. (1996). Family, feminism, and race in America. In N-L. Chow, D. Wilkinson, and M. Baca Zinn (Eds.), *Race, class, and gender: Common bonds, different voices* (pp. 169–183). Thousand Oaks, CA: Sage.

Betances, S. (1973). The prejudice of having no prejudice in Puerto Rico: Part two. *Rican*, 3, 22–37.

Chapa, J., and Valencia, R. R. (1993). Latino growth, demographic characteristics, and educational stagnation: An examination of recent trends. *Hispanic Journal of Behavioral Sciences*, 15, 165–187.

Delgado, R. (1995). Legal storytelling: Storytelling for oppositionists and others: A plea for narrative. In R. Delgado (Ed.), *Critical race theory: The cutting edge* (pp. 64–74). Philadelphia, PA: Temple University Press.

Delgado-Gaitan, G. (1993). Research and policy in reconceptualizing family-school relationships. In P. Phelan, and A. Locke Davidson (Eds.), *Renegotiating cultural diversity in American schools* (pp. 139–158). New York: Teachers College Press.

_____. (1995). Researching change and changing the researcher. In G. Capella Noya, K. Geismar, and G. Nicoleau (Eds.), *Shifting histories: Transforming education for social change* (pp. 119–141). Cambridge, MA: Harvard Educational Review.

Esteves, S. M. (1997). A la mujer borrinqueña. In H. Augenbraum and M. Fernández Olmos (Eds.), *The Latino reader* (p. 384). Boston: Houghton Mifflin Co.

Facio, E. (1993). Ethnography as personal experience. In J. Stanfield, II, and R. Dennis (Eds.), *Race and ethnicity in research methods* (pp. 75–91). Newbury Park, CA: Sage.

Ferré, R. (1995). *The house on the lagoon*. New York: Farrar, Straus and Giroux.

Fine, M. (1994). Dis-stance and other stances: Negotiations of power inside feminist research. In A. Gitlin (Ed.), *Power and method* (pp. 13–35). New York: Routledge.

Flores, W., and Benmayor, R. (Eds.). (1997). *Latino cultural citizenship*. Boston, MA: Beacon Press.

Foster, M. (1994). The power to know one thing is never the power to know all things: Methodological notes on two studies of Black American teachers. In A. Gitlin (Ed.), *Power and method* (pp. 129–146). New York: Routledge.

Gitlin, A. (Ed.). (1994). *Power and method: Political activism and educational research*. New York: Routledge.

Gonzalez, B. (1986). Schools and the language minority parents: An optimum solution. *Catalyst for Change*, 14–17.

Guba, E., and Lincoln, Y. (1994). Competing paradigms in qualitative research. In N. Denzin and Y. Lincoln (Eds.), *Handbook of qualitative research* (pp. 105–117). Thousand Oaks, CA: Sage.

Haney López, I. (1995). The social construction of race. In R. Delgado (Ed.), *Critical race theory: The cutting edge* (pp. 191–203). Philadelphia, PA: Temple University Press.

Hidalgo, N. (1992). *"I saw Puerto Rico once": A review of the literature on Puerto Rican families and school achievement in the United States.* Boston: Center on Families, Communities, Schools and Children's Learning, Report no. 12.

Hidalgo, N. (in press). Puerto Rican mothering strategies. In S. Nieto (Ed.), *Puerto Rican students in U.S. schools: Cambiando camino/Charting a new course.* Hillsdale, NJ: Lawrence Erlbaum Associates.

Hidalgo, N., Siu, S.-F., Bright, J., Swap, S., and Epstein, J. (1995). Research on families, schools, and communities: A multicultural perspective. In J. Banks and C. Banks (Eds.), *Handbook of research on multicultural education.* New York: Macmillan.

Hurtado, A. (1995). Variations, combinations, and evolutions: Latino families in the United States. In R. Zambrana (Ed.), *Understanding Latino families* (pp. 40–61). Thousand Oaks, CA: Sage.

Maack, S. (1995). Applying anthropology in urban non-profit organizations. *Urban Anthropology and Studies of Cultural Systems and World Economic Development,* 24, 137–188.

Maldonado-Dennis, M. (1975). Puerto Rican emigration: A socio-historical interpretation. *Journal of Contemporary Puerto Rican Thought,* 2, 30–36.

Marín, G., and Van Oss Marín, B. (1991). *Research with Hispanic populations.* Newbury Park, CA: Sage.

Massey, D., Zambrana, R., and Alonzo Bell, S. (1995). Contemporary issues in Latino Families: Future directions for research, policy, and practice. In R. Zambrana (Ed.), *Understanding Latino families* (pp. 190–226). Thousand Oaks, CA: Sage.

McCollum, H., and Russo, A. (1993). *Model strategies in bilingual education: Family literacy and parent involvement.* Washington, DC: Department of Education.

McGoldrick, M., Pearce, J., and Giordano, J. (1982). *Ethnicity and family therapy.* New York: Guilford Press.

Montoya, M. (1995). Máscaras, trenzas, y greñas: Un/masking the self while Un/braiding Latina stories and legal discourse. In R. Delgado (Ed.), *Critical race theory: The cutting edge* (pp. 529–539). Philadelphia, PA: Temple University Press.

Mullings, L. (1994). Images, ideology, and women of color. In M. Baca Zinn and B. Thornton Dill (Eds.), *Women of color in U.S. society* (pp. 265–290). Philadelphia, PA: Temple University Press.

Nieto, S. (1998). Fact and fiction: Stories of Puerto Ricans in U.S. schools. *Harvard Educational Review,* 68, 133–163.

Perez, S. M., and De La Rosa Salazar, D. (1993). Economic, labor force, and social implications of Latino educational and population trends. *Hispanic Journal of Behavioral Sciences,* 15, 188–229.

Perry, W. (1998). Memorias de una vida de obra (Memories of a life of work): An interview with Antonia Pantoya. *Harvard Educational Review,* 68, 244–258.

Pessar, P. (1997). Dominicans: Forging an ethnic community in New York. In M. Seller and L. Weis (Eds.), *Beyond Black and White: New faces and voices in U.S. schools* (pp. 131–150). Albany, NY: State University of New York Press.

Ramos-Zayas, A. Y. (1998). Nationalist ideologies, neighborhood-based activism, and educational spaces in Puerto Rican Chicago. *Harvard Educational Review,* 68, 164–192.

Rodríguez, C. (1989). *Puerto Ricans born in the U.S.A.* Boston: Unwin Hyman.

Rogler, L., Cooney, R., and Ortiz, V. (1980). Puerto Rican families in New York City: Intergenerational processes. *Marriage and Family Review,* 16 (3/4), 331–349.

Rosales, J. (1991). Forging an alliance in a multiethnic school community. *School Community Journal,* 1, 53–55.

Roy-Fequiere, M. (in press). *When gender meets race: Women, creole identity, and intellectual life in early twentieth-century Puerto Rico.* Philadelphia: Temple University Press.

Sabogal, F., Marín, G., and Otero-Sabogal, R. (1987). Hispanic families and acculturation: What changes and what doesn't? *Hispanic Journal of Behavioral Sciences,* 9, 397–412.

Sherrard Sherraden, M., and Barrera, R. (1995). Qualitative research with an understudied population: In-depth interviews with women of Mexican descent. *Hispanic Journal of Behavioral Sciences,* 17, 452–470.

Son, D. (1996). *R.A.W. ('Cause I'm a woman).* Play performed at the Hallie Flanagan Studio Theatre, Smith College, Massachusetts, November 2.

Stacey, J. (1991). Can there be a feminist ethnography? In S. Gluck and D. Patai (Eds.), *Women's words: The feminist practice of oral history* (pp. 111–119). New York: Routledge.

Stanfield, J., II (1994). (Response) Empowering the culturally diversified sociological voice. In A. Gitlin (Ed.), *Power and method* (pp. 166–180). New York: Routledge.

Stanfield, J., II, and Dennis, R. (Eds.). (1993). *Race and ethnicity in research methods.* Newbury Park, CA: Sage.

Tandon, R. (1988). Social transformation and participatory research. *Convergence,* 21, 5–15.

Tate, W. F., IV. (1997). Critical race theory and education: History, theory, and implications. In M. W. Apple (Ed.), *Review of research in education,* vol. 22, pp. 195–250. Washington, DC: American Educational Research Association.

Torres, A. (1988). Explaining Puerto Rican poverty. *Centro,* 2, 9–21.

_____. (1998). La gran familia Puertorriqueña "es prieta de belda" (The great Puerto Rican family is really Black). In A Torres and N. E. Whitten, Jr. (Eds.), *Blackness in Latin America and the Caribbean* (pp. 285–306). Bloomington: Indiana University Press.

Torres, A., and Whitten, Jr., N. E. (Eds.). (1998). *Blackness in the Caribbean.* Vol. 2. Bloomington: Indiana University Press.

Valdés, G. (1996). *Con respeto: Bridging the distances between culturally diverse families and schools.* New York: Teachers College Press.

Valle, S. D. (1998). Bilingual education for Puerto Ricans in New York City: From hope to compromise. *Harvard Educational Review,* 68, 193–217.

Vélez-Ibáñez, C., and Greenberg, J. (1992). Formation and transformation of funds of knowledge among U.S.-Mexican households. *Anthropology and Education Quarterly,* 23, 313–335.

Villenas, S. (1996). The colonizer/colonized Chicana ethnographer: Identity, marginalization, and co-optation in the field. *Harvard Educational Review, 66,* 711–731.

Voiland-Sánchez, E., Sutton, C. P., and Ware, H. W. (1991). *Fostering home-school cooperation: Involving language minority families as partners in education.* Washington, DC: National Clearinghouse for Bilingual Education.

Walsh, C. E. (1998). "Staging encounters": The educational decline of U.S. Puerto Ricans in [Post-]colonial perspective. *Harvard Educational Review, 68,* 218–243.

Zambrana, R. (Ed.). (1995). *Understanding Latino families.* Thousand Oaks, CA: Sage.

6

Formations of *Mexicana*ness: *Trenzas de identidades múltiples* (Growing Up Mexicana: Braids of Multiple Identities)

FRANCISCA E. GONZÁLEZ

Una mujer se tiene que dar su propio lugar todo el tiempo, donde esté para que la respete la gente, ¿verdad? Te tienes que dar tu lugar porque eres persona, tienes tus sentimientos, y tienes que respetarte a ti misma. [*A woman always has to give herself a place so that people will respect her, right? You have to give yourself your place because you are a person, because you have feelings, and you have to respect yourself.*]

—*La de Michoacán y La de Sinaloa*

Claiming a Space and Situating Ourselves

En un sitio y con una lengua (in our space and in our language), young *Mexicanas*[2] claim a space of self-respect and fashion transnational identities with cultural meanings and feelings (Alarcón, 1990; Chabram-Dernersesian, 1994; Delgado, 1995a; Hurtado, 1989, 1996; Pérez, 1993; Segura, 1990; Torres and Milun, 1995). *La de Michoacán* and *La de Sinaloa* speak, in their language, about a space where the formations of *Mexicana*ness intersect and transform as complexities of ethnicity, sexuality, gender, and

---

The reporting of young voices in this work represents a sensitive cultural approximation of meaning(s) translated from Spanish into English. Guided by the cultural intelligence and knowledge of my mother, *una mujer Mexicana,* I detail close approximations—translations on the formations of *Mexicana*ness. I am very grateful to my mother and to the young *Mexicanas*, to their mothers, to Mrs. Contreras, and to Yvonne Esquivel for sharing their meanings and feelings with me. I am also grateful to the editors of the special issue of *QSE*—Sofia Villenas, Laurence Parker, Donna Deyhle, Claudia Torres, James Scheurich, and to Jon Wagner, Karen Watson-Gegeo, and Otis Scott.

class identities within multiple contexts (Caldwell, 1995; Crenshaw, 1995b; Davis, 1981; Montoya, 1994; Segura, 1990). From this space, young *Mexicanas* and I converse to construct narratives that examine and analyze how we sift through cultural knowledge and meanings to create our own identities. With "a daring and forward-looking consciousness" (Chabram-Dernersesian, 1994, p. 284), a group of young *Mexicanas* render accounts of contestations and possibilities against a sociopolitical landscape. Their narratives bring to light the articulation of their social agency and offer valuable knowledge for current social analysis and for formulating educational policies and practices about school cultures (Freire, 1970; Tate, 1997). Thus, popular conversation told by those on the bottom, through their situated knowledge, constructs realities of a gendered, ethnic culture and moves the writing of what it means to be *Mexicana* into the forefront of the research community (Castillo, 1994; Chow, 1993; Delgado, 1995a; Montoya, 1994).

Situated in a constellation of shifting and changing social spaces, young *Mexicanas* talk back and construct narratives in opposition to stereotypic representations (Canclini, 1992; González and Habell-Pallan, 1994; Saldívar-Hull, 1991; Torres, 1991). As a necessity to talk back, Emma Pérez (1993) reminds *mujeres* (women) of the space and language that Chicanas have always had and that these are powerful strategies and tools to break the silence, name oneself, and reconstruct the text:

> I wish to point out that our works emerge from *un sitio y una lengua* [a space and language] that rejects colonial ideology and the by-products of colonialism and capitalist patriarchy, sexism, racism, homophobia, etc. The space and language is rooted in both the words and silence of Third-World-Identified-Third-World-Women who create a place apart from white men and women and from men of color . . . where we create for each other. (pp. 47–48)

In our space and with our language, thoughts and meanings form and flow to transform consciousness. As part of this space that writes against the current of the master narrative, its theoretical and methodological conventions and outcomes, I situate myself in the current of the intellectual community to claim presence and power to my voice as a Chicana researcher and interpreter of the voices of young *Mexicanas*. By the same declaration, I recognize the tensions and contradictions associated with my positionality and respective actions, and I move forward in learning and problematizing the master's tools and writings to construct counternarratives with community. These I do as acts of self-determination, commitments, affirmations, and to inform public policies (Castillo, 1994; Padilla, 1997; Pérez, 1993; Villenas, 1996). William F. Tate (1997) argues that researchers must work "against structural determinism, essentialism, and academic neo-imperialism" (p. 225). In so doing, counternarratives create subversive texts of gendered, ethnic cultural formations written as developing and changing relationships in the contexts of family and community networks situated in a mesh of structural, political, and sexual dynamics (Baca Zinn, 1994; Crenshaw, 1995b; Ruiz, 1993; Segura, 1990; Segura and Pierce, 1993).

The constellation of relationships I refer to are the lived experiences and realities of growing up *Mexicana*. This experience is marked by distinct gender roles, difference, and social location. Through cultural expectations, *Mexicanas* are socialized to learn particular values, behaviors, and ways of thinking and knowing (Chabram-Dernersesian, 1994). From these experiences and realities, *Mexicanas* grow up in U.S. society and develop a consciousness that includes an awareness of oppression, poverty, and racism (or what Kimberlé Crenshaw [1995b] calls multiple systems of subordination). Simultaneously, from this site oppositional strategies and skills are born and transformed to challenge and affirm intersecting realities, relationships, and identities. To a large extent *Mexicanas'* specialized strategies and experiential knowledge are a response to the politics of rejection. Historically and to the present day, *Mexicanas*, as well as all women of color, are textually represented as the "other." In social and sexual realms "othering" creates differences in what constitutes acceptable heterosexual and lesbian social and intimate relations. Consequently, because of these differences, *Mexicanas* and women of color are named inferior to both European American men and women and are subordinated through rejection because of race/ethnicity and class differences (Hurtado, 1989, 1996; Matsuda, 1995; Pérez, 1993; Quintana, 1996; Sandoval, 1991; Villenas, 1996).

I seek, therefore, to foreground the voices and experiential knowledge of young *Mexicanas*, including my own, by creating counternarratives to name "one's own reality" (Tate, 1997, p. 219). In the first part of this chapter, I offer a Chicana feminist approach to constructing narratives with *trenzas* (braids) of analytic frames, methodology, and with the engagement of my researcher-self and the young *Mexicanas* participating in the study (Montoya, 1994). In the second part, through qualitative data, I explore how *Mexicana* identities are created, shaped, and developed. More specifically, I examine the braids of multiple identities among young *Mexicanas* as they come to womanhood in U.S. society.

In beginning this chapter, I detail the theoretical context and qualitative strategies from critical race theory (CRT) and feminist and womanist theorists for examining the structural and ideological factors that shape the context of *Mexicana* lives. In my analysis of the qualitative data, I focus on two group *pláticas* (popular conversations) from a larger study that asked for meanings and feelings about language, *Aztlán* culture and identity, and womanhood. From this I provide counternarratives from young *Mexicanas* who correct stereotypic representations that render *Mexicanas* vulnerable and dismissed from U.S. civic life and public education. I conclude with reflections on writing *Mexicana*ness as subversive narratives of "our own realities" (Tate, 1997, p. 219), and I propose directions for transforming educational research, curriculum, and the building of education partnerships.

At a time when the browning of the nation is causing such hysteria, CRT provides direct and contextual analysis for examining and "identifying a structural feature of human experience that separates people of color because they see and experience acts of blatant or subtle racism all the time" (Tate, 1997, p. 219). Through the lens of CRT, I call attention to the details of ethnic, gendered meanings and culture as a foundation for human rights and property rights, and as a strategy to break out of the paradigmatic insulation of dominant white-controlled discourse. As a way of introducing the chapter's theoretical context I look specifically to selected reconstructions and *trenzas* of multiple perspectives.

Critical Race Feminisms: *Trenzas* of Our Lives

Learned in woman's knowledge and schooled in the scholarly enterprises, CRT feminists and womanists of color rise as intellectual activists. Their presence and voice embodies multiple identities and multilingual semantics, and from these experiences they intervene to place at the center of articulations the material and emotional experiences by and about people of color (Austin, 1995; Montoya, 1994; Williams, 1995). What these women make known, with pen in hand, are the daily realities of their peoples' lives through their interrogations and contestations of dominant ideologies of racial power. From a position of resistance to the color-blind approaches and perspectives on race as neutral and apolitical, CRT feminists and womanists weave and reconfigure representations and facts about people of color as citizens exercising rights through oppositional strategies.

Through their scholarly writings, feminists and womanists of color dismantle androcentric and Eurocentric paradigmatic inclinations with several mediums of expression. In *Critical race theory: The key writings that formed the movement*, women of color who are also legal scholars advance interrogations on gender, race, and the law by problematizing the existing extrapolations of colored women's identities, bodies, and spirits. Most directly, Kimberlé Crenshaw (1995b) and colleagues write:

one is race-d in tandem with other social factors, such that one can say that being race-d as a woman of color may diverge significantly from the means by which those engendered as male are race-d. Yet, antidiscrimination law as well as liberal race and gender politics overlook the ways that race-ing and en-gendering are interpolated. Just as race is presumed to be a natural category existing independently and apart from law, so too, other identity components are regarded as natural and mutually exclusive. The rigidity of this framework and its continued centrality in law, politics, and public policy create a host of problems. (p. 354)

Taking to heart their traditions of commitment, women of color interrogate and work to correct the rigidity and problematics of extrapolating identities. They interrogate the intersecting dynamics of structural, political, and sexual realities and construct innovative meanings and approaches, several of which I consider and rework for writing *Mexicana*ness.

In "Mapping the margins," Kimberlé Crenshaw (1995b) proposes an analytic frame of intersectionality to account for the complexities of social power and its relationship to identities of race, gender, class, and sexuality. Unlike mainstream liberal discourse where race, gender, and other identities are treated as mutually exclusive, Crenshaw's details the various ways in which race and gender intersect in shaping structural, political, and representational systems in the lives of women of color. This frame brings to the fore the need to account for multiple identities and dimensions in the analysis and construction of a social world.

The mapping of identities locates women of color within a marginal existence and across multiple and successive spaces. With a multidimensional analytic frame, Professor Crenshaw (1995b) examines the systems of subordination beginning with the structural dimension. This includes the facts and realities of immigration and social policies, poverty, language barriers, low level of education, and a service-labor occupational category. The second dimension is the political experience of a split in the subordinated groups' political energies/activism on issues of race and gender. One's energies are split on either gender or race, as if these are two separate political agendas. The third dimension is representational images and categories, known as stereotypes, that socially and culturally devalue women of color. This imagery represents a critical aspect in the treatment of women of color and their place in society. These three dimensions—structural, political, and representational—make up the frame of intersectionality and are central to our understanding and explication of the process and the experiences of subordination. Kimberlé Crenshaw (1995b) argues, "Through an awareness of intersectionality, we can better acknowledge and ground the differences among us [women of color] and negotiate the means by which these differences will find expression in constructing group politics" (p. 377).

In theorizing about gender subordination, feminists of color share expressions on difference and group politics. Various frameworks constructed by Maxine Baca Zinn (1975, 1994), Yvette Flores-Ortiz (in press), Aída Hurtado (1989, 1996), Chela Sandoval (1991), Denise Segura (1990), and Patricia Zavella (1991) add to Kimberlé Crenshaw's (1995b) conceptualization a constellation of sociohistorical factors, social location, family dynamics, sexism, differences, and tensions within groups and communities as being central to any analysis. Other important articulations include the works of feminists of color questioning the homophobia in their communities and writing about the lives of lesbians of color (Moraga and Anzaldúa, 1983; Pérez, 1996; Trujillo, 1991). This collection of perspectives, existent within groups and communities, constructs a rigorous frame of intersectionality for examining meanings and feelings about "our own realities" (Tate, 1994) and identities. With these shared expressions womanist and feminist legal scholars and feminists of color transform knowledge and approaches for writing the *trenzas* of our lives.

Rooted in traditions of resistance, critical race theory and feminist approaches give affirmations and validations to and through narrative scholarship (Austin, 1995; Delgado, 1995a; Lawrence, 1995; Montoya, 1994; Tate, 1997). In a forthright assertion Austin (1995) declares that the construction of knowledge is to include voices

> grounded in the material and ideological realities of minority women and in their cultural and political responses; as the lives of minority women change, so too should the analysis. The voice and vision reflected in her work should contain something of the essence of the culture she has lived and learned. (p. 427)

To Regina Austin's declaration, I add that the culture lived and learned by women includes linguistic diversity so as to hear many voices in different languages. Margaret Montoya's (1994) assertion is that this approach challenges dominant society's indifference to non-English speakers:

> One of the central issues of feminism is the cultural construction of subjectivity. Language, images, and masks are key factors in that de/construction. For Latinas, this endeavor entails the use of Spanish with English. (p. 212) . . . New narrative forms give power to stories that fashion new authentic identity, an identity made stronger and more resilient because it braids together the disparate. (p. 213) . . . Our conceptual *trenzas*, our rebraided ideas, even though they may appear un-neat or *greñudas* to others, suggest new opportunities for unmasking the subordinating effects of legal discourse.

Our rebraided ideas, the *trenzas* of our multicultural lives, offer personally validating interpretations. (p. 220) . . . From a discursive space formerly denied to Latinas are regenerative acts which can transform self-understanding and reclaim for all Latinas the right to define ourselves and to reject unidimensional interpretations of our personal and collective experiences. (p. 214)

Rebraided ideas make possible hearing linguistically diverse gendered voices and interpretations for fashioning transnational identities. Reworking Margaret Montoya's (1994) conceptualization of *trenzas*, I conceptualize it as braids of Crenshaw's (1995b) analytic frame of intersectionality with a broader constellation of social, cultural, and personal dynamics, a multimethodological approach of *pláticas* (popular conversations) with my insider's cultural intuition, from the vantage of an earlier generation, and the active engagement-voices of my researcher-self and the participants of my study. From *trenzas* of different analytical and experiential meanings, self-descriptions and counternarratives of transnational and intersecting realities are collected and written as *trenzas de identidades múltiples* (braids of multiple identities). The counternarratives tell of the meanings and feelings about a culture woven with threads of language, behaviors, expectations, values, history, and experiences of personal and group identities pronouncing social recognition (Fregoso and Chabram, 1990; Laforest, 1996; Torres, 1991; Torres and Milun, 1995; Williams, 1995). This is the creation of the formations of *Mexicana*ness rising from currents of social and racial tensions within the context of violence, anti-immigrant political sentiments, sexism, and global and domestic shifting economic realities.

The crafting of CRT and feminist analytic frames brings to light the material and emotional experiences by and about people of color. These subversive strategies signify a commitment to self-determination and revisionist scholarship. I consider these practices most useful in writing an accurate and valid story about young *Mexicanas* and my researcher subjectivities.

La de aquí y las del otro lado: Detailing the Research Project

I am a Chicana researcher and community member who was born and still lives in California, and I am writing this scholarship from my home in Barrio Oak Park. I situate myself in my *barrio* with pride and dignity and refer to *barrio* as a term of endearment and a site of social and cultural grounding. I am committed to the social and political articulation of research by, for, and about the Chicana experience, Chicana and *Mexicana* dignity and self-respect, and the responsibility of our leadership in the struggle for human rights and access to higher education. In ascribing to the political ethnic signifier *Chicana*, I am referring to a gendered, ethnic life experience in a racially, economically, and sexually oppressive society. Adaljiza Sosa-Riddell (personal communication, June 1991), a Sacramento Chicana community activist and co-founding member of Mujeres Activas en Letras y Cambio Social (MALCS), names the Chicana experience as that of:

> Mexican-, Central American–, or other South American–origin women who are currently residing in the United States and who share one or more of the following similar experiences: retention of indigenous roots and/or indigenous memory; knowledge and/or experience of conquest and/or imperialism by Spain, Portugal, and/or the United States; forced or induced migration, and living in the United States; exploited as part of the working class, racially/ethnically oppressed, and controlled because of gender.

Sosa-Riddell's enunciation is not without reference to the different cultural, language, and sexual experiences. It is not without the tensions and contradictions among our membership as Chicanas and our relationships with *Mexicanas* and other indigenous women. "Given our *mestizaje* as Chicanas, we have attempted to address our diverse identities, and we are still learning what it means to us as Chicanas" (Facio, 1997, p. 2). I expect that I will also continue to explore and name "Chicananess" with personal, sociocultural, and political meanings, as I live and write the truth about our own realities.

For quite some time now, I have engaged in activism and research both through commitment and as inquiry. In crossing over to and from the barrio, the city, and the university, I am in communication with various concerns about the rising tides of racism, sexism, and homophobia. Also, in my personal experience, because of my prominent brownness, I too encounter forms of racism and sexism on a daily basis. My communication and personal experiences tell about a social landscape painted with fears of the increasing racial/ethnic and language diversity in the state of California and the United States generally. Concerns about the rapidly changing racial identity and presence of Mexican and Latino immigrants prompted a movement calling itself "Save Our State" to place Proposition 187, a proposal to deny undocumented immigrants the few public benefits to which they are legally entitled, on the California November ballot in 1994. The intention was to save the state's racial identity and to stop the depletion of the state's resources. Interrogating immigration and rights through a racial lens in "Critical race theory and Proposition 187," Rubén García (1995) details sentiments and fears in a racialized landscape:

Propelled by hegemonic fears, Proposition 187 is consistent with the racism underlying the history of United States immigration law and policy. . . . Politicians have used anti-immigrant rhetoric to mobilize white voters who feel that immigrants are "taking jobs" from them. . . . Intragroup tensions are also exacerbated by pitting racially and economically subordinated groups against one another in a competition for scarce resources (p. 120). . . . Thus, many view Latinos as not belonging in the United States because of the immigrant history of their ancestors. Measures such as Proposition 187 stigmatize Latinos regardless of their immigration status (p. 121). . . . In addition, Governor Wilson and other politicians have proposed an amendment of the United States Constitution to deny citizenship to the children of undocumented immigrants (p. 129). . . . Finally, Proposition 187 aims to exclude undocumented children from both public elementary and secondary schools as well as public postsecondary institutions (p. 131).

On November 7, 1994, voters in California passed this measure by a margin of 59 to 41 percent. On November 20, 1995, U.S. District Judge Mariana Pfaelzer ruled portions of the initiative an unconstitutional infringement on the federal government's power to regulate immigration (García, 1995).

Because of the severe racial attacks against *Mexicanas* and their children and my social and political commitments, I, *la de aquí* (U.S.-born Chicana), thought it imperative to learn more about the lives of *Mexicanas, las del otro lado* (women from Mexico), and their children. Fully recognizing my Chicana experience of growing up in the United States; of communicating with English as my first language and my *pocha* Spanish; the realities, tensions, and contradictions of my researcher position; and knowing that I could make mistakes and unintentionally offend someone, I set out with my commitments, *corazón* (heart), and the light of Our *Virgen de Guadalupe-Tonantzin* to ask mothers and daughters, against the backdrop of a hostile political landscape, what does it mean to be a *Mexicana*? What does it mean to be a woman? Just how important are the *consejos* (nurturing advice) mothers impart to their daughter? How do young *Mexicanas* create their own identities within the context of family and in the face of intersecting oppressions? These questions and my own concerns about *Mexicana* youth shaped the design of my study, interactions, and an interview script consisting of the following questions: (1) What does it mean to be a *Mexicana*?; (2) What does it mean to be a woman?; and (3) What does it mean to be *la mujer Mexicana*? From the responses to these questions, I identified the issues of language, *Aztlán* culture and identity, and womanhood as central.

My research design is also informed by several kinds of knowledge. This includes insights of practical knowledge, feminist practice, interdisciplinary training, and a blend of research knowledge and activism that give meaning and direction to realize my own dreams and desires as a Chicana feminist researcher. This weaving is grounded in the perspective of "Chicana self-determination which encompasses a struggle against both personal and institutional manifestations of racial discrimination, patriarchy, and class exploitation" (Pesquera and Segura, 1993, p. 106). From here, I situate my academic and practical knowledge across disciplines to refashion *Mexicana* multiple identities and desires. With a different set of questions and *trenzas* of analytical frames and multiple methodological strategies, I examined the salient and changing relational meanings in the lives of young *Mexicanas*.

As part of a larger study, this research project was conceptualized as an exploratory qualitative study of eight young *Mexicanas*. For one academic year, in the setting of a local suburban high school, I interacted and talked with the young *Mexicanas* at various moments in a school day, after school, during weekends, and in their homes. I simultaneously collected and analyzed what I saw, heard, learned, and experienced through participant observations and from *pláticas* (popular conversations) (Blea, 1995; Sherraden and Barrera, 1995). Through participant observation and interactions I looked and listened for contextual exchanges, expressions, and interpretations of *Mexicana*ness. With *pláticas*, a strategy that gives considerations of cultural relevance and shared, gendered meanings, I listened to young *Mexicana* voices and feelings (Sherraden and Barrera, 1995). To this project, I added my own cultural intuition and memory of growing up Chicana with a *Mexicana* mother (Blea, 1995; Castillo, 1994; hooks, 1994; Quintana, 1996). My intuitive memory also included my heterosexual feelings, the power in communicating with *La Virgen de Guadalupe-Tonantzin*, and a life of motherhood. In braiding this study's various data collection strategies to my experiential knowledge and feelings, I made possible *un encuentro* (a group meeting) of generations situated in *Aztlán*.

This qualitative study is broadly contextualized in *Aztlán*, the homeland of *la de aquí y las del otro lado*, a Chicana and *Mexicanas*. The concept of *Aztlán* was recovered and named, during the Chicana/o Movement, as a geographical region of spiritual and political union and as a philosophical basis for self-determination. Carlos Muñoz (1989) defines *Aztlán* as "the name used by the Aztecs to refer to the place of their origin. Since the Aztecs had migrated to central Mexico from 'somewhere in the north,' Chicano activists claimed that *Aztlán* was all the southwestern United States taken from Mexico as a result of the Mexican-American War" (p. 77). "*Aztlán* symbolizes the spiritual union of the Chicanos, something that is carried within the heart, no matter where they may live or where they may find themselves" (Hurtado, 1996, p. 108). In this study I conceptualize *Aztlán* as the geographic space where economic shifts, tensions, and new developments shape the spiritual and political feelings of young *Mexicanas* with what is carried in their hearts and memories. *Aztlán* symbolizes the absence and presence of the homeland where young *Mexicanas* live acts of self-determination and negotiate ways of knowing.

Central to this study is the formation of personal complexities. I have detailed the contextual complexities of a political, economic, and spiritual landscape that dictate a power relationship in the constellation of family life environments, quality of life, and changes in family roles (Baca Zinn, 1994; Delgado-Gaitán, 1990, 1993; Flores-Ortiz, in press; Segura and Pierce, 1993; Solís, 1995; Valdés, 1996). These intersecting realities shape and reshape a homeplace for children and adolescents learning to resist assimilation and develop cultural integrity (Deyhle, 1995; Evans, 1995). Monica J. Evans (1995) describes homeplace as a site for intense cultural activity that gives young family members "a place to revel in their culture, to resist negative representations of their culture, and to support each other in locating and defining the self within their culture" (p. 509). This cultural activity is the complex learning of knowledge and strategies from the experiences of gendered cultural socialization, where *consejos* (nurturing advice) and *educación* (education of the whole person) are imparted largely, but not exclusively, by mothers and a maternal community.

The research of Concha Delgado-Gaitán (1994) and Karen Ann Watson-Gegeo and David W. Gegeo (1994) supports my formative thoughts on *consejos* and the shaping of the mind. Professor Delgado-Gaitán (1994) describes *consejos* as "cultural narratives of nurturing through a cultural domain of communication, imbued with emotional empathy, compassion, and familial expectations" (p. 314). Professors Watson-Gegeo and Gegeo's (1994) research on the indigenous culture in rural Solomon Islands describes *educación* as "*Fa'amanata'anga* that literally means 'shaping the mind.' In its specialized meaning, it refers to a formal, serious-to-sacred speech event in which direct teaching and interpersonal counseling are undertaken. . . . In the family, *fa'amanata'anga* begins in early childhood and continues throughout life" (p. 46–47). Considering all the socializing complexities of familial *consejos* and *educación*, I name the formations of *Mexicana*ness as the experience of young *Mexicanas* sifting through cultural knowledge and strategies to weave threads of cultural morality, life energy, transformation of vitality and desire, spirituality, and personal and societal relational behaviors into *trenzas de identidades múltiples* (Alarcón, 1990; Castillo, 1993; Espin, 1984; Lawhn, 1993; Quintana, 1996). In this experience young *Mexicanas* are active agents in naming their identities and in creating a youth culture of various feelings, meanings, and symbols.

The study's eight participants share variations of experiences and racial attributes of light and dark skin and hair. With the exception of one young woman from a family of four, they all come from large families of seven to eleven members as well as extended family members residing in the home. The young women are first-year and second-year high school students, between the ages of fourteen and seventeen, and self-identify as *Mexicana*. They meet the criteria of Mexican-oriented students born in Mexico and have lived in the United States for seven years or less (Matute-Bianchi, 1986; Rumbaut, 1995). They are primarily Spanish speakers and share bicultural identities and communication networks with *Mexicana* communities in both Mexico and the United States (Canclini, 1992; Chabram-Dernersesian, 1994). In their discussions with me and in their patterns of association, the young *Mexicanas* position themselves very distinctly in relation to Chicanas. These young *Mexicanas* represent a category of women who differ from Chicanas and European American young women. They are of a *Mexicana* orientation coming of age and attending school in a changing U.S. society.

This study was situated across several settings. A local suburban high school was the major site of my field research. Other sites included the young *Mexicanas'* homes and communities. All eight *Mexicanas* attended the one high school and commuted from a sprawling working-class and low-income part of town. They left their homes in the east to go westward and crossed the tracks into the nicer part of town. During the course of my school site interaction with the young *Mexicanas*, I engaged in two *encuentros* (group meetings) with them. What follows is a detailing of our active engagement and hearing of our voices.

Formations of *Mexicana*ness:
Beginning with Language

The sun was shining, and I felt loads of energy this morning. I woke up earlier than usual to gather my documenting materials, and I placed everything in a bag near the back door so I could just jet over to the school *a platicar con las muchachas* (to talk with the girls). It was going to be my first group meeting with the girls. I was not sure whether they all knew each other.... The second lunch bell rang, and it was time for them to go to their next class. We said bye to each other, and I watched them walk out of the classroom. I gathered my materials and cleaned up the classroom area where we were sitting. I thought about our *encuentro*, and I realized I had learned a lot from the young women.

As my field notes indicate, at the end of the *encuentro* I realized it was a day of learning about the formations of *Mexicana*ness. In our space and in our language, I listened to a group of young women speak with maturity and strength about their feelings and identities. They spoke with tones of self-confidence and with assertive body language about their knowledge and power to define themselves. Just the night before and the morning prior to my *encuentro* with the *Mexicanas,* I had perceived them as girls, not quite sure about their feelings of the world around them. They proved otherwise through their confidence and affirmations of their emerging meanings of womanhood and their negotiation of ideological and symbolic features.

Inside Mrs. Contreras's ESL classroom I learned about the importance of language and its meaning in being *Mexicana.* One day, during the first and second lunch periods, I ate lunch with a group of the young *Mexicanas.* We sat in a circle, in the back corner of the classroom, surrounded by bookshelves, textbooks, and global maps. A few students were in the classroom taking English proficiency tests and a couple of others were there helping Mrs. Contreras. Our backs were to them, and we shut out the other part of the classroom world as we conversed in Spanish, laughed, and ate. They asked me, "Where are the *jalapeños*?" I had taken them lunch, but I forgot the *jalapeños.* I made a quick mental note to remember them for the next time. In a very casual way I asked for their attention. "Do you all know each other?" They replied "yes" and explained how they knew each other. "Because we are so few at this school, we know each other, and we live near each other." They laughed and ate, and I began our *plática,* conversation, by introducing the idea of *Mexicananess.* I told them that *Mexicananess* is the experience of developing their identities with cultural memories and practices from Mexico and their changing life and present realities in the United States (Anzaldúa, 1987; Canclini, 1992; Gilroy, 1996). To explore this further I asked the young women, what does it mean to be a *Mexicana*? I watched them as they talked with each other, and I observed that their engagement shifted from laughter to attention and looking outward to think while they were eating. From our *plática,* I illuminate the young *Mexicana* voices into a sequence of enunciations and affirmations:

> For me it means to continue with the traditions of speaking Spanish and to give yourself your place and not to hide that you are a *Mexicana,* to not be ashamed of talking in Spanish, even if people make fun of you. . . . For me to be *Mexicana* is to live my culture and continue with our traditions and talk a lot of Spanish and English at school. . . .
>
> *Como en la escuela, nosotras, que nos sentamos puras Mexicanas, y hablamos español, me fijo que nos hacen burla. Todos, hasta los mismos Chicanos y eso es lo que me cae gordo. Solamente porque no hablamos inglés nos hacen burla.* [In school when we sit together, just the *Mexicanas,* and we talk in Spanish, I notice they make fun of us. Everyone, even the Chicanos, and that makes me mad. Just because we do not talk English, they make fun of us.] . . . Don't try to be

someone else, just be yourself. If someone asks you what you are, don't be ashamed to tell them you are *Mexicana*. . . . I am proud to be *Mexicana* because I was born there and my parents and grandparents were also. We have a language and a beautiful country. When I think about this I feel proud. . . . I am proud that I have *Mexicano* parents and that I was born in Mexico. When I lived there, I attended school and learned about the history of Mexico. This was very important. . . . I can't say how I feel about being *Mexicana* but I feel it. . . . Being *Mexicana* is very important to me because I was born there and my family is there. I have only been here a short time, but, no matter where I am, *nadie me va a hacer negar mi nacionalidad* [no one will make me deny my nationality]. In California, *Mexicanos* have to live with discrimination. Who is going to do the work that *Mexicanos* do?

En un sitio of a high school classroom *y con una lengua*, young *Mexicanas* talked through the social predicament of naming identities and claiming social entitlement (Quintana, 1996). I listened to the young women speak, in their own words, about developing themselves and their self-worth in the face of denigration and racial discrimination. They assertively and repeatedly claimed their birthrights through cultural memory rooted in family life, their homeland, and their present social realities. The young *Mexicanas* claimed entitlement to talk about their cultural integrity, resisting dominant social and educational practices of assimilation (Deyhle, 1995; Ooka Pang, 1995). They connected their feelings and meanings of differentness to a sense of personal and collective power to challenge the silencing of their language and the obliteration of their cultural memory and identities. No one would ever deny them their linguistic preference of speaking with each other in Spanish, no matter where they were. The necessity of speaking one's language was also discussed in a classroom that was predominantly Latina/o and was taught by a Latino professor. In Padilla's (1997) story about teaching, learning, and liberating education Latina/o students voiced their feelings:

The way we speak and the language that we use is one of the most important parts of our culture because it gives direction to the way we communicate, and what our thoughts are . . . or when I'm arguing, conversing or debating with my mom and dad, (usually my mom), I not only speak in Spanish but the concepts that I try to develop are those of a culture whose language is Spanish. I have discovered over time that these Spanish concepts, concepts that have to do with the Latino culture, have no English counterparts. So you see, the language you want us to speak, this English language, does not always provide us with the concepts that we can apply to us. . . . Speaking in Spanish to my friends and to my classmates tells me that we are bonding. We connect even tighter when we speak in our native tongue. And that's something that no one will deny me of. That's my language, that's the language of my ancestors, of my people. I'm sorry, but I get very, very angry about this issue. (pp. 130–131)

The feelings and meanings voiced by the *Mexicanas* in my study and the students in Padilla's (1997) classroom, about the power of language and communication, are important considerations in the formation of young racial/ethnic identities (Locke-Davidson, 1996). Meanings of language and the development of identities also reflect the strength of family networks and interdependence and the constant negotiation of personal histories, values, and the fact that intersecting and oppressive realities of life socialize young people (Deyhle, 1995; Mendoza Strobel, 1996; Ooka Pang, 1995; Ward, 1995). These complex considerations of identity development challenge the fixed binaries of meanings and representations "to show how meaning is never finished or completed, but keeps on moving to encompass other, additional or supplemental meanings which disturb the classical economy of language and representation" (Hall, 1991, p. 229). In the *encuentro* with the young *Mexicanas*, I listened and watched them sift through a traditional past and the U.S. future to braid the ongoing formations of *Mexicana*ness (Quintana, 1996). I listened to them navigate across the absence and presence of the homeland and move on to talk about culture and identity in *Aztlán*.

Aztlán Culture and Identity, Tensions, and Realities

I sensed that the classroom energy had subsided, and when I looked around, there were fewer students in the room. The young *Mexicanas* had finished their lunch, and they took turns throwing their empty bags into the garbage can placed in the center of our circle. *La de Sinaloa* pulled out a bag of cookies from her back pack, and she proudly announced that the cookies were from Mexico, like the kind she used to eat when living in Sinaloa. She grabbed a few and smiled when she gave me the bag. All eyes were on me as I ate one cookie, wanted another, but passed the bag around the circle because I saw eagerness to have a taste of Mexico. Before I could introduce the next *encuentro* question, *La de Michoacán* looked at the cookie in her hand and said: "I like these kind of cookies because they are different from the kind my mother and I buy in the grocery store. Sometimes we have *galletas y dulces*, cookies and candy, *de México*, but not enough." I made a quick note in my field notes to remember that observation because I saw their connection to the absence and presence of the homeland; no matter where they live or where they find themselves they will always be culturally connected. My field note elaborations also included this analysis:

> As I listened to the young *Mexicanas,* I looked at each one, with a bit more attention to *La de Michoacán.* As they sat in a peripheral place, a U.S. classroom, they recuperated the flavors and sweetness of *México* by transcending the borderlines with longing and memory of their homeland and forgetting for the moment their displacement in the U.S.

As we occupied a space in *Aztlán,* I saw and heard the strengthening of identities through sweet memories and young nostalgia (Chabram-Dernersesian, 1994; Clifford, 1994; Gilroy, 1996; Hall, 1991).

From this observation and others, I found that the young *Mexicanas* were a collective who consciously set themselves apart from others. I remember one day, I gave four of the young women a ride home after school. As we drove by the front of the school, I saw a large group of students waiting for the bus. I heard a yell from the back seat telling me to stop because one of their friends was at the bus stop. When we pulled up near the bus stop, one of the *Mexicanas* rolled down the window and quickly motioned to her friend to come to the car, while the other three *Mexicanas* told me about their new friend from Los Angeles. I was introduced to their new friend and at the same time asked if I could give her a ride home. They were so excited to be in each other's company, how could I say no. We rearranged ourselves in the car, turned the radio a little louder, and drove off to cross the tracks and go home. There was such a feeling of happiness in the car, and in many ways it felt like nothing could go wrong. We talked and laughed and listened to the radio, switching it back and forth to hear the latest songs in English and in Spanish. For every song we heard on the radio, there was a personalized interpretation, and I listened attentively to each young voice. As we approached their neighborhood, one of the young women began to give me directions to their homes. They all lived within a couple of blocks from each other, and they asked me to first take our new friend home. As I pulled up to the first home, they all began to say their good-byes and said they would see each other at school the next day. I finally arrived at the last home of two sisters who were the closest friends of the new *Mexicana* at school. Before they got out of the car, they looked around to make sure they had everything, and one of them turned the radio off while the other rolled up the back windows. By that time the energy was calm, it was quiet, and I watched them as they walked up their driveway and into their home. As I drove away in silence, I thought about all the energy and action and its connection to "a collective identity to know that one is not alone, that one is inextricably connected to others and embedded in a network of interdependent relationships" (Ward, 1995, p. 183).

I learned that in forming their own friendships, the young *Mexicanas* strengthened their homeland connections and culture. They claimed space in *Aztlán* to create culture and meanings that are similar to the research findings on collective engagement and cultural integrity among youth of the same racial/ethnic group (Deyhle, 1995; Padilla, 1997; Ward, 1995). What I also learned about young *Mexicana* social interactions was a further distinction between themselves and other young women of Mexican descent. In our second *plática*, as a follow-up to *Mexicana*ness, they talked about culture intertwined with tensions. Listen to the sequence of their feelings and meanings:

> *De allá soy* [I am from there]. *A veces no lo puedo explicar* [Sometimes I cannot explain it]. . . . Our culture is our traditions. This means our language, our families, and our celebrations. We have to struggle and fight more so that they do not remove us from this country. . . . *Y, como yo por Mexicana y los Mexicanos que sí pudieron ser algo en su vida, pues somos ejemplo para los otros Mexicanos* [And I as a Mexicana and the other Mexicanos who were able to accomplish something in life, well, we are examples for the other Mexicanos.] . . . I do not understand why the different cultures do not get along. But what I do not really understand is why among ourselves we do not get along. There are some Mexicanas that do not like us because we speak Spanish and because we are from Mexico. . . . I want to be *Mexicana* first and to practice my culture the way I know it. I cannot be a Chicana because I was not born here. They are born here, and they are Chicanas. They do not speak Spanish, and they act embarrassed to speak Spanish or to say they are *Mexicanas*. Just because they are born here, they think they are better than us. I am going to tell the truth; they think they are better. . . . Because we [*Mexicanas*] are different, they [Chicanas] say, Look at her, she is born over there [Mexico], and how she came over here and how she looks in comparison to us [U.S.-born Chicanas]. . . . So when we go to school we are *bien Mexicanos* and the girls that are born here just stare at us because of the way we are dressed. I do not like that. We cannot always afford to buy new clothes or the latest fashions. . . . *Nos hacen burla de la forma en que nos vestimos. Pues, como unas de mis amigas, recién llegadas de México se visten como de allá de pantalón apretado. No se visten a la moda por eso nos hacen la burla y se ríen de nosotros.* [They make fun of us because of the way we dress. Like some of my friends who just came from Mexico, they dress Mexican style, wearing tight pants. They do not dress in style. That is why they are made fun of and they (Chicanas) laugh at us.] . . . The Chicanas, they separate themselves from us Mexicanas who are born in Mexico.

This was a very intense part of our *plática*. The young *Mexicanas* moved from talking about culture and integrity to their tensions with and distance from the Chicana students at school. I remember how their facial expressions became serious, and when they talked, they sat up straight and leaned forward. As I listened to the young *Mexicanas'* sentiments about group differences, I was reminded of a conversation I had early on in the academic year between myself and a Chicana staff person at the school field site. She had expressed her concern about not being able to bring the two groups together. She had organized special meetings for the Chicana/o and *Mexicana/o* students and their families, but very few attended; the reasons included *Mexicano* familial responsibilities and parents working out of town. The demands of providing for a family and the intersecting realities of social and economic pressures spill over into the tensions and differences between *Mexicanas* and Chicanas. Through the voices of young *Mexicanas* these tensions elucidate complex experiences of signification, inclusion, exclusion, and difference that render obsolete monolithic notions of homogeneity within race and ethnic groups (Alarcón, 1990; Fregoso and Chabram, 1990).

From our *pláticas* and other interactions, the young *Mexicanas* taught me about the significance of their parents and their family life. They did not specifically talk about their family histories or their migration experiences, but they did share stories with me in other ways. My field notes and participant profile forms indicate that between two and seven years earlier, each of the young *Mexicanas* had moved north with their parents and/or relatives. They left their regional homelands of Sinaloa, Jalisco, and Michoacán and a life of poverty in search of something more. Since all the families had relatives or friends residing around the northern California area, this was the homeland destination. When they arrived, the parents and older family members sought employment in the labor and service sectors. They lived with family or friends for a year or longer, until the family could afford to move into an apartment or a home.

I also learned about family life and feelings from my early visits to the young *Mexicanas'* homes. I met with mothers, and I listened to them tell me about the poverty in their lives and their concerns about the effects of Proposition 187. One morning after taking my children to school, I went to visit one mother, and after telling her about my research and my concerns about *Mexicanas*, she immediately began to tell me about the discrimination she had recently experienced. We sat at the kitchen table, and all around me were empty bowls of menudo and toasted, curled corn tortillas. The kitchen table was long, and it occupied all of the kitchen space. I remember that the older daughter gave attention to her mother's voice while she moved from the table, to the sink, and over to the stove. She cleared off the table, washed the dishes, and listened to our conversation.

When I looked at the table, it was covered with tortilla crumbs and little menudo stains. When I looked at the pot on the stove, it had just a little bit of menudo in it, and the older sister graciously offered me the last serving. I expressed my appreciation and respect. For what I really wanted was to hear their views and feelings about the hostile climate and social realities of *Mexicana* life.

As the mother told me her story, she looked directly at me, and I heard sadness in her voice. The older daughter turned around, looked at us, and walked over to her mother, who proceeded to tell me about a social encounter. The mother and the older daughter had taken the youngest child to a medical clinic, and when requesting, through the daughter's translation, to see the doctor and providing the medical card as proof of payment, the receptionist interrogated the mother as to her citizenship status and that of the child. The older daughter remembered the incident and gave testimony to her mother's account. Both the mother and daughter said they questioned the receptionist's authority to interrogate them about their citizenship status. The mother told me she felt insulted and was concerned about her child receiving proper medical attention, and they left the clinic. The mother's final comment was about another social service encounter with a food stamp eligibility worker who informed her of a possible reduction in the family's food stamp allocation. The benefit change called into question family size and the citizenship status of the family members, thus compounding the mother's daily challenges in feeding her family. As I listened to her story, I drifted between reality and disbelief.

I heard similar stories from other mothers about their racial encounters and their fears. Interrogations about citizenship at medical clinics were the most common. One mother feared termination of the welfare benefits she received for her two younger children born in the U.S. As I listened to them talk about the realities of their lives, I remembered reading about another *Mexicana* mother's concern: "I was buying groceries one day with my two-year-old daughter, when she was stopped by an older man who shoved her aside. I think he threw her aside because she is dark, because she is Mexican. I don't speak English and he didn't speak Spanish, but the language of hatred was clearly understood" (Quiroga, 1995, p. 22). The mothers tell it like it is, and their stories tell about how words and actions hurt people and how children suffer from the affects of a lack of public *educación*. These stories detail the various ways in which race/ethnicity and gender intersect with the structural, political, and representational systems of subordination. In a culture of shifting and changing realities, life is seen through the multidimensional frame of intersectionality where meanings and feelings of displacement, poverty, and racism are acknowledged and written as different kinds of truth (Crenshaw, 1995b; Segura, 1990; Thornton-Dill, 1994). Yet, from this space young *Mexicanas* sift through knowledge and experiences to braid transnational realities, identities, and relationships into womanhood.

Being a Woman: *La mujer Mexicana*

We were well into our *plática* and into the second lunch period of the school day. There were only a few other students in the classroom, and we continued to have our space and to talk. I was amazed that the young *Mexicanas* were not distracted or bored but very engaged in discussion. They had set the social context and described an *Aztlán* culture, and next they moved on to talk about what it meant to be a woman. The young voices gave themselves their place to express their feelings with generational alterations through this weaving of their interpretations:

> To be a woman is to be a woman, and it is like an African American woman, an American [*gringa*] woman and like a woman from another country. We are all the same gender but different colors and with different cultures. . . . I think we [the young *Mexicanas*] feel the same about being a woman, but I think it is different from how our mothers feel. The most important thing I feel is that as a woman I have to claim my place and give myself respect. . . . *Nomás vas a vivir una vez y te tienes que dar tu lugar y tienes que hacer algo. A veces no se como explicarlo, lo sé pero, no tengo palabras para decirlo. Yo pienso que así es la mujer y ya.* [You are only going to live once and you have to give yourself your place and you have to do something. Sometimes, I cannot explain it. I know it, but I do not have the words to say it. I think that is what it means to be a woman and that is it.] . . . I have *tías* [aunts] that do not give themselves their place and they are controlled by men, by what people tell them about themselves, and they let people tell them what to do. They listen to other people and let themselves be disrespected. . . . *Tienes que respetarte ti misma y así para que una sepa valorarse a sí misma. Sí, hace falta en la vida y siempre lo necesitas. Sentirte bien de lo que eres y saber de donde vienes. La mujer piensa en mucho: de su vida, del futuro, de su familia, y de mucho.* [You have to respect yourself, and that way you value yourself. Indeed, it is something you need in your life. You will always need that. To feel good about yourself and to know where you came from. A woman thinks about a lot of things, about her life, her future, her family, and about a lot of things.] . . . Regardless of what people tell you, you have to give yourself your place as a woman, and you have to be careful with young men, about getting married, marrying in white, and the Catholic church. You have to show self-respect, so that men will respect you and take you serious. You have to behave like a young woman. Even though they are going to call you names because you do not

let them kiss you. Not just to please them am I going to give in, not me. That is why I am giving myself respect. That is being a *Mexicana*.

The young *Mexicanas platicaron tocante* [talked about] the cultural interpretations of an essentialized *Mexicana* womanhood. They claimed *un sitio* and in their language resisted this broad expression and the gendered socialization of their female elders with their meanings about womanhood as culture in motion. The young voices recreated *Mexicana* cultural and symbolic representations as active naming of female heterosexuality with styles of desire. In a letter written to her mother, Colindres (1993) tells about her feelings that are generationally different from her mother's. "These new perceptions of womanhood are at odds with our traditions, and I am afraid that these differences in the way we express our femaleness may cause friction between you and me. I don't want to betray your teachings. . . . For me, mom, the story is different" (p. 73). Colindres's feelings resonate closely with the young voices I heard talking through symbolic and ideological social expectations, behaviors, restrictions, and the tensions and contradictions in negotiating their pleasures. These tensions and contradictions are also evident in the music of Selena, the Chicana/*Mexicana* crossover: "I could only wonder how touching you would make me feel. But, if I take that chance right now, tomorrow will you want me still? So, I should keep this to myself and never let you know. . . . *Siempre estoy soñando en ti"* [I am always dreaming of you] (1997). Contemplating the social molding and the Catholic ideology of morality, Selena (1997) and the young *Mexicanas* speak about nuanced meanings and feelings of being a woman coming of age in an *Aztlán* culture and the changing U.S. society (Castillo, 1993; Moraga, 1993). These young voices name their own gendered, ethnic script to unmask resistance against the circumscribed cultural and social powerlessness that injure in the name of protection.

Womanhood and *Aztlán* culture become intertwined when giving meaning to the formations of *Mexicana*ness. In their discussion of what it means to be *la mujer Mexicana*, transregional identities came to the fore in this blend of meaning:

La mujer Mexicana es el orgullo de Mexico [The Mexican woman is the pride of Mexico]. *Somos la de Michoacán . . . la de Sinaloa . . . la de Morelia* [We are: the one from Michoacán, the one from Sinaloa, and the one from Morelia]. . . . The meaning of *la mujer Mexicana* is personal, and I think it means something different for each one of us. I learn about the meaning of *la mujer Mexicana* from my mother's *consejos* [nurturing advice]. My mother tells me not to do bad things because later I am going to regret it. . . . All that I think is based on the *consejos* my mother gives me. But sometimes I tell myself they are not true. But now I see what is happening, and I think about it and real-ize it is true. My mother is right and has reasons for what she thinks and tells me. Because she has lived longer and has more experience and because she tells you for your own good. . . . *Me sirven mucho, los consejos de mi mamá porque no quiero vivir como mis padres. Que mi papá trabaja en el campo y mi mama en el restaurante. Entonces, a mi ni me gusta trabajar en el campo ni en el restaurante. Entonces ya con una carrera puedo hallar un mejor trabajo. Con un trabajo que me gusta hacer y saber como hacerlo puedo salir adelante.* [My mother's *consejos* help me because I do not want to live like my parents. My father works in the fields and my mother in the restaurant. I do not like ei-ther working in the field or in the restaurant. With a career I can find a bet-ter job. With a job that I like and that I know how to do I can come out ahead.] *Los consejos te los dan para tu futuro.* [The *consejos* are given to you for your future.]

The *consejos* and *educación* imparted from a previous generation form the foundation for becoming *la mujer Mexicana* (Delgado-Gaitán, 1994; Quintana, 1996; Valdés, 1996). With "nurturing advice" and "education of the whole person" and various forms of personal, cultural, and social knowledge, young *Mexicanas* braid their meanings and desires into their development of womanhood. Situated in a mesh of intersecting dynam-ics, *la mujer Mexicana* embodies transregional pride, a linguistic prefer-ence, and the right to claim a space for creating agency and cultural in-tegrity, thus rejecting unidimensional interpretations of personal and collective experiences (Alarcón, 1990; Anzaldúa, 1987; Montoya, 1994). These are the formations of *Mexicana*ness woven with young energy and a responsibility to name *Mexicana* honor and dignity.

Reflection and Future Directions

What I learned through my research and community involvement with young *Mexicanas* is that cultural knowledge and the foundations of *edu-cación* are sources of power, affirmations, and contradictions of real-life complexities. I saw a beautiful transformation of consciousness-maturity, with movements of rebellion, and I listened to voices name women's tra-ditions of our *cultura*—that is, to value and love oneself amid the lies, dis-tortions, rejection, and displacement across our overlapping intimate and public spaces. From our *pláticas*, young *Mexicanas* asserted agency to cre-ate subversive narratives to challenge the representations that render *Mexicanas* vulnerable and dismissed from U.S. civic life and public edu-cation. In talking with *Mexicana* mothers, not only did they challenge rep-resentations, but they positioned themselves as policy analysts and criti-cally interrogated and evaluated California political actors, policies, and public sentiments. Our voices crossed the boundaries of policy making and conventional research, and with our words and bodies we transformed the writing on race/ethnicity into "a more complex and less neat and less rigid definition of identity" (Nieto, 1997, p. 177). In constructing ethnicity with their ideologies and power, the young *Mexicanas'* meanings resonate with Sonia Nieto's *Puertorriqueña*, Puerto Rican perspective, presented in *un encuentro*, a gathering, at the Harvard Graduate School of Education:

> On a personal level for me, ethnicity means my language and it means my languages. And how I combine my languages, and how I express myself. And it's a primary part of my identity, but it's only a part. It means my birth family, and my home, and my childhood memories, and the senses and smells of my past and also of my present. (Nieto, 1997, p. 177)

These kinds of feelings and meanings braided with a critical race theory and feminist analytic lens illuminate what is needed in creating research about young women's multiple identity formations. These dimensions of fact must be considerations for writing racial/ethnic identities, as the state of California's complexion and social panorama change in color and class. I conclude this chapter by proposing directions for writing subversive narratives with affiliation and accountability to communities of color and their personal and social realities (Flores, 1997; González, 1996). I also propose tools for transforming educational research, curriculum, school cultures, and the building of education partnerships.

Respecting the writing of stories, the following theoretical and methodological considerations can only enhance the insistence to create social and intellectual knowledge and to "continue the battle to have our experiences and voices heard in academic discourse" (Tate, 1994, p. 264). Across the interdisciplinary and qualitative spaces of inquiry, I suggest writing narrative research as subversive texts of material and emotional realities with feminist and womanist multidimensional, intersecting webs of analysis (Crenshaw, 1995b; Flores-Ortiz, in press); multimethodological approaches (González, 1996; Stanfield, 1994); indigenous epistemologies; and the interpretation of ideologies as texts (Gotanda, 1995) to give the researcher(s) the authority to challenge the ideal of colorblindness, racialism, homophobia, meritocratic ideology, and claims of universality.

With these insights and approaches, writing about the intersection of gender, race/ethnicity, class, and sexualities weaves stories of multiple feelings and meanings. In particular, theorizing about sexualities challenges and "dissolves the sexist and heterosexist conception of [ethnic] group unity and inclusion and complicate[s] the meanings of [ethnic] claims and affirmations" (Flores, 1997, p. 213). In exploring the formation of the sexual identities, desires, and behaviors of young women of color, some guiding questions include, but are not limited to, the following: (1) Within particular ethnic spaces, situated within the broad context of intersecting systems of subordination, how do young women of color transform their sexual identities? (2) Within that ethnic space, how do language, *educación* (education of the whole person), cultural socialization, and cultural memory shape or avert the formation of heterosexual and lesbian feelings and identities? (3) How different is this experience, or is it, when talking about lesbian identity and desire? (4) How is the formation of sexual identities complicated by transnational migration—connections, translocality, and global economic and political shifts? and (5) How can young women of color claim power through voice, scholarship, and a safe space, and talk through their feelings and desires? (Delgado, 1990; Pérez, 1993)

From a distinct positionality, the researcher assuming her subjectivities and commitments makes possible the acquisition of power for herself and communities of color. By telling it like it is and writing "against structural determinism, essentialism, and academic neo-imperialism" (Tate, 1997, p. 225), researchers can move discussion, conceptualizations, and projects by means of new paradigms and analytic tools—Specifically, those situated in ethnic studies, Chicana/o studies, and the other interdisciplinary enterprises. From these galaxies, new social research with an oppositional vision of racial justice transcends boundaries to shape the formulation of culturally appropriate social and educational policy and critiques of legal discourse and court rulings.

The directions, I have suggested, for crafting research and shaping policy also serve as tools for transforming the field of education. More specifically, a systematic analysis of critical race theory in education makes known the tensions of the racialized, ideological foundations of the genetic and cultural deficit models that shape educational research, policies, curriculum, pedagogy, and the subordination and marginalization of students of color (Solórzano, 1997; Tate, 1997). By accounting for the place of race and racism in education, critical educators, students, parents, and communities challenge these models and the practices of K–12 public education. With regard to curriculum, the implementation of ethnic studies with particular and comparative examinations of the histories and experiential knowledge of people of color and of European Americans creates interactions and learning about oneself and each other, among students and teachers. By creating a classroom community for learning, through multiple pedagogical strategies, students can begin to interrogate social tensions and the notion of race, systems of subordination, public policies, their personal and worldviews, and their interactions with each other.

This kind of interrogation attempts to recreate learning and a school culture that are grounded in the identities and culture of each student. In so doing, school relationships, behavior, and rules transform to weave the assertion of cultural knowledge, *educación* (education of the whole person), and formal education. This kind of learning with the praxis of community service and research makes possible, for students, the expression and formation of multiple identities, leadership and responsibility in the broader struggle of social justice and the preservation of dignity and respect (hooks, 1994; Scott, 1994; Stanfield, 1994; Tate, 1997; Wagner, 1987, 1993). Thus, critical race theory in education proposes change and directives for the building of education partnerships.

Notes

1. I begin this chapter with the voices of two young *Mexicanas* whom I identify with signifiers of transregional identity. I withhold their actual names, and I elaborate on their transregional identity further into the chapter.

2. An explanation of the ethnic signifier *Mexicana(s)* unfolds from the analysis of *Mexicana*ness in this article. Somewhat related to the political ethnic signifier *Chicana*, as detailed in the text of this article, *Mexicana* is distinguished by a preference to a particular ethnic signifier, a difference in place of birth, and variations in cultural memory. For purposes of defining *Mexicana* in social science literature: "The term *Mexican* is used to refer specifically to immigrants from Mexico. *Mexicana* typically refers to immigrant women" (de la Torre and Pesquera, 1993, p. xiii). Two other important references include Valdés (1996) and Suárez-Orozco and Suárez-Orozco (1995).

References

Alarcón, N. A. (1990). Chicana feminism: In the tracks of the native woman. *Cultural Studies*, 4 (3), 248–255.

Anzaldúa, G. (1987). *Borderlands/La frontera: The new mestiza*. San Francisco: Spinsters/Aunt Lute.

Austin, R. (1995). Sapphire bound! In K. Crenshaw, N. Gotanda, G. Peller, and K. Thomas (Eds.), *Critical Race Theory: The key writings that formed the movement* (pp. 426–437). New York: New Press.

Baca Zinn, M. (1975). Political familism: Towards sex role equality in Chicano families. *Aztlán: Chicano Journal of the Social Sciences and the Arts*, 6 (1), 13–26.

———. (1994). Feminist rethinking from racial-ethnic families. In M. Baca Zinn and B. Thornton Dill (Eds.), *Women of color in U.S. society* (pp. 303–314). Philadelphia: Temple University Press.

Blea, I. I. (1995). *Researching Chicano communities: Social-historical, physical, psychological, and spiritual space*. Westport, CT: Praeger.

Caldwell, P. M. (1995). A hair piece: Perspectives on the intersection of race and gender. In R. Delgado (Ed.), *Critical Race Theory: The cutting edge* (pp. 267–279). Philadelphia: Temple University Press.

Canclini, N. G. (1992). Cultural reconversion. In J. Franco, G. Yudice, and J. Flores (Eds.), *On edge: The crisis of Latin American culture* (pp. 29–43). Minneapolis: University of Minnesota Press.

Castillo, A. (1993). The distortion of desire. In N. Alarcón, A. Castillo, and C. Moraga (Eds.), *The sexuality of Latinas* (pp. 147–150). Berkeley, CA: Third Woman Press.

———. (1994). *Massacre of the dreamers: Essays on Xicanisma*. Albuquerque: University of New Mexico Press.

Chabram-Dernersesian, A. (1994). Chicana? Rican? No, Chicana-Riqueña? Refashioning the transnational connection. In D. T. Goldberg (Ed.), *Multiculturalism: A critical reader* (pp. 269–295). Cambridge: Blackwell.

Chow, R. (1993). *Writing diaspora: Tactics of intervention in contemporary cultural studies*. Bloomington: Indiana University Press.

Clifford, J. (1994). Diasporas. *Cultural Anthropology, 9* (33), 302–338.

Colindres, C. (1993). A letter to my mother. In N. Alarcón, A. Castillo, and C. Moraga (Eds.), *The sexuality of Latinas* (pp. 73–79). Berkeley, CA: Third Woman Press.

Crenshaw, K. W. (1995a). Introduction. In K. Crenshaw, N. Gotanda, G. Peller, and K. Thomas (Eds.), *Critical Race Theory: The key writings that formed the movement* (pp. xiii–xxxii). New York: New Press.

———. (1995b). Mapping the margins: Intersectionality, identity politics, and violence against women of color. In K. Crenshaw, N. Gotanda, G. Peller, and K. Thomas (Eds.), *Critical Race Theory: The key writings that formed the movement* (pp. 357–383). New York: New Press.

Davis, A. (1981). *Women, race, and class*. New York: Vintage Books.

de la Torre, A., and Pesquera, B. M. (1993). A note on ethnic labels. In A. de la Torre and B. M. Pesquera (Eds.), *Building with our hands: New directions in Chicana studies* (pp. xiii–xiv). Berkeley: University of California Press.

Delgado, R. (1990). When a story is just a story: Does voice really matter? *Virginia Law Review, 76* (9), 95–111.

———. (1995a). Legal storytelling: Storytelling for oppositionists and others: A plea for narrative. In R. Delgado (Ed.), *Critical Race Theory: The cutting edge* (pp. 64–74). Philadelphia: Temple University Press.

———. (1995b). Introduction. In R. Delgado (Ed.), *Critical Race Theory: The cutting edge* (pp. xiii–xvi). Philadelphia: Temple University Press.

Delgado-Gaitán, C. (1990). *Literacy for empowerment: The role of parents in children's education*. New York: Falmer Press.

———. (1993). Researching change and changing the researcher. *Harvard Educational Review, 63,* 389–411.

———. (1994). *Consejos*: The power of cultural narratives. *Anthropology and Education Quarterly, 25,* 298–316.

Deyhle, D. (1995). Navajo youth and Anglo racism: Cultural integrity and resistance. *Harvard Educational Review, 65,* 403–444.

Espin, O. (1984). Cultural and historical influences on sexuality in Hispanic/Latin women: Implications for psychotherapy. In C. S. Vance (Ed.), *Pleasure and danger: Exploring female sexuality* (pp. 149–164). Boston: Routledge and Kegan Paul.

Evans, M. J. (1995). Stealing away: Black women, outlaw culture and the rhetoric of rights. In R. Delgado (Ed.), *Critical Race Theory: The cutting edge* (pp. 502–515). Philadelphia: Temple University Press.

Facio, Elisa (1997). Saludos de Colorado. *MALCS [Mujeres activas en letras y cambio social] Noticiera*, 2 (Summer).

Flores, J. (1997). Latino studies: New contexts, new concepts. *Harvard Educational Review*, 67 (2), 208–221.

Flores-Ortiz, Y. (in press). Voices from the couch: The co-construction of a Chicana psychology. In C. M. Trujillo (Ed.), *Xicana theory and consciousness*. Berkeley, CA: Third Woman Press.

Fregoso, R. L., and Chabram, A. (1990). Chicana/o cultural representations: Reframing alternative critical discourses. *Cultural Studies*, 4 (3), 203–212.

Freire, P. (1970). *Pedagogy of the oppressed*. New York: Continuum.

García, R. (1995). Critical race theory and Proposition 187: The racial politics of immigration law. *Chicano-Latino Law Review*, 17 (Fall), 118–154.

Gilroy, P. (1996). Route work: The Black Atlantic and the politics of exile. In I. Chambers and L. Curti (Eds.), *The postcolonial question: Common skies, divided horizons* (pp. 17–29). London: Routledge.

González, F. E. (1996). *Growing up Mexicana: Multiple identity formations*. Unpublished dissertation proposal. Davis: University of California.

González, J. A., and Habell-Pallan, M. (1994). Heterotopias and shared methods of resistance: Navigating social spaces and spaces of identity. *Enunciating Our Terms: Women of Color in Collaboration and Conflict*, 7, 80–104.

Gotanda, N. (1995). Critical legal studies, critical race theory, and Asian American studies. *Amerasia Journal*, 21 (1), 127–135.

Hall, S. (1991). Cultural identity and diaspora. In A. D. King (Ed.), *Culture, globalization and the world-system: Contemporary conditions for the representation of identity* (pp. 222–238). Minneapolis: University of Minnesota Press.

hooks, b. (1994). *Teaching to transgress: Education as the practice of freedom*. New York: Routledge.

Hurtado, A. (1989). Relating to privilege: Seduction and rejection in the subordination of white women and women of color. *Signs*, 14 (Summer), 833–855.

_____. (1996). *The color of privilege: Three blasphemies on race and feminism*. Ann Arbor: University of Michigan Press.

Laforest, M. H. (1996). Black culture in difference. In I. Chambers and L. Curti (Eds.), *The post-colonial question: Common skies, divided horizons* (pp. 115–120). London: Routledge.

Lawhn, J. L. (1993). *El regidor and la prensa:* Impediments to women's self-determination. In N. Alarcón, A. Castillo, and C. Moraga (Eds.), *The sexuality of Latinas* (pp. 134–142). Berkeley, CA: Third Woman Press.

Lawrence, C. R., III (1995). The word and the river: Pedagogy as scholarship as struggle. In K. Crenshaw, N. Gotanda, G. Peller, and K. Thomas (Eds.), *Critical Race Theory: The key writings that formed the movement* (pp. 336–351). New York: New Press.

Locke-Davidson, A. (1996). *Making and molding identity in schools: Student narratives on race, gender, and academic engagement*. New York: State University of New York Press.

Matsuda, M. (1995). Looking to the bottom: Critical Legal Studies and reparations. In K. Crenshaw, N. Gotanda, G. Peller, and K. Thomas (Eds.), *Critical*

Race Theory: The key writings that formed the movement (pp. 63–79). New York: New Press.

Matute-Bianchi, M. E. (1986). Ethnic identities and patterns of school success and failure among Mexican descent and Japanese American students in a California high school: An ethnographic analysis. *American Journal of Education*, 95, 233–255.

Mendoza Strobel, L. (1996). Born-again Filipino: Filipino American identity and Asian panethnicity. *Amerasia Journal*, 22 (2), 31–53.

Montoya, M. E. (1994). Máscaras, trenzas, y greñas: Un/masking the self while un/braiding Latina stories and legal discourse. *Harvard Women's Law Journal*, 17 (1), 185–220.

Moraga, C. (1993). *Algo secretamente amado*. In N. Alarcon, A. Castillo, and C. Moraga (Eds.), *The sexuality of Latinas* (pp. 151–156). Berkeley, CA: Third Woman Press.

Moraga, C., and Anzaldúa, G. (1983). *This bridge called my back: Writings by radical women of color*. New York: Kitchen Table Press.

Muñoz, C. (1989). *Youth, identity, power: The Chicano movement*. London: Verso.

Nieto, S. (1997). Ethnicity and education forum: What difference does difference make? *Harvard Educational Review*, 67, 169–187.

Ooka Pang, V. (1995). Asian Pacific American students: A diverse and complex population. In J. A. Banks and C. A. McGee-Banks (Eds.), *Handbook of research on multicultural education* (pp. 414–424). New York: Macmillan.

Padilla, F. M. (1997). *The struggle of Latino/a university students: In search of a liberating education*. New York: Routledge.

Pérez, E. (1993). Sexuality and discourse: Notes from a Chicana survivor. In MALCS (Eds.), *Chicana critical issues* (pp. 45–69). Berkeley, CA: Third Woman Press.

_____. (1996). *Gulf dreams*. Berkeley, CA: Third Woman Press.

Pesquera, B. M., and Segura, D. A. (1993). There is no going back: Chicanas and feminism. In MALCS (Eds.), *Chicana critical issues* (pp. 95–115). Berkeley, CA: Third Woman Press.

Quintana, A. (1996). *Home girls: Chicana literary voices*. Philadelphia: Temple University Press.

Quiroga, A. (1995, April). Copycat Fever. *Hispanic Magazine* (18–24).

Ruiz, V. L. (1993). "Star struck": Acculturation, adolescence, and the Mexican American woman, 1920–1950. In A. de la Torre and B. M. Pesquera (Eds.), *Building with our hands: New directions in Chicana studies* (pp. 109–129). Berkeley: University of California Press.

Rumbaut, R. G. (1995). The new Californians: Comparative research findings on the educational progress of immigrant children. In R. G. Rumbaut and W. A. Cornelius (Eds.), *California's immigrant children: Theory, research, and implications for educational policy* (pp. 17–69). San Diego: Center for U.S.-Mexican Studies.

Saldívar-Hull, S. (1991). Feminism on the border: From gender politics to geopolitics. In H. Calderón and J. D. Saldivar (Eds.), *Criticisms in the borderlands: Studies in Chicano literature, culture, and ideology* (pp. 203–220). Durham, NC: Duke University Press.

Sandoval, C. (1991). Feminist theory under postmodern conditions: Toward a theory of oppositional consciousness. *Sub/Versions*, 1, 1–6.

Scott, O. (1994). *The veil: Perspectives on race and ethnicity in the United States*. Minneapolis: West.

Segura, D. A. (1990). Chicanas and triple oppression in the labor force. In T. Cordova, N. Cantú, G. Cárdenas, J. García, and C. M. Sierra (Eds.), *Chicana voices: Intersections of class, race, and gender* (pp. 47–65). Colorado: National Association for Chicano Studies.

Segura, D. A., and Pierce, J. L. (1993). Chicana/o family structure and gender personality: Chodorow, familism, and psychoanalytic sociology revisited. *Signs*, 19 (1), 62–91.

Selena. (1997). I could fall in love. On EMI Latin and Q Productions, *Selena: The original motion picture soundtrack* [CD]. Hollywood: EMI Latin.

Sherraden, M. S., and Barrera, R. E. (1995). Qualitative research with an understudied population: In-depth interviews with women of Mexican descent. *Hispanic Journal of Behavioral Sciences*, 17 (4), 452–470.

Solís, J. (1995). The status of Latino children and youth. In R. Zambrana (Ed.), *Understanding Latino families: Scholarship, policy, and practice* (pp. 62–81). Thousand Oaks, CA: Sage.

Solórzano, D. G. (1997). Images and words that wound: Critical race theory, racial stereotyping, and teacher education. *Teacher Education Quarterly*, 24 (3), 5–19.

Stanfield, J. H. (1994). Ethnic modeling in qualitative research. In N. K. Denzin and Y. S. Lincoln (Eds.), *Handbook of qualitative research* (pp. 248–261). Thousand Oaks, CA: Sage.

Suárez-Orozco, C., and Suárez-Orozco, M. (1995). *Transformations: Migration, family life, and achievement motivation among Latino adolescents*. Stanford: Stanford University Press.

Tate, W. F. (1994). From inner city to ivory tower: Does my voice matter in the academy? *Urban Education*, 29, 245–269.

_____. (1997). Critical race theory and education: History, theory, and implications. *Review of Research in Education*, 22, 195–247.

Thornton-Dill, B. (1994). Race, class, and gender: Prospects for an inclusive sisterhood. In L. Stone (Ed.) and Gail Masuchika Boldt, *The education feminism reader* (pp. 42–56). New York: Routledge.

Torres, G., and Milun, K. (1995). Translating *Yonnondio* by precedent and evidence: The Mashpee Indian case. In R. Delgado (Ed.), *Critical Race Theory: The cutting edge* (pp. 48–55). Philadelphia: Temple University Press.

Torres, L. (1991). The construction of the self in U.S. Latina autobiographies. In C. Talpade Mohanty, A. Russo, and L. Torres (Eds.), *Third world women and the politics of feminism* (pp. 271–287). Bloomington: Indiana University Press.

Trujillo, C. (1991). Chicana lesbians: Fear and loathing in the Chicano community. In C. Trujillo (Ed.), *Chicana lesbians: The girls our mothers warned us about* (pp. 186–194). Berkeley, CA: Third Woman Press.

Valdés, G. (1996). *Con respeto: Bridging the distances between culturally diverse families and schools: An ethnographic portrait*. New York: Teachers College Press.

Villenas, S. (1996). The colonizer/colonized Chicana ethnographer: Identity, marginalization, and co-optation in the field. *Harvard Educational Review*, 66, 711–731.

Wagner, J. (1987). Teaching and research as student responsibilities: Integrating community and academic work. *Change: The Magazine of Higher Education,* 19 (5), 26–35.

_____. (1993). Educational research as a full participant: Challenges and opportunities for generating new knowledge. *Qualitative Studies in Education,* 6 (1), 3–18.

Ward, J. (1995). Cultivating a morality of care in African American adolescents: A culture-based model of violence prevention. *Harvard Educational Review,* 65 (2), 175–188.

Watson-Gegeo, K., and Gegeo, D. (1994). Keeping culture out of the classroom in rural Solomon Islands schools: A critical analysis. *Educational Foundations,* 8 (Spring), 27–55.

Williams, P. J. (1995). *Metro Broadcasting, Inc. v. FCC:* Regrouping in singular times. In K. Crenshaw, N. Gotanda, G. Peller, and K. Thomas (Eds.), *Critical race theory: The key writings that formed the movement* (pp. 191–200). New York: New Press.

Zavella, P. (1991). *Mujeres* in factories: Race and class perspectives on women, work, and family. In M. de Leonardo (Ed.), *Gender at the crossroads of knowledge: Feminist anthropology in the post-modern era* (pp. 312–336). Berkeley: University of California Press.

7

Race, Class, Gender, and Classroom Discourse

MARLIA BANNING

This chapter examines what is often left unmarked in the discourses of emancipatory pedagogy and research: the discursive practices that reproduce white privilege. I juxtapose two research accounts, both of which revolve around and are derived from my ethnographic classroom study of a feminist course that fulfills a diversity requirement at the university at which it is offered.[1] The first account, which I refer to as the main "text," derives from observations and analysis of my field notes, classroom transcripts and notes, and student interview transcripts. This account focuses on the research "results." I refer to the second account as the "subtext." Subtexts can contain the stories, assumptions, beliefs, norms, and/or discursive codes that usually are left implicit and unspoken. The subtext that I recount here tells of the research relations constituting my study, relations marked by struggle and conflict.

I juxtapose segments of the subtext against the text in this chapter deliberately, in order to give readers a sense of fragmentation, since in this case the subtext is one that has been explicitly displaced and silenced. I include the subtext here, however, because it is an effective illustration of the ways in which a power-evasive discourse is mobilized to protect the privilege, power, and entitlements of speakers occupying privileged "axes of social difference" (Fiske, 1993, p. 8). Power-evasive discourses are discourses in which speakers do not acknowledge what power and advantages they have as a result, for example, of whiteness and white supremacy, but also as a result of middle- or upper-class status, or masculine or heterosexual privilege. I specifically want to address how power-evasive white discourse also can be deployed by those professing to hold emancipatory agendas—such as those posited by feminist pedagogy and research—and can subvert their goals of disrupting relations of domination.

In both of the accounts that I give here, I highlight issues of power, conflict, and control as they are expressed in a feminist pedagogy and are performed between two white female feminists in the academy. I view "discourse" as a significant site for the construction and reproduction of power, knowledge, and subject positions, and I assume that positionality can shape discursive practices in myriad ways. Numerous critical race theorists have suggested that the counternarratives of subjugated groups are strategically essential to transgressing hegemonic knowledge (Collins, 1990; Crenshaw, Gotanda, Peller, and Thomas, 1995; Delgado, 1995; Fine, Weis, Powell, and Wong, 1997; Frankenberg, 1993). They also argue that although it is crucial to center the narratives and knowledges of those historically excluded and marginalized—in order to challenge the "racist repertoires that characterized much of the 'knowledge' generated in the context of racial domination in the United States," it is also necessary to examine the silence on whiteness itself (Frankenberg, 1993, p. 16). A number of theorists have begun to address this task (Fine, Weis, Powell, and Wong, 1997; Frankenberg, 1993; Maher and Tetreault, 1997; McIntyre, 1997).

In this chapter, I extend the work of these theorists and presume that the effort to expose and destabilize white privilege is one of the discursive strategies that can transgress dominant cultural narratives. Throughout the juxtaposition of accounts and my analyses of classroom practices and my research interactions, I particularly focus on how the silencing of conflict and the deployment of a power-evasive discourse work to reproduce white power, privilege, and entitlement.

Text #1: Research Design and Central Dilemma

Feminist and critical pedagogues are particularly concerned with understanding classrooms as sites in which to challenge dominant relations of power and with developing pedagogies that subvert the subject-object relations that characterize traditional teacher-student interactions. These pedagogies are centrally concerned with disrupting relations of domination. Although there has been a stream of feminist and critical pedagogical literature, most of these works have tended to articulate the visions of emancipatory pedagogy more fully than the practices that will implement these visions. What gets said in the classroom, who says it, and what doesn't get said are largely left unspoken. In response to this relative dearth in the feminist and critical pedagogical literature, I designed a study to trace emancipatory pedagogical practices and enlisted the participation of two professors, both of whom taught the same feminist course and both of whom were white women in their fifties.

One of these professors is especially recognized as a "master"[2] feminist teacher on the campus where she works. During my classroom observations and interviews, however, I found myself becoming increasingly uncomfortable with, and troubled by, the discourses and practices of this exemplary teacher's classroom. The professor, whom I will call "Jan Gordon,"[3] told students that she intended to critique and deconstruct all relations of domination, including the power hierarchy that normally exists between students and professors within the classroom. However, the central dilemma of her classroom is that whereas its explicitly stated goals are to critique and deconstruct all relations of domination, its micropractices both reproduce these relations and attempt to obscure their reproduction. Gordon's pedagogy, although marbled throughout by a critical feminist vision, is deeply marred by problems of power in practice.

Through the discursive assignments and practices of the class, Gordon not only reproduced conventional teacher-student relations of power and control but denied, both in conversations with me outside of class and during class discussions, that this was what was occurring. As a result, it became difficult for all participants in the class, including the undergraduate students and me—a white woman in her early forties, a feminist, a graduate student, and a classroom researcher—to resist, contradict, or speak "out loud" the paradox occurring and encoded between class practice and course rhetoric.

Subtext #1: Design, Relationship, and Positioning

I designed the study to use feminist action ethnographic methods like those suggested by Lather (1991) in *Getting Smart*, Fine (1992) in *Disruptive Voices*, and Reinharz (1992) in her chapter on feminist action ethnography in *Feminist Methods in Social Research*. These methods emphasize the importance of establishing close, nonhierarchical, intersubjective relations between researcher and researched and aim both to examine efforts toward social change and to contribute to these efforts. Lather, who perhaps writes most extensively about how to accomplish this kind of research, advocates that research relations be collaborative, egalitarian, and reciprocal. Research relations should further be based on trust, friendship, and shared decisionmaking. As a way to facilitate and achieve some of these goals, she advocates that researchers provide their data, initial interpretations, and final analyses to research participants for responses and input.

I enlisted Gordon's participation in part because of her status as a master teacher and in part because she expressed interest in participating when I first began to talk with her about what shape my research was taking. I also enlisted her participation out of my great respect for her as a teacher and feminist. Gordon had received multiple awards for her teaching, some of which are highly prestigious. Although she was an adjunct professor in women's studies, by the time I initiated and conducted my study she had already secured a permanent, non-tenure-track, contract position on the merits of her teaching performance at this university.

I had known Gordon for more than a decade. We initially met when I was an undergraduate student in her class. Over time we became friends, occasionally dog- and cat-sitting for each other, going for walks, and meeting for conversation over lunch or dinner. It was during one of our lunch meetings that I initially discussed the possibility of conducting this study as part of my dissertation research. Although I was still a student during the period of time in which I designed and conducted the study, I was now a graduate student and doctoral candidate, and this study was to be part of my dissertation research. At that meeting, Gordon expressed an interest and willingness to participate in the sort of study I was describing. When my prospectus for the study was approved, Gordon and I met again to walk and to discuss the project.

During the quarter of my observation and involvement in her classroom, Gordon and I met once a week and engaged in open-ended, conversational interviews about the class. Each interview lasted about two hours, and at the end of the quarter, there were about twenty hours of taped interviews. From our first interview, however, I noticed that I felt awkward, uncomfortable, and tongue-tied when I expressed my opinions, especially ones that diverged from Gordon's. I wondered if this was perhaps due to my new role as researcher vis-à-vis Gordon, or to the power of the gaze that I held through my observations of her classroom practice, or to our former teacher-student relationship. It was not clear to me *why* our research relationship felt so strained, only that it was. It would take me a long time to understand why I felt tongue-tied during our conversations and so uncertain and anxious afterward.

Text #2: Classroom Practices and Deconstructing and Reconstructing Power

What are the practices of this classroom and how do they reproduce dominant relations of power and control? During my observations throughout the quarter, Gordon urged relational closeness and student identification with course positions. She emphasized to students that her classroom was a safe one in which to take risks and face fears. She also emphasized that it was important to the course objectives that students make themselves vulnerable in the classroom. At the same time, Gordon used a variety of speaking, writing, and reading assignments and discursive strategies that supported unilateral vulnerability and risk taking, and tightly controlled and suppressed the voicing of disagreement and conflict with the professor.

I suggest that it is questionable to presume that any classroom attempting to deal with the controversial issue of race (or gender) in the United States is actually a "safe" space, particularly if an attendant presumption is that disagreement is unsafe. The controversial nature of diversity issues is highly likely to produce some "risky" disagreement. However, the assumption of safety is particularly problematic when the discursive practices of a diversity classroom are marked by mainstream and dominant white, middle-class codes around control, conflict, and power; and when student disagreement and divergence from course materials and positions result in silencing, dismissal, and potential exiling (Wing, 1997; Solórzano, 1998).

As I stated at the outset of this chapter, the feminist course that Gordon taught satisfies the diversity requirement at the university in which the course is offered. To fulfill this requirement, undergraduate students must take a course that critically examines power relations between dominant and nondominant groups in the United States. This agenda, according to the university bulletin, is the central goal of diversity courses. The specific course I observed, "Gender Hierarchies,"[4] focuses on feminist theory and the study of gender relations. Gordon used feminist, postmodern, poststructural, and psychoanalytic theories, such as the feminist revisioning of Lacanian theory, to deconstruct how hierarchical, binary logic orders gender and other relations of domination and subordination. Goals of the course included, as Gordon stated the first day of class, teaching students to "become more adept at empathy" and to get close to those different from themselves without making them "other." Throughout the quarter, Gordon emphasized that a central course focus was to deconstruct relations of domination. Across all class discussion and activity, Gordon juxtaposed closeness, identification, vulnerability, and empathic relations against distance, mastery, objectivity, and the conventional relations endorsed by institutionalized professionalism.

From the first day of class, Gordon, like other feminist pedagogues, particularly second-wave feminist teachers, attempts to establish her class as a "safe space." She literally states on day one that her class is "a very safe room." On this day, she faces a room overflowing with about sixty-five students, most of whom are white (as the majority of students on this campus are), and roughly half of whom are female. A small percentage of students appear to be of American Indian, Asian, Latin American, Middle-Eastern, and Pacific Islander heritage. As is the case with the many other classes that fulfill a university-wide requirement on this campus, more students want to add this class than there are seats available.

Gordon's comment that the class is a safe space is surprising, given that the course is on feminist theory and that feminist theory is routinely viewed by both feminists and nonfeminists as political, controversial, and debatable (e.g., Faludi, 1991; Hirsch and Keller, 1990; Minh-ha, 1989; Mohanty, Russo, and Torres, 1991; Moraga and Anzaldúa, 1981; and Walker, 1983). Although this claim may not become more believable as I discuss the discursive practices of the classroom, it may become less surprising why she might suggest this when we consider the kinds of speaking, writing, and reading practices Gordon asks students to perform.

In a variety of ways, Gordon needs her students to believe that her classroom is a safe space since what she asks students to do in the class is to assume a very specific learning position—that of identification, unilateral vulnerability in relation to her, and closeness to positions and people students might otherwise find unfamiliar, perhaps even threatening and frightening. Throughout the quarter, Gordon presents feminist materials and positions, including scholarly arguments, fiction, and films, with which she asks students to identify. At minimum, it is highly likely that some of the fifty-five or so students who ultimately remain in the class might label these feminist materials and positions as radical or alien to them. Given this likelihood, from the very first day of class, Gordon attempts to position students and frame materials so that students identify with them rather than contest, dismiss, or fear the feminist messages of the course.

In this section I will describe six classroom practices that illustrate how power and control are deployed in this classroom, confounding the course goal of deconstructing relations of domination. In the following analysis of these practices, I detail how this classroom employs a power-evasive discourse that both characterizes and reproduces white privilege.

Identification

Student identification with course positions and materials is one of the central goals of Gordon's pedagogy. This is illustrated by Gordon's most common in-class refrain: "Raise your hand if you identify with that statement!" Gordon repeatedly and consistently used this statement, or a variation of it, to urge students to identify with course positions. By contrast, she rarely asked students to assume the counterpart of this position, to indicate when they disagreed with arguments being made or did not identify with the positions argued for, the characters in the stories read, or the narratives told in class. The often-repeated call for identification, coupled with the lack of more open-ended requests for students' reactions—including disagreement—worked together to suppress the expression of divergent opinions.

Gordon also elicits student identification with course materials via reading and writing assignments. One such assignment consisted of having students read a series of feminist scholarly arguments that she instructs students to accurately and succinctly summarize in writing. Early in the quarter, she explains to the class that this assignment requires students solely to comprehend the arguments, some of which are rather complex. Without giving students further rationale for the practice, Gordon tells students that this homework assignment requires that they *only* summarize, and not interpret, evaluate, or react to the readings. Despite her explicit instructions to students to write only summaries, however, one white male student in his mid-twenties apparently included his reaction to the article in the assignment he handed in. He spoke to Gordon after the first summaries were handed in and returned during class break, and Gordon told him: "This is where you went wrong. This assignment is not about your reaction—summarize the main ideas that are being presented." Like the one-sided calls for student identification, limiting students to writing summaries and only summaries of these articles diminishes the discursive space in which students might otherwise voice divergent reactions or oppositions.

Write This Down

Increasingly, through class lectures, assignments, and discussion, it became clear that the control of conflict was central to this pedagogy. A number of classroom practices were designed to direct students' responses to course materials and processes so they would identify and not disagree with course positions. One of these practices was Gordon's repeatedly issued directive to students to "write this down." She used the command "write this down" to discipline students, to direct students' attention to what they should or should not view as important in the course, and to survey students' reactions when students appeared reluctant to speak in class. This practice displaced other kinds of interactions that might have occurred at these points in the class interaction, such as allowing student questions or interpretations to guide discussion. Like most direct commands, this command also explicitly positioned students in a one-down position in relation to Gordon. Gordon gave the orders, and students received them.

Throughout the first half of the quarter, at several points in discussion she gave the command "write this down" before proceeding to deliver a lengthy lecture. During these injunctions, Gordon stood behind a podium at the front of the room and the students, who sat in rows that faced the front of the room, writing fast and furiously and groaning out loud when Gordon signaled that she was about to proceed to the next point. Although it is possible to view her explicit directives to students as good, clear teaching, the students' groans appear to indicate that they experienced the directions to "write this down" and their writing performance as a form of discipline.

Direct commands are only one in a range of discursive strategies available to professors to clarify student confusion, to engage students, and to direct their attention toward what is significant and necessary for them understand. In the context of the explicit goal of this pedagogy (to deconstruct relations of domination), Gordon's reliance on direct commands appears curious. At times, for example, she used the directive "write this down" to indicate that what she (or someone) had said was significant. This is illustrated in an exchange between Gordon (JG) and a female student (FS):

JG: *Write down what you have learned.* How the eye functions in film. How do cultural signs perpetuate the status quo? In what ways?
FS: Turns woman against woman.
JG: Watch for this too, and *write this down, too,* popular media, advertising, TV, films and so on, not only represent power relations, but they produce them, women and minorities, it is a matter of being constructed. One last comment.

In another interaction between Gordon and male (MS) and female students, she uses the injunction "write this down" not only to signal what students should hear as most significant but to indirectly alert students to the possibility that she might ask to review their thoughts (in writing) at any time:

JG: For the next three weeks, we are going to look at evidence for these hierarchical, binary oppositions. At the same time, these binaries tell none of the truths. The first aspect of class is a critique of binary logic. *Write that down* and tell me what it means.
MS: Do you think there is factual basis for stereotypes?
JG: How much influence do cultural myths—in some sense, are we so soaked in cultural assumptions about masculinity and femininity that I can't even separate them? *Write this down:* Do gender roles go so deep they constitute our senses of self? What is hierarchical, binary logic?
FS: Doesn't that mean if one is one, then the other is the other?

JG: Gender identities are an unequal opposition. Structured in unequal oppositions. We almost cannot escape thinking in a dualistic pattern. So, if I say "day," you say?
Students (in chorus): Night.
JG: Good?
Students: Bad.
JG: Next time will give more practice. Right now, *write down what
you have learned*. What ideas have you learned? Put your name
on it.

[Gordon then instructed students to hand their writing in to her].

This excerpt simultaneously demonstrates several discursive strategies
that Gordon uses to suppress and control divergent opinions. "Write this
down" functions not only to signal what should be viewed as significant
by the students, but since Gordon finishes the class period by asking students to write down what they have learned, put their names on their
writing, and hand this in for review, students quickly understand that
they may be called on to report their thoughts to Gordon at any point
during the class period. Although they can choose what to write down,
this practice implies that Gordon may survey students' thinking at any
time.

This writing practice is coupled with Gordon's claims that she has a
powerful ability to "see" students. She makes this point early in the quarter:

> Secondly, a couple of people in your introductory papers said "Oh, I'm re-
> ally afraid because I am not a person to talk in class and 25 percent of the
> grade comes from whenever I talk." If you feel that way, please come and
> talk to me, and also please be aware that you have many ways of inserting
> energy in the group, and it's pretty easy, you may not believe it, but I can see
> and know . . . I see who is paying attention. I see who has gotten excited. I
> see who has gone to sleep.

Gordon emphasizes her powers of surveillance and thus attempts to
focus her students' attention on the fact that they are under scrutiny.

Call and Refrain

Gordon also uses rhetorical questions—questions that are not really
questions—coupled with a call-and-refrain pattern of interaction to position students in ways that make it more difficult for them to express disagreement. In the transcript excerpt above, for example, although it is

constructed in question form, the sentence, "Do gender roles go so deep they constitute our senses of self?" is rhetorical. It implies that students are to answer in the affirmative.

Furthermore, in the transcript excerpt I have been discussing, and repeatedly in class discussions during the quarter, direct commands and rhetorical questions were used in conjunction with a call-and-refrain pattern of interaction. Call-and-refrain interaction functions both as an effective illustration device and to engage students in an interaction in which Gordon closely controls the content of what becomes spoken in class. This pattern is demonstrated in the latter part of the transcript excerpt, when Gordon asks students to complete the term implied by its binary other, such as "good" and "bad." The use of call and refrain asks students to summarize what has just been said, to supply the right answer, and/or to speak out loud the positions being read about or discussed in class. Usually, the pace of this interaction is fast. Both the speed and tone of Gordon's speech indicated little tolerance for lag time in response. It is difficult to fully capture speech tone and pace from a written transcript, but this interaction between Gordon and the class early in the quarter illustrates some sense of the pacing:

> JG: O.K. Remember what Aristotle says, woman is?
> FS: Body.
> JG: Body, material. Man is?
> Students (in chorus): Soul.

In call-and-refrain interactions, the "call" question is generally close-ended, and discussion moves fast, leaving little room for variation in answer. Together, these kinds of discursive moves channel students' responses to move in very particular directions. They function to engage students in speech, to suppress variation in reactions, and to control the expression of conflict and disagreement in the class.

Speak the Truth

Along with these discursive strategies, Gordon attempts to establish the discursive norm that students speak truthfully in class discussions. When students are silent and do not respond to her prompts to speak, Gordon uses a variety of strategies to press students to speak. For example, at times she instructs students to take out a piece of paper and write down what they are resisting in the course, telling students to answer—in writing—the question: "What is your fear?" This exchange illustrates her response when students are unwilling to speak:

> MS: I had kind of a "wow" experience when I saw that movie [*Powder*] Friday night. A lot of things I am learning I think I have rejected because of things in my past.
>
> JG: Raise your hand if you identify with that—"I think I am trying to reject it because of things in my past." [students do not raise their hands] O.K., let's bring that into the room—what is—O.K., you need to do a resistance journal then if you can't bring it into the room. If we can't talk about it, you will have to write about it. Because there is serious resistance every single time and it gets in the way of our connecting. And what are we resisting? Do you think I am going to make feminazis out of everyone? [a number of the students laugh]

Gordon's comment suggests that students' silences are an unacceptable or incomplete response, and when she feels that students are not sufficiently responsive to her prompts to them to raise their hands or to speak, she tells students, "Now you are going to write—What's the fear; What is the resistance? Free write!", and she adds, "Tell the truth." Thus, Gordon uses a variety of tactics to urge students not only to speak but to speak (and write) about their fears and about what they are unwilling to say.

Unilateral Vulnerability and Powerlessness

Not only does Gordon press students to identify with the feminist materials presented, to speak and to tell the truth, but she also tells students to take risks, to make themselves vulnerable, and to feel destabilized. She does this both during in-class discussion and via course assignments. Early in the quarter, she explains the importance of feeling vulnerable in this statement:

> A basic rule in here is that we listen. A lot of people keep looking at me to see what I am thinking. This is my view. I believe that destabilization and humility and lack of arrogance are the best places in which to learn anything. So, yeah, I privilege destabilization. A lot of people are saying, "I am afraid, I am confused. I don't know what is going on." That is a viewpoint for me of a learner. To be destabilized. You are not going to learn anything unless you get a little bit uncomfortable. A little bit close to your own border of what you think you know.

Gordon explicitly, and without any irony, states that she privileges a learning position that is characterized by a sense of destabilization, uncertainty, and discomfort. She does not explain that she privileges a uni-lateral destabilizing in which her students assume a vulnerable position to her and she remains invulnerable. She does not question whether it is appropriate or desirable for students to assume these positions of vul-nerability when she herself does not assume such a position. Nor does she acknowledge the irony implicit in her asking students to be vulnera-ble to her even as she denies the institutional power she holds in relation to them.

For at the same time that Gordon tells students that the class is a safe space in which to take risks and face their fears, she also tells them that she is not in a position of power. This became evident several times dur-ing the quarter, when she made statements suggesting she does not oc-cupy a position of power, as in this response to a male student the third week of class:

> MS: It just seems like in our system going to school we are always the objects, teachers are sometimes the subjects, and it's just to the whim of the teacher.
> JG: So you are sort of investing me with subjectivity even if I'm sup-posedly trying to say this isn't a power position, that I want at least to begin to critique the question?

Later she says, "It matters to me that we begin to deconstruct a little more the opposition between teacher and student so that I am not always re-sponsible for your learning, even if it is talk that you are learning." The meaning of the phrase "even if it is talk you are learning" is not entirely clear; however, I believe that Gordon is suggesting in this statement that she is deconstructing, not reconstructing, traditional relations of domina-tion and control between the teacher and students in her classroom. Based on these classroom observations and despite the explicitly stated course goal of deconstructing these relations, I argue that Gordon's prac-tices maintain these relations of control.

Gordon also draws attention to her lack of power in discussions in which she emphasizes her socialization, position, and subjugation as a "feminized subject." In one such discussion, she reminds the class of an incident in which she apologized to a male student, and argues that this apology was a feminized response. By emphasizing her lack of power and denying the importance of her Ph.D. and her institutional rank as ad-junct professor on a long-term contract, Gordon implies she is as vulner-able and at risk as the students in her course.

Gordon claims to lack power and emphasizes her subjugation at the same time as she instructs students to take risks and make themselves vul-nerable, yet Gordon does not make herself vulnerable in the classroom.

This is evident at several key points in the quarter—such as, for example, during a discussion of works by lesbian theorists, when she makes a point of telling the class that she has been married but neglects to state that she now is a member of the lesbian and bisexual community. Granted, there are clear professional risks involved with identifying oneself as lesbian, gay, or bisexual when one is a professor or teacher. This self-disclosure is risky for Gordon in part because of the conservative religious and cultural environment of the university at which she teaches, and in part because her disclosure may detract from whatever power is accorded her by virtue of being a professor. However, a central ethical dilemma emerges when professors choose not to make themselves vulnerable yet prescribe practices to exact this kind of self-disclosure and vulnerability from their students. In any case, Gordon herself does not perform any of the assignments in which she asks students to position themselves as vulnerable.

Relations of unilateral vulnerability are particularly evident in the structure and performance of the final class assignment. In this assignment, Gordon instructed students to perform narratives—read out loud—texts that they had written and of which they were the subjects. She asked students to position themselves in these narratives as "lack . . . beyond the illusions of mastery, phallus, identity, certainty" and to "take a risk, put yourself at the border, edge, for you." The assignment is based on in-class discussions and a one-page hand-out summarizing feminist revisionings of Lacanian theory of phallus and lack that Gordon has compiled.

As she orally delivers the various sets of instructions for this final assignment, Gordon tells students to assume a very particular position from which to write, a position in which they do not feel masterful, in control, or powerful, but in which they feel powerless, afraid, and/or vulnerable, or in which they experience themselves as shameful, "other," or lacking. For this final assignment, students write and read narratives about being bulimic, about being racially discriminated against, and about being in physically and emotionally abusive relationships, among other experiences. These performances were intended to express narratives of students' experiences of subordination, to explore feelings of shame and loss, and to illustrate how students can reconstruct a sense of self to include an aspect of themselves rejected by mainstream society. Gordon herself, however, does not perform a narrative alongside her students. Class relations are constructed so that vulnerability is performed unilaterally by students.

Silencing Dissent

When students do take positions that could be characterized as expressing "distance," including in-class expressions of conflict and disagreement, or seem to resist course materials or practices, Gordon does not validate their responses. This lack of validation includes talking over, ignoring, suppressing, and redirecting these kinds of student expressions. To suppress and redirect these student responses, Gordon changes the topic, does not respond, and/or tells students who are diverging from a course position to hold that thought for later but then never returns to address the point.

In one example of redirecting a student's response, Gordon apparently spoke with a white male student in his early twenties after the previous class period. In the following class, she prompted him to repeat what he said to her outside of class. He did not talk about what she hoped he would, however, and instead took the opportunity to critique a film shown in the course:

> MS: I thought *Dreamworlds*, when I was watching it, I noticed it was really manipulative with the wording and the background music and everything, and I think when it tried to make its point it was going in the right direction but didn't quite have the factual case built. So what happened I think, is they had to use a motion film to say, well, if you view people as objects, you are going to rape them or you are going to do that, when I think a crime is committed against someone—rape, murder, or war— they view people as objects in order to do it. I think what happened was, it seems a little backwards to me in how they presented it.
>
> JG: You had something else to say, too.
>
> MS: I think some people in the class have a tendency to dominate the discussion in how things go, and I hope that we can all share our viewpoints a little more.

When he finished, Gordon directed discussion away from his critique of the film to elaborate on the point regarding participation that she wanted him to bring into class discussion.

In a separate situation, during a discussion of Genesis, a white female student in her early twenties offered an alternative interpretation to Gordon's position that the Bible positions wives as subordinate to their husbands. This student said, "Just to add to the record, there are versions of the Bible that say man and woman are yoked together." In response, Gordon paused, looked at her, and said, "Go and find them." This student, a women's studies major, was seated next to me on this day and sighed heavily after the exchange. When I asked, "More work?", she turned and whispered, "Oh, it is so hard to go against the grain." At another point in the quarter, students critiqued a text that Gordon had introduced using language that clearly indicated her admiration of the scholarship. When this first occurred during the class period, Gordon tried to redirect students by asking them to read specific passages, but the students persisted in returning to their critique in the ensuing discussion. At that point, Gordon threatened to dismiss class an hour early.

In certain cases, Gordon "invited" students who continued to be vocal about their disagreement, or obvious in their resistance, to drop the course. One of these students, a young white male who initially was very vocal in disagreeing, told me in an interview that Gordon had asked to speak with him after class during the third week of school, and during this meeting asked if he wanted to drop the class. This invitation occurred after the point in the quarter when students could either add another class or receive reimbursement for the tuition they had paid for a class dropped. He said he decided after the meeting to only speak up if he agreed with her. In a similar vein, at midterm, Gordon announced that students could make alternative arrangements to complete the course if they "couldn't bring their learning edge into the classroom." When I asked her what kinds of arrangements she made, she told me she offered to let students complete the writing assignments for the course and receive a lower grade in exchange for no longer attending class. Clearly, although Gordon introduces this classroom as a safe space in which relations of closeness and positions of identification will deconstruct relations of domination, her pedagogy relies on practices that control, direct, and place students in subordinate positions. If at this point some readers are tempted to dismiss Gordon as an ineffectual or simply manipulative teacher, I want to remind them that Gordon is a well-recognized and popular teacher among many administrators, faculty members, and students on the campus at which she teaches.

Subtext #2: The Power Vortex

Although, in retrospect, it took me what seemed an inordinately long time to understand the tension I felt and my feelings of being tongue-tied during my conversations with Gordon, I finally came to understand that they were connected to two conversational moves. First, I felt a tension anytime I offered an opinion or interpretation that diverged from Gordon's. In response to this tension, I struggled to respond to her in ways that were both supportive and critically reflexive. Second, I felt a tension during any attempt to discuss power, whether it was an attempt by me to attribute power to Gordon or an attempt by Gordon to attribute power to me; to discuss the power between us; or to discuss the power relations of the classroom. Gordon, for example, attributed power to me because I am heterosexual, married to a tenured academic, and had the power of the gaze in the classroom. I, on the other hand, attributed power to Gordon because she had already attained her Ph.D., was employed as a professor, and was a renowned feminist teacher on the campus at which we both work. Both of us, in other words, consistently positioned ourselves as powerless in relation to each other and identified ourselves with positions of relative powerlessness: by status in the academy, by sexual preference, and by status in the dominant culture. We each saw power as located away from our own subject positions. What was left unspoken but what I assumed we "shared" was the subjectivity of being women and feminists in a masculinist culture and academy.

As I stated in my introduction, I have included the subtext in this essay because I want to problematize the ways in which discourse is mobilized to protect the privilege, power, and entitlements that speakers hold by virtue of occupying particular axes of social difference. I also have included the subtext here because it illustrates, to some degree, the depth of investment and struggle involved in collaboration, and thus problematizes the increasing, often facile, calls to collaborate in research.

At the beginning of the term following my classroom observations, student interviews, and conversations with Gordon, my "collaborative" research relationship and friendship with Gordon ended. We had a severe disagreement over what I would do next. I had initially intended to observe the classroom of a different professor; but due to unexpected circumstances that transpired in her family, this professor did not return my messages to set up our research arrangements until the night before the quarter started. By then, I had already asked Gordon for permission to sit in on her class again, and she had agreed. After the first week and a half of class, however, I began to think it would be more productive to withdraw from a second quarter of classroom observations to focus on transcription and analysis. Gordon did not want me to withdraw. At the end of our exchange on this issue, she forbade me to use any data from the study. After lengthy negotiation, Gordon finally agreed to allow me to use classroom transcripts and student interviews but did not want me to use any of our interview-conversations. I do not, in fact, directly draw from or reference any of our taped conversations here, as Gordon requested.

This agreement between us has had multiple effects. One immediately tangible effect is, as an author, I now can write more directly about the contradictions I observed and tensions I experienced than I was ever able to speak with Gordon about them; I can also be more direct in my analysis than would have been likely had I presented all of my data, interpretations, and possible analyses to her for review. In other words, this disagreement/agreement and ultimate rupture freed me to conduct a critical reading. Scholes (1989) has argued that critical readings cannot rely on a stance defined by closeness, identification, and agreement but must entail a measure of distanced reflection that is generative of new insight. At minimum, critical work requires moving back and forth between a position of closeness and a position of distance for reflection.

At the same time, however, by agreeing not to use our interviews, I accepted the condition that I would not include any transcript excerpts that represented the relational dynamics between Gordon and me or that included Gordon's account of and reflections on what had occurred in her classroom. In a sense, one effect of our agreement is that it restricted the possibility of producing a text that was polyvocal and that contained both of our voices and our points of contestation, and my stance as a writer became, as a result, more monovocal. I now think, however, that without conscious transgression and interruption, the norms and codes of white, middle-class, female, and feminist discourse and its attendant press for consensus are unlikely to produce a truly polyvocal or dialogic account. And although I agree with Scholes about the importance and need for distanced reflection in critical, reflexive work, I think methodological and theoretical discussions of critical activity have left unstated the costs (physical, temporal, emotional, and mental) that can accompany the achievement of a critical distance.

Text #3: Coding Conflicts in White, Middle-Class, Female and Feminist Discourse

As the author of these accounts, I could emphasize the injustice of what occurred between Gordon and me, my pain, and my position as a victim of these circumstances. Or I could emphasize my power of knowing, offering an analysis ultimately aimed at displacing and silencing other understandings. What I would like to do, however, is to avoid either of these authorial positions. There are multiple stories that could be told and multiple ways to analyze these events. Representation and meaning, always polysemic, ideological, and political, are in this case clearly contested as well.

I first want to suggest several ways to understand the power of this classroom and the power between Gordon and myself. Ultimately, however, although I do not dismiss the alternative ways to understand the text and subtext that I introduce, I will privilege an account that I believe to be more generative. This account emphasizes the ways in which race, class, and gender code how power, control, and conflict are expressed and suppressed within the discourse of many classrooms and research relationships in predominantly white, middle-class institutions.

First, I consider how the situational and subjective intersect with the systemic and institutional to shape the micropractices of this classroom.

Although not immediately apparent from the practices that I describe here, Gordon's pedagogical vision is underpinned by the egalitarian tenets of second-wave feminist pedagogy. Second-wave feminist pedagogy, as represented in such earlier works as *Gendered Subjects* (Culley and Portuges, 1985) and more recently in *The Feminist Classroom* (Maher and Tetreault, 1994), for example, is strongly affiliated with the second wave of the women's movement in the United States and advocates the establishment of nonhierarchical, dialogic, and egalitarian relations in the classroom. Although the practices of this classroom do not immediately evidence the tenets of second-wave feminist pedagogy, these become more visible when we consider Gordon's statements that "this is not a position of power" and her other comments about deconstructing the traditional relations of power between teacher and student alongside these pedagogical tenets.

What is at stake in this line of inquiry is questioning whether the kinds of micropractices and relations advocated by second-wave feminist pedagogy are ever possible to implement in classrooms, given that most feminist classrooms are housed in institutions of higher education in the United States. These institutions historically have been, and currently continue to be, neither egalitarian nor nonhierarchical. As Ferguson has illustrated, modern bureaucracies have increasingly become the key sites for enforcing power relations in society (1984). Given this institutional backdrop for these classrooms, the question of feasibility, of whether it is possible to implement these kinds of practices in these institutions, merges with the question of whether it is desirable for teachers and students to attempt to overlook, downplay, or dismiss the differences in rank and status (to mention just two sources of social difference) that exist and that are otherwise clearly marked, enforced, and reinforced by institutional bureaucracies.

Still another way to trace how the situational intersects with the systemic is to ask how the social construction of female authority in Western cultures may work to shape the pedagogy of this classroom. Specifically, in this line of questioning, I ask whether or to what extent the classroom efforts to control and suppress conflict while denying the power that is in play and in place reflect a deep social (and feminist) ambivalence about female authority.

Numerous feminists (e.g., Code, 1991; Walkerdine, 1990; Carroll, 1992; Luke and Gore, 1992) have carefully and extensively critiqued the social construction of female authority in Western cultures. These analyses illustrate that female authority is socially constructed in ways that either negate its possibility at all—via social definition or evidence of experience—or construct it as nearly unattainable—a precarious position that is conflicted at best, a negative attribute or characteristic at worst, and usually oxymoronic. When these understandings and critiques of the construction of female authority are coupled with two assumptions—(1) that any effort by a female feminist to implement a feminist pedagogy is likely to involve the introduction of content and processes that are considered controversial and even contentious, or at minimum, debatable; and (2) that this pedagogical production is likely to occur in the face of an American culture that is becoming increasingly conservative—pedagogical efforts that tightly control student responses and communicative behaviors can be seen from a different vantage point. From this perspective, the construction of female authority problematizes any attempt to level relations or to introduce conflict into the classroom, and provides insight into Gordon's efforts to suppress the conflicts and challenges to course materials, positions, and processes that as a female professor she expected to face.

Articulating how Gordon's classroom practices intersect with systemic and cultural impulses sheds some insight into why this classroom contains these contradictions and tensions. However, it is insufficient to say that we simply need to understand why white female feminist professors may choose sets of practices such as these. Any class that claims to deconstruct relations of domination at the same time as it actually obscures and reproduces them, and that implements relations premised on unilateral vulnerability, raises ethical, political, and pedagogical questions. This point about unilateral vulnerability is taken up by hooks (1994), who argues that an education that is truly emancipatory and for "freedom" occurs when "students are not the only ones who are asked to share, to confess" (p. 21). In situations of unilateral vulnerability, she states, in which professors "expect students to share confessional narratives but are themselves unwilling to share, [these professors] are exercising power in a manner that could be coercive" (p. 21). This concern is amplified given the context for the course that Gordon teaches, a course slated to fulfill the university diversity requirement and premised on critically examining and deconstructing relations of domination.

As I already have stated, I ultimately privilege one account. Even though the dilemma for women of gaining and maintaining authority remains a troubling problematic and provides a powerful framework through which to understand the contradictions of this classroom, it is not the account that I privilege. It is neither a sufficient nor an acceptable account, particularly in service of generating further insight into the discursive workings of power. By centering on the problematic of female authority alone, this account reduces all problems of power in practice to one axis of social difference, that of gender. It ignores the axes of race and class, indices of social difference fundamental to understanding how power and conflict come to be framed in this classroom and in any given set of discursive practices.

The discourse of this classroom, and the conversations between Gordon and myself, are power- and conflict-evasive. However, the relations and the conflict between Gordon and myself should not be discounted as idiosyncratic or due to the personal characteristics of the two persons involved in this research. To do so would imbue this discourse with liberal individualistic overtones, overtones that function to veil the patterns across and between individual persons, and thus miss the opportunity to identify and challenge the powerful discursive strategy of power evasion. Instead, the discourse and classroom practices that I describe here need to be recognized as being implicitly but deeply shaped by white female, middle-class, and feminist norms around issues of power, control, and conflict. It is a discourse that African American scholars Marsha Houston (Houston and Kramarae, 1991) and bell hooks (1990) each have separately described as encoded by race, class, and gender, and it is a discourse that suppresses conflict.

Houston (Houston and Kramarae, 1991), for example, has developed a list based on her own cross-racial conversations for over twenty years, which she calls "Why the Dialogues Are Difficult, or 15 Ways a Black Woman Knows When a White Woman's Not Listening" (p. 389). She notes that when she has spoken at public forums in which she shared this list, other African-American women in the audience not only have validated her observations but have extended the list. Houston names the suppression of conflict and avoidance of confrontation by white feminists the "Talk like me, or I won't listen" speaking style (p. 389). hooks (1990) also derives her observations from her own difficulties in engaging white academic feminists in dialogue, describing these interactions as inscribed by white, middle-class, and gender-based "nice, nice" behavior (p. 89).

These kinds of observations about how class and whiteness code discourse are extended in Frankenberg's (1993) treatise on the subject, *The Social Construction of Whiteness: White Women, Race Matters.* Throughout this work, Frankenberg, a Jewish white woman, interviews numerous white women, and illustrates how the discourse of white women tends to be power-evasive, a discourse that "apparently valorizes cultural difference but [does] so in a way that leaves racial and cultural hierarchies intact" (p. 297). Frankenberg found that the women she interviewed selectively engaged with comfortable aspects of race and class differences but neglected to address the privileges accorded to them by their whiteness or middle-class status. Most of the white women she interviewed did not see their whiteness, yet within their discursive repertoires, still treated both "[w]hiteness and Americanness . . . as normative and exclusive categories in relation to which other cultures were identified and marginalized" (p. 198). Whiteness functions invisibly to norm this discourse.

Frankenberg's description of the discursive repertoires of white women echoes, although differently, the analysis of culture and power that Rosaldo offers (1989). Rosaldo argues that those who occupy positions of power (generally the white, upper middle class) position themselves in ways that maintain their own cultural invisibility while working to reveal the cultures of those less powerful. In these politics of visibility and invisibility, whiteness and upper-middle-class status function to conceal dominance.

A number of the authors who contributed to *Off white: Readings on race, power, and society* (Fine, Weis, Powell, and Wong, 1997) argued that white discourse is consistently characterized by a form of power-evasiveness in which speakers of the discourse do not talk about racial formation or white domination, privileges, or entitlements. This discourse is not only power-evasive but actively resists acknowledging that "racial inequities . . . [are] attributable . . . increasingly to acts of cumulative privilege quietly loaded up on whites" (Fine, 1997, p. 57). I want to draw attention to the modifier "quietly" in this statement. What I hope to have established by this point is that one of the significant privileges of white discourse is to proceed "quietly" while using a variety of discursive strategies to displace and silence dissent and disagreement. This growing "body" of work illustrates that silences over real social differences, the selective marking and invisibility of white racial identity, and the suppression of overt conflict not only continue to be shaped and coded by race, class, culture, and gender, but these silences, absences, and unmarked differences themselves constitute forms of discursive power.

Whereas the majority of these race theorists focus on how the presence of race, class, and gender code power in cross-cultural interactions, Rosenberg (1997), a self-described "white teacher educator," targets the importance of the "presence of an absence" via a discussion of interactions in one of her classrooms (p. 79). She argues that there can be "a figurative presence of race and racism, even in the virtual absence of people of color" (p. 80). I would like to extend her point here by arguing that the suppression of conflict, disagreement, and confrontation, both in the discourse of the classroom and in the research relations outside of the classroom, is an expression or "presence" of a racialized discourse, even though within the research relations between two white women there was not a race difference. The norms of the discourse around conflict and the expression of power still continue to function.

Text, Subtext, and Implications

I mentioned twice in Subtext #1 that it took me a very long time to understand my sensation of being tongue-tied in conversations with Gordon. The difficulty that I had understanding what was going on between us was due to my implication in this discourse. My intimacy with, and positionality within, this discourse made it harder for me to see and hear what was occurring. It often is more difficult to identify the codes and norms with which one is closely familiar than it is for an "outsider" or non–group member.

Like the white women Houston and hooks each describe, I too am uncomfortable with confrontation. In fact, I try to avoid confrontations whenever possible. As I stated in Subtext #2, I too engaged in a power-evasive discourse in conversation with Gordon. I attributed power to Gordon, whereas I felt and expressed a sense of relative powerlessness in relation to her. To understand how this discourse was coded, I had to establish a position that allowed me to distance and "defamiliarize" myself from these discursive practices.

I must report, however, that this was neither as neat nor as rational a process as terms such as "defamiliarization" seem to imply. First, I had to work through a series of almost overwhelming emotions that I experienced in response to the rupture and outcome of our research (and personal) relationship. This took more than a year. To "defamiliarize" myself, I had to move through waves of emotions, including my initial responses of outrage, anger, betrayal, and a sense of (not surprisingly) powerlessness. Only after I had divested myself of these reactions could I begin to engage in the kind of critical activity that I present here. I mention this to indicate some of the costs that can be involved in efforts to achieve critical distance.

Recently, when I have presented this work at conferences or for review for publication, however, I invariably find that at least one audience member or reviewer is deeply disturbed by what I have to say. In one case, a reviewer wrote in her evaluation that I was "not feminist." Her point was that real feminists do not critique each other. In earlier versions of this paper, a number of different audience members, women who presented themselves as aligned with feminisms and feminist pedagogy, questioned what, if any, "good" could come from my analysis. In a later version of this same paper, during a discussion of my presentation at a conference, one audience member, a white woman who appeared to be in her late forties or early fifties, was troubled by the ethics of my "exposing" Gordon. I mention these incidents as illustrations of the pervasiveness of the efforts among feminists, specifically white women, to suppress and silence the research report and analysis I present here. There is a tendency among white women feminists to attempt to force and enforce consensus, a point made both by Ebert (1996) and by Patai and Koertge (1994).

Ebert (1996) has argued that there is a press for consensus and rejection of critique among feminists that precludes critical readings and engagement. She argues that there must be "a constructive space for engagement in critique within feminism" (p. 4), adding that "A collectivity of critique does not need polite conversations so much as it requires strong, rigorous advocacy of the silenced positions and sustained, rigorous critiques of the limitations and hidden assumptions and effects of the privileged discourses" (p. 44).

Professing Feminism (Patai and Koertge, 1994) exhibits a polemic tone that is unfortunate and ironically similar in kind to the polemics that the authors critique as being characteristic of women's studies pedagogy and scholarship. Patai and Koertge (1994) argue that a "tyranny of consensus" characterizes decisionmaking in women's studies programs, adding that much of its pedagogy is "thinly disguised indoctrination" (p. xvi).

Chow (1993) identifies the discourse that I have been describing throughout this essay as a "discourse of white guilt," which she defines specifically as one in which the speaker is not necessarily white, but which "continues to position power and lack against each other, while the narrator of that discourse . . . speaks with power but identifies with powerlessness" (p. 14). The implications of a white-guilt discourse are multiple. In both pedagogy and research, deploying this discourse reduces the complexity of subject positioning to a dichotomous framework. The implications also include simplifying understandings of how power works. Walkerdine (1990) makes these points when she argues that it is necessary to understand

> Individuals *not* as occupants of fixed, institutionally determined positions of power, but as multiplicities of subjectivities . . . [to understand, for example] an individual's position [a]s not uniquely determined by being "woman," "girl" or "teacher." It is important to understand the individual signifiers [girl, woman, teacher] as subjects within any particular discursive practice. We can then understand power *not* as static, but produced as a constantly shifting relation. (p. 14)

Another implication of the white-guilt discourse that Chow (1993) identifies is that it involves a discursive currency that inverts Robin Hood logic: It takes from those who are less privileged the very terms from which they might be able to develop their own sets of discursive tactics. Those deploying a white-guilt discourse further their privileges and entitlement while "robbing the terms of oppression of their critical and oppositional import, thus depriving the oppressed of even the vocabulary of protest and rightful demand" (p. 13).

Within much discourse, whether located in a pedagogical or research situation, inside or outside the academy, whiteness is often invisible, not marked. This omission has powerful ramifications. Discursive strategies such as power-evasion confuse power with powerlessness, and most importantly, they confound and defeat emancipatory agendas. It is time to closely and critically examine how class, race, and gender code what is spoken, what is not, and who and what get silenced.

Notes

1. I designed my classroom study of a feminist course to utilize feminist action ethnographic methodology, an emerging method oriented to social change. Feminist action ethnography is offered as an alternative to conventional social science methods, and as a methodology premised on developing collaborative, reciprocal, and egalitarian intersubjective relations between researchers and participants. Feminist action ethnography, Lather suggests (1991), "invites reciprocal reflexivity and critique, both of which guard against the central dangers to praxis-oriented empirical work: imposition and reification on the part of the researcher" (p. 59). It is a methodology that makes a place for producing critical, reflexive empirical work using data collection techniques such as interviewing, participation-observation, and textual analysis of artifacts such as interview transcripts. In the process of conducting this study I attended class, did the reading, took class notes and field notes, and recorded classroom discussion on audio tape. I also conducted twelve two-hour interviews with the professor over the course of an eleven-week quarter, most of which I recorded on audio tape. These interviews were open-ended—we both initiated topics and posed questions to each other. I also conducted open-ended interviews with eighteen students. In the course of this study, however, I ran into difficulties that greatly complicated my ability to report on this work. In this study, as a graduate student conducting research with a professor—whom I refer to here as "Gordon"—I was "studying-up." In other words, by institutional rank I occupied a one-down position of power in relation to her. Despite my presumption that we were working collaboratively, as soon as we had a significant disagreement, Gordon unilaterally deployed the institutional power and privilege that she held and forbade me to use any of the data I collected. After this interaction, I exchanged several letters with her and met several times with my dissertation committee. Gordon met alone with my dissertation committee chair to discuss how I could proceed. Although her initial injunction forbade me to use any of my study data, after extended negotiation, she agreed in writing to allow me to use classroom transcripts but not any of my taped conversations with her. I honor this agreement by not referencing any of our taped conversations here. The implications of this collapse in "collaboration" for me were multiple. One significant outcome was that this conflict appeared to have made some members of my dissertation committee nervous. Eight months after the initial disagreement with Gordon, my chair requested that I reconceptualize my project to write a theoretical dissertation. This project of reconceptualization took well over a year. Another significant result of this issue is that I have come to read emancipatory discourse "within but against the grain." In other words, I now read emancipatory discourses and practices more critically, with an eye focused on their contradictions and an ear to their silences about power. The forbidden data now sit boxed up in the back of a closet.

2. The phrase "master teacher" is widely circulated and has been normalized within educational circles to designate someone who has achieved teaching excellence. Whereas this phrase does not appear to be problematic for many, I find it problematic because of its connotations derived from relations of domination, such as master-slave relations. I also think it an ironic phrase to apply to exemplary emancipatory pedagogues because of this master-slave connotation.

3. A pseudonym.

4. A pseudonym.

References

Carroll, B. (1992). Originality and creativity: Rituals of inclusion and exclusion. In C. Kramarae and D. Spender (Eds.), *The knowledge explosion: Generations of feminist scholarship* (pp. 353–361). New York: Teachers College Press.

Chow, R. (1993). *Writing diaspora: Tactics of intervention in contemporary cultural studies.* Bloomington: Indiana University Press.

Code, L. (1991). *What can she know? Feminist theory and the construction of knowledge.* Ithaca, NY: Cornell University Press.

Collins, P. H. (1990). *Black feminist thought: Knowledge, consciousness, and the politics of empowerment.* New York: Routledge.

Crenshaw, K., Gotanda, N., Peller, G., and Thomas, K. (Eds.). (1995). *Critical race theory: Key writings that formed the movement.* New York: New Press.

Culley, M., and Portuges, C. (Eds.). (1985). *Gendered subjects: The dynamics of feminist teaching.* Boston, MA: Routledge and Kegan Paul.

Delgado, R. (Ed.). (1995). *Critical race theory: The cutting edge.* Philadelphia: Temple University Press.

Ebert, T. (1996). *Ludic feminism and after: Postmodernism, desire, and labor in late capitalism.* Ann Arbor: University of Michigan Press.

Faludi, S. (1991). *Backlash: The undeclared war against American women.* New York: Crown.

Ferguson, K. E. (1984). *The feminist case against bureaucracy.* Philadelphia: Temple University Press.

Fine, M. (1992). *Disruptive voices: The possibilities of feminist research.* Ann Arbor: University of Michigan Press.

_____. (1997). Witnessing whiteness. In M. Fine, L. Weis, L. C. Powell, and L. M. Wong (Eds.), *Off white: Readings on race, power, and society* (pp. 57–65). New York: Routledge.

Fine, M., Weis, L., Powell, L. C., and Wong, L. M. (Eds.). (1997). *Off white: Readings on race, power, and society.* New York: Routledge.

Fiske, J. (1993). *Power plays, power works.* New York: Verso.

Frankenberg, R. (1993). *The social construction of whiteness: White women, race matters.* Minneapolis: University of Minnesota Press.

Hirsch, M., and Keller, E. F. (Eds.). (1990). *Conflicts in feminism.* New York: Routledge.

hooks, b. (1990). *Yearning: Race, gender, and cultural politics.* Boston: South End.

_____. (1994). *Teaching to transgress: Education as the practice of freedom.* New York: Routledge.

Houston, M., and Kramarae, C. (1991). Speaking from silence: Methods of silencing and resisting. *Discourse and Society*, 2 (4), 387–399.

Lather, P. (1991). *Getting smart: Feminist research and pedagogy within/in the postmodern.* New York: Routledge.

Luke, C., and Gore, J. (Eds.). (1992). *Feminisms and critical pedagogy.* New York: Routledge.

Maher, F. A., and Tetreault, M. K. T. (1994). *The feminist classroom.* New York: Basic.

_____. (1997). Learning in the dark: How assumptions of whiteness shape classroom knowledge. *Harvard Educational Review*, 67 (2), 321–349.

McIntyre, A. (1997). *Making meaning of whiteness: Exploring racial identity with white teachers.* Albany: State University of New York Press.

Minh-ha, T. (1989). *Woman, native, other.* Bloomington: Indiana University Press.

Mohanty, C. T., Russo, A., and Torres, L. (Eds.). (1991). *Third world women and the politics of feminism.* Bloomington: Indiana University Press.

Moraga, C., and Anzaldúa, G. (Eds.). (1981). *This bridge called my back: Writings by radical women of color.* New York: Kitchen Table.

Patai, D., and Koertge, N. (1994). *Professing feminism: Cautionary tales from the strange world of women's studies.* New York: Basic.

Reinharz, S. (1992). *Feminist methods in social research.* New York: Oxford University Press.

Rosaldo, R. (1989). *Culture and truth: The remaking of social analysis.* Boston: Beacon.

Rosenberg, P. M. (1997). Underground discourses: Exploring whiteness in teacher education. In M. Fine, L. Weis, L. C. Powell, and L. M. Wong (Eds.), *Off white: Readings on race, power, and society* (pp. 79–89). New York: Routledge.

Scholes, R. (1989). *Protocols of reading.* New Haven, CT: Yale University Press.

Solórzano, D. G. (1998). Critical race theory, race, and gender microaggressions, and the experience of Chicana and Chicano scholars. *International Journal of Qualitative Studies in Education*, 11, 121–136.

Walker, A. (1983). *In search of our mothers' gardens: Womanist prose.* New York: Harcourt Brace Jovanovich.

Walkerdine, V. (1990). *Schoolgirl fictions.* New York: Verso.

Wing, A. K. (Ed.). (1997). *Critical race feminism.* New York: New York University Press.

8

Critical Race Theory and Interest Convergence in the Desegregation of Higher Education

EDWARD TAYLOR

Local and national leaders periodically attempt to refocus public attention on the need for racial dialogue with the goals of reconciling our differences and laying a foundation for our cooperation in a shared future. Americans are quickly learning, however, that such conversations often go down paths that are not only arduous and frustrating but that also lack road maps or guideposts. If the quest for racial equity in higher education can be described (as it often is) as a long, long journey requiring considerable intellectual effort and sturdy footwear, this chapter is about finding some "cognitive road map" to better understand our segregated past and help direct a course toward reconciliation.

Educators attempting to foster cross-racial understanding face a lack of direction due, in part, to theoretical frameworks that are contradictory, disingenuous, or both (Ladson-Billings and Tate, 1995; Tate, 1997). Omi and Winant (1994) assert that most policies and practices relating to race operate without a coherent theoretical basis. Moreover, the various theories of positivism, postpositivism, and constructivism have faced criticism for being derived from European-based perspectives and rarely addressing other-race viewpoints (Stanfield, 1994). Against this backdrop, educational theorists and practitioners are looking for paradigms to understand the racialization of education. One development in this conflict of paradigms has been the increasing use of critical theory to promote educational reform using social justice and equity as a moral compass. Critical theory has been criticized, however, for marginalizing race (West, 1995), and as a result, race-based epistemologies such as critical race theory (CRT) have emerged (Scheurich and Young, 1997). However, the central tenets of CRT have yet to be extended into analyses of higher education, and their potential to inform strategies for reform has yet to be fully explored. In writing this chapter, therefore, I have three primary goals. The first is to describe and critique CRT and its tenets. The second is to briefly trace the history of desegregation in higher education by examining the case of Tennessee State University through the lens of CRT. The final goal is to analyze CRT's explanatory strengths and weaknesses for analyses of higher education in general. Although I recognize the inherent dangers of using the "retrospectoscope" to interpret the past, I submit that unless some such analysis is attempted, the tenets of CRT will either go unquestioned or be dismissed without serious consideration.

Theoretical Framework

This analysis of CRT rests on two primary assumptions. First, it assumes that historical/legal analysis of racially segregated education and the litigation that challenged it is critical to understanding systemic racism. An all-too-common tendency in discussions about race is to oversimplify complicated dynamics and to disregard the historical context in which a specific conflict developed. This amnesia is often not deliberate but reflects the broader, ordinary narcissism of each age. Bond contends that this widespread historical illiteracy reveals "an astounding ignorance of our racist past" (1991, p. 222). Educators and education policy makers may be at particular risk from this ahistoric tendency. For African Americans in higher education, distance from the social context and the corresponding legal history in which *de jure* segregation was both born and battled breeds a certain "objectivity" that can be damaging in its naiveté. African American access to higher education has never been an assumed right or privilege; the courts have been (and continue to be) the gatekeeper. As a result, lack of familiarity with the pertinent legal issues creates a particularly potent form of illiteracy.

The second assumption of this analysis is that CRT should demonstrate some explanatory powers if it is to be considered a theoretical construct. Although critical race theorists do not generally trust conventional forms of empirical verification, Farber and Sherry (1995) maintain that CRT has not empirically demonstrated (for example) the existence of a distinct African American voice, nor has it clearly conceptualized its claims. Kennedy (1995) notes that there is a significant difference between a *plausible hypothesis* and a *persuasive theory* (p. 436). My point here is not to argue the relative merits of traditional, positivist methodologies against scholarship that challenges the narrative of objectivity (although I will outline some contours of this controversy) but to begin the process of bringing CRT into the consciousness of educational researchers and theorists. There are many ways one could do this. I have chosen to explore desegregation litigation in higher education as a means to understanding both some of the origins of CRT and its place in educational thought and practice. Such an analysis may therefore reveal the strength of its presumptions as well as its limitations.

Critical Race Theory

Critical race theory, an eclectic and dynamic area of legal scholarship, developed in the late 1980s as a result of the perceived failure of traditional civil rights litigation to produce meaningful racial reform. Its founders include legal scholars Derrick Bell, Charles Lawrence, Richard Delgado, Mari Matsuda, Patricia Williams, and Kimberle Crenshaw. What began as informal exchanges between law professors and students gradually grew into a movement. Watching the gains of the civil rights movement slowly erode sparked interest in new strategies for achieving racial justice, strategies informed by critical theory, feminism, postmodernism, and other intellectual traditions. This scholarship gradually grew into a group identity that has not only significantly affected the legal field but has also been extended into areas such as education (Ladson-Billings and Tate, 1995), women's studies (Wing, 1996), and economics (Rubin, 1996).

As a form of oppositional scholarship, CRT is not an abstract set of ideas or rules. However, critical race scholars have identified some defining elements (Lawrence, Matsuda, Delgado, and Crenshaw, 1993). The first is that racism is a normal, not aberrant or rare, fact of daily life in society, and the assumptions of white superiority are so ingrained in our political and legal structures as to be almost unrecognizable (Delgado, 1995). Racial separation has complex, historic, and socially constructed purposes that ensure the location of political and legal power in groups considered superior to people of color (Calmore, 1995a). Racism is also likely permanent, and periods of seeming progress are often followed by periods of resistance and backlash as social forces reassert white dominance (Bell, 1992). In reaction, CRT challenges the experience of whites as the normative standard (Calmore, 1995b) and grounds its conceptual framework in the distinctive experiences of people of color. This "call to context" insists that the social/experiential context of racial oppression is crucial for understanding racial dynamics.

CRT is grounded in the lived experience of racism, which has singled out, with wide consensus among whites, African Americans and others as worthy of suppression (Crenshaw, 1988). CRT thus embraces this subjectivity of perspective and openly acknowledges that perceptions of truth, fairness, and justice reflect the mind-set, status, and experience of the observer. In contrast, traditional legal definitions claim neutrality and color blindness as the basis for the ideology of equal opportunity and meritocracy (Brown, 1992; Litowitz, 1997). CRT challenges those claims, noting the way "objective" facts are used to promote the interests of the majority. Delgado points out an important distinction between the viewpoints of blacks and whites, however. Whites don't see their understanding of reality as a specific perspective but as the truth (1989).

One powerful way to challenge the dominant mind-set of society—the shared stereotypes, beliefs, and understandings—is through telling stories. Stories can both challenge the status quo and help build consensus by creating a shared, communal understanding. They can simultaneously describe what is and what ought to be. As a result, CRT scholars often engage and contest negative stereotyping through storytelling/narrative/autobiography/personal history. This strategy uses the experiences of people negatively affected by racism to confront the beliefs held *about* them by whites. This is what Crenshaw calls a condition for the development of a distinct political strategy informed by the actual conditions of black people (1988, p. 1387).

CRT proponents are deeply dissatisfied with traditional civil rights litigation and liberal reforms. Having watched an increasingly conservative judiciary erode the gains of the 1960s, CRT scholars lost faith in traditional legal remedies. They have seen restrictive definitions of merit, fault, and causation render much current antidiscrimination law impotent. Progress in employment and contracting laws designed to end discrimination has been stalled as courts promote popular preferences at the expense of minority interests. Two commonly held ideologies have contributed to the backlash against civil rights litigation—the myths of meritocracy and colorblindness. By relying on merit criteria, or standards, the dominant group can justify its exclusion of blacks to positions of power, believing in its own neutrality (Harris, 1993). CRT asserts that such standards are *chosen*, not inevitable, and should be openly debated and reformed in ways that no longer benefit privileged whites alone. The neoconservative color-blind view calls for the repeal of affirmative action and other race-based remedial programs, arguing that whites are the true victims. CRT notes that color blindness makes no sense in a society in which people, on the basis of group membership alone, have historically been, and continue to be, treated differently. The danger of color blindness is that it allows us to ignore the racial construction of whiteness and reinforces its privileged and oppressive position. Thus, whiteness remains the normative standard and blackness remains different, other, and marginal. Even worse, by insisting on a rhetoric that disallows reference to race, blacks can no longer name their reality or point out racism.

Not all critical race theorists agree in their criticism of liberal legal ideology. Crenshaw (1988) has argued that liberal ideology, although far from being perfect, has visionary ideals that should developed. She also notes that given the limited range of options for blacks to challenge racism, liberalism should not be too quickly discarded.

A central tenet of CRT's criticism of liberalism is Bell's theory of "interest convergence"—that is, whites will promote advances for blacks only when they also promote white interests (Bell, 1980). The concept of interest convergence has its roots in the Marxist theory that the bourgeoisie will tolerate advances for the proletariat only if these advances benefit the bourgeoisie even more. Class conflict is therefore intractable and progress is possible only through revolution.

The following story illustrates the dynamics of interest convergence. In Bell's parable *The space traders* (1992), he describes an invasion of space aliens that offer to solve the planet's fiscal, environmental, and fuel needs in exchange for all persons of African descent. Although many whites were against it, the majority, like their colonial forebears, were ultimately willing to exchange the lives, liberty, and happiness of Africans for their economic, educational, and social desires. Bell's point is that, historically, white Americans have been willing to sacrifice the well-being of people of color (Africans, indigenes, and others) for their economic self-interests, and that continued subordination of blacks is sustained by economic and legal structures that promote white privilege.

Olivas (1990) holds that people respond to *The space traders* in predictable ways, largely along racial lines. People of color, including American Indians, Japanese immigrants, and others whose interests have been sacrificed to promote white concerns, find its explanatory power compelling. Whites are less enthusiastic. Olivas's contention is not that Bell's theory is too far-fetched but that it is based on what already has happened repeatedly. His review of the treatment of Cherokees, Hispanic immigrants, and Chinese laborers confirms the principles that have guided white interests.

Examining desegregation litigation for evidence of interest convergence requires some familiarity with this history, which I will briefly describe. The case of Tennessee State University will then be used as an example. A note of caution, however: The phrases "black interests" and "white interests" are not meant to imply the concerns of *all* persons designated black or white; rather, the intent is to summarize those opinions generally held by the majority, or at least by those holding political power. Dissenting voices, such as those of whites opposing the racial subordination of blacks or blacks objecting to civil rights litigation, although important, are not addressed.

Desegregation of Higher Education

The *Plessy v. Ferguson* (1896) standard of "separate but equal" legitimized modern American apartheid. Segregation was so deeply woven into the fabric of educational institutions that only a few colleges were willing to accept even a token number of exceptionally qualified black students (Anderson, 1988). "Equal" education in the South produced an ugly record of deceit, deprivation, and shamefully inferior schooling for blacks (Kujovich, 1987). In Bell's words, "A belief in black inferiority and even simple greed are insufficient explanation for the relentlessness of the disparities, the meanspiritedness of the deprivations, and the utter devastation of hopes that the policies wreaked among blacks wanting only the schooling needed to make their own way" (1987, p. 25). This era of legalized apartheid produced increasingly entrenched social separation and acts of lawless violence, conditions that contributed to the rise of organized protest by blacks.

In 1935, the National Association for the Advancement of Colored People (NAACP) appointed Charles Houston chief legal counsel. Houston, with others, devised a strategy for attacking discrimination in higher education, particularly in professional schools, with the goal of establishing enough precedence in small cases to overturn *Plessy* (Humphries, 1994).

Most states where blacks lived had separate primary schools, secondary schools, and colleges for black and white students, making it difficult to argue lack of access to education (however inferior) at those levels. However, because almost no professional school opportunities for Negroes existed, this area was targeted. Houston also reasoned that white judges might be more personally sympathetic to undeniably able students barred from law or medical school solely because of their race (McNeil, 1983).

Claiming protection under the Equal Protection Clause of the Fourteenth Amendment, Houston and his team, including Thurgood Marshall, first argued the case of Donald Murray, a student denied admission to the University of Maryland School of Law solely because of race, in 1935. In a crucial early victory, the Maryland district court ordered that Murray be admitted (*Murray v. Maryland*, 1936, 1937). Soon after, Houston took up the case of Lloyd Gaines, another young African American attempting to go to law school, in *Missouri ex rel. Gaines v. Canada* (1938). Like Murray, Gaines had been denied entry to the state university's law school, but the state of Missouri offered to build a separate law school just for him. The U.S. Supreme Court agreed to hear Houston's case. He argued that preventing Gaines from attending the only law school in Missouri violated his right to equal protection under the law. The Supreme Court justices agreed, and ordered (for the first time) the admission of a black student to a segregated school, agreeing that separate but equal professional schools denied African Americans equal protection.

In *McLaurin v. Oklahoma* (1950) the Supreme Court again outlawed efforts to force African Americans in state universities to use separate facilities. It ruled that a black graduate student (pursuing a doctorate in education) could not be required to sit at a separate table in the library, use the cafeteria only when whites were not present, and have a designated desk. Ruling on the same day on a similar case at the University of Texas Law School (*Sweatt v. Painter*, 1950), the Court concluded that separate facilities inherently interfered with legal education. The Court found the restrictions in both Oklahoma and Texas stigmatizing, confining, and illegal.

Although these smaller cases did not end segregation in higher education, they weakened the primacy of *Plessy*. They also demonstrated the interests of certain states in protecting the educational and economic advantages reserved for whites by maintaining racial separation. Could interest convergence have predicted the outcomes of these two cases? Other cases, such as *Sipuel v. Oklahoma State Board of Regents* (1948), did not have favorable outcomes. Were the judgments the outcome of the guilt and anxiety of those holding power, or motivated by progressive interpretations of the Fourteenth Amendment? Judging *intent* in these cases is speculative and inconclusive. However, the cases were argued so personally (McNeil, 1983) that white judges' identification with aspiring and struggling law students may have inspired favorable rulings.

As hoped, the U.S. Supreme Court reversed the *Plessy* decision in 1954. The ruling in *Brown v. Board of Education of Topeka, Kansas* (1954) stated that racial segregation in public schools at all levels was inherently unequal. This unanimous, watershed ruling promised enormous change and suggested dramatic racial progress. However, several factors other than the interests of equitable education for black children may have played a seminal role, including increasing international media coverage of white racism against blacks, especially stories involving torture and lynching. Dudziak (1988) found evidence of considerable pressure from the U.S. Justice Department to overturn *Plessy*. The department's amicus brief argued that desegregation was in the national interest due to foreign policy concerns. As the United States was attempting to position itself as the leading force against communism, continual and negative foreign reporting of its system of racial apartheid threatened to undermine its role as a model of democracy. In fact, within an hour of the *Brown* decision (written briefly, in lay terms), the Voice of America was broadcasting the news, particularly to Russian satellites and communist China (Dudziak, 1988).

Other majority interests may have been served as well. Bell (1980) posits that increasing black unrest, especially among black World War II veterans victimized by violent, unprovoked attacks by whites, was also of concern. The ensuing publicity threatened to undercut military morale and further undermine U.S. foreign policy concerns as well as foment civil disorder. In addition, increasing numbers of Northern whites felt that strict racial apartheid posed a barrier to further industrialization in the South (Bell, 1980).

Despite the dramatic nature of *Brown*, there was no sudden end to racial separation in education. Although a number of black schools were immediately closed, black children were hardly welcomed into neighboring white schools. Nor were institutions of higher education, particularly in the South, interested in ending traditional dual, strictly segregated systems.

Systematic legislation and the passage of the 1964 Civil Rights Act established federal agencies responsible for the enforcement of federal nondiscrimination policies. These included the Office for Civil Rights (OCR) and the Equal Employment Opportunity Commission (EEOC). The OCR developed numerous programs to cultivate and support opportunities for and equal treatment of ethnic minority students. By 1965, of the 600,000 African Americans enrolled in college, 65 percent attended historically black colleges and universities (HBCU) (Wilson, 1994).

Southern Resistance

In Southern states, *Brown* was actively ignored, resisted, or both, for more than fifteen years (Kujovich, 1987; Ware, 1994). When Title VI of the Civil Rights Act was enacted in 1964, nineteen states were operating openly segregated higher education systems. The massive, sustained resistance of whites in Southern states to comply with *Brown* would have come as no surprise to seasoned racial realists. Whites, particularly underclass ones, were incensed that elite whites would allow a restructuring of the social class system that had always guaranteed even the poorest whites a higher status than blacks (Bell, 1980). Elite whites, particularly those in Washington, D.C., however, had some other interests at stake, particularly as they related to promoting the rule of law and federalism. When one examines the reaction to Southern universities' refusal to segregate despite federal intervention (however ineffectual), it becomes apparent that the federal government and its agencies worked to enforce *Brown* not entirely out of a sense of concern for the education of black children but in response to the obvious disregard for federal statutes and the rule of law (Bell, 1980).

In 1969 and 1970, after intensive investigative work, OCR notified a number of states that they were in violation of Title VI for having failed to disassemble racially segregated systems of higher education. This notification carried with it no enforcement provision or penalty, but it helped set the stage for direct legal challenge.

In 1969, the Legal Defense Fund of the NAACP filed suit against the Department of Health, Education, and Welfare (HEW) for failing to initiate enforcement action against ten state higher education systems. *Adams v. Richardson* (1973) was the first suit challenging the federal government's lack of progress in dismantling state-sanctioned segregation in higher education as well as blatantly discriminatory state funding practices. In 1973, the U.S. Court of Appeals for the District of Columbia mandated that HEW enforce Title VI and ordered that the states formulate specific plans for integrating predominantly white colleges *(Adams v. Richardson)*. This ruling held that enforcement by HEW must follow in absence of voluntary compliance within a reasonable time "to the extent that their resources permit" (1973, p. 1165). In addition, the court explicitly recognized that HBCUs provided more and better training to minority group doctors, lawyers, and other professionals, and ordered the ten mandated states to improve funding for their public black colleges.

HEW accepted desegregation plans from the ten states in 1974, but in 1977 the district court held that these plans failed to meet the requirements of HEW. In *Adams v. Califano* (1977), it was also found that these plans achieved no progress in desegregation. Despite clear violation of Title VI, HEW continued to provide federal funding to these states. The court reiterated its support for HBCUs:

> These black institutions currently fulfill a crucial need and will continue to play an important role in black higher education. The process of desegregation must not place a greater burden on black institutions or black students' opportunity to receive a quality public higher education. The desegregation process should take into account the unequal status of the black colleges and the real danger that desegregation will diminish higher education opportunities for blacks. (1977, p. 120)

After this ruling it appeared that HBCUs would not be sacrificed at the altar of integration. Hailed as a milestone in desegregation law, *Adams* established that the federal government, in its pursuit of a just and fair society, had a legitimate interest in encouraging and supporting remedial efforts to ensure educational access and opportunity. Since HBCUs are remedial in nature and intended to reverse the effects of past discrimination, there could be no legitimate claim for desegregation laws to apply to them. This would not long be the case, however.

Over the next few years, the public fallout from *Adams* grew to colossal, unmanageable proportions as women's groups and advocates for the visually impaired joined to protest Title IX violations, as the Departments of Education and Labor became involved, and as the mandate of *Adams* expanded to include all fifty states. Finally, in 1987, based on the argument that the plaintiffs lacked "standing," the Federal District Court dismissed the entire litigation. According to the court's narrow definition of standing, which is the legal status necessary to sue, the plaintiffs could not proceed in their case. Although the plaintiffs could show evidence of "distinct and palpable" injury from discriminatory practices, this was the fault of the institutions and the states, not the federal government. The government, which was charged with providing financial assistance to states and institutions engaged in discriminatory practices, claimed that since it did not *cause* these "customary" practices, it could not be held responsible (*Adams v. Bennett*, 1987). The court also held that it was speculative to predict that close monitoring or withholding of federal funding would necessarily remedy the situation and pointed out that withholding money from HBCUs could be particularly damaging.

On appeal, the U.S. Court of Appeals disagreed and felt the plaintiffs did have standing to sue (*Women's Equity Action League v. Cavazos*, 1989), and it gave them a chance to argue their case. After this hearing, Judge Ruth Bader Ginsberg sided with the District Court and upheld the dismissal (*Women's Equity Action League v. Cavazos*, 1990). If *Adams* had been properly settled, HBCUs would probably have been protected from the same pressures to desegregate as white colleges (Williams, 1987). As institutions intended to remediate against racial discrimination, they would not only have been exempt from desegregation laws but they also would have been eligible for improved funding. The unusual plight of Tennessee State University would never have happened.

Tennessee State University

Located in Nashville, Tennessee State University (TSU) is a historically black college. In 1968, the University of Tennessee (historically white) proposed building a new campus in Nashville. Faculty at TSU objected. Arguing that another state university was unnecessary and provided evidence of Tennessee's continued commitment to segregation, Rita Geier, a professor at TSU, filed suit to prevent the construction. The U.S. Justice Department entered the suit, siding with TSU's position that Tennessee was perpetuating duplicate programming and a dual system of higher education in violation of Title VI. The federal government also wanted to force Tennessee to submit a desegregation plan. While the case languished over the next eleven years, Tennessee built and began operating its new facility.

Although the intent of the case was to focus attention on Tennessee's unwavering support of racial segregation, TSU, not the historically white universities (HWUs), became the target of litigation. In a 1972 ruling, Federal District Court Judge Gray stated, "The phenomenon of a black Tennessee State, so long as it exists, negates both the contention that defendants have dismantled the dual system of public higher education in Tennessee, as ordered by this court, and the contention that they are, in any realistic way, on their way to doing so" (*Geier v. Dunn*, 1972). In 1977, after failed negotiations, Gray presented his "radical remedy" (*Geier v. Blanton*, 1977). He ordered the merger of TSU and UT—Nashville, to be accomplished by 1980. Because TSU was the senior institution, the merged college would retain its name and governing board. In addition, the state was ordered to submit desegregation plans for its remaining institutions and to set up a system for monitoring progress.

When the final settlement came up for approval in 1984, the federal government, which had intervened in 1968 to force Tennessee to develop a desegregation plan, reversed itself. Under the Reagan administration, the U.S. attorney general's office argued that racially conscious remedies violated the Fourteenth Amendment unless there was evidence of discrimination against each individual. The Justice Department asserted that any black students selected for programs designed to increase access at a historically white college or professional school must prove they had personally been victimized by that institution.

The federal district court disagreed with this "victim specificity" claim and rejected it. Judge Wiseman (*Geier v. Alexander*, 1984) held that the court did not need to trace a specific child's life to prove racial discrimination when there is a preponderance of evidence that *group membership* resulted in suffering:

> In dealing with the broad and paramount issue of public education, this Court takes judicial notice of the long history of social, economic, and political oppression of blacks in Tennessee—a history marked by years of slavery followed by years of Jim Crow laws. It is the past and present state of Tennessee's universities that the Court identified as the specific instance of racial discrimination; its effects are pervasive throughout the black community, affecting practically all black men, women, and children in the state. (p. 1265)

Paradoxically, the next section of his ruling identified TSU as "the heart of the problem" of desegregation in Tennessee (p. 1266). Wiseman accused TSU of seeking to maintain its black identity, noting that black students had marched and given public statements and black faculty had written letters to the editor—all opposing the loss of TSU's historic mission. He also expressed regret that community leaders (presumably blacks) had not spoken out against this effort.

The court then set specific desegregation goals—to have 50 percent of TSU's faculty and administrators white by 1989 and 50 percent of its undergraduates white by 1993. White institutions, in contrast, were asked only to broaden access by recruiting "qualified" black high school students, but no specific goals were set other than recruiting 75 "qualified" blacks for professional school. The court did not challenge the racial identifiability of historically white colleges, nor did it provide definitions of "qualified." The Sixth Circuit Court of Appeals approved this plan in 1984 (*Geier v. Alexander*, 1984), finding it "truly ironic" that the federal government would be trying to block integration after years of promoting it. So it came to be that the centerpiece of Tennessee's desegregation plan placed the burden of desegregation not on white colleges but on an HBCU. In 1979, the first year of merged operations, TSU gained almost 3,000 students, about 50 percent of whom were white. By 1986, however, total enrollment had dropped by 1,700 (Davis, 1993), and to compensate, faculty and administrative staff were reduced. Sixty-seven percent of faculty are now black (down from 92 percent in 1976); administrators are 61 percent black (down from 85 percent). Enrollment of white students has steadily declined, dropping from 27.7 percent in 1994 to 22.1 percent in 1996, and to 18.8 percent in 1997 (Garrigan, 1997). However, TSU is the most racially integrated university in the state. In addition, it continues to educate the majority of black students in the state—56 percent of black undergraduates and 70 percent of black graduate students attend TSU (Davis, 1993).

Whites are increasingly making the thirty-mile drive to the nearest HWU, Murfreesboro's Middle Tennessee State University (MTSU).

TSU's efforts to increase white enrollment have hinged on two strategies. The first was a capital improvement project, investing more than $100 million in new building and in renovation.. The second is better financial aid for whites, who are now offered a full-ride scholarship for a high school grade-point average (GPA) of 2.5. These desegregation strategies have created considerable controversy among faculty. Some white faculty members have accused the administration of being hostile to white students: "What non–African Americans suffer at TSU is very much like what African Americans experienced in historically white institutions in the not-so-distant past" (Garrigan, 1997). Calls have been made for more advertising and recruitment directed toward whites. A number of white faculty members asked the federal government to merge TSU with MTSU (Mercer, 1994).

Black faculty members note that TSU was distinctly underfunded compared to the UT system until it became a campus for white students, at which point the money began to flow. They also note that black high school students with 2.5 GPAs are certainly not offered full scholarships at the predominantly white UT campuses.

Both the state of Tennessee and the TSU Alumni Association are now appealing for the court order to be lifted. Judge Wiseman refused to lift the order in 1997, calling such action premature. The state argues that Tennessee has eliminated all policies and procedures traceable to segregation and is moving forward at a good pace. The Alumni Association maintains that the local (white) community cannot be forced to attend or support the university. They also note that since white colleges continue to resist changing their essential character, TSU is being targeted unfairly (Mercer, 1993). George Barrett, the attorney who represents the original plaintiff in the case, thinks some attention should be paid to desegregation at the University of Tennessee at Knoxville. Its 5 percent black enrollment is below the 11 percent goal. According to Barrett, "My constant theme has been that TSU should not bear the burden of dismantling the dual system of higher education. TSU has an obligation to be as non–racially identifiable as UT, but I don't think they should bear the whole burden" (cited in Garrigan, 1997, p. 8).

TSU Through the Lens of CRT

To decide whether the case of TSU provides supportive evidence for the central tenets of CRT, certain questions must be answered.

Racism as Normal

As Judge Wiseman saw it, dual systems of education are illegal, and TSU is at the center of this problem. What made TSU problematic was its *blackness;* the *whiteness* of the UT system was not the central issue. The other state universities are presumably normal; TSU, in its blackness, is not. Thus, having historically designated white schools with white faculty and administrators to serve an exclusively white population, generously supported by a white state legislature using tax dollars from black and white citizens, although not entirely adequate, is not particularly worrisome. It is acknowledged that these schools (never identified as white) should improve blacks' access, but the problem of access is only peripheral. The assumption of whiteness as normative is so pervasive that it can hardly be seen. In contrast, blackness is highly visible; and TSU, despite its much smaller size, marginal status, and minimal funding in the state budget, became the high-profile institution targeted for change.

The federal government went one step further. It had no objection to TSU's desegregation plan, nor any concern that racial disadvantage for black students be corrected. What bothered the government was the possibility that whites could lose something in the remediation process—

that is, that the seventy-five seats for minorities in professional schools would displace the (presumably) more deserving whites.

Given its initial support of desegregation in higher education, this marked a significant turnaround. Tushnet (1996) calls this the "we've done enough" theory of school desegregation. He asserts that after whites have one of their periodic outbursts of support for assisting African Americans, they eventually decide that they have done enough and reverse themselves. This pattern, though championed by the Reagan administration, is hardly new. Its roots are located in the post–Civil War period of reconstruction. Slavery had hardly been laid to rest before whites felt they had done enough. Supreme Court Justice Bradley stated, "When a man has emerged from slavery, and by the aid of beneficent legislation has shaken off the inseparable concomitants of that state, there must be some stage in the progress of this elevation when he takes the rank of a mere citizen, and ceases to be the favorite of the law" (*Civil rights cases*, 1883, p. 25).

The Role of Social/Historic Context

The construction of TSU as the desegregation centerpiece rests on the assumption that TSU achieved its racial identifiability just as did the UT system—by choice. Although it claimed to understand the long, ugly history of segregation in the state of Tennessee, the court ultimately treated TSU as an equivalent practitioner of racial separation. In fact, HBCUs have never limited admissions by race; they exist only in reaction to black exclusion at HWUs. Overlooking this historical reality, the justice system held TSU even more culpable for segregation. Meanwhile, HWUs continue, from their stronger economic and political position, to delay or resist change indefinitely.

The allegation that white students at TSU are now treated as badly as African Americans have been treated in the past (made by Professor Broad at TSU) has generated considerable controversy. What makes his assertion so powerful is its reference to the epic dimensions of suffering visited upon blacks; elevating the experience of whites at TSU to this level not only engenders sympathy for whites but also effectively silences blacks. When blacks can no longer lay exclusive claim to the wrongs of segregation, their objections are neutralized.

Narrative

In a public debate about rights, entitlements, and discrimination, one would hope that those negatively affected would have their chance to speak. For example, when African Americans generally do not enroll in, or only briefly attend, HWUs that have been required to adopt race-neutral admissions policies as a result of desegregation cases, it seems that their reasons should be ascertained. What is their experience at these institutions? Is the campus climate hostile or welcoming? What are student, faculty, and staff attitudes toward African Americans? The court, however, did not seek these voices. Instead, students and faculty at TSU who objected to the potential loss of their university's historic mission and purpose were singled out for criticism and contempt. Judge Wiseman admonished:

> This Court does not live in a vacuum. During the pendency of this matter there has been a march of TSU students on the courthouse, public statements by student leaders, and letters to the editor by faculty members all urging and insisting upon the retention of TSU's black identification. Regrettably, this Court has not observed any public statements by community leaders pointing out the paradoxical inconsistency of this position. (*Geier v. Alexander*, 1984, p. 1267)

The story of why black students chose to attend TSU, why alumni value it, and why the administration is unwilling to give up its blackness is not heard. Not only do their experiences not help inform mediation strategies, they are taken as examples of recalcitrance.

Interest Convergence

Assessing interest convergence requires an attempted tally of black gains versus those of whites; or more precisely, what interests of blacks were allowed as long as white interests were also promoted. TSU gained long-needed money for maintenance and construction of its physical plant. This financial support has also improved programming, teaching, and research. The business school now offers a top-ranked program. In addition, seventy-five black students have access to professional schools on other state campuses, including schools of law, medicine, pharmacy, and dental training. Black high school students now have letters of recruitment sent to them from white colleges.

White colleges retain their historic mission and status. Although they are asked to broaden access, they are not required to challenge their essential whiteness. Concerns around racial identifiability can be immediately referred to the "problem" institution: TSU. And since TSU is unlikely to change its commitment to its African American heritage, this subterfuge might go on for years. Not only do whites remain in control of state funding for all institutions, but white students willing to go to TSU are offered the advantage of a free education in return for an academic performance that would not entitle blacks to a full ride anywhere. Whites also remain in control of the standards of admissions "qualification," which can be (and have been) set in race-neutral language that effectively excludes most blacks.

One outcome of interest convergence is the unlikely political alliance of TSU's Alumni Association and the state. To the extent that both seek to preserve and defend their institutions, their interests converge. Like most organizations, both seek to grow and thrive. TSU and other HBCUs will likely persist in their stance against state-sponsored solutions that could result in their eradication (Davis, 1993; Jones, 1993). Similarly, HWUs will likely resist structural changes in governance, structure, or curriculum that would affect their racial identifiability.

Summary

The TSU case not only illustrates and confirms the tenets of CRT but also demonstrates CRT's power as an explanatory model. The counterpoint, however, is this: If you look at this situation from the viewpoint of the court, it is upholding undeniably valuable legal principles: (1) segregated higher education must be eliminated; (2) admissions requirements must be race-neutral; and (3) any remaining racial identifiability (at least on the UT campuses) must only result from the personal choices of students, which the state cannot control. In fact, TSU is seen as a model for desegregation by some (Patterson, 1994). Yet CRT scholars criticize the court for being racist.

Taking the good faith of individual judges as given, what has gone wrong? CRT asserts that the problem lies in the processes and methods of legal scholarship itself, where neutrality and choice are the guiding values. Paradoxically, centering these values serves to negate the importance of historical context. By mentioning but refusing to act on the full ramifications of certain social and economic realities faced by blacks in Tennessee for hundreds of years (segregated residential patterns, educational deficiencies resulting from underfunded and stigmatized primary and secondary state schools, and so on), the judicial system reveals no contextualized picture. Importantly, the flip side—the social and educational advantages accorded to whites—is missed entirely. When such disparities are rendered invisible, equality is assumed. Thus, black and white students chose colleges on the basis of personal choice. This freedom justifies, at least on white campuses, the fact that few blacks attend.

In analyzing the principles of neutrality and choice as applied to desegregation litigation, Brown (1992) points out that the court's fallacious assumption is that blacks and whites occupy equal positions in society. Then, by a process termed "disaggregation," the court disengages the case from its historic context, removes (or ignores) the voice of people negatively affected by racism, and refuses to acknowledge the deeply held beliefs of black inferiority and white superiority that drive state resistance to integration. The principle of neutrality dictates that blacks cannot name their reality; the principle of choice justifies further racial inequality and segregation. What in fact happens, however, is that white students have their choices widened to include black colleges, whereas black students continue to face a hostile environment at white colleges. In short, white choice trumps that of blacks.

The challenges that CRT places before the court are now apparent—to acknowledge racism, understand cases in their historical/social context, listen to the realities of the lives of black people, and see how even well-meaning whites can unconsciously reinforce and perpetuate a system designed to protect majority interests. In the case of TSU, at least, CRT's argument is effective. Here, the theory gains force.

Critiques of CRT

Although this example suggests that CRT is helpful for understanding the nature of some litigation on desegregation in education, its usefulness in resolving the general dilemmas of segregation has not yet been demonstrated. Important issues and obstacles remain.

Narrative

Narrative is a methodological format that has been used in legal scholarship for years and has only become a focus of criticism since CRT embraced it (Johnson, 1994). Farber and Sherry (1995) have disputed the value and applicability of narrative on several grounds. One is the issue of verifiability: That is, can the stories people tell be proven as truth? Farber and Sherry question whether narrative meets the standards of traditional legal scholarship, asserting that it fails to explicate through the usual methods of fact, logic, and linear reasoning.

A related concept, the unique voice of color, is relatively new and has also been questioned. According to Farber and Sherry, CRT has not clearly conceptualized a "black" voice or proven its existence. Kennedy (1995) agrees, maintaining that meritocratic legal scholarship is indifferent to the color of the scholar. Traditional legal methods rely more on universality and typicality. In his critique, Litowitz (1997) says that the job of lawyers is to look beyond stories to issues of doctrine, policy, and argument. He admonishes minority law professors to produce "exhaustively researched law review articles" rather than to present themselves as storytellers without analytic skills (p. 523). Critics of CRT are concerned that narrative and rhetoric may replace legal doctrine in a domain that values abstract and formal reasoning over empathy and context (Kennedy, 1995). They also object to the supposition that members of the judiciary could have different opinions based on their race, a possibility that seems (to some) unlikely in a neutral and objective arena such as a courtroom (Litowitz, 1997).

This controversy may have less to do with CRT than with the broader debate within both legal and educational research as to what constitutes valid scholarship. Because there are no universal standards for scholarship in general, Johnson (1994) argues that neither traditional methods nor nontraditional methods (such as narratives) can be said to meet those standards. It may be that both approaches can explicate legal (and educational) principles: one through traditional, empirical, and apersonal means; the other through experience. Johnson believes that neither one can be shown to be better or worse than the other, just different (1994). As the academy struggles to find answers to the complex and multilayered issues confronting a pluralistic and multiracial/multiethnic society, perhaps both methods can contribute. Indeed, perhaps CRT should be informed by both qualitative and narrative research methodologies. Because the stakes are high, however, this debate remains far from resolution.

Racism as Normal

Another concern for the future of CRT relates to its assumption that racism is normative cultural behavior. Since many whites have embraced the "color-blind" perspective, constructs built upon the premise that racism is a normal activity in American society will be resisted. Because it is less painful and upsetting, most whites simply deny, usually not maliciously, that racism exists (Tatum, 1994). This barrier may prove so intransigent as to limit the potential of CRT.

Minorities are commonly accused of balkanization when they challenge majority interests and perspectives. Litowitz (1997) levels the same charge against CRT, arguing that its focus on ethnic concerns has a "splintering" effect on what he sees as the common interests (p. 519). CRT scholars would rightly point out that this society has a long and painful history of balkanizing people based on race, gender, class, and other factors of group membership; identifying oppression does not create balkanization. To suggest otherwise is disingenuous, at best.

Stereotyping of Scholars

CRT's manner of describing whites and blacks suggests they think and act in monolithic, predictable, and homogeneous ways. Kennedy (1995) has objected to the stereotyping of scholarship by race and rejects the assertions that academicians write/think/act in uniform ways that are racially determined. Litowitz (1997) is more direct: "It simply will not do to say that *all* whites are equally complicitous in this country's legacy of racism and that *all* blacks are innocent victims" (p. 527). CRT does not argue the agency of individuals. It does speak to race as a social construction, and it critiques systems that promote and sustain majority interests. More specifically, CRT would assert that although individual whites are "innocent," they do, by no personal intent, benefit from dominant group membership in numerous ways.

It can be argued, however, that as institutions of higher education become more diverse, with African Americans and other nonwhites increasingly represented as faculty members, administrators, and admissions officers in HWUs, historically "white" goals may be altered. For example, it is not uncommon for university presidents and faculty members at HWUs to have adopted the goal of attracting a multiracial student body on its own merits (On the importance of diversity, 1997).

Interest Convergence

At once provocative and compelling, interest convergence has yet to be fully problematized. The theory of interest convergence raises a host of questions: What does it imply? Is its only effect one of fatalism (Litowitz, 1997)? Can it inform strategies for achieving racial justice? Is it possible for disparate groups to find common interests, and in so doing, to forge an antiracist agenda? Can the theory of interest convergence inform remedies that include other groups (Araujo, 1997)?

Interest convergence engenders considerable debate, with liberals naturally reluctant to surrender their sense of pride when pointing to civil rights progress and conservatives unwilling to admit naked self-interest. At least in the abstract, many from both camps embrace the broad goals of racial equity. There is, however, convincing evidence that problems arise for many whites when black progress engenders a personal cost to positions of power and privilege (Ladson-Billings and Tate, 1995). As Bell states, "Whites simply cannot envision the personal responsibility and the potential sacrifice inherent in [the] conclusion that true equality for blacks will require the surrender of racism-granted privileges for whites" (1992, p. 22). Even morally compelled believers in racial equality, when faced with their son's rejection from law school, might look for a scapegoat. More likely than not, the target will not be the other beneficiaries of affirmative action such as white women, or the "legacy" admits of alumni and university benefactors, but the handful of African Americans assumed to be unqualified and undeserving.

Definitions of "white" interests contain additional problems around assumptions of homogeneity. *Anti*racist activism among whites is not a new phenomenon; its roots extend deep into American abolitionist history (Loewen, 1995). Although its impact has often been overshadowed by a variety of forces, its relevance has continued to assert itself. Currently a number of whites, including educators, are deconstructing whiteness and critiquing educational institutions from a white perspective (Sleeter, 1993). In addition, the psychological, social, and economic impact of whiteness has been advanced by racial identity development theory (Helms, 1990; Tatum, 1994) and holds considerable promise for promoting cross-racial dialogue. CRT would benefit from white narratives that examine and critique white privilege in its varied forms. White opposition to racial oppression could serve as a valuable strategy for challenging other whites to actively oppose racism.

CRT has received support from white legal scholars such as Brooks and Newborn (1994), who acknowledge that CRT brings an "outsider" perspective with both new knowledge and fresh insight that has the potential to transform (p. 845). It is possible that the acknowledgment of interest convergence will have positive effects if educational quality, not desegregation *per se*, is made a central and guiding vision. Legal strategies, using the goals of *Brown,* have ended up too narrowly attached to achieving "correct" numbers rather than also attending to issues of educational quality (Bell, 1980). Racial balance *per se* is no guarantee of an adequate education for blacks or whites. Clearly, the interests of blacks and whites in quality of education must be linked, since Southern legislatures will not likely take the concerns of African Americans in higher education seriously unless white interests are also promoted. As a strategy for resolving future cases against segregation and a possible alternative to protracted litigation, mediation—supported by a deeper public awareness of and appreciation for interest convergence—could be very effective. However, much remains to be done in this area, with respect to public higher education.

Conclusion

CRT offers considerable explanatory power for the racial separations that have plagued our past and continue to compromise our hope for equitable education. Its usefulness in mainstream dialogue may be limited to the extent that many will not accept its assumptions; I anticipate critique from both the left and right. Theorists, researchers, and practitioners who agree to "try it on" will have the opportunity to test whether or not CRT has additional explanatory or predictive powers, and perhaps more importantly, whether or not it can inform strategies for action across the color line.

There may come a day when all Americans will be able to pursue higher education without concern for protecting or defending race-based positions. Such an educational system will move smoothly from its segregated past to reveal itself as the genuinely multiracial and multicultural ideal that has long been sought. It will be a long time before we see this. While we are waiting, however, those of us who seek direction on the road to racial reconciliation will have to find it ourselves by openly debating, discussing, and, yes, dialoguing.

References

Adams v. Bennett, 675 F. Supp. 668 (D.D.C. 1987).

Adams v. Califano, 430 F. Supp. 118 (D.D.C. 1977).

Adams v. Richardson, 480 F. 2d 1159 (1973).

Anderson, J. D. (1988). *The education of Blacks in the South, 1860–1935*. Chapel Hill: University of North Carolina Press.

Araujo, R. J. (1997). Critical race theory: Contributions to and problems for race relations. *Gonzaga Law Review, 32* (3), 537–575.

Bell, D. (1980). *Brown v. Board of Education* and the interest-convergence dilemma. *Harvard Law Review, 93*, 518.

_____. (1987). Introduction to *Equal opportunity in higher education and the Black Public College: The era of separate but equal*, by Gil Kujovich. *Minnesota Law Review, 72* (1), 23–27.

_____. (1990). Racial realism—After we're gone: Prudent speculations on America in a post-racial epoch. *St. Louis Law Journal, 34*, 393.

_____. (1992). *Faces at the bottom of the well: The permanence of racism*. New York: Basic Books.

Bond, J. (1991). Reconstruction and the Southern movement for civil rights—Then and now. *Teachers College Record, 93* (2), 221–235.

Brooks, R. L., and Newborn, M. J. (1994). Critical race theory and classical liberal civil rights scholarship: A distinction without a difference. *California Law Review, 82* (4), 787–845.

Brown v. Board of Education, 347 U.S. 483 (1954).

Brown, W. R. (1992). The convergence of neutrality and choice: The limits of the state's affirmative duty to provide equal educational opportunity. *Tennessee Law Review, 60*, 63–133.

Calmore, J. O. (1995a). Critical race theory, Archie Shepp, and fire music: Securing an authentic intellectual life in a multicultural world. In K. Crenshaw, N. Gotanda, G. Peller, and K. Thomas (Eds.), *Critical race theory: The key writings that formed the movement* (pp. 315–329). New York: New Press.

_____. (1995b). Racialized space and the culture of segregation: "Hewing a stone of hope from a mountain of despair." *University of Pennsylvania Law Review, 143*, 1233–1273.

Civil rights cases, 109 U.S. 3 (1883).

Crenshaw, K. W. (1988). Race, reform, and retrenchment: Transformation and legitimation in antidiscrimination law. *Harvard Law Review, 101* (7), 1331–1387.

_____. (1995). The intersection of race and gender. In K. W. Crenshaw, N. Gotanda, G. Peller, and K. Thomas (Eds.), *Critical race theory: The key writings that formed the movement* (pp. 357–383). New York: New Press.

Davis, E. B. (1993). Desegregation in higher education: Twenty-five years of controversy from Geier to Ayers. *Journal of Law and Education, 22* (4), 519–524.

Delgado, R. (1989). Legal storytelling: Storytelling for oppositionists and others: A plea for narrative. *Michigan Law Review, 87,* 2411.

Delgado, R. (Ed.). (1995). *Critical race theory: The cutting edge.* Philadelphia: Temple University Press.

Dudziak, M. L. (1988). Desegregation as a Cold War imperative. *Stanford Law Review, 41,* 61.

Farber, D. A., and Sherry, S. (1995). Telling stories out of school: An essay on legal narratives. In R. Delgado (Ed.), *Critical race theory: The cutting edge* (pp. 283–292). Philadelphia: Temple University Press.

Foner, P. S. (1970). *W.E.B. DuBois speaks: Speeches and addresses, 1890–1919.* New York: Pathfinder.

Garrigan, L. M. (1997). Lightening up. *Nashville Scene* [On-Line]. Available: http://www.weeklywire.com/ww/nash_cover.html

Geier v. Alexander, 593 F. Supp. 1263 (1984).

Geier v. Blanton, 427 F. Supp. 644, 661 (M.D. Tenn. 1977).

Geier v. Dunn, 337 F. Supp. 573, 580, 581 (M.D. Tenn. 1972).

Geier v. University of Tennessee, 597 F. 2d 1056, 1065 (6th Cir. 1979).

Harris, C. I. (1993). Whiteness as property. *Harvard Law Review, 106,* 1721.

Helms, J. E. (1990). *Black and white identity: Theory, research, and practice.* Westport, CT: Greenwood Press.

hooks, b. (1994). *Teaching to transgress.* New York: Routledge.

Humphries, F. S. (1994). A short history of blacks in higher education. *The Journal of Blacks in Higher Education, 6,* 57.

Johnson, A. M. (1994). Defending the use of narrative and giving content to the voice of color: Rejecting the imposition of process theory in legal scholarship. *Iowa Law Review, 79* (4), 803–852.

Jones, D. K. (1993). An education of their own: The precarious position of publicly supported black colleges after *United States v. Fordice. Journal of Law and Education, 22* (4), 485–517.

Kennedy, R. (1995). Racial critiques of legal academia. In R. Delgado (Ed.), *Critical race theory: The cutting edge* (pp. 432–450). Philadelphia: Temple University Press.

Kujovich, G. (1987). Equal opportunity in higher education and the black public college: The era of separate but equal. *Minnesota Law Review, 72,* 30–172.

Ladson-Billings, G., and Tate, W. F. (1995). Toward a critical theory of education. *Teachers College Record, 97,* 47–68.

Lawrence, C. R., Matsuda, M. J., Delgado, R., and Crenshaw, K. W. (1993). *Words that wound: Critical race theory, assaultive speech, and the First Amendment.* Boulder: Westview Press.

Litowitz, D. E. (1997). Some critical thoughts on critical race theory. *Notre Dame Law Review, 72* (2), 503–529.

Loewen, J. W. (1995). *Lies my teacher told me.* New York: Simon and Schuster.

McLaurin v. Oklahoma State Regents for Higher Education. 339 U.S. 637 (1950).

McNeil, G. R. (1983). *Groundwork: Charles Hamilton Houston and the struggle for civil rights.* Philadelphia: University of Pennsylvania Press.

Mercer, J. (1993). The ambiguous success of desegregation at Tennessee State U. *Chronicle of Higher Education, 39* (35), A32(2).

_____. (1994). Contradictory proposals offered in Tennessee's college-desegregation case. *Chronicle of Higher Education, 40* (38), A24(1).

Missouri ex rel. Gaines v. Canada, 305 U.S. 337 (1938).

Murray v. Maryland, 182 A. 590 (1936): 169 Md. 478 (1937).

Olivas, M. (1990). The chronicles, my grandfather's stories, and immigration law: The slave traders chronicle and racial history. *St. Louis Law Journal, 34*, 425.

Omi, M., and Winant, H. (1994). *Racial formation in the United States: From the 1960s to the 1990s* (2nd ed.). New York: Routledge.

On the importance of diversity in University admissions. (1997). *New York Times* (24 April), p. A17.

Patterson, C. M. (1994). Desegregation as a two-way street: The aftermath of *United States v. Fordice. Cleveland State Law Review, 42*, 377–433.

Plessy v. Ferguson, 163 U.S. 537 (1896).

Rubin, E. L. (1996). The new legal process, the synthesis of discourse, and the microanalysis of institutions. *Harvard Law Review, 109* (6), 1393–1438.

Scheurich, J. J., and Young, M. D. (1997). Coloring epistemologies: Are our research epistemologies racially biased? *Educational Researcher, 26* (4), 4–16.

Sipuel v. Oklahoma State Board of Regents, 332 U.S. 631 (1948).

Sleeter, C. E. (1993). How white teachers construct race. In C. McCarthy and W. Crichlow (Eds.), *Race, identity, and representation in education* (pp. 157–172). New York: Routledge.

Stanfield, J. H. (1994). Ethnic modeling in qualitative research. In N. K. Denzin and Y. S. Lincoln (Eds.), *Handbook of qualitative research* (pp. 175–188). Thousand Oaks, CA: Sage.

Sweatt v. Painter, 339 U.S. 629 (1950).

Tate, W. F., IV. (1997). Critical race theory in education: History, theory, and implications. In M. W. Apple (Ed.), *Review of research in education*, vol. 22, pp. 195–250. Washington, DC: American Educational Research Association.

Tatum, B. D. (1994). Teaching white students about racism: The search for white allies and the restoration of hope. *Teachers College Record, 95* (4), 462–476.

Tushnet, M. V. (1996). The "we've done enough" theory of school desegregation. *Howard Law Journal, 39* (3), 767–779.

Ware, L. (1994). The most visible vestige: Black colleges after *Fordice. Boston College Law Review, 35*, 619, 633–680.

West, C. (1995). Foreword. In K. Crenshaw, N. Gotanda, G. Peller, and K. Thomas (Eds.), *Critical race theory: The key writings that formed the movement* (pp. xi–xii). New York: New Press.

Williams, J. L., III. (1987). *Desegregating America's colleges and universities: Title VI regulation of higher education.* New York: Teachers College Press.

Williams, P. J. (1991). *The alchemy of race and rights: Diary of a law professor.* Cambridge: Harvard University Press.

Wilson, R. (1994). The participation of African Americans in American higher education. In M. J. Justiz, R. Wilson, and L. G. Bjork (Eds.), *Minorities in higher education* (pp. 195–209). Phoenix, AZ: Oryx Press.

Wing, A. K. (1996). Critical race feminism and the international human rights of
women in Bosnia, Palestine, and South Africa: Issues for LatCrit Theory. *University of Miami Inter American Law Review*, 28 (2), 337–360.

Women's Equity Action League v. Cavazos, 879 F. 2d 880 (D.C. Cir. 1989).

_____, 906 F. 2d 742 (D.C. Cir. 1990).

9

Negotiating Borders of Consciousness in the Pursuit of Education: Identity Politics and Gender of Second-Generation Korean American Women

LENA DOMYUNG CHOE

In a keynote address at the first national conference on Korean American studies, Elaine Kim recounted how some people respond when she relates stories about various kinds of racial bigotry she and her family have experienced. "Sometimes, white people said to me, 'At least you are not black,' or 'You should be grateful that you are not black'" (Kim, 1997, p. 71). These sentiments express the ambiguous position in which Korean Americans,[1] and all Asian Americans,[2] are situated: Neither black nor white, yet nevertheless an *eternal other*.[3] The dichotomous black-white racial paradigm is established and entrenched in the American psyche. And in recent historical times, Asian Americans have been elevated to the precarious status of *honorary whites*. The perpetuation of generalized stereotypes of Asian Americans, such as the *model minority* and its derivatives, have further contributed to the *deracing* and the absence of Asian Americans in the dialogue regarding race and ethnicity.

Currently, however, the voice of second-generation Korean American attorney Angela Oh, the only Asian American member of the advisory board to President Clinton's Initiative on Race, *is* challenging U.S. conventional notions of civil rights by advocating a new paradigm of race relations that encompasses all individuals and groups:

> That paradigm is one that must be multifaceted in terms of race, culture,
> and generational differences. It must strike a balance between individual
> and social responsibility and, finally, it must reflect appreciation for the fact
> that advancing race relations is a new frontier. (Oh, 1998, p. 9)

Literary scholar Shirley Hune (1993), along with other scholars, has
noted that Asian American policymakers, researchers, and politicians
alike recognize the necessity of a shift in paradigm from exclusion to inclusion. The racial formation theory of Omi and Winant (1994), which asserts, in general, that race needs to be understood as a sociohistorical
concept, is paramount to understanding the position of Asian Americans;
however, to deconstruct the construction of race [and gender] is not to
deny the determining effect these categories have on our worldviews. As
pervasive as this current, limiting paradigm is, how can we begin to tran-
scend this ostensible archetype in the educational context?

Critical race theory is a useful tool for reconsidering this racial paradigm. Richard Delgado (1990) has argued for the need of people of color
to "name one's own reality." With the understanding that "reality is socially constructed" and that "stories are a powerful means for destroying
and changing mind-sets," Delgado (1995), along with other critical race
theorists, uncovered and challenged the processes by which racial paradigms have been, and are, manifested within legal discourse. In addition,
he afforded legitimacy to the multiple voices of others, including Asian
Americans.

This process of deconstructing in order to reconstruct a portrayal that
reflects the complexity of Asian Americans' lives, as well as those of other
people of color, requires contextualization. All too often ahistorical understandings of racial representations distort reality. The overlooking
and the limited documentation of significant historical events perpetuate
existing perceptions in addition to silencing[4] oppositional voices. Despite
the momentum of multiculturalism, the history of racial oppression (social and legal) against Asian Americans, as well as information in general
about Asian Americans, continues to be treated inadequately by mainstream history courses and books, thus perpetuating limited knowledge
in the classroom with regard to Asian Americans.

Because of the deracialized Asian American voice, oral histories and
other narratives function to enhance critical race theory scholarship on
the Asian American experience. Oral histories further provide epistemological significance to race-based theory. As Lawrence (1995) pointedly
argues, the power of the narrative "to build bridges of validation, understanding, and empathy [is what] makes it so powerful as an intellectual
and political tool" (p. 344). Moreover, as historian Paul Thompson (1978)
stated: "Oral history gives history back to the people in their own words.

And in giving a past, it also helps them towards a future of their own making" (p. 226).

This essay analyzes the oral histories of Jin Bai, Susie Jang, Lynda Lee, and Eun Hee Park, all second-generation Korean American women.[5] The stories these young women tell of their schooling experiences permit us to recognize the limited and distorted perceptions of Asian Americans that dominate the academy. Through the voices of these articulate undergraduate and graduate students recalling their secondary school experience in the Chicago area and surrounding suburbs, the unidimensional perceptions of Asian Americans are challenged, and the complex borders that a Korean American woman must negotiate to be successful in obtaining higher education become apparent.

Shifting of Consciousness

Essentialist notions of identity politics typically have obscured intragroup differences, and Asian Americans are not exempt from this predicament. The Asian American "intragroup" is complicated by the diversity of Asian ethnicities it comprises (with a range of histories, immigration patterns, cultures, religions, and languages), as well as by gender differences. Kimberlé Williams Crenshaw (1995) describes the tension experienced by women of color as they are often confronted with the decision to "choose" between feminist legal and political efforts or antiracist efforts, which are too frequently mapped on "mutually exclusive terrains" (p. 357). Crenshaw's analysis of how *structural intersectionality* and *political intersectionality* situate women of color within overlapping structures of subordination is beneficial to understanding the lives of Asian American women generally, and in this case, of Korean American women in particular. Critical race theory seeks to expose the complexity of Asian American voices and to unmask the stereotype that lumps all Asians together as one *Oriental* voice.

Oral histories do not represent one voice singing a single note but a chorus of intricate harmony, responding in synchrony to rhythms of consciousness. Within the racial category of Asian Americans, each individual lives in a world created and adapted to juggle daily with multiple identities that are reflexive socially, politically, and culturally. These identities are fluid within the individual lives of Asian Americans. What Mari Matsuda (1996) refers to as a *shifting of consciousness,* as a woman of color negotiates multiple worlds, depends very much on the structural and political context in which she finds herself. In their study of second-language learning among adolescent Chinese immigrant students, McKay and Wong (1996) recognize the agency that these students had in negotiating multiple identities in an environment of asymmetrical power relations, despite the failure of teachers to observe this *shifting of consciousness*. Matsuda's (1996) assertion that Asian American communities are like "bamboo—bending but never breaking when the typhoons come" (p. 161) is definitely pertinent to the individual lives of second-generation Korean American women as well. Themes of strength, resiliency, and survival reverberate in the lives of many young Korean American women as they negotiate various structural and political spheres. Jin Bai described this phenomenon in a personal interview with me:

> It's funny—for some reason I've always identified with blacks. Because I don't know enough about Korean Americans. [There isn't much offered in high school regarding Korean Americans.] In college, especially in feminism, because I've done papers before, or women artists were black. Just because of that dual identity that they have. (Bai, 1996)

Despite the lack of a Korean/Asian American role model in her past educational environments, Jin illustrates her flexibility in adapting to the resources available to her by finding common ground in the understanding of the *dual identities* of African American women. And, as indicated in the previous statement, this *shifting of consciousness* between what appear at times to be very different worlds resonates within the lives of many second-generation Korean American women.

Eun Hee Park demonstrated this shifting of consciousness in discussing with me the significance of her name in relation to her identity: "[Although given a Korean first name when born in South Korea, Eun Hee immigrated to the United States at the age of 1 with her family.] My parents changed my name officially to . . . [an American name]. But in September, I legally changed to my Korean name again." Eun Hee's name is very symbolic of her recognition of her racial and ethnic identity. Her name both reflects her understanding of the multiple worlds and identities that she must contend with and represents her choice of the identity she wants to publicly dominate. Eun Hee's choice of her name also served as a form of resistance to some of her past experiences in school.

The multiple worlds with which second-generation Korean American women need to contend are further complicated in regard to race because of additional dynamics. Through parents and the transnational nature of the Korean American community, the domain of second-generation Korean Americans expands to accommodate racial and ethnic identities within the parameters of the "Koreanness" of traditional first-generation Korean cultural values, the "Americanness" of Asian American panethnicity and awareness of the American politics of race, and the "Korean Americanness," or bicultural development, of a growing Korean

American identity. For Korean American women, it is at times difficult to maneuver between the boundaries of identity politics and gender. Although it may seem that I am disconnecting these identities, the two elements in praxis are multiple and interconnected; as Wing (1997) articulates, "[our layered experience is] multiplicative" (p. 31).

Koreanness:
Nationalism, Transnationalism, and Gender

The fact that second-generation Korean Americans are still living in the period dominated by first-generation Koreans is essential to understanding all Korean Americans, for it means that the heritage from traditional Korea cannot be ignored. According to the 1990 U.S. Census (U.S. Dept. of Commerce, 1993), almost three-quarters of Korean Americans are foreign-born.

In the 1980s, the Korean American population more than doubled, with approximately 35,000 Koreans legally immigrating to the United States each year. It can therefore be concluded that the proportion of foreign-born Koreans will remain high for some time (Hing, 1993). The Koreans immigrating during this time period are less educated than the immigrants who arrived in the period just after the passage of the 1965 immigration law (U.S. Dept. of Commerce, 1993, p. 84). Since 1990, however, the number of Koreans immigrating to the United States has steadily decreased.[6] Given the recent extreme economic instability of South Korea, it would not be surprising to see immigration to the U.S. begin to increase again.[7] Nevertheless, many Korean Americans still attempt to maintain a strong connection to Korea.

Although the phenomenon of transnationalism is often alluded to loosely and without specificity by social scientists, a discussion of transnationalism in regard to Korean Americans helps to shed some light on the experience of the second generation.[8] In an obvious institutionalized demonstration of this desire for movement across national borders, a section of Lawrence Avenue in Chicago officially had its name changed to Seoul Drive at the request of the Korean businesses and the Korean American community residing along that stretch. South Korean newspapers, videos, music, and other media are sold in Korean grocery stores and other small businesses owned by Koreans. The transnationalism of the Korean American community is not confined to the lives of Korean immigrants living in the U.S. but also has implications for the lives of second-generation Korean Americans.[9] It is not uncommon for parents to send their 1.5- and second-generation Korean American children to participate in collegiate summer school language programs in South Korea—basically, to visit family and to foster a deeper connection to their parents' homeland.

Perhaps the silences of Korean Americans can be explained within the context of transnationalism. As Chon (1995) suggests, these silences "signify the actively engaged listening of those positioned between cultures, who must exert enormous energy to understand and mediate among two or more different cultural sign systems" (p. 11). Korean Americans have been interconnected and somewhat mobile, and their identities have been fluid, multiple, and contextualized.

In addition, as second-generation Korean American women assert their agency by adjusting their *consciousness*, this *multiplicative* existence serves as a method of survival in a competitive educational system. To some extent, survival knowledge is attributed partially to Korean culture itself. As Lynda Lee disclosed during my interview with her:

> Because of continually domination over Korea, Koreans have learned to survive. Even if they outwardly survive, assimilate, it does not mean they internalize it. It starts before coming to the U.S. Their perceptions are shaped before coming here. They are *nunchi balla*.[10] Koreans have learned quickly what to do to survive. (Lee, 1994)

Unfortunately, within the generations of grandparents and parents, Korea has experienced Japanese subjugation, a dreadful war dividing the nation in half, and political unrest as well as economic growth and more recently economic instability. Despite Korea's historical turmoil, "Koreans have remained remarkably homogeneous, so much so in fact that they use the same term, *Han minjok*, to mean both 'Korean nation' and 'Korean race,' and, indeed, do not clearly differentiate between the two ideas" (Eckert, Lee, Lew, Robinson, and Wagner, 1990, p. 407).

Post–Korean War Korean nationalism has served as a cultural factor in the economic growth of South Korea; it has been an ideology of popular mobilization and legitimacy during the hardships and social disruption of South Korea's rapid economic growth. Many Korean immigrants (mostly the parents) were raised and shaped in this culture of nationalism, which is also transmitted, directly and indirectly, to their children through observation and by practice. Hurh, Kim, and Kim's (1979) study of Korean assimilation patterns found that an overwhelming majority of immigrants considered it important to teach Korean language, history, morals, and customs to their children. These findings seem to suggest the tenacity with which Korean immigrants preserve their ethnic identity and their desire to perpetuate it through generations. Lynda Lee described the significance of continuing Korean cultural values:

> I prefer to marry a Korean man. I would like to keep the 100-percent Korean bloodline going. There is no logic to this. When I consider the centuries of

the Korean bloodline, I feel too much guilt to break the Korean bloodline. I don't want to disappoint my grandfather. And it's also for the sake of the children's identity. There is less strife to marry a Korean man. It's easier to understand without explanation. . . . I like a man who can speak Korean fluently. It's sexy. *Fobby*.[11] My Korean friends used to call me a *Twinkie*.[12] I like a man who is respectful of elders. I want kids to have these ideas. . . . I want, I like the physical closeness of Koreanness. I want someone who thinks of other people. (Lee, 1994)

In addition, since the arrival of the first Korean immigrants, they have demonstrated an interest in maintaining Korean language and culture by establishing Korean language classes for children and schools as early as 1906 (W. Kim, 1971). These classes have evolved into Korean weekend schools that provide instruction in Korean language, arts, history, music, dance, and/or tae kwon do, which are generally not taught in American public or private schools. P. Choi (1991) observed that the Korean weekend schools try to instill a sense of Korean ethnic identity in their students and at the same time to help them adapt to mainstream American life so as to become successful Korean American citizens—comprehending the complexity of life for Korean Americans. This desire to maintain a Korean ethnic identity contradicts the widespread perception by Asian Americans that assimilation is a process in which individuals take on dominant cultural characteristics and cultural identity and move into the dominant society, thereby relinquishing their own ethnic identification.

The pressures of adapting to two cultures simultaneously are most pronounced for immigrant youths or for those whose parents were immigrants (Berry, 1980; Phelan, Davidson, and Cao, 1991). As is somewhat apparent in the following excerpt, generational differences can lead to confusion and cultural misunderstandings. As Eun Hee Park recounted:

If I was in Korea, I would've seen my parents as normal and not so odd. My parents don't listen to me much. They just want me to be an obedient daughter. They never support me emotionally like you see other American kids. . . . I used to wonder why my parents were so psychotic. It wasn't until I met other Koreans that I realized it was Korean. (Park, 1994)

If the cultural values and behaviors at home are not necessarily recognized or valued among peers or at school, children and youth may experience daily conflict and stress. Despite this particular initially negative experience, children and youth learn to adapt and develop an understanding of their experiences. Moreover, validation and even minimal recognition of coexisting cultures by the family, peers, or school can facilitate this development.

Although nationalism can be advantageous and family and cultural lineage are significant to an individual's sense of belonging and history, this does not imply that there are no weaknesses in the cultural values and norms of nationalism. As Chungmoo Choi (1998) wrote, "In the sacred mission of anti-colonial nationalism, the object of which is often to restore national masculinity, women of the colonized nation are doubly oppressed" (p. 14). Although Korean culture continues to be influenced by many social, religious, and philosophical systems of thought—Buddhism, shamanism, Confucianism—it is recognized that Confucian virtues of loyalty, filial piety, and chastity still constitute a dominant value system within Korean culture (Eckert, Lee, Lew, Robinson, and Wagner, 1990). The Confucian House Rules, prepared in 1468 but still embedded within current cultural practices, prescribe to Koreans the essence of the moral capabilities of the Confucian society to encompass the domestic and public realms (Lee and de Bary, 1997). The domestic domain of the Korean woman is clearly defined by the role of obedient wife, and she has an even more limited role to play in the public domain. In addition, many Korean Americans attend Korean Christian churches, mostly of conservative religious doctrine, further defining the status and role of women.

Nonetheless, the women's movement in South Korea to revise family law has moved forward toward eliminating the discrimination against women in marriage, family, and kinship that has been rooted in a constructed tradition of official nationalism (Moon, 1998). Who knows how these changes will impact the cultural values in Korean society and hence in Korean American society?

Traditional values still filter into the lives of second-generation Korean American women residing within U.S. borders. The separate private and public domains for women are evident in Eun Hee Park's (interview) remarks:

> I have an older brother. And we were treated really differently. He was always pushed academically [he was in medical school at the time], but I was not. Actually, my mom is quite sexist. My brother only had to mow the lawn. I had to do everything else. All the housework. My brother was an overachiever and an ideal student. I was only a mediocre student. He got to go out later and had more leeway. I was never given any leeway. My brother got to take tae kwon do.[13] I really wanted to take tae kwon do. But I wasn't allowed because they didn't like the idea of boys touching me.

It is not uncommon for Asian American women, including Korean Americans, to face socialization into traditional roles both at home and at school. Although the women I interviewed were encouraged to pursue a college education and degrees beyond college, it happened that these women pursued advancement in *traditional female* occupations. And, as in Mau's (1995) responses from a sample of Asian American girls, many indicated that the proper role of females is still to cook, clean, and watch their younger brothers and sisters. Emphasis is often placed on the private domain for women regardless of their potential in the public realm. This conclusion is supported by Eun-Young Kim's (1993) study of career choice among second-generation Korean Americans. Kim found that the powerful influence of gender identity on career identity is also often demonstrated when Korean American female students who initially plan professional careers drop those plans after graduation in order to prepare for marriage. Kim concluded that the pattern of career choice reflects the cultural model of their first-generation parents.

Some aspects of traditional Korean culture encourage all Korean Americans to achieve academically, but this is true to a lesser extent for Korean American women. The statistics tend to support this assertion: Regardless of nativity, Korean American men have completed college and advanced degrees at much higher rates than Korean American women (U.S. Dept. of Commerce, 1993). The disproportionate support of the favored son to achieve academically is exemplified in Lynda Lee's (interview) comments:

> I think because my brother was older and a boy, my parents received him better. Especially my mom. She listened to him. Although there wasn't a language problem, my brother still had to translate for me in high school. . . . In high school my brother didn't have to work at all, but I had to. And my mom always soothed my brother's ego. He was supposedly more sensitive. But she was always more blunt with me. . . . We had no choice in picking out our college majors. Our parents picked it. And at the time, I just accepted it. . . . My parents pushed both of us, especially him, for SATs. They worked with him to get a better score but not with me. Academically they pushed him more. My brother was very helpful to help me get my way with my parents. I needed him for legitimacy. My parents really respected his opinion, but I always struggled for their respect.

Lynda's parents' support of and belief in her brother extended to the educational realm, as her parents encouraged their children to pursue their academics at different levels.

Within Confucian philosophy, the presumed moral superiority of the educated man was the basis for his attainment of responsibility and power. If one actually held an official position, the reputation for learning itself brought with it great moral prestige. This is consistent with the common belief that Asian cultures regard education highly, although

Asian American achievement levels tend to be inversely related to the number of generations a family has been in the United States (Sue and Okazaki, 1990). However, this is not to say that a high regard for education is particular to Asian cultures. And, as significant as the desire for education is to Korean cultural values, it is also bolstered by immigrant middle-class aspirations to succeed in the United States. Educational attainments of Asian Americans are highly influenced by the opportunities present for upward mobility, not only in educational endeavors but also in non-education-related areas (Sue and Okazaki, 1990).

The significance of formal education is reinforced for Korean Americans by the traditional Korean cultural values of education and family honor; therefore, Korean parents place a great deal of pressure on their children to achieve academically. Several studies have found that Asian parents have a significant influence and place considerable pressure on their children to excel in formal educational settings (Wong, 1995; E.-Y. Kim, 1993). It is not uncommon for Korean children's careers to be predetermined by their parents, whether parental advice is solicited or not (E.-Y. Kim, 1993). However, when Korean children's talents and interests do not match those valued by their families and their community, Korean American youths are often left with little choice but to suppress them, and this suppression can result in serious problems.

Americanness:
Panethnicity, Stereotypes, and Their Effects

Shifting to the parameters of strictly American politics, panethnic Asian American coalitions are gathering momentum due to the political realities, similar histories within the United States, and the unfortunate confrontations with and survival against racism. Although many Asian Americans still feel a strong sense of their separate ethnic identities, an increasing number of young Asian Americans are coming together to form panethnic Asian coalitions—even catching the attention of national newspapers. [14] Although it is predominantly driven by the energy of many 1.5- and second-generation Asian Americans, this emerging racial consciousness is even manifested at an institutional level—in the increasing demand for Asian American studies programs across the nation as well as in the formation of pan-Asian community organizations, Asian American news media, and electoral politics (Espiritu, 1992).

Omi and Winant's (1994) theory of racial formation examines the evolution of an Asian American identity, which did not exist prior to the 1960s. With the opening of the golden doors to myriad Asian nations, Asian American panethnicity has been a product of political and social processes rather than of cultural bonds. According to Espiritu (1992), for many Americans of Asian descent, an Asian American identity requires a sophisticated knowledge of the American political system:

> In a political system in which numbers count, this political strength is derived from a unified front rather than from the separate efforts of individual subgroups. Thus, such an identity is not only imposed from above but also constructed from below as a means of claiming resources inside and outside the community. (pp. 13–14)

As a racial category, *Asian American* is a fairly new formal classification; prior to the 1990 U.S. Census, data were available only by Asian ethnicity. However, according to Lowe (1996), the racialization of Asian Americans is apparent when examining the immigration history of Asian Americans:

> While immigration has been the locus of legal and political restriction of Asians as the *other* in America, immigration has simultaneously been the site for the emergence of critical negations of the nation-state for which those legislations are the expression. . . . Immigration regulations and the restrictions on naturalization and citizenship have thus racialized and gendered Asian Americans, and this history has situated Asian Americans, even as citizens, in a differential relationship to the political and cultural institutes of the nation-state. (pp. 8–12)

Although ethnicity theorists might object to the race-based process of aggregating people of various Asian descents in America into the category of Asian Americans, the majority of Americans cannot differentiate between Asian ethnicities. "They are racially identified—their identities are racially constructed—by processes far more profound than mere state policy formation" (Omi and Winant, 1994, p. 24). Given racial politics in the United States, an Asian American identity can be beneficial, but it can also contribute to the misunderstanding of the differences between various Asian American ethnicities. Especially when students and teachers treat Asian American identity as monolithic, it can contribute to feelings of alienation and isolation in addition to the typical teenage angst. Jin Bai illustrates this process in describing how Asian Americans of East Asian and Southeast Asian descent are often perceived as being the same:

> So in high school there were mostly Chinese Americans at my high school. And people always thought I was Chinese in high school. I guess because of my name and I guess I look more Chinese than Korean. . . . I was on pompons. I'm really embarrassed to say that now. Again I was the only Asian and there was another white girl but she thought she was black and every-

one else was black. I don't mean to be stereotyping but I didn't have the language. I wasn't really able to connect with them culturally. I didn't know all
the songs. . . . I mean, I was familiar with it but it wasn't a part of me. So and
I had no interest in the football team. Everyone was dating someone from
the football or basketball team. And I didn't live anywhere near them. And
you know I was just this flexible Chinese girl to them. You know, that's
funny, because I'm not even Chinese. (Bai, 1996)

Although Jin expresses clearly throughout her interviews a strong identification with Korean Americans, she was very aware of how others perceived her racially.

Although a panethnic Asian American coalition has been productive,
"the Asian American identity which had been allowed was fixed,
closed, and narrowly defined, dividing *Asian American* from *Asian* as
sharply as possible, and whereas, Asian American identities are fluid
and migratory" (E. Kim, 1995, p. 14). Current American mainstream politics and the dominant American cultural milieu has enhanced this division, with the increased anti-immigration legislation and the Democratic national campaign finance scandal further questioning Asian
Americans regarding *their allegiance to Asia or to America*. Since classrooms do not exist in a vacuum, these sentiments are voiced by some
students and perhaps even some teachers. Because of the transnational-
ist nature of the Korean American community—and for that matter, of
many other Asian American communities—this is an extremely discon-
certing position. This understanding of the Asian American identity as
fixed is similar and related to the dominant image of Asian Americans
as the model minority.

Keith Osajima (1988) has analyzed the image of Asian Americans as
the model minority—the dominant image of Asian Americans that
emerged in the 1960s and has since pervaded all facets of American society and institutions. Regardless of whether an individual identifies
him/herself as Korean, Korean American, Asian, Asian American,
and/or American, all Asian Americans are affected by the prevalent
image of Asian Americans as the model minority.[15] A significant problem
of this stereotype is its static, monolithic portrayal of Asian Americans—
even if some Asian Americans adhere to this image, it is extremely problematic for this stereotype to serve as the premise regarding all Asian
Americans. Although the phrase *model minority* began to be used in various mainstream publications to describe Asian Americans only fairly recently, the popular view of Asian Americans as a model for other groups
to emulate is not such a recent concept. For instance, after the abolition of
slavery, Chinese laborers were used by Southern planters as examples of
good workers (Takaki, 1995).

However, before the articulation of the model minority image, another stereotype had prevailed: that of the Yellow Peril. The racist fear of the yellow peril was so pervasive at the turn of the century that it resulted in the passage of the Immigration Act of 1924. What began as anti-Chinese immigration exclusion laws eventually were extended to include all Asians. This act essentially restricted and halted immigration from the "Asiatic-barred" zone until the Immigration Act of 1965.[16]

Some may perceive the prevailing stereotype of Asian Americans as the model minority as a positive, novel image when compared with the Yellow Peril image; however, as historian Gary Okihiro (1994) demonstrates, the concepts of the Yellow Peril and the model minority

> form a seamless continuum. While the yellow peril threatens white supremacy, it also bolsters and gives coherence to a problematic construction: the idea of a unitary *white* identity. Similarly, the model minority fortifies white dominance, or the status quo, but it also poses a challenge to the relationship of majority over minority. . . . It seems to me that the yellow peril and the model minority are not poles, denoting opposite representations along a single line, but in fact form a circular relationship that moves in either direction. We might see them as engendered images: the yellow peril denoting a masculine threat of military and sexual conquest, and the model minority symbolizing a feminized position of passivity and malleability. Moving in one direction along the circle, the model minority mitigates the alleged danger of the yellow peril, whereas reversing direction, the model minority, if taken too far, can become the yellow peril. In either swing along the arc, white supremacy is maintained and justified through feminization in one direction and repression in the other. (pp. 141–142)

Robert Chang (1993) views responses to oppression in three stages: denial of difference, affirmation of difference, and liberation from difference. He presents these stages as a framework for analyzing legal scholarship, but the framework can be extended to aid us in understanding the development and persistence of the stereotype of Asian Americans as *model* minorities, and hence, the educational implications of such a perception. Unfortunately, denial can be persuasive; for some Korean Americans, it may be easier to swallow this position than to recognize the reality. As Lynda Lee observed during our interview:

> Korean Americans want to believe they're almost white. So they support whites and turn the other way when they're discriminated against or when something racist happens to them. . . . The reason why Koreans like to think they're almost white is because they understand the hierarchy in the U.S. So they place themselves there. It's easy to spread the *model minority* myth

because Asian Americans want to believe it. Who wants to recognize the reality? Denial. Asian American women are much more marginalized than Asian American males. This just reflects the severity of oppression for women. Since Asian American males are the tokens, they don't realize they are until they reach that glass ceiling. By then, it's too late. (Lee, 1994)

Coming to such conclusions about these manifestations of race is definitely uniquely American.

Korean Americanness, or Biculturalism

The construction of Asian Americans as the model minority often assumes complete assimilation, denying the retention of any aspect of Asian culture. However, Hurh (1980) argues that Korean Americans are a distinct ethnicity, and this cultural identity is in the process of formation. This new cultural identity and understanding is an amalgamation of traditional Korean values and the American experience and values—some combination of Americanism (assimilation) and Koreanism (ethnic identity), which are not necessarily mutually exclusive. To some degree, Korean Americanness is a by-product of juggling multiple identities. Nevertheless, because it is still in its developmental stages, only time will determine how this identity will evolve.

The discussion of what is Korean and what is Korean American is still more complicated because of the contemporary sociopolitical and cultural history of Korea. Because of the relationship between the United States and South Korea after the latter's liberation from Japanese colonial rule, most Koreans who emigrated to the United States came directly from South Korea (although some Koreans in America are from North Korea). The U.S. Army Military Government *officially* ruled Korea from September of 1945 to August of 1948, and the impact of those three years of intensive control is still evident in South Korea (G. Lee, 1989). South Korea has been subjected to intensive and extensive Western influences—mainly American—spiritually, materially, and politically. Although information from South Korea continues to be accessible within the United States, the transmission of Korean cultural values passed from parents to their children appears to be fairly static. Jin Bai (interview) describes this phenomenon:

And the other thing I realized is that times have changed in Korea. Our parents came here in the seventies and the sixties, but what they brought with them is Korea of the seventies. And that hasn't evolved. That hasn't progressed. Whereas, now Korea is into a lot more things and so when Koreans come here I tell them. . . . So it's funny. What I was passed down was the Korea of the seventies. So I don't know what that really means.

Depending on the year of arrival, the cultural values and practices of Korean immigrants tend to remain stagnant despite the transnational flow of information. Through the proliferation of foreign publications, Western ideas and values have been transferred to South Korea. This is not to say that contemporary South Korean culture is exactly the same as Korean American culture; however, the two cultures have developed into separate and distinct, yet similar, cultures of American and Korean hybridity.

Implications for Educators and Educational Practice

When compared to the deracialized stereotype of Asian Americans as the model minority, the voices of the second-generation Korean American women I interviewed both illustrate the contradictions of such a monolithic understanding and serve to dispel the race-neutral dialogue with regard to Asian Americans. Despite the interviewed women's awareness of the process of negotiating through the borders of Koreanness, Americanness, and Korean Americanness, these women were not always entirely conscious of the extent of their agency at all times. Educators need to be aware, as some already are, of the multiple identities that their students are sustaining. Although some students do not appear cognizant of such identities, educators should still assume that these students are required to *shift consciousness*. In some cases, depending on a student's sense of agency, the student may not even be aware of all the choices that she/he may really have. In light of multiple identities with at times contradicting values, a teacher can play a significant role in helping students with the process of negotiating identities (for example, in the case of career choice for Korean American women).

In addition, Keith Osajima's (1993) study of Asian American students' "educational life stories" found that the Asian American student experience continued to be profoundly shaped by racism, and the hidden impact of racism is best understood by examining the hidden manifestations. For the Asian American students in his study, silence became a survival mechanism formed in the context of a racially discriminatory society. Chun (1980) recognized that the misleading "success" image of Asian Americans had several important educational implications: resentment against the success stereotype, self-limiting occupational aspirations, and a sense of lost identity.

Asian American scholar Kenyon Chan made the following comment on a local radio program: "If you ever go to a Chinese, Korean, or Asian food restaurant on campus, you will notice how exciting and noisy the environment becomes with a roomful of Asian American students. Then in the classroom, the same students are so quiet that they are hardly noticeable. What is silencing these Asian American students?"[17]

What *is* silencing these Asian students? Unfortunately, the silence of an Asian American voice in mainstream racial and cultural politics has only further reinforced this stereotype. Curriculum omissions of Asian American voices within traditional American history courses at the primary and secondary level also have perpetuated this silence.

In addition, perhaps in some cases an explanation can be derived from the stereotypes and expectations that teachers and students themselves hold. During her student teaching experiences as an adult, Jin Bai observed:

> I think that although teachers favored Asians because they were smarter in their own way or whatever, but still they weren't as quite as . . . I think there were still differences which prevented . . . I don't know how to say it. I think there were some prejudices. . . . Because oftentimes the Asian kids would be the favorite. The teacher would call upon them because this kid knows all the answers. And say, "See, this person is studying," and things like that, in passing. But I don't think that these teachers took these kids in. You know how sometimes teachers get attached to kids. I didn't see this happen as much with Asians. It was only for an example for a standard or merit or a quality and maybe even trusting them enough to do certain errands because they can afford to miss that work time or something. But I don't know about that personal—there was still that distance. I don't know if that was a race issue. But would they allow themselves to take in this kid to mentor? Would they take this kid in to be their apprentice or to be their prodigy or whatever, as their own? As I'm sure teachers have a heart for, once in a while. But do they really do that with Asian kids, or do they feel that they're too different? (Bai, 1996)

Bai is questioning both the extent to which perceived racial difference affects teacher mentoring, and how the stereotype of the model minority, especially in the case of a good student, can mask the limited *real* attention and guidance an Asian American student may be receiving from a teacher. Bai's question deserves consideration by all educators.

Jin Bai also recounted how in another situation she was able to manipulate to her own advantage the perceptions some teachers held of Asians as model students:

> In high school, like I said, I got away with cutting school. They didn't think twice to call my parents. . . . A lot of my other friends who were smart and

good kids and all these things, who weren't Asian—a lot of them called their parents to double-check. And I don't have hard evidence it was because I was Asian. But it was the general assumption that I would make—. . . . I remember saying that, and my friend would laugh and say that I was right. No hard feeling, but he kind of laughed at it too when he got caught and got in school suspension.

The stereotype of the model minority obscures the differences that exist among Asian Americans. There is tremendous diversity among the various Asian ethnicities and also within ethnicities; these differences are based on history, reasons for immigration, educational attainment, occupation, class, adaptability to American society, and generation, to name just a few. The story of Susie Jang's precollege years dispels the idea that all Korean Americans have model family lives. Like Susie, many suffer from family-related stresses and difficulties that can affect educational performance:

This is so weird. My father is a minister. Actually. He actually went to prison. . . . [As a senior, Susie changed from a straight-A student to a straight-F student.] It started out okay. . . . It was when, I guess, my rebellious stage peaked. And I was really rebellious to my mom. . . . And after my parents got divorced, I just really isolated myself. I didn't go out anymore. I was just really depressed and didn't know how to deal with it. . . . So junior, senior year, I started to hang out with different people. Senior year, we all started to cut school a lot and do whatever. . . . We would just leave and go downtown or go to somebody's house. Well, a lot of people would have parties during school hours, so we would do that or whatever. . . . Just like somebody's parents were out working so they'd call 'em *daytimes*. And we all just hang out at that person's house. . . . Drink. . . . Some of us would go back to school later in the day, but that's basically what we would do . . . the spring of my senior year. So they called one of those parent-student-teacher conferences. A couple of times. Actually. . . . Yeah [my mother went]. The first one was pretty emotional I guess. . . . This school suggested that I see a therapist. Which I actually did a couple of times. . . . The administration really wanted to help me. I had gotten kicked out of the National Honor Society because of all F's. They got the faculty sponsors of NHS. They'd gotten involved. They all did. All my teachers. And it just got to a point. I'm about to graduate. Why can't they just leave me alone? You know, 'cause I'm going to go to college. It's not a big deal. So when I felt like, I didn't bother speaking to them anymore, the teachers. I didn't go to classes. You know my mother started ignoring. It just didn't matter anymore. . . . They pretty much gave up on me. I still just had a semester left. I was still going to graduate. . . . I never expressed at home to my mother like what I had felt about the

whole thing. Like the divorce. And everything else that had happened to my
family. I had never said anything before about it. You know. I guess it just
kept building up and up. . . . It wasn't until high school it really started to
bother me. And I really needed to tell somebody. (Jang, 1996)

Although her teachers were, fortunately, able to identify Susie Jang's
problems because of her change in behavior, this situation raises a concern: To what degree does seeing Asian Americans through the *model minority* lens distort a teacher's ability to recognize problems with Asian
American schoolchildren and youth? Susie had been severely depressed
and withdrawn for quite some time before anyone intervened. Could her
situation have been prevented from escalating to the crisis level if her
problems had been identified earlier? However, this is not to place all the
burden on her teachers.

Unfortunately, Koh and Koh's (1988) study of psychological evaluation
data collected from Korean American children demonstrate that teachers,
although able to identify the learning problems of children and to provide appropriate educational services, were not able to identify psychological and emotional problems in Korean American children. In addition, the schools or community mental health agencies did not treat
Korean American children even when a psychologist strongly recommended counseling. It is unclear to what extent the inability of teachers
to recognize problems and the failure of schools to treat the students are
related to a belief that Asian American children and youth, as members
of a model minority, do not have special needs or concerns.

The model minority stereotype also has implications for whether
school systems recognize and deal with institutional concerns or problems of Asian Americans. For example, in 1979 the *Chicago Sun Times* reported that all Asian students were counted as whites rather than as minorities by drafters of local and federal desegregation plans for the
Chicago public schools. This practice was followed despite the fact that a
substantial number (about 9,000) of Asian pupils were enrolled in the
Chicago public school system and an additional 2,000 Asian students
were expected to enter during the 1979–80 school year.[18] The failure to
distinguish between Asian and white students prevented administrators
and policymakers from addressing any special needs or concerns particular to the Asian American students.

Because of this focus on Asian Americans' high levels of educational
achievement, an unfortunate unidimensional understanding of the educational experience of Asian Americans has developed. The problem
with this understanding is that it masks the differences between ethnicities and among individuals: The Asian American *success* in educational
attainment is generalized to Korean Americans and to other aspects of

the educational experience. In other words, Asian Americans are deracialized. The implications of this stereotype must be examined not only at the individual level (as in the case of teachers) and the institutional level but also within the theoretical framework of the research conducted in and on education. Unfortunately, this model minority image underlies past educational theories, as Hurh and Kim (1989) demonstrate through examining its theoretical validity and practical implications. In addition, recent literature, such as the research by Stacey Lee (1996) and Wendy Walker-Moffat (1995), is examining the validity of this image.

Another contradiction of the model minority stereotype is that it denies the direct racism that Asian American children and youth may experience even within the boundaries of the schoolyard. The U.S. Commission on Civil Rights (1992) and other organizations have documented an increase of anti-immigration, anti-Asian sentiment and anti-Asian hate crimes in the United States. Unfortunately, this trend has not been addressed in the nationwide media but only in local Asian American media sources. Such problems contradict the notion that Asian Americans have been easily accepted into mainstream American society. In fact, as recently as 1981 the latent anti-Japanese sentiment of World War II resurfaced in the widely publicized, brutal murder of Vincent Chin.[19]

As one would expect, the classroom is a reflection of the larger society. Public high school campuses throughout the United States are characterized by a high level of racial tension and are often marred by incidents of bigotry and violence; especially affected are immigrant and refugee students in public schools (U.S. Commission on Civil Rights, 1992). A study by Bok-Lim Kim (1980) found that most of the children interviewed did not attribute any school problems they had to their Korean ethnicity, but some did report that they had problems in school because they were Korean. In the following account, Eun Hee Park relates how her experience of discrimination encompassed multiple racist beliefs regarding various Asian ethnicities:

I don't have important memories in the classroom because it was miserable. I got called many racial slurs all the way up to high school. . . . Examples? Did you swallow napalm this morning? Are you fat because of fried rice and saki?[20] Two football players in my sophomore year geometry class harassed me every day. The teachers always ignored the blatant racism that happened to me. My classmates would say: it's because she's Chinese. And the teachers would say nothing. Basically it was encouraged by the teachers. . . . I always used to think it was just I was a target, unpopular kid, but by high school, I realized it was a racial thing. Maybe I always knew but didn't want to admit it. . . . I didn't know that I didn't deserve it because I was raised my entire life as isolated. I saw this always normal. . . . I'm Korean because I look Korean. People see me as Korean. If people didn't see me as Korean, I wouldn't feel the need to be Korean as much. (Park, 1994)

The teacher's inaction and insensitivity to the vicious verbal attacks against this second-generation Korean American woman are unconscionable. Teachers wield enormous power in the classroom—legitimizing situations by their action and inaction.

In some cases, females are protected from more threatening advances to some degree, because of their status as females. As Jin Bai (interview) observed:

I know there were incidents of name-calling. But I think they were just isolated and never followed up by anything. . . . All through school, I remember people saying *chink* or *Chinese* and doing this with their eyes [she made a motion of pulling on her eyelids so they appeared slanted]. And I learned that I should do this back to them [she made a motion pulling on her eyelids so that her eyes appeared abnormally large]. . . . You get hurt at that moment, but it's not followed up by a bully threatening me. You know, to kill you. But that was fine. I think also it's partly because I was a girl. Girls just get treated better because you have that identity as well.

Korean American and Asian American males tend to be victimized by aggressive verbal and physical attacks at a greater rate. However, this is not to imply that such incidents do not occur against Asian females. The concern is not only the specific situation itself but also the possible ramifications of such abuse. Racism and racial insults can have profound psychological, sociological, and political effects. Hopefully, and in light of the efforts of multiculturalism, teachers can also be further educated in teacher education programs to develop an understanding of the harmful effects of racism—not only for Asian Americans but for all minorities.

As we move toward the twenty-first century, the nations of the world are undergoing a monumental transformation as global political, economic, and social structures continue to develop. By the year 2000, the Korean American population is projected to number 1,320,759 (Gardner, Robey, and Smith, 1985, p. 37); and in the year 2020, the projected Asian Pacific American population is 20.2 million (Ong and Hee, 1993, p. 16). These changes, driven by immigration and refugee resettlement patterns as well as by differential fertility rates, have important ramifications for educational policy because linguistic, cultural, and socioeconomic profiles vary widely by ethnicity. The number of Asian Pacific children and young adults under the age of 24 is expected to increase from 3 million in 1990 to 7.4 million in 2020 (Ong and Hee, 1993, p. 17). Because of the projected growth of the Asian American population, in particular the number of Asian American school-aged children and youth, it is important to develop further our knowledge of the Asian American experience through educational research and in the classroom.

Notes

1. In general and very inclusive terms, *Korean Americans* can be used to describe anyone of Korean heritage living in the United States, regardless of citizenship status and age of immigration. In the Midwest, however, most Korean Americans fall into the following generational categories (of somewhat common understanding among Korean Americans): (1) first, or 1.0, generation: persons who were born in Korea and immigrated to the United States as adults; (2) 1.5: persons born in Korea who immigrated to the United States as children or teenagers and who have some Korean and U.S. precollege educational experience; and (3) second, or 2.0, generation: persons who were either born in the United States or were born in Korea and came to the United States before obtaining any substantial formal primary schooling, and who have attended U.S. primary and secondary schools.

2. My definition of this phrase follows that of Yen Le Espiritu: "I use the term *Asian American* to refer to American-born Asians and to post-1965 arrivals, most of whom come to this country with the intention of settling permanently" (Espiritu, 1992, preface).

3. For an example of the unfortunately pervasive *eternal other* encounters, see Ronald Takaki's account of his experiences in *A different mirror: A history of multicultural America* (1993). Takaki is a Japanese American scholar who despite the fact that his family has been in the United States since the 1880s is forever perceived as a foreigner. He recounts the all-too-familiar experience of many Asian Americans asked the question, "How long have you been in this country?" (p. 1).

4. Although "silence can be read in many nuanced ways, including as active resistance" (see Chon, 1995, p. 11), I am referring here to what Chon describes as the "undesirable silences—speechlessness induced by shame and guilt, the oppressive or protective withholding of words in the family, or the glaring oversight in official history . . . denial."

5. All interviewees were either born in the United States or immigrated to the United States by the age of 4 and had no schooling in South Korea. All interviewees have been given pseudonyms to protect their privacy.

6. See Brenda You's article, "American dream wearing out many Koreans," *Chicago Tribune*, March 13, 1994, p. 19.

7. The total Korean American population, excluding Koreans residing illegally in the United States, is less than 1.0 percent of the total U.S. population—0.32 percent, to be exact—and it is interesting that such a small number has received as much attention as it has in the public eye (U.S. Dept. of Commerce, 1993). The attention in the media contrasting the success of Korean Americans with the plight of the urban underclass has been a particularly interesting focus. Refer to the chapter on "American Ideologies on Trial," in Nancy Abelmann and John Lie's book, *Blue dreams: Korean Americans and the Los Angeles riots.*

8. I rely on Basch, Schiller, and Blanc's (1994) definition of transnationalism as "the processes by which immigrants forge and sustain multi-stranded social relations that link together their societies of origin and settlement. . . . An essential element of transnationalism is the multiplicity of involvements that transmigrants sustain in both home and host societies . . . [and that] connect them simultaneously to two or more nation-states" (p. 7). They go on to assert: "By living their lives across borders, transmigrants find themselves confronted with and engaged in the nation building process of two or more nation-states. Their identities and practices are configured by hegemonic categories, such as race and ethnicity, that are deeply embedded in the nation building processes of these nation-states" (p. 34).

9. Although I use the term *transnationalism* to describe the process by which Korean Americans juggle their racial and ethnic existence daily, this is not necessarily the terminology a nonacademic Korean American would use to articulate the experience him/herself (although Gloria Anzaldúa [1987] wonderfully constructs in her fictional writing a fully articulated voice of the transnational identity and the state of "in-betweenness"). Nevertheless, for second-generation Korean Americans, the effects of transnationalism are strong.

10. Born out of reasons for survival in unequal power dynamics, especially due to the history of Korea, *nunchi balla* refers to a Korean expression which roughly translates into quickly understanding the personal, social, and political dynamics of a situation or interaction so as to prevail.

11. Slang to describe an Asian or Asian American who is "fresh off the boat."

12. Slang to describe an Asian American who is "yellow on the outside but white on the inside."

13. Tae kwon do is a Korean martial art.

14. See Norimitsu Onishi's *New York Times* article, "New sense of race arises among Asian-Americans," May 20, 1996.

15. Only after the passage of the Immigration Act of 1965 did the Asian American population begin to steadily increase. The law actually did not take effect until 1968. One of the significant features of this legislation was the abolition of the national origin quota system. In the period immediately following this change in immigration law, commonly referred to as the "Asian brain drain," a high proportion of South Korean professionals—many in health-care professions—entered the United States, as did many professionals from other Asian countries. This select group of Asian professionals further enhanced the "model minority"; however, the educational and professional attainments of these Asians in their home countries did not necessarily translate into the same opportunities for all Asian immigrants in the United States.

16. Even Filipinos/as were eventually restricted by the Tydings-McDuffie Act of 1934, which changed their status from nationals to Asian aliens almost a decade before the Philippines attained independence.

17. Kenyon Chan, guest speaker on the National Public Radio Focus 580 Program, broadcast on March 9, 1998, from Champaign-Urbana, Illinois.

18. See the *Chicago Sun Times* article "Overlooked in Hannon Plan, Asians assert," by Karen Koshner (September 21, 1979).

19. Vincent Chin, a Chinese American, was killed by an unemployed white American Detroit auto worker who had mistakenly assumed Chin was Japanese.
20. Saki is a traditional Japanese alcoholic beverage.

References

Abelmann, N., and Lie, J. (1995). *Blue dreams: Korean Americans and the Los Angeles riots.* Cambridge, MA: Harvard University Press.

Anzaldúa, G. (1987). *Borderlands/La frontera: The new mestiza.* San Francisco: Spinsters/Aunt Lute.

Bai, J. (1996, May). Tape-recorded interview in Urbana, Illinois.

Basch, L., Schiller, N., and Blanc, C. (1994). *Nations unbound: Transnational projects, postcolonial predicaments, and deterritorialized nation-states.* Newark, NJ: Gordon and Breach.

Berry, J. (1980). Acculturation as varieties of adaptation. In A. Padilla (Ed.), *Acculturation: Theory, methods, and some new findings* (pp. 9–25). Boulder, CO: Westview Press.

Chan, K. (1998, March 9). Guest speaker, WILL-AM, *Focus 580 Program,* Champaign, Illinois.

Chan, S. (1991). *Asian Americans: An interpretative history.* Philadelphia: Temple University Press.

Chang, R. (1993). Toward an Asian American legal scholarship: Critical race theory, post-structuralism, and narrative space. *California Law Review,* 81, 1241–1258.

Chang, R., and Aoki, K. (1997, October). Centering the immigrant in the inter/national imagination. *California Law Review,* 85 (5), 1395–1447.

Choi, C. (1998). Nationalism and construction of gender in Korea. In Elaine H. Kim and Chungmoo Choi (Eds.), *Dangerous women: Gender and Korean nationalism* (pp. 9–32). New York: Routledge.

Choi, P. (1991). *An analysis of the functions of weekend schools in the U.S.* Unpublished doctoral dissertation, George Mason University, Virginia.

Chon, M. (1995, Fall). On the need for Asian American narratives in law: Ethnic specimens, native informants, storytelling and silences. *UCLA Asian Pacific American Law Journal,* 3 (1), 3–32.

Chun, K. (1980, Winter/Spring). The myth of Asian American success and its educational ramifications. *IRCD Bulletin,* 1–12.

Crenshaw, K. (1995). Mapping the margins: Intersectionality, identity politics, and violence against women of color. In K. Crenshaw, N. Gotanda, G. Peller, and K. Thomas (Eds.), *Critical race theory: The key writings that formed the movement* (pp. 357–383). New York: New Press.

Delgado, R. (1990). When a story is just a story: Does voice really matter? *Virginia Law Review,* 76, 95–111.

_____. (1995). Legal storytelling: Storytelling for oppositionists and others: A Plea for Narrative. In R. Delgado (Ed.), *Critical race theory: The cutting edge* (pp. 64–74). Philadelphia: Temple University Press.

Eckert, C., Lee, K., Lew, Y., Robinson, M., and Wagner, E. (1990). *Korea old and new: A history.* Seoul: Ilchokak (distributed by Harvard University Press).

Espiritu, Y. (1992). *Asian American panethnicity: Bridging institutions and identities.* Philadelphia: Temple University Press.

Gardner, R., Robey, B., and Smith, P. (1985, October). Asian Americans: Growth, change, and diversity. *Population Bulletin, 40,* 4.

Hing, B. (1993). *Making and remaking of Asian America through immigration policy, 1850–1990.* Stanford: Stanford University Press.

Hune, S. (1993). An overview of Asian Pacific American futures: Shifting paradigms. In *The state of Asian Pacific America: Policy issues to the year 2020* (pp. 1–10). Los Angeles: LEAP Asian Pacific American Public Policy Institute and UCLA Asian American Studies Center.

Hurh, W. (1980, October). Towards a Korean-American ethnicity: Some theoretical models. *Ethnic and Racial Studies, 3,* 4.

Hurh, W., Kim, H., and Kim, K. (1979). *Assimilation patterns of immigrants in the United States: A case study of Korean immigrants in the Chicago area.* Washington, DC: University Press of America.

Hurh, W., and Kim, K. (1989, October). The "success" image of Asian Americans: Its validity, and its practical and theoretical implications. *Ethnic and Racial Studies, 12,* 4.

Jang, S. (1996, November). Tape-recorded interview in Urbana, Illinois.

Kim, Bok-Lim C. (1980). *The Korean-American child at school and at home: An analysis of interaction and intervention through groups.* Washington, DC: U.S. Department of HEW.

Kim, Elaine. (1995). Beyond railroads and internment: Comments on the past, present, and future of Asian American Studies. In G. Okihiro, M. Alquizola, D. Rony, and K. Wong (Eds.), *Privileging positions: The sites of Asian American studies* (pp. 11–20). Pullman: Washington State University Press.

———. (1997). Korean Americans in U.S. race relations: Some considerations. *Amerasia Journal, 23,* 2.

Kim, Eun-Young. (1993). Career choice among second-generation Korean-Americans: Reflections of a cultural model of success. *Anthropology and Education Quarterly, 24,* 3.

Kim, W. (1971). *Koreans in America.* Seoul: Po Chin Chai.

Koh, T., and Koh, S. (1988, March). *Cognitive and affective adaptation of Korean American schoolchildren in Chicago: Service and research priorities.* Paper presented at the annual meeting of the Association for Asian Studies, San Francisco, CA.

Koshner, K. (1979, September 21). Overlooked in Hannon Plan, Asians assert. *Chicago Sun Times,* p. 42.

Lawrence, C., III. (1995). The word and the river: Pedagogy as scholarship as struggle. In K. Crenshaw, N. Gotanda, G. Peller, and K. Thomas (Eds.), *Critical race theory: The key writings that formed the movement* (pp. 336–351). New York: New Press.

Lee, G. (1989). *Ideological context of American educational policy in occupied Korea, 1945–1948.* Unpublished dissertation, University of Illinois—Urbana-Champaign.

Lee, L. (1994, May). Tape-recorded interview. Urbana, Illinois.

Lee, P., and de Bary, W. (Eds.). (1997). *Sources of Korean tradition: From early times through the sixteenth century.* Vol. 1. New York: Columbia University Press.

Lee, S. (1996). *Unraveling the "model minority" stereotype: Listening to Asian American youth.* New York: Teachers College Press.

Lowe, L. (1996). *Immigrant acts: On Asian American cultural politics.* Durham, NC: Duke University Press.

Matsuda, M. (1996). *"Where is your body?" and other essays on race, gender, and the law.* Boston: Beacon Press.

Mau, R. (1995). Barriers to higher education for Asian/Pacific-American females. In D. Nakanishi and T. Yamano Nishida (Eds.), *The Asian American educational experience* (pp. 235–245). New York: Routledge.

McKay, S., and Wong, S. (1996, Fall). Multiple discourses, multiple identities: Investment and agency in second-language learning among Chinese adolescent immigrant students. *Harvard Educational Review, 66,* 577–608.

Moon, S. (1998). Begetting the nation: The androcentric discourse of national history and tradition in South Korea. In E. Kim and C. Choi (Eds.), *Dangerous women: Gender and Korean nationalism.* New York: Routledge.

Oh, A. (1998, February 5). Voices—Ideas and opinions from the Asia Pacific American community: The future of race relations. *Asianweek, 19,* 24.

Okihiro, G. (1994). *Margins and mainstreams: Asians in American history and culture.* Seattle: University of Washington Press.

Omi, M., and Winant, H. (1994). *Racial formation in the United States: From the 1960s to the 1990s.* 2nd ed. New York: Routledge.

Ong, P., and Hee, S. (1993). The growth of the Asian Pacific American population: Twenty million in 2020. In *The state of Asian Pacific America: Economic diversity, issues and policies* (pp. 11–24). Los Angeles: LEAP Asian Pacific American Public Policy Institute and UCLA Asian American Studies Center.

Onishi, N. (1996, May 20). New sense of race arises among Asian-Americans. *New York Times,* pp. A1, A16.

Osajima, K. (1988). Asian Americans as the model minority: An analysis of the popular press image in the 1960s and 1980s. In G. Okihiro et al. (Eds.), *Reflections on shattered windows: Promises and prospects for Asian American studies* (pp. 165–74). Pullman: Washington State University Press.

_____. (1993). The hidden injuries of race. In L. Revilla et al. (Eds.), *Bearing dreams, shaping visions: Asian Pacific American perspectives* (pp. 81–91). Pullman: Washington State University Press.

Park, E. H. (1994, May). Tape-recorded interview. Champaign, Illinois.

Phelan, P., Davidson, A. L., and Cao, H. T. (1991). Students' multiple worlds: Negotiating the boundaries of family, peer, and school cultures. *Anthropology and Education Quarterly, 22,* 225–250.

Sue, S., and Okazaki, S. (1990, August). Asian-American educational achievements: A phenomenon in search of an explanation. *American Psychologist, 45,* 8.

Takaki, R. (1993). *A different mirror: A history of multicultural America.* Boston: Little, Brown and Company.

_____. (1995). Race as a site of discipline and punish. In G. Okihiro, M. Alquizola, D. Rony, and K. Wong (Eds.), *Privileging positions: The sites of Asian American studies* (pp. 335–348). Pullman: Washington State University Press.

Thompson, P. (1978). *The voice of the past: Oral history.* New York: Oxford University Press.

U.S. Commission on Civil Rights. (1992). *Civil rights issues facing Asian Americans in the 1990s.* Washington, DC: Government Printing Office.

U.S. Department of Commerce. (1993). *1990 Census: Asian and Pacific Islanders in the United States.* Washington, DC: Government Printing Office.

Walker-Moffat, W. (1995). *The other side of the Asian American success story.* San Francisco: Jossey-Bass.

Wing, A. (1997). A multiplicative theory and praxis of being. In A. Wing (Ed.), *Critical race feminism: A reader* (pp. 27–34). New York: New York University Press.

Wong, M. (1995). The education of White, Chinese, Filipino, and Japanese students: A look at "High School and Beyond." In D. Nakanishi and T. Yamano Nishida (Eds.), *The Asian American educational experience* (pp. 221–234). New York: Routledge.

You, B. (1994, March 13). American dream wearing out many Koreans. *Chicago Tribune,* p. 19.

10

Separate and Still Unequal: Legal Challenges to School Tracking and Ability Grouping in America's Public Schools

PAUL E. GREEN

We are seeing kids, particularly minority kids, being placed in remedial and other kinds of programs for the same reasons they were put in separate schools 40 years ago, and that's wrong. (Edmonds, Usdansky, and Davis, 1994, p 3A)

Increasing reliance on special ability programs raises the specter of another form of segregation in America's public elementary and secondary schools, namely tracking (Bell, 1992; Oakes, 1985, 1992, 1995; Oakes, Wells, Jones, and Datnow, 1997). Research reveals that white students are admitted to accelerated schools and programs, whereas African Americans and Latinos are relegated to inferior schools and low tracks (Oakes, 1985, 1992, 1995; Gomoran and Robert, 1989; Glazer, 1990; England, Stewart, and Meir, 1990; Kilgore, 1991; Braddock and Dawkins, 1993; Kean, 1993; Argys, Rees, and Brewer, 1996; Avery, 1995; Backus, 1995; Welner and Oakes, 1996; Dickens, 1996; Hutto, 1996; Oakes, Wells, Jones, and Datnow, 1997). Such tracking internalizes the bias and stigma of segregation, nullifying the benefits of intraschool desegregation (Oakes, 1985, 1992, 1995; Page, 1991; Welner and Oakes, 1996; Oakes, Wells, Jones, and Datnow, 1997).

This chapter explores the potential social and legal ramifications of academic tracking, which is often also referred to as "ability grouping." *Tracking* involves the division of students of similar age and educational level into groups that are to receive instruction according to different curricula. For example, tracking in high school separates students into academic, general, and vocational programs that determine which subjects they will have the opportunity to learn. In a similar fashion, elementary schools track student classes when they divide them into separate groups for the entire day. *Ability grouping* in elementary schools, however, most commonly refers to divisions among students within particular subjects. These divisions might be informal, as with special math assignments given to certain students and not to others; or formal, as with class divisions into separate groups for reading periods.

The processes of tracking and ability grouping involve sorting students into high, average, and low tracks based on prior achievement and perceived intellectual ability (Oakes, 1985, 1992; Kilgore, 1991; Avery, 1995; Hutto, 1996). The division of the class into instructional groups is designed to facilitate instruction and enable schools to better meet the needs of a large and increasingly diverse student population (Argys, Rees, and Brewer, 1996). In the process of creating a more efficient means of instruction, however, students are labeled and assigned to advanced or to remedial levels of instruction (Oakes, 1995). The practice is problematic because actual ability is not always the criterion for grouping; students are typically divided according to measured or *perceived* performance in school. Oakes (1992) asserts that because school performance is related to social inequality outside the school, tracking and ability grouping contribute to the segregation of students based upon differences in racial, ethnic, and social background (Oakes, 1992, 1995; Oakes, Wells, Jones, and Datnow, 1997).

The central purpose of this chapter is to examine the policy and practice of de facto segregation created by tracking systems in America's public elementary and secondary schools. *De facto segregation* is defined as unintentional discrimination caused by laws or policies (Bell, 1992). The central issue is whether tracking denies schoolchildren assigned to lower tracks an equal educational opportunity. In *Brown v. Board of Education* (1954; hereafter, *Brown I*) the Supreme Court ruled that states must provide an equal education to all students enrolled in public schools on equal terms. A key question explored in this chapter is whether the court's concept of equal educational opportunity applies to policies and practices of tracking as well as to racial segregation. A number of education researchers have argued that tracking results in differential access to curriculum and instruction among racial groups and therein violates the intent of *Brown I* by denying African Americans and other children of color in lower tracks equal educational opportunity. Their argument, in brief, is that the sorting of students by ability creates divisions within a student body in much the same manner as do policies and practices of school segregation based on race (Kean, 1993; England, Stewart, and Meir, 1990; Hutto, 1996; Welner and Oakes, 1996; Dickens, 1996). Ability grouping often leads to de facto racial segregation within school sites as students of color, particularly African Americans, are denied access to higher levels of curriculum (Oakes, 1985; Kean, 1993; Hutto, 1996).

The chapter explores these issues in four stages. In the first, I use critical race theory as a lens for examining the role of the courts in advancing policies and practices of segregation. In the second, I discuss the origins of tracking and ability grouping in educational reform. In addition, this section briefly explores the *Brown v. Board of Education* (1954) decision and its significance for policies and practices of tracking and ability grouping. The third part illuminates key assumptions undergirding arguments for and against tracking and ability grouping as a policy of educational reform. In the fourth part, I outline a number of important court cases challenging tracking and ability grouping in public elementary and secondary schools beginning in the 1960s and continuing through 1995. Within this context, I review the effects of tracking on public education. The chapter thus explores the social, political, and legal contexts in which the tracking controversy is centered. Since the trial courts' opinions provide critical insights into the future legal status of tracking policies, I conclude with a brief discussion of the future of tracking in public schools.

Conceptual Framework:
Critical Race Theory and Educational Inequality

The conceptual framework used in this chapter borrows from the paradigm of critical race theory to examine the role of judicial policy making in maintaining racial segregation and educational inequality. Research in this tradition is critical to understanding racial injustice and its connection to equal access and equal educational opportunity for students of color in elementary and secondary education (Tate, 1997). What follows is a definition and explanation of critical race theory, embedded in the larger analysis of tracking and ability grouping as tools for racial segregation and educational inequality.

Critical race theory began in the 1970s with the realization that after the civil rights movement of the 1960s stalled, many social, economic, political, and legal gains eroded (Delgado, 1995; Caldwell, 1996). Scholars such as Derrick Bell and Alan Freeman argued that traditional approaches of filing amicus briefs, staging social protests, and marching were producing fewer gains than they had in previous decades (Ladson-Billings and Tate, 1995). Critical race theory emerged from the notion that racism is normal, not aberrant, in American society (Delgado, 1995).

Critical race theorists admit that although antidiscrimination laws often remedy the more extreme forms of racial injustice, equality as a judicial remedy can do little about the subtle forms of racism that persons of color confront daily (Delgado, 1995). Hence, critical race theory evolved as an important tool used to evaluate and question the American judicial system and its purported impact or lack thereof on race and racism as a system of equal justice (Delgado, 1995; Tate, 1997). It further suggests that racism is so entrenched in the fabric of our social, economic, political, cultural, and legal discourse, that it appears both ordinary and natural (Ladson-Billings and Tate, 1995). In Bell's *Faces at the bottom of the well: The permanence of racism* (1992a), racism is considered as an immutable fixture in American life. The goal of critical race theorists is to unmask and expose societal racism in all its forms.

Critical race theory examines the complex relationship between and among race, racism, and American jurisprudence (Delgado, 1995; Ladson-Billings and Tate, 1995; Caldwell, 1996; Tate, 1997). Critical race theorists articulate issues and concerns that have been ignored or marginalized by the dominant discourse, discuss concepts that appear immune from judicial scrutiny, and suggest resolutions that are frequently at odds with the prevailing demands of convention or fashion. Tate asserts, "A major goal of critical race theory is the elimination of racial oppression as part of the larger goal of eradicating all forms of oppression" (Tate, 1997, p. 234). Therefore, critical race theorists focus on the struggle for racial justice and the persistence of the racial hierarchy (Delgado, 1995; Aleinikoff, 1991, 1992; Bell, 1987a). Moreover, they challenge the efficacy of both liberal and legal theory and of communitarian ideals as vehicles for racial progress; destabilize the supposedly neutral criteria of meritocracy and social order; and call for a reexamination of the concept of race (Guinier, 1991; Matsuda, 1991; Bell, 1987b, 1992; Minow, 1990; Delgado, 1995).

With these goals in mind, careful inquiry regarding the role of judicial policy making and its effect on equity in education is essential when examining the policies and practices of tracking and ability grouping in public elementary and secondary schools. Tate (1997) suggests a number of important questions that educational scholars might ask in trying to shed light on the politics of educational equity and the role of courts in limiting the educational opportunities of students of color in general and African Americans in particular. For example, according to Tate, the primary question is not whether or how racial discrimination can be eliminated while maintaining the political status quo (i.e., federalism, traditional values, educational standards, choice, property interests). The issue, rather, is whether established political interests and traditions of meritocracy serve to limit access and deny educational opportunity to students of color (Tate, 1997).

Second, critical race theory reexamines civil rights law in light of its limitations, noting that laws intended to remedy racial inequality are often undermined before they can be implemented. For instance, multi-cultural education and educational diversity are linked to civil rights laws; yet practices such as tracking can undermine the positive effects of civil rights and diversity policies. Critical race scholars might examine such practices in greater depth, seeking to discover and measure their specific effects on the education of students of color.

Third, critical race theory questions the dominant legal claims of neutrality, objectivity, color blindness, and meritocracy, because such claims often have been used to buttress dominant groups' political, economic, and social self-interest. In education, the critical scholar might therefore seek to determine whether tracking and ability grouping support or undermine the dominant claims.

Finally, critical race theory challenges ahistoricism and insists on a historical reexamination of the law and a recognition of the experiential knowledge of people of color in analyzing law and society. Therefore, in education, critical thinkers might well question the ahistorical treatment of educational reform initiatives, equity, and students of color. Further, they might seek to show how experiential knowledge of race, class, and gender could better inform education discourse and policy.

Historical Background

Demographic Changes and Educational Reform

In the early 1900s, change swept through public education in the United States. A reform movement in public education began in response to demographic shifts taking place in cities in the northeastern and midwestern United States (Tyack, 1974; Zinn, 1980). Jobs created there by rapid industrialization attracted rural Americans as well as immigrants from northern and eastern Europe. Concomitantly, black families in search of job opportunities abandoned the rural communities of the South and relocated to cities in the hopes of securing employment in the growing industrial centers of the Northeast and Midwest (Tyack, 1974; Trotter, 1984). This growth placed enormous pressure on public school systems ill-equipped to support the growing numbers of immigrant and African American students entering elementary and secondary schools (Trotter, 1984).

Federal and state governments looked to the public educational system for solutions to the rapid growth in immigrant and African American populations. Community and public school leaders, in turn, turned to business and industry in search of a solution to the problem of equal educational opportunity for these groups (Tyack, 1974). In response, business and civic leaders recommended the application of Frederick

Taylor's model of organizational efficiency, and a number of educators who were proponents of school reform picked up their refrain, advocating Taylor's model in public elementary and secondary schools. Public schools should operate like factories, wrote Ellwood Cubberly, "in which the raw products (children) are to be shaped and fashioned into products to meet the various demands of life." Cubberly continued: "The specifications for manufacturing come from the demands of the twentieth-century civilization, and it is the business of the school to build its pupils according to the specifications laid down" (Hanson, 1996, p. 21).

According to efficiency advocates, public schools were responsible for educating all students in the same manner, as had been the practice of public schools since their inception. The purpose of public education was no longer a matter of developing an educated citizenry so much as it was to prepare students for their roles in the workforce. Hence students with various abilities had to be prepared for different types of employment. The factory model thus called for a differentiated curriculum in public elementary and secondary schools (Oakes, 1985, 1992; Hanson, 1996).

A differentiated curriculum required the classification of children in public schools (Crews and Counts, 1997). First, students were grouped by age into grade levels. Specific courses were taught at each grade level. Students were also grouped by their intellectual abilities as perceived by school officials. In other words, students were not considered equals (Hanson, 1996). Charles Elliot, the president of Harvard University and a leader in the school reform movement, explained to the Harvard Teachers Association in 1908 that society "is divided into layers" that have "distinct characteristics and educational needs." It would be foolish, said Elliot, to educate each child to be president of the United States when some were destined to membership in the "thick fundamental layer engaged in household work, agriculture, mining, quarrying, and forest work" (Tyack, 1974, p. 129).

The result of this educational philosophy was the track system. Tracking was conceived as a system of meritocracy, with the most deserving and able students rising to the top of the class. Educational reformers claimed that grouping students would enable public schools to meet the diverse needs of a large number of children efficiently (Hanson, 1996; Crews and Counts, 1997), as instruction could be tailored to prepare pupils for life after graduation. According to reformers, not every child needed to study classical literature and Latin if factory work was his destiny. Tracking would provide scholarly students with the academic education necessary for college entrance and would emphasize vocational training for the slower pupils. In this manner, tracking would benefit society as well as students. The track system appeared to offer equal educational opportunity to every student (Tyack, 1974; Oakes, 1985, 1992).

Not everyone, however, supported tracking. John Dewey, one of the leading educators of the time, firmly opposed the practice. Dewey (1990) believed an education should be comprehensive, based on the experiences of the student. He rejected the idea of classifying students and offering them a fractured course of study. Dewey believed the school should be a "community of individuals" and that categorizing students would isolate them and create divisions in the school community. According to Dewey, under a track system "the only measure of success is a competitive one, in the bad sense of that term—a comparison of results in the recitation or in the examination to see which child has succeeded in getting ahead of others in storing up, in accumulating, the maximum of information" (Dewey, 1990, p. 15). Dewey feared that education would become a commodity under the factory model.

Dewey's beliefs represented the minority opinion in contemporary educational theory. In fact, as the reform movement gained momentum, newly developed scientific concepts of intelligence added credibility to ideas advanced by reform-minded educators. Moreover, many aspects of the educational reform movement had their roots in Herbert Spencer's theory of social Darwinism. Social Darwinism applied the evolutionary idea of survival of the fittest to modern society, implying that intellectual differences between individuals were biological in nature (Oakes, 1985, 1992; Ladson-Billings and Tate, 1995; Tate, 1997).

The development of the first tests of "intelligence quotient" (hereafter, IQ) around the turn of the century seemed to validate Spencer's ideas. Psychologists such as Alfred Binet and Carl Brigham developed IQ tests based on the assumption that intelligence was a tangible quality capable of being identified and measured through scientific analysis. The first IQ tests were designed by and for the U.S. Army (Oakes, 1985). State boards of education quickly realized their potential for use in public elementary and secondary schools. David Tyack (1974) noted that intelligence tests could be used to "identify the able, the normal, and the slow from the start, to provide them with appropriate instruction, and by secondary school to sort them out according to their likely careers" (pp. 203–204). In brief, IQ testing provided scientific justification for tracking students in public schools.

With this purpose in mind, school boards rapidly incorporated testing into the standard operating procedure in school districts across the nation (Tyack, 1974). Psychologists adapted the IQ test for use in public schools in 1919, and more than 400,000 copies of the National Intelligence test were sold to state boards of education during the following six months. The U.S. Bureau of Education reported in 1925 that 215 cities across the country used intelligence tests either to classify students for ability grouping or to diagnose causes of academic failure. The Bureau of

Education surveyed 40 cities in the United States with populations exceeding 100,000 and found that 37 of those cities used ability grouping in some or all elementary grades. A slightly smaller percentage of school districts tracked students in junior and senior highs (Tyack, 1974). Aided by the widespread use of intelligence tests, tracking was firmly established in American schools by the end of the 1920s (Tyack, 1974; Zinn, 1980; Oakes, 1985, 1992; Dickens, 1996).

Educational Reform and Racial Segregation in America's Public Schools

The use of IQ tests and tracking during the educational reform movement initially had little impact on children of color. Even with the enforcement of compulsory attendance laws, few children of color enrolled in public schools (Tyack, 1974; Crews and Counts, 1997). In fact, education was a privilege not readily extended to African Americans. States in the Northeast, Midwest, South, and West operated dual, racially segregated systems of public education. Moreover, white students often attended schools that had an abundance of instructional and staff resources, whereas black students most often attended schools with limited or no resources (Bell, 1992; Franklin, 1997). Segregated systems of education were common, even in states in the Northeast that traditionally advocated racial and educational equity (Franklin, 1997).

Aided by federal and state court decisions, segregated public elementary and secondary schools flourished through the first half of the twentieth century. Following World War II, however, attitudes toward race began to change (Franklin, 1997). Racial desegregation slowly evolved in public arenas such as the armed forces and professional sports. In the field of education, a new wave of reformers questioned the morality of segregated schools (Oakes, 1985, 1992). Few local school systems voluntarily made the attempt to desegregate; rather, most continued to operate segregated schools until and even after *Brown v. Board of Education* (1954). In *Brown I*, the Supreme Court declared that in the field of public education, the doctrine of separate but equal was unconstitutional. In brief, the operation of segregated school systems violated the Equal Protection Clause of the Fourteenth Amendment (Bell, 1992).

In *Brown I*, the Court emphasized the importance of public education in America. Writing for a unanimous Court, Chief Justice Earl Warren described education as "perhaps the most important function of state and local governments" (*Brown v. Board of Education*, 1954, p. 691). He continued: "In these days, it is doubtful that any child may reasonably be expected to succeed in life if he is denied the opportunity of an education. Such an opportunity, where the state has undertaken to provide it, is a right which must be made available to all on equal terms" *(Brown v. Board of Education,* 1954, p. 691). As a matter of law, the Supreme Court replaced the doctrine of "separate but equal" with "equal opportunity for all," at least in regard to public education *(Brown v. Board of Education,* 1954, p. 691). More importantly, *Brown I* restricted the power of state and local school boards to classify pupils based on race. The *Brown I* ruling did not, however, specifically mention the classification of students based on perceptions of ability. In order to understand the significance of subsequent court cases challenging equal educational opportunity and ability grouping, it is important to examine some key assumptions surrounding tracking.

Proponents and Opponents: Tracking as Policy and Practice

At the forefront of the tracking debate are differing notions of the value of ability grouping and its implementation as sound educational policy and practice. Proponents assert that tracking provides an efficient means of ensuring appropriate instruction for a diverse student population. Tracking advocates base their arguments on two fundamental assumptions. First, they claim that students learn more effectively when they are grouped with others at the same academic level. Higher achievers can challenge each other (Allan, 1991). They can explore issues at a quicker pace and in greater depth because they do not have to wait for slower learners to catch up. Moreover, ability grouping allows lower achievers to move at a slower, more appropriate pace. Lower achievers can take more time to grasp concepts and practice basic skills in homogeneous groups. They are less likely to feel inferior, since they no longer have to compete with higher achievers (Allan, 1991). Second, proponents argue that it is easier for teachers to accommodate the individual differences of students if they are grouped according to ability. Smaller groups are easier to manage, and curriculum can be tailored to a variety of different learning styles. In sum, ability grouping allows teachers to meet the needs of a greater number of students (Feldhusen, 1989).

Opponents of tracking argue that a differentiated curriculum maintains inequality in educational opportunity, especially for African Americans (Oakes, 1985, 1992; Braddock and Dawkins, 1993; Hallinan, 1987; Page, 1991; Slavin, 1987, 1990). In most instances, the content and quality of instruction differ across academic tracks. For example, students in higher tracks cover more academic material, explore issues in greater depth, conceptualize problems, interact more meaningfully with teachers, and receive higher quality instruction than do students in lower tracks (Hallinan, 1987; Slavin, 1990; Braddock and Dawkins, 1993; Welner and Oakes, 1996). Consequently, children placed in lower tracks and ability groups do not receive the same instructional opportunities provided to higher-track students (Oakes, 1985, 1992; Page, 1991; Slavin, 1990).

Tracking inevitably produces educational winners and losers (Oakes, 1985, 1992, 1995; Oakes, Wells, and Datnow, 1997), as teachers often place African Americans in lower tracks at a much higher rate than white students (Oakes, 1985; Glazer, 1990; Bell, 1992; Kean, 1993; Braddock and Dawkins, 1993; Welner and Oakes, 1996). According to data compiled by Braddock and Dawkins (1993), African Americans were more than twice as likely as whites to be placed in a low track. Almost 24 percent of African Americans in the tenth grade were placed in a vocational track, whereas only 10 percent of whites at the same grade level were assigned to a similar track. In addition, 32 percent of African Americans were assigned to academic tracks, compared to 39 percent of whites. Among Latino students, only 30 percent took classes in higher tracks, and 16 percent were placed in low tracks (Braddock and Dawkins, 1993). Data collected by the U.S. Office of Civil Rights shows that in more than half of the school districts in the country students of color are overrepresented in nonacademic or vocational tracks (Levine and Levine, 1996).

Tracking opponents note that the conceptions of intelligence that were used to justify ability grouping at the turn of the twentieth century have changed dramatically in the intervening decades. Many psychologists and social scientists now view intelligence as influenced at least to some degree by environmental factors rather than as a matter of innate quality. According to this theory, human knowledge is socially constructed (Oakes, 1992; Oakes, Wells, Jones, and Datnow, 1997). Hence, equal access to curriculum allows all students the opportunity to build upon their base of knowledge.

Research also indicates that the quality of teaching varies between tracks (Oakes, 1985, 1992; Slavin, 1990; Page, 1991). Teachers with more professional experience tend to be assigned to higher academic tracks, leaving less-experienced teachers to deal with students who need the most help (Dawson, 1987). Teachers in lower-track classrooms have shorter interactions with students and expect less of them than do teachers in academic tracks. Consequently, lower-track teachers develop less-supportive relationships with pupils (Oakes, 1992, 1995).

As a consequence of low expectations, teachers tend to face more disruptive behavior from students in lower tracks. Good and Marshall (1984) found that during class discussions, the behavior of children in the lower-track classrooms "could be characterized as challenging teachers, obstructing academic activity, and misusing educational resources" (p. 22). Some of this behavior may be attributed to the fact that in homogeneous classrooms lower-track students are deprived of academic role models. Not only do they lose out in class discussions and group activities but they do not get to see appropriate classroom behavior modeled on a regular basis (Good and Marshall, 1984). According to Good and Marshall (1984), classrooms structured in this manner often produce passive learners who show little interest in school.

Furthermore, the impact of tracking on African Americans extends far beyond the classroom. Studies indicate that children placed in lower tracks are limited severely in their employment and educational opportunities after high school. According to Oakes (1992), "Tracking influences students' attainment and life chances over and above their achievement" (p. 13). Students assigned to lower tracks are disadvantaged in comparison to higher-track students, in their prospects for completing high school, attending college, and securing high-status jobs. Lower-track students are more likely to drop out of school prior to graduation. They are also less likely to see a relationship between academic success and future opportunities (Oakes, 1985; Wells and Crain, 1996; Smith-Maddox and Wheelock, 1995).

With this evidence in mind, Oakes (1995) has demonstrated that tracking systems have a discriminatory effect upon African Americans. Further, Oakes asserts that the intent behind tracking is to segregate (1995). Beginning in the 1960s, legal challenges began to focus on the unconstitutional and harmful effects of tracking and ability grouping.

Litigation and Tracking in the 1960s and 1970s

The 1960s and 1970s witnessed a gradual erosion of support for equal access and equal educational opportunities in the courts. According to plaintiffs, tracking and ability grouping resulted in intraschool segregation. Cases such as *Hobson v. Hansen* (1967), *Moses v. Washington Parish School Board* (1972), and *McNeal v. Tate County School District* (1975) challenged the policies and practices of tracking.

Hobson v. Hansen

Argued in 1967 before the federal district court of the District of Columbia (hereafter, Washington, D.C.), *Hobson v. Hansen* (1967) was the first case to address tracking in public schools. Public schools in Washington, D.C. operated under a dual system of education until *Brown I*. Although policies had been implemented to bring about desegregation in Washington, D.C., the plaintiffs in *Hobson* alleged that tracking perpetuated racial segregation of students since African Americans were disproportionately represented in vocational and lower academic tracks in the district schools. Like many other districts across the country, Washington,

D.C. used a combination of standardized tests and teacher recommendations to classify students into ability groups. According to Superintendent Carl Hansen, students were assigned to tracks based solely on their
abilities and educational needs, not on the basis of race (*Hobson v. Hansen*,
1967).

The court, however, did not agree, and it ordered that the tracking system in Washington, D.C. public schools be abolished. Citing *Brown v.
Board of Education* (1954), the Court ruled that the track system "uncon-
stitutionally deprived African American and poor school children of
their right to equal educational opportunity with white and more affluent public school children" (*Hobson v. Hansen*, 1967, p. 401). As was ruled
in *Bolling v. Sharpe* (1954)—a companion case to *Brown I* dealing with separate and unequal education in Washington, D.C. public schools—the
Fourteenth Amendment of the constitution did not extend to Washington, D.C. Hence the court ruled that tracking procedures in Washington,
D.C. schools violated the due process clause of the Fifth Amendment. In
writing the opinion of the court, Judge J. Skelly Wright found: "Even in
concept, the track system is undemocratic and discriminatory. Its creator
[Hansen] admits it is designed to prepare some children for white-collar,
and other children for blue-collar jobs" (p. 407).

Judge Wright based his decision on two essential findings. First,
African Americans were assigned to lower tracks at a much greater rate
than whites, resulting in a segregated student body (Oakes, 1985, 1992).
Second, children assigned to lower tracks did not receive the same educational opportunities provided to children in higher tracks. Not only
was instruction in lower tracks inadequate, but according to the court,
students placed in these tracks suffered from the stigma of being labeled
inferior academically (*Hobson v. Hansen*, 1967). The track system in Washington, D.C. public schools was also rigid—students were rarely reas-
signed to higher tracks. This inflexibility condemned students to an inferior status at a very early age (Oakes, 1985, 1992).

Moses v. Washington Parish School Board

Moses v. Washington Parish School Board (1972) provided the next legal challenge to tracking. Washington Parish in Louisiana operated a segregated
educational system until 1965. In reaction to a court mandate requiring
desegregation, the school board adopted a plan to group students by ability (Welner and Oakes, 1996). As in *Hobson*, the plaintiffs claimed that ability grouping resulted in the segregation of students within the district.
Specifically, the plaintiffs charged that the use of IQ tests to determine
track placement undermined the educational ability of African American
students who had previously been educated in segregated schools.

The plaintiffs asserted that culturally biased IQ tests placed African Americans at a disadvantage to whites, who had received a superior education *(Moses v. Washington Parish School Board,* 1972). The Fifth Circuit Court agreed, ruling that the use of standardized achievement tests for classification purposes deprived African American students of their constitutional rights. The court ordered that the district discontinue its use of the track system on the grounds that it resulted in a further segregated student body, violating the Equal Protection Clause of the Fourteenth Amendment. According to the court, homogeneous grouping was educationally detrimental to students assigned to lower tracks, and African Americans constituted a disproportionate number of the students in these lower tracks.

McNeal v. Tate County School District

The use of IQ tests in tracking was the focus of another case before the Fifth Circuit three years after *Moses. McNeal v. Tate County School District* (1975) clarified some of the legal questions about track assignment procedures raised in *Hobson* and *Moses.* In *McNeal,* the court ruled that testing could not be used to determine track placement in a desegregated school system until a district had remedied the results of de jure segregation and achieved "unitary status." *Unitary status* is a phrase used by the Supreme Court to describe and define remedies available to district courts to dismantle all vestiges of the unconstitutional, de jure segregation until the injuries and stigma inflicted upon the group disfavored by the violation are no longer present. The court found this provision necessary to ensure that "the assignment method is not based on the present results of past segregation" *(McNeal v. Tate County School District,* 1975, p. 1018). As with previous legal challenges to ability grouping, however, the Fifth Circuit upheld the validity of tracking as district policy:

Ability grouping, like any other non-racial method of student assignment, is not constitutionally forbidden. Certainly educators are in a better position than courts to appreciate the educational advantages or disadvantages of such a system in a particular school or district. School districts ought to be, and are, free to use such grouping whenever it does not have a racially discriminatory effect. If it does cause segregation, whether in classrooms or in schools, ability grouping may nevertheless be permitted in an otherwise unitary system if the school district can demonstrate that its assignment method is not based on the present results of past segregation or will remedy such results through better educational opportunities. *(McNeal v. Tate County School District,* 1975, p. 1020)

The Fifth Circuit's decision left open the possibility that segregation in public education might be constitutionally permissible. Schools may legally continue to classify and group students by race so long as the segregation is a de facto outcome rather than an explicit goal of district policies. *McNeal* reflected the court's view of tracking as an acceptable practice, undergirded by the meritocratic principle according to which the most deserving and capable students naturally rise to the top whereas slower or less motivated students are relegated to lower tracks. Given this approach, any resulting segregation is not the responsibility of the school system so long as appropriate placement procedures are implemented. *McNeal* also implied that there could be exceptions to the Supreme Court's finding in *Brown I* that "separate educational facilities are inherently unequal" (*Brown v. Board of Education*, 1954, p. 692).

Legal Challenges and Educational Inequality

In the 1980s and 1990s the court system made a judicial retreat from equal access and equal educational opportunity for persons of color. Further, during the presidencies of Ronald Reagan and George Bush, the courts became increasingly conservative and less inclined to issue desegregation orders to remedy policies and practices of segregation in public schooling (Bell, 1992; Stanfield, 1994). In fact, the judicial appointments of the Reagan and Bush administrations to the federal courts, coupled with a lack of decisionmaking in the area of civil rights policy, exacerbated the growth of racial segregation in the nation's public schools (Bell, 1992; Stanfield, 1994). For example, the federal courts often deferred to the judgment of school officials who employed pedagogical policies and practices such as tracking and ability grouping (*Quarles v. Oxford School District*, 1989; *Montgomery v. Starkville Municipal Separate School District*, 1987).

Georgia State Conference of Branches of NAACP v. State of Georgia

In 1985, an important case involving tracking was argued before the Eleventh Circuit Court of Appeals (Bell, 1992; Stanfield, 1994). In this case, the National Association for the Advancement of Colored People (NAACP) filed a civil rights class action suit on behalf of schoolchildren in several Georgia counties claiming that tracking procedures restricted the educational opportunity of African Americans. The Third Circuit upheld the district court and found in favor of the state of Georgia. As in *McNeal* and *Moses*, the court determined that ability grouping did not violate the Equal Protection Clause of the Fourteenth Amendment. Plaintiffs failed to prove that segregation in Georgia's public schools was intentional or that it was the result of past discriminatory practices. Furthermore, the verdict explicitly stated that tracking did not violate either the Equal Education Opportunities Act of 1974 or Title VI of the Civil Rights Act of 1974. The Eleventh Circuit found that

> Achievement grouping practices used by school districts to place students in classes bore manifest demonstrable relationship to classroom education and, thus, did not violate Title VI of the Civil Rights Act of 1964 in that achievement grouping per se was educationally desirable, and methods used by school districts to assign students to achievement groups adequately measured students' true abilities in each particular class. *(Georgia State Conference of Branches of NAACP v. State of Georgia*, p. 1405)

Once again, the grounds on which tracking opponents could file suits had been narrowed.

With the appointment of President William Clinton in 1992, a backlog of civil rights cases in employment and education was tackled. In education, the Clinton administration led an attack on classroom tracking. The Justice Department's new assistant attorney general for civil rights, Patrick Deval, decided that tracking was the segregating tool of the 1990s. Forty years after the Supreme Court's ruling in *Brown I*, Deval stated, "Tracking will be challenged in the context of laws and rulings that outlaw school segregation" (Edmonds, Usdansky, and Davis, 1994, p. 3A).

As a result, the 1990s saw cases challenging the harmful effects of policies and practices of tracking and ability grouping. Four cases, *People Who Care v. Rockford Board of Education* (1994), *Vasquez v. San Jose Unified School District* (1994), *Simmons on Behalf of Simmons v. Hooks* (1994), and *Coalition to Save Our Children v. State Board of Education* (1995), resulted in de-tracking mandates issued by the courts.

People Who Care v. Rockford Board of Education

People Who Care v. Rockford Board of Education was argued before the Northern District Court of Illinois in 1994. In this case the plaintiffs needed to prove both discriminatory effect and discriminatory intent. What the plaintiffs had to demonstrate was that the school system's use of tracking was unfair. In order to do so, they based their claims on racial disparities resulting from ability grouping.

What distinguished *Rockford* from *Hobson*, *Moses*, and *McNeal* was the variety of supporting evidence presented by the plaintiffs. Prior to *Rockford*, tracking litigation consisted primarily of a single plan of attack.

Plaintiffs focused on the discriminatory intent of the classification techniques used by schools to assign African Americans to lower tracks. Although this strategy led to victory in all three cases, the effects of the verdicts were mixed. Courts ordered the cessation of tracking in the districts involved not due to any biases inherent in tracking but because the districts had implemented tracking policies in a discriminatory manner. As soon as the violations had been remedied, courts allowed the districts to resume ability grouping (Welner and Oakes, 1996).

In *Rockford*, expert witness and tracking authority Jeannie Oakes focused the attention of the court on inequities that affect all lower-track students and minority students. She used data supplied by the district, such as curriculum guides, district reports, instructions and forms, enrollment figures (by grade, race, track, and school), standardized test scores, and teacher recommendations for course enrollment. Moreover, Oakes made use of the Rockford school district's discovery responses, including deposition testimony.

Oakes's expert testimony and analysis convinced the court that placement practices skewed enrollments in favor of whites over and above what could be reasonably explained by measured achievement (Oakes, 1992, 1995). In its decision, the court noted:

> There is ample evidence to support the . . . conclusion [that it was the district's policy to use tracking to intentionally segregate White students from minority students], including, but not limited to: the assignment of minority students to lower track classes in consistently disproportionate numbers . . . , knowledge of these racial disproportions and woefully inadequate efforts to correct them . . . , placing students whose achievement scores qualified them for two or more tracks in lower tracks . . . , and corroboration by District personnel. (*People Who Care*, 1994, p. 934)

On the basis of the evidence and testimony provided, the court ordered the elimination of ability grouping and tracking in the Rockford schools.

Conclusion

Groups that are striving to eliminate policies and practices of tracking in America's public schools face a protracted battle in the federal courts and state legislatures. The tracking of students into high and low ability groups remains entrenched in the meritocratic culture of American public education. In 1990, approximately 86 percent of students attending public middle schools and high schools were placed in tracked classes for mathematics instruction. In the same year, nearly 85 percent of students in public secondary schools were grouped by ability in English (Mostellar, Light, and Sachs, 1996). Because de-tracking in public schools would cause upheaval in the social and academic structures of many middle and high schools, educational policy makers, administrators, teachers, and parents are unlikely to voluntarily initiate a policy retreat. In addition, the long-term effects of de-tracking on student performance are not yet fully known; only short-term data are available for the school districts that have reversed their tracking policies under court mandate.

In sum, public support for meritocracy, coupled with public resistance to the elimination of tracking as an educational policy, ensures the survival of ability grouping as an educational practice. Moreover, courts have traditionally deferred to local school boards and educators when pedagogical and instructional issues become causes for legal action. Although cases such as *Hobson v. Hansen* (1967) and *People Who Care v. Rockford Board of Education* (1994) established legal precedents for tracking opponents, the increasingly conservative nature of the U.S. Supreme Court and the lower federal courts makes the prospect of a federal mandate outlawing tracking unlikely. However, recent court decisions challenging tracking and ability grouping in public elementary and secondary schools have weakened proponents' arguments in favor of tracking. Unfortunately, even where schools have been desegregated system-wide, tracking and ability grouping continue to segregate public school students along racial lines. Until the promises of *Brown* are fulfilled, tracking will remain a battlefield on which the fight for equal access and equal educational opportunity is waged.

References

Addis, A. (1992). Role models of policy recognition. *University of Pennsylvania Law Review,* 144 (4), 137–146.

Aleinikoff, T. A. (1991). A case for race-consciousness. *Columbia Law Review,* 91 (5), 1060–1125.

_____. (1992). The constitution in context: The continuing significance of racism. *University of Colorado Law Review,* 63, (2), 324–373.

Allan, S. D. (1991). Ability grouping research reviews: What do they say about grouping and the gifted? *Educational Leadership,* 48 (6), 60–65.

Argys, L. M., Rees, D. I., and Brewer, D. J. (1996). De-tracking America's schools: Equity at zero cost? *Journal of Policy Analysis and Management,* 15 (4), 623–645.

Avery, A. (1995, May). Do magnet schools exacerbate tracking? Yes. *NEA Today,* 13 (9), 39.

Backus, L. (1995). No. (Do magnet schools exacerbate tracking?). *NEA Today,* 13 (9), 39.

Bell, D. (1987a). *And we are not saved: The elusive quest for racial justice.* New York: Basic Books.

_____. (1987b). *Race, racism and American law.* Boston: Little, Brown.

_____. (1992a).*Faces at the bottom of the well: The permanence of racism.* New York: Basic Books.

_____. (1992b). *Race, racism and American law* (3d ed.). Boston: Little, Brown.

Bolling v. Sharp, U.S. 347 (1954).

Braddock, J. H., and Dawkins, M. P. (1993). Ability grouping, aspirations, and attainments: Evidence from the National Educational Longitudinal Study of 1988. *Journal of Negro Education,* 62 (3), 324–337.

Brown v. Board of Education, 74 S. Ct. 686 (1954).

Caldwell, V. F. (1996). Critical race theory: The key writings that formed the movement. *Harvard Civil Rights–Civil Liberties Law Review,* 30 (5), 1363–1374.

Coalition to Save Our Children v. State Board of Education, 901 F. Supp. 784 (D. Del. 1995).

Crews, G. A., and Counts, M. R. (1997). *The evolution of school disturbance in America.* Westport, CT: Praeger.

Dawson, M. M. (1987). Beyond ability grouping: A review of the effectiveness of ability grouping and its alternatives. *School Psychology Review,* 16 (3), 348–369.

Delgado, R. (1995). *Critical race theory: The cutting edge.* Philadelphia: Temple University Press.

Dewey, J. (1990). *The school and society.* Chicago: University of Chicago Press.

Dickens, A. (1996). Revisiting *Brown v. Board of Education:* How tracking has resegregated America's public schools. *Columbia Journal of Law and Social Problems,* 29 (4), 469–506.

Edmonds, P., Usdansky, M., and Davis, R. (1994, May 4). "School 'tracking' to be challenged as biased," *USA Today,* p. 3A.

England, R. E., Stewart, J., and Meir, K. J. (1990). Excellence in education: Second generation school discrimination as a barrier. *Equity and Excellence,* 24 (4), 35–41.

Fehrenbacher, D. E. (Ed.). (1964). *Abraham Lincoln: A documentary portrait through his speeches and writings.* Stanford, CA: Stanford University Press.

Feldhusen, J. F. (1989). Synthesis of research on gifted youth. *Educational Leadership,* 46 (6), 6–11.

Franklin, J. H. (1997). *From slavery to freedom.* New York: Knopf.

Georgia State Conference of Branches of NAACP v. State of Georgia, 775 F. 21403 (1985).

Glazer, S. (1990). Why schools still have tracking. *Editorial Research Reports,* 1 (48), 746–758.

Gomoran, A., and Robert, D. (1989). Secondary school tracking and educational inequality: Compensation, reinforcement, or neutrality? *American Journal of Sociology,* 94 (5), 1146–1184.

Good, T. L., and Marshall, S. (1984). Do students learn more in heterogeneous or homogeneous groups? In P. L. Peterson, L. C. Wilkinson, and M. Hallinan (Eds.), *The social context of instruction: Group organization and group processes* (pp. 15–38). Orlando, FL: Academic Press.

Gotanda, N. (1991). A critique of "Our constitution is color-blind." *Stanford Law Review,* 44 (1), 1–68.

_____. (1995). Critical legal studies, critical race theory and Asian American studies. *Amerasia Journal,* 12 (1–2), 127–136.

Guinier, L. (1991). The triumph of tokenism: The voting rights act and the theory of black electoral success. *Michigan Law Review,* 89 (5), 1077–1154.

Hallinan, M. T. (1987). Ability grouping and student learning. In M. T. Hallinan (Ed.), *The social organization of schools: New conceptualizations of the learning process* (pp. 41–69). New York: Plenum.

Hanson, E. M. (1996). *Educational administration and organizational behavior.* (4th ed.). Boston: Allyn and Bacon.

Hobson v. Hansen, 269 F. Supp. 401 (1967).

Hutto, J. (1996). Beyond tracking: Finding success in inclusive schools. *Educational Leadership,* 54 (2), 90.

Kean, P. (Jan.-Feb. 1993). Blowing up the tracks: Stop segregating kids by ability and watch kids grow. *Washington Monthly,* 25 (1–2), 31–34.

Kelly, A. V. (1978). *Mixed-ability grouping: Theory and practice.* London: Harper and Row.

Kilgore, S. B. (1991). The organizational context of tracking in schools. *American Sociological Review,* 56 (2), 189–204.

Kulik, J. A., and Kulik, C. C. (1987). Effects of ability grouping on student achievement. *Equity and Excellence,* 23 (1–2), 22–30.

Ladson-Billings, G., and Tate, W. F. (1995). Toward a critical race theory of education. *Teachers College Record,* 97 (1), 47–68.

Levine, D. U., and Levine, R. F. (1996). *Society and education* (9th ed.). Needham Heights, MA: Allyn and Bacon.

Matsuda, M. J. (1991). Voices of America: Accent, antidiscrimination law, and a jurisprudence for the last reconstruction. *Yale University Law Review,* 100 (5), 1329–1407.

McNeal v. Tate County School District, 508 F. 2d 1017 (5th Cir. 1975).

Minow, M. (1990). The constitution and the subgroup question. *Indiana University Law Journal,* 71 (1), 1–25.

Montgomery v. Starkville Municipal Separate School District, 665 F. Supp. 487 (N.D. Miss, 1987).

Moses v. Washington Parish School Board, 456 F. 2d 1285 (1972).

Mostellar, F., Light, R. J., and Sachs, J. A. (1996). Sustained inquiry in education: Lessons from skill grouping and class size. *Harvard Educational Review,* 66 (4), 797–828.

Oakes, J. (1985). *Keeping track: How schools structure inequality.* New Haven, CT: Yale University Press.

_____. (1992). Can tracking research inform practice? Technical, normative, and political considerations. *Educational Researcher,* 21 (4), 12–21.

_____. (1995). Two cities' tracking and within-school segregation. *Teachers College Record,* 96, 681–690.

Oakes, J., Wells, A. S., Jones, M., and Datnow, A. (1997). Detracking: The social construction of ability, cultural politics, and resistance to reform. *Teachers College Record,* 98 (3), 483–510.

Quarles v. Oxford School District, 868 F. 2d 750 (5th Cir. 1989).

Page, R. N. (1991). *Lower-track classrooms.* New York: Teachers College Press.

People Who Care v. Rockford Board of Education, 851 F. Supp. 905 (N.D. 111 1994).

Simmons on Behalf of Simmons v. Hooks, 843 F. Supp. 1296 (E.D. Ark, 1994).

Slavin, R. E. (1987). Ability grouping and student achievement in elementary schools: A best-evidence synthesis. *Review of Educational Research, 57* (3), 293–336.

_____. (1990). Achievement effects of ability grouping in secondary schools: A best-evidence synthesis. *Review of Educational Research, 60* (3), 471–499.

Smith-Maddox, R., and Wheelock, A. (1995). Untracking and students' futures: Closing the gap between aspirations and expectations. *Phi Delta Kappan, 77* (3), 222–228.

Stanfield, R. L. (1994, March 2). The split society. *National Journal,* pp. 762–767.

Tate, W. F., IV. (1997). Critical race theory and education: History, theory, and implications. In M. W. Apple (Ed.), *Review of research in education,* vol. 22, pp. 195–250. Washington, DC: American Educational Research Association.

Teaching inequality: The problem of public school tracking. (1989). *Harvard Law Review, 102* (6), 1318–1341.

Trotter, J. W., Jr. (1984). *Black Milwaukee: The making of an individual proliterate, 1915–1945.* Urbana: University of Illinois Press.

Tyack, D. B. (1974). *The one best system: A history of American urban education.* Cambridge, MA: Harvard University Press.

Vasquez v. San Jose Unified School District, No. C–71–21320, unpublished stipulation (N.D. 1994).

Wells, A. S., and Crain, R. L. (1996). Perpetuation theory and the long-term effects of school desegregation. *Review of Educational Research, 64,* 531.

Welner, K. G., and Oakes, J. (1996). (Li)Ability grouping: The new susceptibility of school tracking systems to legal challenges. *Harvard Educational Review, 66* (3), 451–470.

Zinn, H. (1980). *A people's history of the United States.* New York: HarperCollins.

11

Conclusion

WILLIAM F. TATE IV

To the editor of the *Los Angeles* (The Angels) *Times*:

As immigrants now residing on the East Coast, we await with heightened anticipation the inevitable arrival of local versions of Proposition 227, recently passed by the prescient voters of California to do away with bilingual education. We never got any of that bilingual coddling when we came here as kids, so everyone else might as well go through what we did, much as fraternity hazing rituals are handed down through the years. In fact, in the spirit of better citizenship, we urge Californians concerned with the insidious effects on children of public exposure to a Babel of non-English tongues to go a logical step further with a Prop 227(b) to really drive home the point that the foundation of civics and national unity is English Only. For history has burdened California with what is likely the largest concentration in the U.S. of unpatriotic names, and that could send bilingual kids a wrong and confusing signal. Get out the maps, Californians, roll up your sleeves, and let's get to work.

We hereby propose renaming into English, within one year of the passage of Prop 227, all of the places in California that are now provocatively named in foreign languages, particularly that all-too-common Spanish, all the way from The Jewel (misspelled "La Jolla" as it is), Hidden (Escondido), Big Box (El Cajon), and Saucy Sight (Chula Vista), to Old Mission ("Mission Old Man," if you want to get technical), and St. Anne, Green Sticks and the Port of St. Peter, proceeding up to Oaks Pass (Paso Robles), Mount King, and along the coast through beautiful Big South to Tall Stick (Palo Alto). There would be new Butterfly, Skeletons, and Feathers Counties (Mariposa, Calaveras, and Plumas), to name a few. As a cost-effective move, we can leave the old Catholic saints, so long as they are given their linguistically correct names: St. Ferdinand Valley, Bishop St. Louis, St. Bernard, St. Joseph, and St. Francis, while the name of the capital can become The Sacrament, keeping Holy Cross company. . . . "California" itself will have to go, along with truly foreign names like Yosemite, Mojave, Sequoia, Ahwahmee, and Tekachapi, although we are at present unable to translate those names and will have to find someone who is, well, bilingual, in the appropriate tongues.

The work involved would be well worth the effort. What passes in California usually goes nationwide a short time later, so imagine the useful work that lies ahead! The Renaming of America (a name that is itself of impure origins) will require the earnest efforts of all concerned citizens, from Alabama to Wyoming. Amarillo, Baton Rouge, Chicago, Corpus Christi, Des Moines, Detroit, El Paso, Honolulu, Miami, Milwaukee, San Antonio, Santa Fe, Seattle, Tallahassee, Valdez, Weehawken, and Wichita, here we come!
   —Rubin G. and Luis E. (Reubin and Louis) Rumbaut

What constitutes important knowledge in our society? Opinions on this question can be found in both academic and nonacademic sources. As the above letter to the editor illustrates, many voters who support certain kinds of knowledge—English only—either don't care to know or have not thought about the historical origins of this country. The names of geographic regions are only a surface indicator of the contributions of people of color to that early history. Those charged with the responsibility to dig beneath the surface—academics—have also contributed to efforts to minimize the importance of our knowledge of people of color. Some academics have argued and/or inferred that knowledge about people of color is not important knowledge. This argument has emerged in recent debates about the university curriculum, bilingual education, and affirmative action. For example, in the winter 1997/1998 issue of the *Journal of Blacks in Higher Education* (*JBHE*), the editors crafted an article entitled "Top African-American Military Brass Are a Highly Educated Bunch." The focus of the article is on the higher education of twenty African American armed forces generals and admirals with at least two stars. As you would expect, all twenty have college degrees. Many of these men also held graduate degrees. The article concluded with the following remarks:

> Notice that among the group of black generals there is no [sic] majoring in *soft* [our emphasis] academic fields. There is not one African-American studies major in this group. Some of the master's degrees are in such fields as architectural engineering, computer systems management, and mechanical and nuclear engineering. (*JBHE*, 1997/98, p. 55)

This kind of discourse—*soft academic field*—is often used in academic circles. The organizational structures of higher education—schools, colleges, departments—have for many years distinguished between the sciences (physics, chemistry, mathematics, and so on) and social sciences (psychology, sociology, education, and the like). Often disciplines positioned in the social sciences are referred to (unfairly) as the "soft" sciences. The distinction between "hard" and "soft" sciences is based on paradigmatic issues, economic opportunities, and other issues of power and control. However, I contend that the editors of *JBHE* could not have built a case against African American studies as a "soft" discipline, based on these officers' choices of academic specialization: The list of generals and admirals included officers who majored in government, history, physical education, psychology, and human relations, and these majors are often housed in the social science divisions of universities. Logic indicates that the editors must have noted the "soft" majors of the military leaders.[2] Thus, the prejudice in this instance is clearly not against all "soft" fields but specifically against a specific curricular focus—on African American studies. I can only infer that the editors view the African American experience as inferior material with which to practice the methods of scholarly inquiry, learn the principles of leadership, and find one's vocation.

The *JBHE* remarks represent an attack from the "liberal" left. I assume the editors consider themselves enlightened and supportive of African Americans. The journal is devoted to "[T]he conscientious investigation of the status and prospects for African Americans in Higher Education" (*JBHE*, 1997/98, p. 4). It is interesting that this kind of "devotion" and argument can come from conservatives such as Ward Connerly. Connerly, the businessman of African descent who led the drive to pass Proposition 209, has focused his attention on evaluating the need for ethnic studies programs in the University of California system. He is not interested in assessing the merits of American literature, British history, or Jewish studies. These areas of scholarship appear safe for now. However, nothing is really safe from this kind of assault.

Ladson-Billings (in this volume) noted that this kind of attack is an effort to mute and erase the experiences of people of color by controlling the curriculum. One strategy to minimize the study of people of color is to associate such inquiry with the relaxation of academic and professional standards (Hu-DeHart, 1995). Further, this argument is often coupled with the myth that the study of people of color is not of value in our capitalistic democracy. Why did the editors choose to use the military leaders as their unit of analysis? Please allow me to speculate. First, the perception exists that the military is a merit-based organization. If you have skills and leadership ability, you will be promoted regardless of race. Thus, the *JBHE* editors' attack on African American studies is a warning to future college students: If you want to compete, don't *mark* yourself with the Black major. How far does this argument extend? Should people of color not study or theorize about their contemporary social interactions, educational experiences, economic conditions, legal possibilities, and medical problems, as well as their history and culture?

A second reason the editors of *JBHE* may have chosen military officers as their subjects is that military vocations represent a high form of patriotic service, symbolizing the ultimate of citizenship. Military service is devoted to the protection of U.S. property and democracy. I feel the editors failed to analyze their own beliefs about the relationship between knowledge production related to people of color, U.S. property, and democratic values. For instance, they noted that no women were included within the pool of African American officers. However, they did not equate this with academic major. Certainly there are highly competent women of color who did not major in "soft" academic fields and who are capable of military leadership. What is the underlying cause of this inequitable outcome in a "merit-driven" organization? As Villenas, Deyhle, and Parker (in this volume) stated, we must look at places where race and gender intersect and create qualitatively different/similar experiences for men and women of color. Thus, to really see race we must recognize gender (see chapters by Gonzalez and Banning, this volume).

Many legal, educational, and political scholars of color question whether the philosophical underpinnings of traditional liberal civil rights discourse—a color-blind and gender-neutral approach—are capable of supporting continued movement toward social justice in a climate of retrenchment (Lawrence, 1987; Wilkins, 1995; Williams, 1991). A product of this thinking is the critical race studies movement.

Critical Race Theory:
A Guide to Knowledge Production

A few years after the *Brown* decision, Thurgood Marshall, then director-counsel of the NAACP Legal Defense Fund, visited Pittsburgh where Derrick Bell, a lawyer by training, was serving as executive director of the NAACP's Pittsburgh branch (Bell, 1993). Marshall offered Bell a position on his legal team and Bell accepted. From Marshall and from NAACP general counsel Robert L. Carter, Bell (1993) learned that "the role of the civil rights lawyer was not simply to understand the legal rules but to *fashion* arguments that might change existing laws" (p. 75). The link between Derrick Bell the civil rights lawyer and Derrick Bell the scholar is important in chronicling the origins and philosophical undergirding of critical race theory. In 1969, Bell accepted a position on the law faculty of Harvard University. In his negotiations with the dean of the law school, Bell (1994) made it clear that he viewed teaching as an opportunity to continue his civil rights work in a new arena. His legal research was greatly influenced by his perspective as an African American and experience as a practicing civil rights litigator. Bell (1994) noted, "Practitioners, often through storytelling and a more subjective, personal voice, examine ways in which the law has been shaped by and shapes issues of race" (p. 171). His writing about race and law was at the forefront of a new school of scholarly inquiry in the academy—critical race theory. There was a strong link between Bell's legal analysis, critical race theory, and the African American scholarship and literature that emerged during and after the civil rights movement (as exemplified by the literary work of Toni Morrison, and the scholarship of Charles V. Hamilton and others writing in the social sciences).

Although no definitive date is associated with the conception of critical race theory, its foundation is linked to African American thought in the post–civil rights era—from the 1970s to the present (Bell, 1980a, 1980b; Matsuda, Lawrence, Delgado, and Crenshaw, 1993). The civil rights movement of the 1960s had stalled, and many advancements associated with the movement were under attack (e.g., *Regents of University of California v. Bakke*, 1978). A number of scholars and activists of this era noted the limitations of attempts to obtain justice using dominant conceptions of race, racism, and social justice. Ladner (1973) in sociology, Cone (1970) in theology, Allen (1974) in political science, and Banks (1971) in education all moved beyond the traditional paradigmatic boundaries of their fields to provide a more cogent analysis of the African American experience.

This intellectual movement permeated the paradigmatic boundaries of legal scholarship as law professors and teachers committed to racial justice began to correspond, meet, debate, and engage in political action in an effort to resist institutional structures that facilitated racism while claiming the objectives of racial harmony and equality (Matsuda, Lawrence, Delgado, and Crenshaw, 1993). Thus, the foundation of critical race theory as a movement and as an intellectual agenda was connected to the development of the new approach to examining race, racism, and law in the post–civil rights period (Barnes, 1990; Crenshaw, 1988).

Given this summary of CRT's origins, one important challenge for scholars of color is to fashion a theory of education that might help to change educational inequities for students of color. The scholars in this volume have chosen to explore the potential of critical race theory to address this challenge. In a review of this length, I cannot deal in detail with every chapter, though each provides numerous insights into the world of schools and education. Furthermore, the historical genesis of critical race theory in the field of law and jurisprudence has been reviewed in this volume by University of Illinois law professor Daria Roithmayr. My aim is to move each of us closer to fashioning a theory of race and education. Toward this end, I highlight the contribution of various chapters to this movement. I also outline the challenge for future researchers in this area of study.

One purpose of this review is to note the relationship between the chapters of this volume and critical race theory. A goal of critical race theory is to eliminate racial oppression as part of a larger project to eradicate all forms of oppression. Several distinctive yet interconnected elements in the CRT literature are key to achieving this goal of racial justice. I have argued elsewhere that these elements provide guidance for developing a set of questions on which a systematic inquiry into the political dimensions of equity in education might be based (Tate, 1997).

1. CRT recognizes that racism is endemic in U.S. society. One element of CRT scholarship is the assumption that racism is a permanent fixture of this society (Bell, 1992a). Many of the authors in this volume appear to be building their arguments with this element of CRT in mind. This CRT tenet is not new or particular to CRT scholarship (see, for example, Omi and Winant, 1994; Takaki, 1993). Yet, this element of CRT does imply we need a greater understanding of prior arguments about race and education. I contend that to build on this tenet of CRT requires tremendous insight into the racial dynamics of society and of education in particular. Without additional insight, this tenet of CRT might suggest that progress has not been made or is not possible. The provocative African American social and literary critic Stanley Crouch made a similar argument:

> What bothered me was the impact that I think that the Derrick Bells have on the minds of young black people—and young white people. It's very psychologically injurious for young people to see a guy with Derrick Bell's credentials and background to stand up in front of them and tell them, "You can forget it. These white folks in power ain't gonna let you do this and they ain't gonna let you do that." You might as well not get out of bed in the morning—which is the essential message. I said to myself, "There's something wrong with this." For me, having been involved with Friends of SNCC [Student Nonviolent Coordinating Committee] and CORE [Congress of Racial Equality] 35 years ago, we'd talk with guys from Mississippi who were not as defeatist then as some are now. These were guys wearing overalls and brogans. If you're gonna say that these guys are not just gonna just roll over and die, then that's true, but to look at what we've been through from 1619 or at how different the United States is since 1960 and stand in front of young kids and discourage them was the height of irresponsibility. (Cobb, 1998, p. 33)

Crouch's response to the work of Bell and others with similar arguments is somewhat overstated in my opinion, yet it is worthy of discussion by scholars contributing to the CRT literature. His argument raises one question for me: "Is it possible to have racial progress in a society where racism is endemic?" My response to this question is "yes." If so, how might scholars interested in race and education approach the subject in a responsible and ethical manner? A colleague of mine often remarks, "Ignorance of history is the mother of invention in education." I could not agree more. Our responsibility as scholars is to capture and develop a historical perspective on society, race, and the nature of educational change. For example, in his historical analysis of twentieth-century black intellectuals, Watkins (1996) noted that Black Nationalists, social reconstructionists, Christian humanists, and progressive liberals have provided insights into the racial inequalities that existed in the United States. Watkins argued that many scholars have decontextualized and separated much of the contemporary debate about the nature of African American schooling from its African American intellectual roots. Thus, many contemporary theories, policies, and practices have historical analogs that could serve as guides for measuring progress in the development of theories of change and real outcomes with people of color.

As I have argued elsewhere, CRT challenges ahistorical scholarship and insists on a contextual treatment of the law and a recognition of the experiential knowledge of people of color in analyzing the law and society (Tate, 1997). In this volume, the chapter by Green represents one effort (he is not alone) to situate an argument in a broader historical literature on race and education. Green provides an overview of the history of judicial decisionmaking on tracking and ability grouping in public schools. He grounds this history in a discussion of the intersection of racism, demographic change, and the organizational structures of public education, enabling readers to better understand the current institutional barriers to racial justice. This well-grounded chronological and descriptive context makes clear the need for further analyses linking critical race theory with the institutional and societal forces perpetuating racial injustice in the public schools—analyses that might eventually help eliminate de facto segregation via tracking, and lead to more-equitable student success groupings.

2. CRT portrays dominant legal claims of neutrality, objectivity, color blindness, and meritocracy as camouflages for the self-interest of powerful groups in society. The important question for the scholar employing CRT is how traditional interests and cultural artifacts—e.g., federalism, traditional values, standards, established property interests, and choice—serve as vehicles to limit and bind the educational opportunities

of students of color. Villenas, Deyhle, and Parker's presentation of qualitative studies and perspectives on racial discrimination attempts to link
critical race theory to practice. The research on African Americans and institutional racism, and the evidence from recent court battles between the
Navajo and school officials in southern Utah, illustrate its utility. *Critical
race praxis* can be used to legally and politically challenge race-neutral
positions in school policies that have a deleterious effect on African
American and Navajo students. Villenas, Deyhle, and Parker's chapter
also shows how the color-blind position in U.S. law, with its emphasis on
merit and individual success, ignores the collective struggles of Latina
mothers and their efforts for human agency in the face of racial and gender oppression.

The challenge to the "color-blind" view of law and meritocracy is also
a key point in a previous article by Parker (1998) on the *Hopwood v. Texas*
anti–affirmative action case. Parker used CRT in order to understand
how the traditional notion of merit was used to challenge affirmative action at the University of Texas Law School. His presentation reminds me
of Duncan Kennedy's (1995) article "A cultural pluralist case for affirmative action in legal academia." Kennedy argued that color-blind, meritocratic fundamentalism is a set of ideas that develop from fragmented personal philosophies. This form of fundamentalism consists of a set of
tenets. Each tenet is a slogan with an appeal of its own; they rarely are argued at the same time. The important tenets of color blindness are as follows:

2(a) "Prejudice" and "discrimination" are defined in opposition to
"assessment of individuals on their merits":

i.   Merit is a matter of individual traits or products.

ii. People are treated irrationally and unjustly—in short,
they are discriminated against—when their merit is assessed
according to their status rather than according to the value of
their traits or products (derived from [i]).

2(b) Racial discrimination as stereotyping:

i.   There is no reason to believe that race in any of its various
socially constructed meanings is an attribute biologically
linked to any particular meritorious or discreditable intellectual, psychological, or social traits of any kind.

ii. Racial discrimination is irrational and unjust because it
denies the individual what is due him or her under the society's agreed standards of merit (derived from [i]). (Kennedy,
1995, pp. 160–161)

From these two tenets, the fundamentalist builds a set of propositions about the construction of rewards and opportunities associated with institutions of higher education. First, higher education institutions should work to optimize the production of valuable knowledge and also to reward and advance individual merit. Second, these institutions charged with distributing honor and opportunity must do so according to criteria that are blind to race, sex, class, and all other particularities of the individual except the one particularity of having produced some product of value. This second proposition is central to Villenas, Deyhle, and Parker's chapter and to Parker's (1998) analysis. These scholars have argued that CRT seeks to de-cloak the institutional and ideological racial purpose behind the "color-blind" myth of merit and individualism embedded in the anti–affirmative action arguments and race-neutral school policies that discriminate against Navajo, Latino/Chicano, and African American students.

My hope is that other education scholars interested in CRT will continue the examination of merit and individualism as these concepts relate to race and education. Merit is a very context-specific term. For example, the National Merit Scholarship program is not really national. Each year about 50,000 students are selected on the basis of PSAT scores to be semi-finalists for this prestigious award. Ironically, this list is not identical to the list of the 50,000 highest scoring students nationwide. Instead, states are given a specific number of slots for semifinalists in proportion to the number of graduating seniors in each state in the previous year. If students were selected on the sole basis of merit (in this case, test scores), many states would not fill their "quota" of semifinalist slots. In fact, data from the NAEP, the SAT, and other indicators of state-level achievement suggest that some states would have few, if any, awardees in an open competition using test scores (NEGP, 1995). The National Merit Scholarship program is actually a state-level competition. I submit that this program is a form of geographic affirmative action. Further, it is biased, given that high school graduation rates are strongly associated with parental education. However, not many people are opposed to this program. I would imagine supporters saying, "It gives everyone a chance to compete." I concur with this argument. Yet why is this form of affirmative action more acceptable to mainstream white America? Of course, it is veiled in the discourse of merit. Moreover, affluent white Americans rarely oppose programs that operate in their self-interest (see Taylor, this volume). These two fundamentalist practices are cornerstone targets for the critical race critique.

Paul Green specifically examines these fundamentalist tenets in his historical analysis of tracking and ability grouping. He reveals how race as a social construct got intertwined with ability and intelligence—

notions of merit—to serve the interests of whites in segregated tracking systems. He challenges ahistoricism and insists on a contextual/historical examination of the law and its connection with tracking and ability grouping. Similarly, in a detailed analysis of higher education desegregation cases, Edward Taylor addresses the question: Was there evidence of interest convergence in these cases? His analysis indicates that the appropriate response is yes. Bell (1980a) defined the interest convergence theory as follows:

> Translated from judicial activity in racial cases both before and after *Brown*, this principle of "interest convergence" provides: The interest of blacks in achieving racial equality will be accommodated only when it converges with the interests of whites. However, the Fourteenth Amendment, standing alone, will not authorize a judicial remedy providing effective racial equality for blacks where the remedy sought threatens the superior status of middle class and upper class whites. (p. 523)

The Green and Taylor chapters are similar in that both critique a form of segregation. However, more importantly, these scholars have started the process of developing a full-scale structural theory combined with the potential for further microlevel analysis of the individual story.

3. CRT crosses epistemological boundaries.   Scholars associated with CRT use a wide variety of methodological tools. The scholars in this volume borrow from several traditions, including liberalism, multiculturalism, feminism, Marxism, poststructuralism, critical studies, cultural nationalism, and pragmatism, to provide a more complete analysis of "raced" people. This is consistent with methods used by legal scholars whose writings are associated with the CRT movement. CRT suggests that scholars in education interested in equity research must question the appropriateness of traditional theories of psychology, sociology, and other disciplines and paradigms that have influenced thinking and policy development related to the education of people of color.

Delgado (1989) argued that the form and substance of scholarship are closely connected. Many critical race theorists use parables, chronicles, stories, counterstories, poetry, fiction, and revisionist histories to reveal the false necessity and irony of many civil rights remedies and arguments. Much of the CRT literature tacks between situated narrative and more sweeping analysis of the law. This kind of analytical and theoretical method was evident in the chapters by Pizarro, Banning, Gonzalez, Choe, Hermes, and Hidalgo. Their arguments are best described as an enactment of hybridity—that is, scholarship that depicts the education scholar as bicultural in terms of belonging to the world of research and the world of everyday experience. Narayan (1993) provided important insight into the enactment of hybridity:

> One wall stands between ourselves as interested readers of stories and as theory-driven professionals; another wall stands between narrative (associated with subjective knowledge) and analysis (associated with objective truth). By situating ourselves as subjects simultaneously touched by life-experience and swayed by professional concerns, we can acknowledge the hybrid and positioned nature of our identities. Writing texts that mix lively narrative and rigorous analysis involves enacting hybridity, regardless of our origin. (p. 682)

Building from their hybrid positions, Pizarro, Gonzalez, and Hidalgo argued for a space within the intellectual terrain of postcolonialism to provide a more comprehensive analysis of the Chicana/o, Mexicana, and Puerto Rican experiences in education. Similarly, Choe noted that a general ignorance or oversight of significant historical events has limited our understanding of racial dynamics related to Asian Americans and specifically Korean Americans. Hermes noted the tension between the academy and the needs of the American Indian tribal nation. She called for research in communities of color that meet some of the needs of the community in which that research is conducted. Each of these scholars was willing to cross the epistemological boundaries of traditional educational research in search of truth and social change. Their work brings to mind a remark made by Theresa Martinez (1996):

> They [Marx, Durkheim, and Weber] were in fact telling "stories," often called theories, about the world. Although they were limited both by experience and time, these very storytellers were able to set forth their "stories"—their theories—the boundaries, facades, building structures, mortar and bones of what we know as sociological thought.
>
> My academic training taught me to place their way of knowing the social world in a sphere above my own, and this effectively silenced my version of the story when it differed from theirs. When I didn't understand the theories of these eminent men, I assumed there was something wrong with my side of the story. . . . It was when I was doing my research on battered women in New Mexico that I realized that sometimes the stories were very different and sometimes, bless their hearts, Marx, Weber, and Durkheim didn't have a clue. . . . I encountered a Chicana discourse on our history, work, poetry, and prose. I was amazed at how very differently the stories could be told. But before I came to this realization I had a great deal of unlearning and learning to do. (p. 108)

The "unlearning" and learning process with respect to discourses on race and education requires a close examination of other paradigmatic and epistemological options. This is a distinct element of CRT. However, I want to note that boundary crossing does not come without a penalty in the academy. Rafia Zafar, formerly on the faculty of the University of Michigan, remarked: "Interdisciplinary is this buzz word, and universities say they want it. . . . But you go to tenure committees made up of people from traditional disciplines, and they say, 'We don't understand what you're doing'" (Wilson, Heller, and Schneider, 1998). Professor Zafar is speaking from firsthand experience. As an assistant professor of English, she was denied tenure at the Ann Arbor campus. The focus of her work is English and Black studies. There is an important lesson to be learned from Professor Zafar's experience. Scholars who produce interdisciplinary work cannot restrict their scholarly lenses to paradigmatic boundaries acceptable to local tenure committees. In essence, such restriction would be akin to an infringement of their free speech or academic freedom. Yet, they must pay for their freedom, being left to the mercy of the academic market. We have little choice but to "trust" that in the marketplace of ideas our work will be valued by colleagues at other institutions. Professor Zafar secured several offers from Research I universities, and eventually accepted a promotion in rank and an increase in salary from Washington University. Perhaps not all stories will end so positively.

Personally, I have had colleagues from across the country question the importance or merit of interdisciplinary scholarship, and specifically CRT. They have warned me of the dangers to my career. Typically they say things like "You will never receive a presidential appointment" or "Don't jeopardize your administrative opportunities with that race writing." These remarks are spoken to me, face to face. I can only imagine what is said when I am not present. My choice is to continue the struggle. We all have to choose.

Fashioning a Theory of Race and Education

For much of world history, craft has been an important practice in human culture. The practice of any craft involves the fashioning of resources into a product through the implementation of skills that can be taught and mastered. The craftsperson develops the product by drawing, counting, measuring, sorting, ordering, cutting, matching, and so on. To the novice or apprentice, the resulting product is often incomprehensible. The apprentice often asks, How did you start with one set of seemingly unrelated materials and end up with this usable product? Can you do it again?

Metaphorically, theoretical development is very similar to a craft. As does a silversmith or a jeweler, a theoretician constructs and reworks ideas, concepts, and experiences until a more comprehensive understanding of the phenomena is fashioned. The process of theoretical development associated with race and education has a long history. Typically, three operations have been central to this process: (1) interpreting the role and meaning of race in education; (2) correlating those interpretations with other interpretations; and (3) assessing the adequacy of the interpretations and their correlations. Note that just as in any craft, however, the processes can interrelate and overlap. The order of the processes does not follow a pattern but shifts back and forth, checking and adjusting to meet the goal of a usable product—the theory.

I do not want to press the analogy beyond its limits. I recognize that race and education have long-standing political roots. These roots often are connected to the agendas of particular groups who desire to order society. Thus, the analogy is naturally limited. I hope to make clear how politics is constantly a part of the fashioning process.

Theory as Interpreting.   We are all ceaseless interpreters. All of us interpret not only spoken and written words but sights, noises, smells, and tastes. In essence, everything we experience is interpreted. Often, the interpretations we make become our views. The individual's view does not necessarily take into consideration other people's views. However, a number of views grouped together into a more or less distinct set of interpretations constitutes a perspective or theory. Theories do not have to be accurate. Rather, a theory's moral and political authority is derived from its consistency with belief systems that reflect the prevailing cultural ethos of a people.

The predominant theories in education related to people of color have been premised on political, scientific, and religious interpretations that characterize people of color as inferior. The writings of Thomas Jefferson in his *Notes on the State of Virginia* illustrate the long history of vilification of African Americans in U.S. discourse. Peters (1982) further posits that the Jeffersonian view of African Americans helped lay the groundwork for segregation. I submit that his perspective is consistent with the paradigmatic view that undergirds theories of racial inferiority.

The concern I have with the inferiority paradigm, and paradigms in general, is that its adherents often fail to consider alternative interpretations. Instead, the concepts and theories of the "accepted" paradigm drive the interpretation of the problem, problem solving, policy development, and policy implementation. A challenge for future CRT educational scholarship is to articulate the language and meaning of equity and social justice in the formation of interpretations that make up the theoretical perspective. For example, Secada (1989) argued that the relationship between educational equity and justice requires examining how changing notions of justice may give rise to different interpretations of equity. I submit that we need a critical race hermeneutics, or theory of interpretation.

Hermeneutics is a methodological approach that seeks to provide meaning to texts, and by extension, to any human activity, production, expression, or institution that can be viewed as text (Balfour and Mesaros, 1994). In contemporary hermeneutics, text is a broad term that refers to a wide variety of written, verbal, and nonverbal communications, across time periods, that are subject to study and interpretation. Thus texts include documents such as institutional files and records, the Constitution, court decisions, legislative bills, policy statements, speeches, interviews, organizational charts, budgets, employment contracts, research papers, letters, and even statistical data. Textual analysis is not limited to phenomena that are literally textual but might include the analysis of ceremonies (as oral and lived text), organizational culture (symbolic text), and even buildings and neighborhoods as artifacts subject to interpretation.

The importance of hermeneutics for the study of education and race derives from its focus on applying this interpretative method to the study of human activity and products (texts). Hermeneutics requires each generation of scholars and interpreters to work out their own interpretations and understandings of both past and present texts. This requirement is a challenge to scholars committed to advancing CRT as an interpretative method.

Theory as Correlation.   Many social scientists view correlation as a statistical coefficient that characterizes the existence of a relationship between variables. However, correlation is a useful term also for thinking about multiple interpretative viewpoints. Theoretical thinking, therefore, involves correlation—that is, the method of framing two or more discrete phenomena in mutual relation with each other (Stone and Duke, 1996). Even though theoreticians may debate the notion of adhering to a formal method of correlation, the fact remains that theoreticians are without a doubt correlators. They attempt to determine if their view of some phenomenon is consistent with or incompatible to other views arising from different positions and ideologies. Cornell West (1995) described the elements of the correlation process undertaken by critical race theorists with a set of questions especially relevant for educational researchers writing within the genre:

> What does it mean to engage in theoretical activity at this downbeat moment in American society and culture? How do we candidly incorporate experiences of intense alienation and subordination into the subtle way of "doing" theory in the American academy? What are the new constructive

frameworks that result from the radical critiques of the prevailing paradigms in United States legal education? How can liberation-minded scholars of color engage with white radical intellectuals without falling into the pitfalls of coalitions between such groups in the sixties? (p. xi)

West elaborates further on the correlation process:

> [T]he movement highlights a creative—and tension-ridden—fusion of theoretical self-reflection, formal innovation, radical politics, existential evaluation, reconstructive experimentation, and vocational anguish. But like all attempts to reinterpret and remake the world to reveal silenced suffering and to relieve social misery, Critical Race Theorists put forward novel readings of a hidden past that disclose the flagrant shortcomings of the treacherous present in the light of unrealized—though not unrealizable—possibilities for human freedom and equality. (p. xi)

A constant challenge for educational researchers incorporating and expanding on tenets of CRT will be to compare and contrast interpretations of race and education. We must recognize that a central part of this process is a correlation of interpretations.

Theory as Assessment. A theoretical perspective is only one of many differing outlooks in a culture, yet it is of central importance to those who ascribe to it. Its worth is grounded in the belief that what is seen through the theoretical lens is accurate.

Offering some evidence for the rationale and trustworthiness of a theory is an integral part of the reflective theoretical process. We must recognize that in the marketplace of ideas alternative theoretical positions exist. Rival theoretical explanations of race and education or additional explanations not being advanced by any particular scholar do exist. These explanations must be explored in any credible analysis, or they weaken the scholar's case for one or more theoretical tenets being proposed. The more plausible the rival theories that cannot be eliminated, the weaker the case for the proposed theory. We must constantly assess the merit of our theoretical propositions against rival theories of race and education. This represents one type of assessment. In addition, other types of assessment of theoretical adequacy are appropriate. Three of the most common tests of theoretical adequacy deserve brief comment here: intelligibility, moral integrity, and validity.

1. Intelligibility is the concern that a theory make sense in light of prior research, evidence, and principles of rational thought. I am not suggesting that a theory must agree with prior research; in-

stead, the theory should recognize prior arguments, then build logical tenets that may or may not support prior theoretical development. The specific goal is plausible coherence, if this is possible.

2. Moral integrity is concerned with a theory's ethical standards. The scholarly literature on race has its share of principled theories on oppressive and racist dogma. A theory of race and education derived from arguments found in the CRT literature should connect to principles of advocacy and social justice not only for people of color but for all people. I argue that an important aspect of theoretical reflection and assessment is the moral dimension.

3. Validity is concerned with the credibility, reality, and truth of a theoretical view. We must always engage in the process of assessing how well the evidence at hand supports our theoretical perspective. This is a natural process that most scholars consider vital to the research enterprise.

Fashioning a theory of race and education will largely depend on the ability of scholars to appropriately interpret, correlate, and assess their theoretical arguments. This is a great challenge for researchers interested in the problems and opportunities of our system of education.

A Note of Caution

The chapters in this volume represent an important contribution to critical race educational (CRE) studies. I categorize the chapters in three groups. First, many of the chapters directly and explicitly link their writings with arguments and elements of CRT. For example, Ladson-Billings, Green, Taylor, and Villenas, Deyhle, and Parker, are clearly using CRT as a lens to focus their writings. Although other chapters mentioned one or two elements of CRT, their analyses are not explicitly driven by tenets of the movement (e.g., Hermes, Pizarro, and Choe). Rather, these authors are linking some elements of critical race theory to specific groups in ethnic/race studies. For example, the Hidalgo chapter on Latino families and research contains the author's own valuable perspective on how we should *critically* see race-based research as centered on families as opposed to single subject data collection. Hidalgo also questions her role as a Harvard-trained Puerto Rican scholar who was seen as an outsider by the Latino community in which she was conducting her research. Choe's chapter on Korean American women provides readers with narrative historical links between the history of Korean and U.S. political, military, and economic relations, and how this history led to immigration issues and images related to the Asian American model-minority myth. The chapters by Pizarro and Hermes also offer important, honest admissions of the paradox of qualitative research related to insider-outsider status and questions of validity to the communities of color versus the academy (Lincoln, 1997).

A next exploratory step in critical race theory research related to education would be to problematize common epistemological and methodological assumptions and terms about transnationality, language, culture, gender, and social class, and their links to the postcolonial racial and ethnic context both within and beyond U.S. borders. Culture, for example, is not static in terms of, say, a specific "Latino" culture; language is not only spoken but it is also a lived experience among some Latino groups. In addition, for the particular situation of Puerto Rico, we have to combine family interviews with Puerto Rican literature and historical research on colonization (and past and current resistance to this) in order to provide counternarratives to the dominant ideological mind-set of cultural deficit and the general acceptance of Puerto Rican failure in the schools (see for example Dobles and Segarra, 1998, and Nieto, 1998).

A third category of useful work, represented by the chapters in this book that are centered on arguments related to social justice and/or equity, does not mention or build specifically on concepts derived from CRT. For instance, Banning describes issues of power and conflict implicit between the researcher and the phenomena under investigation. Banning details how it is possible to use feminist pedagogy and reproduce the very oppressive methods feminist critiques warn against. This analysis is interesting because it examines the relationship between two white female academicians. The notion of whiteness is explored, yet the relationship of this exploration to people of color is not made clear. To be sure, the work is important for those interested in whiteness, power, and privilege—all concerns of the CRT movement. However, future research in this specific area could usefully apply CRT as a method to study the ideology of whiteness and gender and how it creates cultural deficit models of thinking among teachers, faculty, and administrators toward students of color. Furthermore, it is hoped that scholars will link this type of research to critical actions (in concert with concerned community members, parents, students, and teachers) against racism and other manifestations of discrimination.

In the academy, "traditional" scholars often "lump" all theories that are considered "to the left" of mainstream scholarship into broad, sometimes ill-defined categories. Each of the chapters in this volume could be classified as a part of cultural studies, multicultural studies, or the progressive movement. This begs the question: What scholarship should be included within the domain of CRE writing? Certainly this could be an-

swered in more than one way. Many of the authors of this volume may
not agree with my categorization scheme. Others may think we don't
need to have boundaries of inclusion and exclusion. I realize the CRT
movement is fluid and ever changing. Yet, I contend that two very simple criteria should guide those that claim to be writing from the CRT perspective. First, your scholarship should explore the lives, successes, marginalization, and oppression of people of color both within and outside
of the academy. This is the foundation of CRT. Derrick Bell's (1980b) description of his book *Race, racism, and American law* captures the essence
of this notion:

> It is, though, not the goal of *Race, Racism* to provide a social formula that
> would solve either all or any of the racial issues that beset the country.
> Rather, its goal is to review those issues in all their political and economic
> dimensions, and from that vantage point enable lawyers and lay people to
> determine where we might go from here. The goal for us, as it was for all
> those back to the slavery era who labored and sacrificed for freedom, was
> not to guarantee an end to racism, but to work forcefully toward that end.
> (p. 14)

A second criterion should guide those who contend their work is a part
of critical race theory: The scholarship should build on and expand beyond the scholarship found in the critical race legal literature. Delgado
offered a strong rationale for this criterion. In his article "The imperial
scholar: Reflections on a review of civil rights literature," Delgado (1984)
showed that an inner circle of 26 legal scholars, all male and white, occupied the key venues of civil rights scholarship to the exclusion of scholars of color. He noted that when a member of this inner circle wrote
about civil rights issues, he generally referenced other members of the
inner circle for support while ignoring the scholarship of people of color
in the field. It would be hard to imagine why anyone would want to
replicate this kind of behavior. Those scholars in education who are interested in fashioning a theory of race and education that is informed by
CRT should make it clear how they are using the theory and methods of
this movement and describe the limitations that are pushing them beyond it toward the goal of true social justice.

Notes

1. This letter was submitted to the editors of the *Los Angeles Times*. To the authors' knowledge it was never published.
2. Their argument breaks down in many ways. First, how do the editors explain the reality that many white high-ranking military officers majored in "soft"
academic disciplines or graduated without distinction from college? Second,

African American studies is a relatively new option of study. Many of the military officers listed would not have had the opportunity to select this as a major. Third, a recent investigative report conducted by the *Washington Post*, "Few women get generals' top jobs" (Priest, 1997), found that the pipeline to becoming a general is strongly influenced by a mentor selecting you to serve in key positions. At some point in your career, this mentor should be a general. Some of the generals interviewed stated that their criteria for selecting a key assistant were far removed from academic preparation. One general stated, "We selected the person we felt most comfortable with." Another general sought: "[S]omeone who has hobbies like ones I have. I wanted an aide who could golf with me. . . . Everyone just picks someone who they feel the most comfortable with." These remarks don't reflect merit or academic achievement. Rather, this is business as usual. To suggest that one's undergraduate major field of study is the primary factor in promotion through the military ranks is at best naive.

References

Allen, R. L. (1974). *Reluctant reformers: The impact of racism on American social reform movements*. Washington, DC: Howard University Press.

Balfour, D. L., and Mesaros, W. (1994). Connecting the local narratives: Public administration as a hermeneutic science. *Public Administration Review*, 54 (6), 559–565.

Banks, J. A. (1971). Relevant social studies for black pupils. In J. A. Banks and W. W. Joyce (Eds.), *Teaching social studies to culturally different children* (pp. 202–209). Menlo Park, CA: Addison-Wesley.

Barnes, R. D. (1990). Race consciousness: The thematic content of racial distinctiveness in critical race scholarship. *Harvard Law Review*, 103, 1864–1871.

Bell, D. A. (1980a). *Brown v. Board of Education* and the interest-convergence dilemma. *Harvard Law Review*, 93, 518–533.

_____. (1980b). *Race, racism, and American law*. 2d ed. Boston: Little, Brown.

_____. (1992a). *Faces at the bottom of the well*. New York: Basic Books.

_____. (1992b). *Race, racism, and American law*. 3d ed.. Boston: Little, Brown.

_____. (1993). Remembrances of racism past: Getting beyond the civil rights decline. In H. Hill and J. E. Jones (Eds.), *Race in America: The struggle for equality* (pp. 73–82). Madison: University of Wisconsin Press.

_____. (1994). *Confronting authority: Reflections of an ardent protester*. Boston: Beacon Press.

Campbell, J., Donahue, P., Reese, C., and Phillips, G. (1996). *NAEP 1994 reading report card for the nation and the states*. Washington, DC: U.S. Department of Education.

Cobb, W. J. (1998). The clear-eyed wisdom of Stanley Crouch. *Black Book Review*, 5 (3), 17, 33.

Cone, J. (1970). *A black theology of liberation*. Philadelphia: Lippincott Co.

Crenshaw, K. W. (1988). Race, reform, retrenchment: Transformation and legitimation in anti-discrimination law. *Harvard Law Review*, 101, 1331–1387.

Delgado, R. (1984). The imperial scholar: Reflections on a review of civil rights literature. *University of Pennsylvania Law Review*, 132, 561–578.

_____. (1989). Storytelling for oppositionists and others: A plea for narrative. *Michigan Law Review, 87*, 2411–2441.

Dobles, R., and Segarra, J. A. (1998). Symposium: Colonialism and working-class resistance: Puerto Rican education in the United States. *Harvard Educational Review, 68*, 2.

Hu-DeHart, E. (1995). Ethnic studies in U.S. higher education: History, development, and goals. In J. A. Banks and C. A. Banks (Eds.), *Handbook of research on multicultural education* (pp. 696–707). New York: Macmillan.

Jefferson, T. (1954). *Notes on the state of Virginia*. New York: Norton. (Orig. ed. 1784.)

Kennedy, D. (1995). A cultural pluralist case for affirmative action in legal academia. In K. Crenshaw, N. Gotanda, G. Peller, and K. Thomas (Eds.), *Critical race theory: The key writings that formed the movement* (pp. 159–177). New York: New Press.

Kennedy, R. (1989). Racial critiques of legal academia. *Harvard Law Review, 102*, 1745–1819.

Ladner, J. (1973). *The death of white sociology*. New York: Vintage Books.

Lawrence, C. R. (1987). The id, the ego, and equal protection: Reckoning with unconscious racism. *Stanford Law Review, 39*, 317–388.

Lincoln, Y. A. (1997). Reading response-ably: Ethnography and prudential caring. *International Journal of Qualitative Studies in Education, 10*, 161–164.

Martinez, T. A. (1996). Toward a Chicana feminist epistemological standpoint: Theory at the intersection of race, class, and gender. *Race, Class, and Gender, 3*, 107–128.

Matsuda, M. J., Lawrence, C. R., Delgado, R., and Crenshaw, K. W. (Eds.). (1993). *Words that wound: Critical race theory, assaultive speech, and the First Amendment.* Boulder, CO: Westview Press.

Narayan, K. (1993). How native is a "native" anthropologist? *American Anthropologist, 95*, 671–686.

National Education Goals Panel (NEGP). (1995). *The national education goals report: Building a nation of learners.* Washington, DC: National Education Goals Panel.

Nieto, S. (1998). Fact and fiction: Stories of Puerto Ricans in U.S. schools. *Harvard Educational Review, 68*, 133–163.

Omi, M., and Winant, H. (1994). *Racial formation in the United States: From the 1960s to the 1990s.* 2d ed. New York: Routledge.

Parker, L. (1998). "Race is . . . race ain't": An exploration of the utility of critical race theory in qualitative research in education. *International Journal of Qualitative Studies in Education, 11*, 47–56.

Peters, E. (1982). Stereotyping: Moving against consciousness. In *Ethnic notions: Black images in the white mind* (exhibition catalogue). Berkeley, CA: Berkeley Art Center.

Priest, D. (1997, December 29). Few women get generals' top jobs. *Washington Post*, p. A1.

Regents of the University of California v. Bakke, 438 U.S. 265 (1978).

Secada, W. G. (1989). *Equity in education.* London: Falmer.

Stone, H. W., and Duke, J. O. (1996). *How to think theologically.* Minneapolis, MN: Fortress.

Symposium: Colonialism, and working-class resistance: Puerto Rican education in the United States. *Harvard Educational Review,* 68 (2).

Takaki, R. (1993). *A different mirror: A history of multicultural America.* Boston: Little, Brown.

Tate, W. F., IV. (1997). Critical race theory and education: History, theory, and implications. In M. W. Apple (Ed.), *Review of research in education,* vol. 22, pp. 195–250. Washington, DC: American Educational Research Association.

Top African-American military brass are a highly educated bunch. (1997/1998, Winter). *Journal of Blacks in Higher Education,* 18, 54–55.

Watkins, W. H. (1996). Reclaiming historical visions of quality schooling: The legacy of early 20th-century black intellectuals. In M. J. Shujaa (Ed.), *Beyond desegregation: The politics of quality in African American schooling* (pp. 5–28). Thousand Oaks, CA: Corwin.

West, C. (1995). Foreword. In K. Crenshaw, N. Gotanda, G. Peller, and K. Thomas (Eds.), *Critical race theory: The key writings that formed the movement* (pp. xi–xii). New York: New Press.

Wilkins, R. (1995, March 27). Racism has its privileges. *Nation,* pp. 409–416.

Williams, P. J. (1991). *The alchemy of race and rights: Diary of a law professor.* Cambridge, MA: Harvard University Press.

Wilson, R., Heller, S., and Schneider, A. (1998, July 31). Scholar to take Black studies post at Washington U. *Chronicle of Higher Education,* A37.

About the Editors and Contributors

Marlia Banning is a lecturer in the department of history at Northern Arizona University. Her research and teaching interests include the connections between identity, place, and the history of women, race, and class in the United States, and the promises and predicaments of emancipatory educational research and discourse.

Lena Domyung Choe is a Ph.D. candidate in educational policy studies at the University of Illinois, Urbana–Champaign. She has been contributing to the development of Asian American studies at UIUC as the staff associate. Her current research interests broadly include: socio-historical critique of Asian Americans in education, oral histories of Korean Americans, and racial and ethnic identity formation.

Donna Deyhle is a professor of anthropology and education in the department of educational studies and in the ethnic studies program at the University of Utah, where she is also co-director of the American Indian Resource Center. She is a leading scholar in the area of American Indian educational research, and her work has appeared in the *Harvard Educational Review*, the *Journal of American Indian Education, Youth and Society,* and the *Review of Research in Education*. Her research also has been an integral part of the litigation surrounding the Navajo conflicts with Anglo school officials in southern Utah. Prof. Deyhle is a former Spencer Fellow of the National Academy of Education.

Francisca E. González teaches women's studies at San Jose State University. Her areas of interests are Latina/Latino critical theory and the foundations of education and critical race theory. For the future, her plan is to research and write about the interweaving of Mexicana cultural knowledge and formal education.

Paul E. Green is an assistant professor of urban politics and policy in the School of Education at the University of California–Riverside. He has taught and served as an administrator in public secondary education. His research awards and fellowships include a postdoctoral fellowship at Teachers College–Columbia University and the University of California Regents Faculty Fellowship/Faculty Development Award. His research examines policies and practices of equal access and equal educational opportunity in K–12 and postsecondary institutions, as well as other issues of social justice (e.g., housing, poverty, and employment) for African Americans and other persons of color.

Mary Hermes is currently an assistant professor in the educational studies department at Carleton College in Northfield, Minnesota, where she teaches multicultural education, schooling and opportunity, native issues in education, and social studies methods. She is a mixed-heritage descendant of the Fort Peck

Assiniboin (Sioux). She plans to continue her work toward bridging university and reservation communities in the Great Lakes area.

Nitza M. Hidalgo is a professor in the education department at Westfield State College in Massachusetts, where she teaches multicultural education and ethnic studies. She recently coedited (with Aida A. Nevarez-LaTorre of Temple University) a special issue of the journal *Education and Urban Society*, titled *Latino communities: Resources for educational change.*

Gloria Ladson-Billings is a professor in the department of curriculum and instruction at the University of Wisconsin–Madison. Her work examines successful teachers for African American students and the role of critical race theory in education. She is the author of the critically acclaimed book *The dreamkeepers: Successful teachers of African American children*, as well as of more than 30 journal articles and book chapters on diversity, multiculturalism, and African American students. Ladson-Billings has received numerous awards for her work, including the National Academy of Education's Spencer Post-Doctoral Fellowship; the Palmer O. Johnson Award (of the American Educational Research Association [AERA]); and the Early Career Award from the Committee on the Role and Status of Minorities (of the AERA).

Laurence Parker is an associate professor in the department of educational policy studies at the University of Illinois at Urbana-Champaign. His current research and teaching interests are in the areas of critical race theory and educational policy research and analysis (at the K–12 and postsecondary levels), and the politics of school choice. His most recent article, entitled "Race is . . . race ain't: An exploration of the utility of critical race theory in qualitative research in education," appeared in the *International Journal of Qualitative Studies in Education.*

Marc Pizarro is currently a Ford Postdoctoral Fellow in the graduate school of education at the University of California–Berkeley. He is writing a book that explores the relationship between the identities of Chicana/o students and their academic performance.

Daria Roithmayr is an assistant professor of law at the University of Illinois College of Law, where she teaches critical race theory, feminist jurisprudence, evidence, and civil procedure. After graduating magna cum laude and with the Order of the Coif from Georgetown University Law Center, Professor Roithmayr clerked for a federal district court judge in Baltimore, Maryland. She then served as special counsel to Senator Edward Kennedy on the Judiciary Committee, advising him on questions of race and gender in connection with the nominations of Justices David Souter and Clarence Thomas to the United States Supreme Court. Thereafter, Professor Roithmayr practiced law in Washington, D.C. and Phoenix, Arizona, before coming to the College of Law in 1996. Professor Roithmayr writes in the area of critical race theory. Her works include "Deconstructing the distinction between bias and merit," 85 *California Law Review* 1449 (1997) and "Guerrillas in our midst: The assault on radicals in American law," 96 *Michigan Law Review* 1658 (1998).

William F. Tate, IV is an associate professor in the department of curriculum and instruction at the University of Wisconsin–Madison. His research interests include race and American education and the political and cultural dimensions of mathematics education. He has published articles in the *Journal for Research in*

Mathematics Education, Review of Research in Education, Teachers College Record, and other scholarly outlets. He is an editor of the *American Educational Research Journal.*

Edward Taylor is an assistant professor in the department of educational leadership and policy studies at the University of Washington. His teaching and research areas include the history of higher education, policies and programs servicing disenfranchised groups, and the construction of race-based policy. He has published articles in the *College Student Journal* and the *Journal of Race and Ethnicity.* His recent work centers on African American women educators and includes an article in the book *Multicultural education: Transformative knowledge and action,* edited by James Banks.

Sofia Villenas is an assistant professor in the department of educational studies and in the ethnic studies program at the University of Utah. Her research centers on investigating Latino schooling and home and community education within the dynamics of racial/cultural community politics. Critical race theory informs this work, as is evident in her article co-authored with Donna Deyhle entitled "Critical race theory and ethnographies challenging the stereotypes: Latino families, schooling, resilience and resistance," forthcoming in *Curriculum Inquiry.* As a Chicana ethnographer, Villenas also explores positionality and locality in qualitative research, as can be seen in her article "The colonizer/colonized Chicana ethnographer: Identity, marginalization, and co-optation in the field," in the *Harvard Educational Review.* She is also a former Spencer Fellow of the National Academy of Education.

Index

metaphorical, 8–9
within school policies, 33–35
See also Segregation
Reality, naming one's own, 15–16, 206
Reformists, 2
Reno, Janet, 46
Representation, proportional, 10–11
Research ethic, 87–88
Research methodology, 54
 community involvement, 89–91
 developing a theory, 85–86
 feminist action ethnography, 178(n1)
 for Chicana/o social justice, 55–59,
  65–73
 for feminist pedagogy, 156–158
 for Latinas/os, 102–109
 interview techniques, 104–108,
  120(n7)
 Mexicana identities, 131–136
 Ojibwe studies, 83–98
 researcher-researched relationship,
  157–159, 169–171
 research problems, 86–89
 role of researcher, 88–89, 115–117
 student involvement in, 61–65
 the product of, 70–72
Risk-taking, in the classroom, 159–160,
  166–169
Robeson, Paul, 19–20
Roithmayr, Daria, 1–6

Savage inequalities (Kozol), 24
School funding, 24–25
Schools
 access to, 77(n6)
 Chicana/o protests, 63
 Chicana/o student perspective of,
  67–68
 Korean American students, 219–222
 See also Education; Intelligence
  testing; Students; Tracking
Segregation, 186–187
 de facto (*See* Tracking)
 increase under Reagan and Bush,
  244

See also Desegregation; Historically
 black colleges and universities;
 Litigation; Racism
Segregationists, 2
Selena, 145
Sherry, S., 182
Simón, Laura, 35, 66
Simpson, O.J., 12
Sinajini court case, 44–48
*Sipuel v. Oklahoma State Board of
 Regents* (1948), 187
*The Social Construction of Whiteness:
 White Women, Race Matters*
 (Frankenberg), 174
Social Darwinism, 237
Social justice, 32, 76(n2), 77(n9),
 78(n12)
 See also Research methodology
Social justice, Chicana/o
 research methodology, 65–73
The Space traders (Bell), 27(n3), 185
Spender, Herbert, 237
Stereotypes, 258
 of Asian Americans, 216–217,
  219–223
 of Puerto Ricans, 106–107, 111
 of scholars, 198–199
Storytelling, 5, 8, 33, 48(n2), 70, 93–96,
 206–208, 261
 in law, 14–15
 Korean oral histories, 206–208
 Mexicana voices, 136–139
 narrative, 197–198
 oral tradition and, 184
 pláticas, 134
 to improve schools, 89–91
 See also Oral tradition
Students
 as co-researchers, 61–65, 67–68
 Asian Americans, 220–222
 developing Chicana/o studies
  programs, 70–72
 empowering Chicanas/os, 55–59
 involvement in research, 61–65
 Korean Americans, 219–220,
  221–222
 Latinas/os, 35–39, 38

Printed in the United States
79435LV00002B/254

9 780813 390697